Vision and Revision in Maya Studies

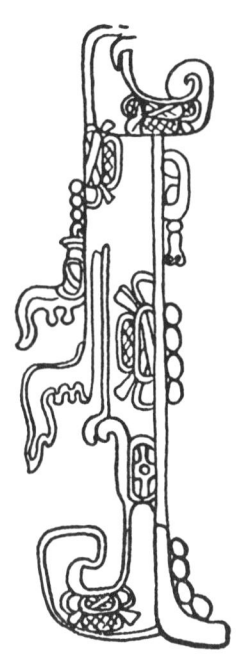

Vision and Revision in Maya Studies

Edited by Flora S. Clancy and Peter D. Harrison

University of New Mexico Press
Albuquerque

Library of Congress Cataloging-in-Publication Data

Vision and revision in Maya studies / edited by Flora S. Clancy and
　　Peter D. Harrison.—1st ed.
　　　　p. cm.
　　Includes bibliographical references and index.
　　ISBN 0-8263-1220-9
　　1. Mayas—Antiquities.
　　2. Mexico—Antiquities.
　　3. Central America—Antiquities.
　　I. Clancy, Florida S. II. Harrison, Peter D., 1937– .
F1435.V724　1990
972'.01'01—dc20　　　90-21266
　　　　　　　　　　CIP

© 1990 by The University of New Mexico Press
All rights reserved
First edition

Contents

Introduction	vii	
Chapter One	The Early Ceramic History of the Lowland Maya.	1
	E. Wyllys Andrews V	
Chapter Two	A Geneology for Freestanding Maya Monuments.	21
	Flora S. Clancy	
Chapter Three	New Perspectives on Old Problems: Dynastic References for the Early Classic at Tikal. 33	
	Juan Pedro Laporte and Vilma Fialko C.	
Chapter Four	The Jester God. The Beginning and End of a Maya Royal Symbol.	67
	David A. Freidel	
Chapter Five	The Birth of the Baktun at Tikal and Seibal.	77
	Clemency Chase Coggins	
Chapter Six	The Revolution in Ancient Maya Subsistence.	99
	Peter D. Harrison	
Chapter Seven	Lowland Maya Wetland Agriculture: The Rio Azul Agronomy Program. 115	
	T. Patrick Culbert, Laura J. Levi, and Luis Cruz	
Chapter Eight	Southern Belize: An Ancient Maya Region. 125	
	Richard M. Leventhal	
Chapter Nine	House Names and Dedication Rituals at Palenque. 143	
	Linda Schele	
Chapter Ten	The Role of Trading Ports in Maya Civilization. 159	
	Anthony P. Andrews	
Chapter Eleven	Up from the Dust: The Central Lowlands Postclassic as Seen from Laminai and Marco Gonzales. 169	
	David M. Pendergast	
Chapter Twelve	Prophets and Idol Speculators: Forces of History in the Lowland Maya Rebellion of 1683. 179	
	Grant D. Jones	
Bibliography	195	
Index	221	

Introduction

by Flora S. Clancy and Peter D. Harrison

The collected papers in this volume are the result of a symposium of the same title presented to the public at the University of New Mexico in Albuquerque in January, 1987. The symposium was an auxiliary function of the traveling exhibition entitled, "Maya: Treasures of an Ancient Civilization," organized by the Albuquerque Museum Foundation which also funded it, along with the University of New Mexico and the National Endowment for the Humanities.

The title for this book and for the symposium was inspired by Barbara Braun's review of the Maya exhibition and its accompanying catalogue. In a review that appeared in *Art In America*, January 1986, Braun took note of many obscure but "vigorous items" of Postclassic date, and suggested that "such extended coverage of later material signals a revisionist interpretation of the Maya."

Revisionism is an analytic approach now associated with a "postmodern" approach toward history. New points of view and new questions stimulate a reexamination of old or known historical data. New data or documents are not necessary for rewriting history when its reinterpretation comes rather from a new perspective. Revisionism, essentially, places a greater faith in the historian and in the questions asked than in the "facts of history" to give new meaning to past events.

Students of prehistory, however, may wonder what is so postmodern about revisionism. Revision, as described above, has been consistently employed by prehistorians to extract as much information as possible from a comparatively small amount of data. Because they lack primary textual sources, prehistorians rely on archaeological and anthropological data, mute sources that are only made comprehensible by interpretative ordering and therefore always susceptible to reinterpretation and revision. Within the dialectic of revision and vision, archaeological data should be understood as the material of revisionism from its recovery through its many interpretations. The "texts" of prehistory are always modern ones.

Maya studies, however, occupy an interesting position with regard to revisionism and new data because the once prehistoric field of Maya studies is becoming historic. Ancient Maya texts are being interpreted and read, and are providing primary historical data for new visions of Maya society and culture. The reading of Maya texts is still at the level where decipherment and not interpretation remains the major problem, but the very different requirements of historical analysis are already being felt in this field that had primarily based its means of understanding on archaeological and anthropological methods.

While the general theme of this volume concerns a rethinking of old premises stimulated by new archaeological data, several papers included deal at least in part with the presentation of primary historical data and texts. Such papers characterize the new "vision" offered by textual studies. The title *Vision and Revision in Maya Studies* is meant to prepare the reader for what is to follow by reflecting this present state of Maya Studies.

The papers collected here revise the chronological frameworks for ancient Maya, envision greater and more complex subsistence and settlement strategies, and address the new potentials of historical text. The results are new and changing methodologies that lead to changing perceptions and to an underlying excitement that can be felt in all the essays.

Another feature of this collection is that several papers interlock with or reinforce one another. Frequently, certain points made in one paper are amplified or further supported by points made in one or more other papers, such that the force of conviction of the whole is greater than the sum of its parts.

The papers are organized chronologically, although since some deal with more than one cultural period in Maya development, it was not always possible to adhere strictly to such an ordering. The papers proceed generally from the Preclassic to the Colonial period.

E. W. Andrews V reassesses ceramic evidence in trying to understand the origins and spread of early Preclassic Maya. In "The Early Ceramic History of the Lowland Maya," Andrews shows that recent archaeological work has supplied data that do not easily fit into current reconstructions of the Preclassic period, and sees reason to emphasize the role of outside, or non-Maya, influences at the earliest stages of development.

Flora Clancy outlines "A Geneology for Freestanding Maya Monuments" by tracing the formal development of monument types and their pictorial compositions from the Middle Preclassic to the beginnings of the Classic Period. Her analysis focuses on the structural aspects of monuments rather than on iconography, and systematically provides an extra dimension for the extraction of information contained in monumental art.

Revision as a result of new archaeological data is presented by Juan Pedro Laporte and Vilma Fialko C. in "New Perspectives on Old Problems: Dynastic References for the Early Classic at Tikal." Reporting on the recent excavations at Tikal, Guatemala, Laporte and Fialko detail and date a sequence of important architectural events in that ancient city during the Early Classic Period. By matching their field data with glyphic texts and previous archaeological interpretations, a historical picture of dynasty and political power is linked to the architectural events.

A link between iconography and archaeology is the basis of David Freidel's contribution, "The Jester God: The Beginning and End of a Maya Royal Symbol." Freidel introduces new thoughts on the complexity of Maya political organization by examining the changing role of a symbol of power as a reflection of changing political structures throughout Maya history. In doing this, he also observes outside influence at the early end of the chronology.

In "The Birth of the Baktun at Tikal and Seibal," Clemency Chase Coggins outlines the practice of monument erection at the turn of the Maya *Baktun*. This event occurred only twice during Classic Maya history, and Coggins, drawing on data from the sites of Tikal and Seibal, shows that there is a pattern of associated iconography. This essay underscores the complexity of tradition central to the Maya calendar. The technique explored in this paper combines a historical approach with a reinterpretation of existing archaeological data.

In "The Revolution in Ancient Maya Subsistence," Peter D. Harrison summarizes the results of the Pulltrouser Swamp Project in northern Belize which contributed to revision of our view of ancient economies. The body of data emerging from this project has established the use of swampy wetlands as opposed to the more spatially limited riverine littoral as a locale of raised field, intensive agriculture. This study has led to perceptions of the spatial arrangements of sites in relation to their ancient functions and economies, as well as to theoretical implications about population sizes.

The contribution by T. Patrick Culbert, Laura J. Levi, and Luis Cruz, "Lowland Maya Wetland Agriculture: The Rio Azul Agronomy Program," describes recent work in Guatemala, which complements Harrison's study. Reporting on the findings at Rio Azul, Culbert, Levi, and Cruz outline the use of a variety of intensive agricultural techniques within a range of topographic situations. It is significant that this material lies geographically outside the Belizean/Mexican examples described by Harrison because it draws the exploitation of intensive techniques closer to the Petén heartland. This work further expands understanding of the complexity and diversity of ancient agricultural techniques employed by the Maya.

New archaeological data are presented by Richard Leventhal in his work, "The Southern Belize: An Ancient Maya Region." His material comes from an area that has remained enigmatic and unknown since Norman Hammond's landmark work at Lubaantun (1975b). Leventhal's contribution describes a field survey that examines the features of a region through settlement patterns and architectural types, as it defines regional patterns and outlines political structures.

Linda Schele's work in "House Names and Dedication Rituals at Palenque," seeks to provide new information by reading ancient texts that tell of the actual function of certain buildings and how these functions were ritually utilized by Maya rulers of Palenque and elsewhere. The elucidation of ritual associated with monumental architectural construction, as read in the texts, depicts a complex interweaving of astronomical events, accession to power, and concepts of architecture that opens avenues for understanding the Maya mind on several levels.

Anthony Andrews's survey of the archaeological evidence for maritime activities, "The Role of Trading Ports in Maya Civilization," was inspired by the archaeological data found in his excavations at Isla Cerritos off the cost of Yucatán. This review caused him to realize that a maritime economy had a longer duration and was more generally effective than what is suggested by the current model of a slowly evolving maritime economy that became culturally important only for the Postclassic Maya. By creating a typology of such sites in an organized framework, Andrews provides a way for future analysis.

From the archaeological information gained by his excavations at Lamanai in Belize, David Pendergast calls for a reassessment of prevailing attitudes about the Postclassic period. "Up From the Dust: The Central Lowlands Postclassic As Seen from Lamanai and Marco Gonzales" establishes a picture of potency for the Postclassic that is contrary to the current paradigm of decadence, and also suggests that the break between the Classic and Postclassic cultures must be locally defined rather than assumed to be a massive general cultural collapse. Pendergast also discusses the role of seaports for this region, reinforcing and expanding the premise of Anthony Andrews's paper.

Another example of historical data providing new vision is found in Grant Jones's work on the Colonial Maya. "Prophets and Idol Speculators: Forces of History in the Lowland Maya Rebellion of 1683" represents a pioneering effort to regain knowledge of a little-known and crucial period in New World history. The new information presented by Jones, especially that from the Archivo General de Indias in Seville, Spain, does much more than detail a history of confrontational politics. It sheds light on the psychology and forms of Maya resistance, rebellion, and warfare and has important implications for historians of both Post- and Precolumbian times.

Most of the papers make it clear that some traditional assumptions and generalizations presently held about the history, quality, and structure of daily life in the Maya culture will have to be carefully reexamined. Furthermore, several of the papers suggest that these assumptions will ultimately be abandoned because they impinge on the way new data are interpreted. In this volume, such "re-vision" is especially true for the Preclassic and Postclassic Maya world. We are faced with strong evidence for complex social and interregional interactions during the Preclassic period where we have originally seen slow, local developments. In trying to maintain the traditional signals for a Postclassic culture, arguments for regional diversity have been put forward to explain the differences, discovered through excavation, concerning when and how these expected signs appear. With the continuing accumulation of data that show cultural vitality instead of the expected decadence and cultural poverty, our definition of Postclassic times is beginning to change. The old assumptions are becoming less useful as models.

The recent work in understanding Maya subsistence and agricultural practices, exemplified by several papers in this volume, challenges long-held ideas about an essentially rural people living within local, self-sufficient agrarian economies. Intensive agricultural techniques, such as raised fields and irrigation, are being extended by the discovery of multiple intensive methods of farming rain forest and riverine environments. Evidence for regional subsistence patterns and interregional distribution patterns begins to suggest agricultural business economies rather than self-sufficient local farming.

New visions of Maya culture are coming to us through the decipherment of glyphs and the advent of a history based on primary historical documents. The interrelationship of archaeological data and historical data will become a more pressing issue to address in the near future of Maya studies. How the discrepancies that will inevitably arise between these two sets of data are understood should become a new focus for discourse among students of Mesoamerica. Several contributions to this volume intimate that such issues exist and must be confronted.

The hope is that this confrontation will lead to strong interdisciplinary cooperation for a reconstruction of Maya culture. Perhaps the relatively new efforts in ethnoarchaeology and historical ethnography will mediate the methodological gap that exists between the disciplines of history and archaeology.

At the threshold of the 1990s there are many gaps in the basic corpus of data for the ancient Maya. Conclusions about the cultural complexity of the Maya must still be essentially tentative until some of these gaps are filled by field research or by other methods of gaining new knowledge. Examples of such gaps which emerge from the discussions in this volume are these:

Demography It is too easy to forget that the Maya Lowlands have not yet been thoroughly explored, so that the numbers, sizes, and locations of Maya settlements remain undefined. In light of this most basic gap, population estimates are inferred by means other than direct calculation from housing. Given the current rate of loss of information due to resettlement and mechanized destruction, as well as looting, this may well be the most serious problem facing Maya studies.

Economy While we now know that the Maya practiced a variety of forms of intensive agriculture, we can still only speculate about the impact of these techniques on the society as a whole. The full spectrum of intensive techniques practiced by the ancient Maya has yet to be demonstrated, as does the possible ubiquitousness of such techniques across the Lowlands. An ancillary problem not addressed in this volume is the explanation of agricultural support for large populations in those parts of the Lowlands which lie outside the wetland zones. In areas such as the northwestern Lowlands, for example, the use of raised fields was not possible or probable. The intriguing question of what types of agriculture and distributional economies were in effect in these areas awaits investigation.

Chronology Existing concepts of the chronological periods and their innate integrity need study and revision. There are two distinct diachronic models for Maya development: one with a collapse and one without. What other disparate models might we expect to find expostulated by the evidence in the future? Papers in this volume bring into question our understanding of several traditional chronological definitions of Maya periods.

Time and Space Studies concerned with the Maya knowledge and uses of time are advancing apace. Sophistication in this area has long been an accepted feature of ancient Maya culture. But what of their knowledge and uses of space?

Culture and Cosmos Our study of these more ephemeral aspects of civilization has engendered perhaps more than their fair share of reconstruction and revision. The decipherment of the glyphs, however, gives a more concrete historical basis to our understanding of ephemeral cultural events. The interpretation of the meanings for the glyphic texts we are beginning to read, however, will require increased efforts in the contextual studies of iconography and ethnography.

It seems inevitable that at some time in the future the information gained by the new perceptions represented herein will be called into question and revised, perhaps by the very scholars contributing to this book. Neither history nor prehistory can provide an immutable or finite body of data. Through vision and revision, each author probes deeply into old concepts and uncovers new directions for interpretation. As we begin to understand Maya history as written by the ancient Maya, we realize it is by these processes of vision and revision, integral to any description of the past, that we are now more truly in the company of the ancient Maya authors.

One

Early Ceramic History of the Lowland Maya

By E. Wyllys Andrews V

Our knowledge of the ancient Maya and their neighbors to the west and the south has increased greatly in recent years. This new understanding stems from rapid and in some cases revolutionary advances in several fields of archaeological and related research. Great changes have been wrought through Maya epigraphy, trace element analysis for sourcing of traded materials, remote sensing, reevaluation of intensive agricultural practices, analysis of craft specialization, especially in lithics, and more detailed study of local and regional settlement patterns. But much of the progress results directly from just doing more archaeology—surveying new areas, digging more sites, and adding new information to the old.

Here lies a danger. The enormous increase in available data makes it increasingly difficult for archaeologists to control or even have reasonable access to all of it. This is perhaps most true of ceramic collections, which provide so much of the historical framework for the Maya and which are stored, almost always in the form of limited type collections, in the country they derived from or in institutions scattered around North America or Europe.

Standards for reporting pottery sherd collections have changed, and in some cases the final presentation is not adequate to allow definitive conclusions about external relationships of a ceramic type of a complex. This problem results partly from the high cost of color illustrations, and partly from the inability of the author to compensate for this by visiting every conceivable comparative collection before drawing his own conclusions. There exists, in addition, no agreed upon set of criteria for judging closeness of relationship—nor should there necessarily be such. The result is that it is often difficult to assess the significance of ceramic collections in a regional or an interregional context without direct study of comparative collections.

Since 1980, as part of the analysis of a large collection of Middle and Late Formative period ceramics from Komchen in northwestern Yucatán, I have been able to visit and study a number of ceramic collections from Mexico, Guatemala, Belize, Chiapas, Tabasco, and Veracruz.[1] These comparative studies began as an effort to place the Komchen ceramics in a Lowland Maya perspective but later came to include the more general goal of understanding early Maya and Olmec ceramic development and interrelationships.

This process has led me to rethink several aspects of internal Maya development and of Maya relationships with the early Isthmian cultures of Chiapas and Tabasco. It has also left me with the growing conviction that we have much to learn from examination and reanalysis of excavated collections. We neglect them at our peril.[2]

In recent years most archaeologists in Mesoamerica have come to accept the existence of an Early Formative Swasey phase in the Maya Lowlands, defined at Cuello, in Belize. The available radiocarbon evidence, however, suggests that Swasey dates to the Middle Formative. This shift, discussed below, has far-reaching implications for early Maya cultural development.

My second concern here is the early Middle Formative Xe ceramic sphere of the southern Petén of Guatemala and what it tells us about the earliest Lowland Maya contacts with the greater Isthmian area of Chiapas and Tabasco to the west. Although remains of the simple Xe culture are limited to one river drainage and to a relatively short time span, it marked an important early stage of expansion and culture contact in eastern Mesoamerica. A consideration of the ethnic identity of Xe leads to the broader subject of ethnic relations in eastern Mesoamerica.

In the centuries immediately following the Xe phase, the Maya expanded rapidly to fill most of the territory they occupied at the time their Classic civilization failed, about a millennium and a half later. We have by now learned enough about Middle Formative ceramics in various parts of the Maya Lowlands to suggest several patterns of population spread and subsequent contacts.

The broken and discarded ceramics of a human society create a poor window through which to glimpse its history or to fathom the reasons for its change. They are, however, often a large part of what we have, and my reconstructions here are based almost entirely upon them. The extent to which pottery reliably reflects ancient Maya events is an underlying issue. We are never justified in assuming a one-to-one correlation between language and culture, but the even more questionable argument is that one aspect of material culture—pottery—accurately reflects language and ethnicity. What follows, then, must obviously be viewed with a robust skepticism. And if we do use ceramics to chart genetic relationships and interaction among the Maya and their neighbors, what are the most useful features of pottery for this purpose?

In attempting to understand relationships among early eastern Mesoamerican ceramic complexes and especially the position of the Xe complex, I have relied most heavily on slip characteristics: color, hardness, thickness, and finish. It is the slips that most readily allow one to place this complex with its closest relatives, although forms and, especially at the site of Altar de Sacrificios, paste and temper are important indicators.

This certainly need not be true in all or even most cases, but I think the ways in which slips are made and applied are often less likely to change than other vessel attributes. Plastic surface decoration is a purely stylistic feature that has no inherent technological stability. Vessel forms, although determined in large part by the uses to which the pots will be put, are subject to great variation and can diffuse easily and rapidly for a number of reasons. Paste and temper, although obviously linked to technological and therefore conservative aspects of manufacture, are restricted partly by the materials that are locally available. The creation of slips that are varied, aesthetically pleasing, and durable is a task requiring considerable skill, and once a group had developed an adequate repertoire of surface finishes and colors, it might have been less likely to change them than other aspects of its pottery.

As a prologue to some suggestions concerning the Xe complex and the development and spread of later ceramics in the lowlands, I outline the history of the acquisition of our knowledge of the basic lowland ceramic sequence.

Development of the Lowland Maya Formative Ceramic Sequence

Raymond Merwin's 1910–11 excavations for Harvard University at Holmul, in the northeast Petén, provided the first secure archaeological indications of an early period of Maya ceramics corresponding in time to Herbert Spinden's "Archaic" culture of nuclear America. A description of the Protoclassic Holmul I vaulted tombs and their pottery was published in 1932 by George Vaillant (Merwin and Vaillant 1932). He noted that this burial assemblage, with its early polychrome decoration, mammiform tetrapod supports, bridged spouts, stucco decoration, and potstands, did not look like the newly excavated sherds from fill under Structure E-VII-sub and its plaza at Uaxactun, that it more resembled stratigraphically early ceramic vessels from El Salvador, and that it "argues a complex origin for the Maya groups" (1932: 93). His last caveat is no less pertinent today than a half-century ago.

Excavations by the Carnegie Institution of Washington from 1926 to 1931 in Group E at Uaxactun, Petén, only 40 km northwest of Holmul, produced detailed evidence of Formative architecture, pottery, and other artifacts from stratigraphic excavations. Edith B. Ricketson (1937) published the first detailed description of early Uaxactun pottery, which came mostly from Structure E-VII-sub and from subfloor trenches, the first of which were excavated in 1928 by George Vaillant (Vaillant 1928). Her Periods 1*a* and 1*b* at the base of the stratigraphic column correspond to Mamom (late Middle Formative) and Chicanel (Late Formative) in Robert Smith's 1955 Uaxactun ceramic sequence.

Although Uaxactun is the site at which the Middle Formative Mamom ceramic complex was defined, the earliest pottery here is late Mamom. Some of the pottery on which Smith based his descriptions would be considered by Maya ceramists today to be transitional to, or within the range of, Late Formative Chicanel ceramics.

In the late 1950s and early 1960s late Middle Formative ceramics came to light at a large number of widely separated sites in the Lowlands, such as Barton Ramie, Tikal, Altar de Sacrificios, and the Mirador Group, near Dzibilchaltún. At most sites, ceremonial or public architecture was absent or rare, and houses were usually not built on raised platforms. A trend toward larger sites with larger buildings at their centers is visible by the end of this period, leading to the increasingly vast construction programs of the Late Formative.

Remains of the early Middle Formative, in contrast to those of the following period, are limited to relatively few areas within the Lowlands. The Xe phase, defined by Richard E. W. Adams at Altar de Sacrificios in 1961 (Adams 1971) and a few years later by Gordon R. Willey (1970) and Jeremy A. Sabloff (1975) at Seibal, where it is called Real Xe, is represented by little more than its pottery, a few postholes and a small pit (A. L. Smith 1972: 142–45), and a La Venta–style cache of jades and pottery. We know next to nothing about Xe dwellings, which were probably perishable and set directly on the ground surface, but both sites must have been small agricultural settlements at this time.

There has been little agreement about where these early farmers in the southern Petén Usumacinta-Pasion drainage might have come from. The Pulestons (1971) speculated that early farming groups spread into the Lowlands along unspecified rivers, a suggestion that still seems likely. Adams (1971: 154; 1972: 8) suggested Xe pottery might have derived from the Veracruz-Tabasco lowlands, that is, the Olmec area. Robert L. Rands's early Middle Formative Chiuaan ceramic complex of Trinidad, Tabasco, was thought perhaps to be similar to Xe (Rands 1969; 1977: 168–69), and this suggestion reinforced the argument for an origin of Xe in the lowlands of Chiapas, Tabasco, or Veracruz. Lorenzo Ochoa (1983: 154–58) has argued that Olmec colonization or impact on the southern Maya Lowlands occurred through both the Usumacinta–San Pedro Mártir drainages and the Highlands of Chiapas and Guatemala, although he considers the contact with the former region to have been concentrated in the late Middle Formative, rather than at the time of early Xe.

Willey (1977b: 135–37) wrote that "it seems most likely that . . . the generic line of ceramic development for the earliest Petén pottery [Xe] is the one which can be traced from Barra-Ocos through Cuadros-Jocotal and Olmec," noting that the closest ties seem to be with the Grijalva Valley (1970: 354–55); but he has preferred to emphasize the likelihood of immigration into the Maya Lowlands from more than one neighboring zone (1977c: 400–401), as has Sabloff (1975: 10, 230). Willey (1977b: 136–37; 1977c: 399) thought it most likely the Xe settlers and their Olmec kin were Maya speakers, but he noted Gareth Lowe's preference for a Zoquean identity for the Olmec.

Lowe (1977: 266, fig. 9.3) suggested immigration into the Lowlands along rivers from the highlands of Chiapas or Guatemala. Robert J. Sharer and James C. Gifford (1970) suggested an origin for Xe in the highlands of western El Salvador, and Sharer's subsequent excavations (Sedat and Sharer 1972; Sharer and Sedat 1987a) in the Salama Valley, Baja Verapaz, and at Sakajut, Alta Verapaz, have produced pottery with form and modal ties to Xe ceramics.

The highlands have been an attractive choice, for this area is Mayan-speaking today, and it is abundantly clear that at a somewhat later date the peoples of the Guatemala Highlands contributed many of the elements that coalesced to form the Classic Lowland Maya civilization. The relevant areas of Chiapas, Tabasco, and Veracruz, in contrast, raised questions of ethnic and linguistic identity, as a commonly held opinion has been that this area was occupied by Mixe-Zoque speakers.

Nearby complexes in the Maya Lowlands have also been suggested to be closely related to Xe and Real; these include the early Eb complex of Tikal, early Jenney Creek at Barton Ramie, and the closely related Bladen and Bolay complexes at Cuello and Colha, Belize. Lowe (1978: 365) argued that, given the other early complexes in the lowlands, Xe derived from both Chiapas and the Maya Lowlands.

One result of these wide-ranging comparisons has been to place Xe firmly in the eastern Meso-

Map 1.1. Eastern Mesoamerica.

american sequence as a developmental lowland Maya stage, anchored by what seemed to be an increasing number of strands to pottery-producing societies on all sides. Perhaps most important in all of the above reconstructions, however, is that Xe was interpreted to be ancestral to late Middle Formative Mamom ceramics and, until the discovery of the Swasey ceramic complex in Belize, as the first evidence of Maya farming populations that had spread north into the lowlands from the highlands of Guatemala.

Reassessment of the Swasey Phase at Cuello, Belize

The position of Xe as the earliest village farming culture in the Maya Lowlands was challenged in 1975 and subsequent years by new discoveries at Cuello, in northern Belize.[3] A series of stratified and internally consistent radiocarbon dates from structural deposits at the base of a Late Formative ceremonial platform (Platform 34) suggested that the earliest ceramic complex, called Swasey, dated to the Early Formative period, a span previously unidentified in the Maya Lowlands (Hammond 1975a; 1977; 1984; Pring 1975; 1977; Hammond et al. 1979; Pring and Hammond 1982). These dates placed the beginnings of the Swasey phase before 2000 B.C.,[4] possibly not long after 2500 B.C., about a thousand years before the first excavated settlements in the Petén and almost that much earlier than the earliest known settlement at Chalchuapa, in the southern Maya Highlands.[5] The Swasey Maya at Cuello lived in a village of perhaps several dozen houses, built pole-and-thatch structures on low, lime-plastered platforms that because of their large size may have served a community ritual or administrative purpose, and grew maize and other crops.

Several aspects of the Swasey phase as it was originally defined, in addition to its early date, disturbed archaeologists (e.g., M. D. Coe 1980: 34–35; 1987: 37; Marcus 1983). The pottery was technically far superior to that of pre–1500 B.C. complexes elsewhere in the Americas. Swasey potters crafted vessels in a variety of shapes, including bottles, used excellent cream-to-buff, red, brown, and black slips, sometimes in combinations, and mastered a complex resist technique of decoration by 1000 B.C. The complex is not at all like the Early or Middle Formative Olmec complexes of the Gulf Coast. Most ceramists would have been happy with a Middle Formative date for Swasey on stylistic grounds, but the radiocarbon ages seemed to preclude that late a placement. Another difficulty was that the Swasey complex appeared to change very little for about a thousand years, far longer than Maya ceramic phases generally lasted.

In an effort to come to grips with this problem, Laura J. Kosakowsky (1983; 1987b) studied a large sample of Cuello pottery excavated in 1980 and was able to subdivide Swasey on the basis of changing frequencies of vessel forms, lip and rim shapes, decorative modes, and the appearance of new cream and honey-brown ceramic groups. She established a new complex called Bladen, corresponding in time to the second half of the original Swasey phase. Although the relationships of Bladen to other early Maya ceramic complexes are not completely understood, Kosakowsky tentatively placed the complex in the Xe sphere and suggested an age of 1500 to 1000 or 900 B.C. (1987b: 90), following Hammond (1984: 823–24).

Material comparable to late Swasey, or Bladen, was excavated in the late 1970s and early 1980s at Colha, 25 km southeast of Cuello (Valdez and Adams 1982; Potter et al. 1984; Valdez 1987). Valdez (1987: 233–37) dates this Bolay ceramic complex to 900–600 B.C. and has suggested that it be placed in a new northern Belize Bolay sphere, rather than in the Xe sphere.[6]

This subdivision of the Swasey sequence in northern Belize seemed to solve neatly the problem raised by a thousand-year-long ceramic phase. The strongly implied relationship between Bladen/Bolay and Xe—although Kosakowsky and Valdez have been careful to note that distinctions between these complexes are as marked as the similarities—also allowed apparent resolution of another thorny issue, namely, the origin of Xe pottery in the Petén. Its origin could now be traced, in large part, to the earlier Swasey complex, from which Bladen and Bolay differ very little and from which they clearly derived. Since the definition of the Bladen and Bolay complexes, the course of ceramic development in the lowlands seemed more direct and relatively straightforward.

But the early date of the Swasey phase must be

reassessed. Compelling evidence indicates that the Swasey phase dates to the Middle Formative and that the Early Formative period in the Maya Lowlands, therefore, remains to be identified. Eight La Jolla radiocarbon determinations from charcoal samples collected during the 1979 excavations at Cuello, published in *Radiocarbon* in 1984 (Linick 1984: 93–94) but neglected until now, conflict with the 1975 and 1976 samples.[7] Three of these runs, from Chicanel and Mamom deposits, are consistent with dates for these phases from other lowland sites. The other five came from Swasey phase excavation units (Construction Phases II and III). The central uncalibrated radiocarbon ages of these five range between 570 and 470 b.c., and the 1–sigma ranges for the calibrated dates fall between 799 and 402 B.C.[8] Norman Hammond (personal communication 1987–88; Linick 1984: 93) states that a similar series of 1979 dates from the same excavation area submitted to Cambridge University produced duplicate results. About ten determinations from 1979, then, date the Swasey and Bladen phases to the Middle Formative period, near the beginning of the Mamom phase and later.

Why is it that an approximately equal number of radiocarbon samples from the 1975 and 1976 excavations yielded dates 500 to 1500 years earlier for the same cultural materials? The answer, I believe, lies in the way the samples were collected. They were small amalgamated samples, generally consisting of pieces of charcoal collected throughout the excavation units (N. Hammond, personal communication 1988), and their provenance and age is therefore uncertain. One date (Q-1574) was described as being from "structural timbers burnt in situ in postholes" (Hammond et al. 1979: 95–96), but even this sample may have contained earlier pieces of charcoal (N. Hammond, personal communication 1988).

The probable origin of the amalgamated samples also explains why the dates become older with increasing depth in the stratigraphic column. When the original Middle Formative settlers moved to Cuello they encountered an environment with small amounts of charcoal from natural fires or perhaps from earlier fires of human origin, although evidence for a preceramic occupation is currently nonexistent. This old charcoal was incorporated in the fill of their first low platforms and resulted in the earliest dates at the base of the Cuello stratigraphy. Later, superimposed units of fill would have incorporated an increasing proportion of recent domestic refuse and charcoal, so that the old charcoal would have constituted a decreasingly significant part of the later amalgamated samples and the radiocarbon ages would have with time come closer to approximating dates for similar ceramic materials elsewhere in the Maya Lowlands. Within a few hundred years, by the late Mamom or early Chicanel phase, the Cuello dates fall where we would have expected them to.

One question remains. Why did the 1979 samples run by La Jolla and Cambridge not yield equally early determinations, since they were collected in the same fashion? The answer may be that those more recently excavated fill units, most of which came from grid square 35/30, contained redeposited midden of recent origin, with very little old charcoal. This is speculation, however, and at this time the question cannot be answered with confidence.

I believe we should reject the Early Formative dates for the Swasey and Bladen phases at Cuello and should accept the dates that range between about 800 and 500 or 450 B.C. The ceramics are more at home in the Middle Formative, and similar materials have been dated between about 850 and 600 B.C. at nearby Colha.[9] Other complexes with general modal similarities to Swasey and Bladen, such as early Eb at Tikal, early Jenney Creek at Barton Ramie, and Xe at Altar de Sacrificios and Seibal, date to the Middle Formative.[10]

Excavations at Santa Rita Corozal, 30 km north of Cuello, have produced ceramics similar to Swasey (Pring 1975). Arlen and Diane Chase (1987: 51, fig. 2a) note that no distinct Mamom complex was isolated in their excavations at this site and that "the Middle Preclassic is characterized by a blending of Swasey [including Bladen] and Mamom" traits. They see "a smooth transition from the earlier Swasey [Bladen]-related ceramics into the Late Preclassic Chicanel-related types." Their interpretation of the sequence supports a Middle Formative date for Swasey.

Robin Robertson (personal communication 1988) see extremely close modal and typological ties between Swasey/Bladen ceramics at Cuello and her earliest Late Formative (Ixtabai complex) pottery

(Robertson-Freidel 1980) at Cerros, 38 km north of Cuello on Chetumal Bay. Her comparison bolsters the argument for a Middle Formative Swasey/Bladen date.

The Cordilleran Origins of Xe

Study of a number of early ceramic collections from the Maya lowlands, Chiapas, Tabasco, Veracruz, and Guatemala has led me to reevaluate the origin and external relationships of the Xe ceramic complex of the Pasion drainage. I have concluded, first, that Xe is not closely related to any of the roughly contemporary ceramic complexes in the southern lowlands.[11] Xe pottery has so far been found only at Altar de Sacrificios and Seibal, and it has not been reported from any Maya site beyond the Pasion River.

Three complexes in northern Belize have been suggested to be roughly contemporary with or related to the Xe sphere, or both; these are the early facet of Jenney Creek at Barton Ramie (Sharer 1976: 61–62; Gifford 1976: 83–84) and the more recently defined Bladen and Bolay complexes at Cuello and Colha (Kosakowsky 1987a; 1987b; Valdez 1987). Early Jenney Creek, although it may overlap with Xe in time (Sharer 1978: 62), shows little similarity in content. Laura Kosakowsky (1987b: 90) says that Bladen, at Cuello, "bears some resemblances to the Xe complex," but that "the dissimilarities are more noteworthy than the similarities." Fred Valdez (1987: 233–34; personal communication 1987) states that the Bolay complex at Colha, which is essentially similar to Bladen at Cuello, shares numerous modal similarities with Xe, especially in vessel forms, but that the differences are sufficient to place Bolay and Bladen in a separate ceramic sphere. Although the modal correspondences between Bolay and Xe clearly exist, I think they are not striking and prefer to see them as the result of contemporaneity in adjacent zones of eastern Mesoamerica. The northern Belize tradition of glossy reds and blacks and of pale, thin orange-buffs is sufficiently different from the Xe and Real complex matte, glittery, and micaceous reds and whites that I consider it likely they derive from different ceramic traditions.

In the northeast Petén, the earliest ceramic materials are currently thought to be those of the Ah Pam Early Mamom complex in the Lake Yaxha and Lake Sacnab basins (P. Rice 1979: 13–22). Prudence Rice begins Ah Pam at about 750 B.C., linking it closely with the early Eb complex at Tikal, which has one radiocarbon date of 800 (784) 558 B.C. (588 ± 53 b.c., P-750) (W. R. Coe 1965: 1406), and somewhat more distantly with the Xe sphere, through "broad resemblances in certain categories of form, decoration, and surface treatment," especially the presence of dull red and cream slips and bolstered lip tecomates (1979: 20). Eb, however, contains polished orange pottery (W. R. Coe 1965: 1406, fig. 2a) that corresponds to early Mamom at Seibal and Altar, and Culbert (1977: 36) sees little or no relationship between this complex and either Xe or Jenney Creek.

My second argument is that Xe pottery was intrusive into the Pasion River drainage from Chiapas or the northern highlands of Guatemala and that it was probably not Maya. The major slipped types, Abelino Red, Huetche White, and Crisanto Black (Adams 1971; Willey 1970; Sabloff 1975), have thin, matte, easily eroded, and powdery slips that are dead ringers for Isthmian slips in color, hardness, and dullness of appearance. Xe pastes and slips at Altar, closer to the Isthmian source than Seibal, are glittery and micaceous, and the paste is usually sand- or ash-tempered, generally unlike contemporary lowland Maya pottery, but indistinguishable from much contemporary pottery in Chiapas. Vessel forms of the Xe complex are more like those of the early Middle Formative in Chiapas and Tabasco than they are like vessel forms of any contemporary complex in the Maya lowlands.

The double-line break, incised on exteriors or interiors of bowls, dishes, and plates, is a common and widespread feature—practically a sine qua non—of early and late Middle Formative complexes in Mesoamerica, especially Tabasco, Veracruz, and Chiapas, as are circumferential lines of connected arcs, or "bouncing lines." The double-line break also occurs on the Pacific Coast and highlands of Guatemala and El Salvador in Early or early Middle Formative contexts.

The distribution of this trait in the Formative Maya Lowlands, however, is spotty and relatively late. On Xe vessels at Altar de Sacrificios the double-line break was a common incised motif, as was the bouncing line (Adams 1971: 42, figs. 1gg, hh, 2f, 6e, 7a–c, i). In the Real complex at Seibal, however, Willey (1970: 328) noted only one double-line break, and bouncing lines are not illustrated. The motifs seem to be absent in the contemporary Swasey, Bladen, Bolay, and early Jenney Creek complexes, but the double-line break appeared on Guitara Incised in the following Lopez Mamom complex at Cuello (Kosakowsky 1987b: 44, 45, 90, fig. 5.3; personal communication 1987). It has also been reported on the same type in the Chiwa Mamom complex at Colha (Valdez 1987: 85, 239; personal communication 1987), where the bouncing line is also common. Valdez also reports a few sherds of white-rimmed black ware, rare in the Maya Lowlands. Double-line breaks persisted especially late in Belize. Gifford (1976: 164, figs. 88a, e) illustrated this motif inside Lucha Incised dish rims at Barton Ramie.

The double-line break occurs in the Late Formative and later outside the Maya Lowlands, so the Middle and Late Formative presence of the motif in the Maya Lowlands, when it seems to be limited mostly to Belize, is perhaps less significant than the fact that it does not appear in early Middle Formative complexes except at Altar de Sacrificios.

A cache that derived from a Xe context at Seibal suggests close ritual relationships and trade in precious commodities with the late Olmec heartland or with areas to the south in Chiapas that were intimately connected with La Venta. Cache 7 contained six jade celts, one jade ice-pick-shaped perforator, and five jars of the Real Xe type Crisanto Black (Willey 1978: figs. 90, 91, 104, 105; A.L. Smith 1982: 118, 243, figs. 188, 189). The cache was laid out in a cruciform or quadripartite arrangement similar to that of three caches of celts, magnetite mirrors, and other ritual objects from La Venta (Drucker 1952: figs. 10b, pl. 8; Drucker et al. 1959: fig. 51). The Seibal cache has a date of 831 (803) 781 B.C. The date of the La Venta celt caches is not clear, but they seem to span most of the time of construction at the site's ceremonial center, or most of the Middle Formative.

About 120 km south of La Venta, the Middle Grijalva Basin site of San Isidro (Lowe 1981) has produced a series of 17 La Venta–style centerline caches and burials in Mound 20 that contain celts or pseudocelts and a few jade ornaments in rows, quadrilateral arrangements, or other groupings. Lowe dates these to the Equipac phase of his Modified Olmec period, about 700–550 B.C.

The 1–sigma ranges of calibrated dates for Xe at Seibal and Altar de Sacrificios are 831–781, 1040–770, and 1253–840 B.C. (see Note 5). Xe pottery appears similar to ceramics of the Dili phase in the Chiapas Central Depression, of Conchas I in southwestern Guatemala, and to approximately contemporary complexes reported elsewhere on the Isthmus (Lowe 1978: figures 11.3, 11.4; McDonald 1983: fig. 3). Xe definitely predates the Escalera and Conchas 2 phases, with their red-to-orange cloudy resist wares that are related to the highly polished orange resist pottery of early Mamom. A span of 900 to 750 B.C. for Xe seems to fit the limited evidence best.

Since Xe pottery formed the entire domestic and ritual assemblage at Altar and Seibal in their earliest phase of occupation, I believe that the complex represents the migration of non-Maya peoples into the southern Petén, which seems to have been largely vacant until this time. Precisely where they came from is uncertain, but we can eliminate some areas in a search for origins and point to other areas and routes as strong contenders.

To the north, the Chontalpa of northwestern Tabasco can be eliminated as a point of origin of the Xe intrusion into the southern Petén. Edward B. Sisson (1976: 604–617) does not believe the ceramics of his Puente phase in the Chontalpa, estimated to date 900 to 700 B.C., are very much like those of the contemporaneous Xe phase. He further suggests (1976: 617) that all of western Tabasco can be ruled out as a source.

The Chiuaan phase of Trinidad, Tabasco, on the Usumacinta floodplain, is suggested to show some correspondences to Xe (Rands 1969: 6; 1977: 160, 170; 1987: 208–211), although Rands's and George R. Holley's (personal communication 1987) description of the Chiuaan-Xot tradition indicates that the similarities are general.

The site of Tierra Blanca, Tabasco, a few kilometers up the Usumacinta from Trinidad, also provides substantial evidence of Formative settlement in the middle Usumacinta drainage. Lorenzo Ochoa and Luis Casasola (1978: 27–28; manuscript in preparation; Ochoa 1983: 154–57; personal communication 1988) describe a group of San Lorenzo and Nacaste phase types, including Aguatepec Thick, a few sherds of Calzadas Carved, and a red ceramic similar to Tatagapa Red, that constitute their Early Formative San Lorenzo-related Chun complex. The following Kub complex has most of these, except Calzadas Carved, as well as Camaño Coarse and Tular Black and White, which continue into the Nacaste phase at San Lorenzo. The most common types in Kub are Achiotes Unslipped and Sapote Striated, Middle and Late Formative Maya Lowlands types, but the typical Middle Formative Maya reds, oranges, creams, and blacks are absent, and the Kub complex is basically unlike anything in the Maya area. The following Payol complex forms only about 1.5 percent of the site total and consists only of the Late Formative Lowland Maya types Sierra Red, Laguna Verde Incised, Polvero Black, Flor Cream, and the Terminal Formative Ixcanrio Orange Polychrome. These relatively few sherds probably indicate a spread of the lowland Chicanel sphere.

The ceramics from Tierra Blanca, therefore, show strong Olmec influences from the northwest in the Early or early Middle Formative, but they lack close ties to either Xe or Mamom in the Maya Lowlands. Xe pottery has not been found on the Usumacinta downstream from Altar.

This portion of the middle Usumacinta was not the home of the earliest farmers entering the Maya Lowlands, and it is by extension unlikely that the bearers of either the Xe or the early Mamom ceramic complex entered the Peten by way of the Usumacinta drainage from the north. Ochoa argues for a "migration from the Olmec metropolitan area into the Usumacinta drainage in the late Middle Formative" (1983: 155), but he refers primarily to the late Olmec sculptural style, and it is in any case the spread beyond the middle Usumacinta that most concerns us here.

The Xe complex is, in contrast, similar in slip characteristics, paste, and forms to a number of Isthmian assemblages that I have examined, but it is not identical to any one of them. Its makers do not seem to have come directly from the Soconusco of coastal Chiapas or the La Victoria–Salinas la Blanca area (M. D. Coe 1961; M. D. Coe and Flannery 1967) in nearby Guatemala. Dili phase ceramics from Chiapa de Corzo, in the Central Depression of Chiapas, are perhaps as close as any I have looked at, but they, too, differ. Full publication of the Chiapa de Corzo ceramic sequence will facilitate future comparisons.

Numerous traits link Xe to the late facet of the Xox complex of the Salama Valley, Baja Verapaz, which is estimated to date to about 1000 to 800 B.C. (Sharer and Sedat 1987a: 276–82, 305; 1987b; David W. Sedat, personal communication 1987). Sharer and Sedat (1987a: 248–53, 468) also excavated ceramics comparable to Xox at Sakajut, near Coban in the Alta Verapaz, where it is associated with a radiocarbon date of 1388 (1044) 830 B.C. (930 ± 190 b.c., P-3208). They believe that the roots of the Xox complex, which they place about 1200 B.C., lead back to Ocos on the Pacific Coast, but they note that preslip grooving, horizontal cut and punched appliques, red daubing or zoned painting, red-on-cream slips, fugitive red embellishments, and pallid red slips, in addition to general similarities in vessel forms and slipped wares, tie Xox to Xe. Although I have not seen this pottery, the published descriptions seem to me to link it more closely to the Pacific Coast than to the southern lowlands. That Xe and Xox are related is certain, but the similarities may result in part from a common ancestry, and I hazard the opinion that Xe did not develop directly from the Xox complex in the highlands. Xe pottery is more like contemporary assemblages in the Central Depression of Chiapas than it is like Xox.

The information now available indicates that Xe did not enter the southern Petén from the Tabasco-Veracruz Lowlands to the north, by way of the Usumacinta, nor is it particularly like the earliest complexes at Kaminaljuyu or Chalchuapa in the southeast Maya Highlands. This leaves a vast area to the west, including the eastern lowlands, low sierras, and central highlands of Chiapas, and to the south and southwest, in the northern highlands of Guatemala, for the origin of Xe. The Verapaz Project and other recent surveys in Alta Verapaz (Sharer and Sedat 1987a: 447–48) indicate a widespread occupation in the Early Formative and early Middle Formative. The most probable entry into the lowlands would have been north and east through the Chixoy-Salinas or the Lacantun drainages, or possibly down the Pasion-Sebol river system. If the last drainage was too far east for the spread of this Isthmian-Cordilleran ceramic tradition, it would likely have been the chief means of access for other early groups in the southern lowlands (Adams 1978; Sharer and Sedat 1987a: 22–24).

Ceramic evidence at Altar and Seibal may be relevant to determining the direction of entry. Sabloff (1975: 48, 49, 229) has suggested that Real at Seibal may be somewhat earlier than Xe at Altar. The evidence he cites is that the early red pottery at Seibal more often has a duller, darker slip than does the early red pottery at Altar, where Abelino Red tended to be lighter colored and waxier, more like the following Mamom complex Joventud Red. The duller slip at Seibal, furthermore, appeared to be stratigraphically earlier than the waxier slip. White pottery and thickened tecomate rims, early traits in the greater Isthmian area, were also more common at Seibal.

Although I have seen only portions of the collections, I believe the Altar dull, dark, matte-slipped reds are as early as any of the Seibal reds, although they may not appear as frequently. Perhaps more significant in considering the age of the earliest material is the nature of the slips and pastes, and in these aspects I find the Altar ceramics more like Chiapas pottery than are the Seibal ceramics. The Altar pottery is sand- or ash-tempered, and the pastes and slips are micaceous and glittery, unlike those at Seibal, which are calcite-tempered and not micaceous. Although there may not be as much of the earliest material at Altar as there is at Seibal, the Xe pottery from Altar probably had diverged less from the ceramics in the area from which it derived. This might reflect the greater distance of Seibal from the point of origin, but I think it more likely indicates an earlier date for Altar. We have only three Xe radiocarbon dates, but the weighted average of the two Altar dates is 1060 (924) 830 B.C., compared to the 831 (803) 781 B.C. Seibal date.

If Xe at Altar is earlier than Real at Seibal, this suggests that the earliest settlers moved east. They would in this case have entered through one of the river systems that drain into the Usumacinta, rather than moving north along the Pasion River from the Alta Verapaz.

My third and final suggestion in this section is that we reconsider the relationship of Xe and Mamom. Because of stratigraphic evidence at Altar and Seibal that Xe pottery was followed by early Mamom, it has been generally accepted that Xe developed in situ into Mamom (Willey 1970: 355; Adams 1971: 4; Sabloff 1975: 230–31). But Xe and Mamom are very different from each other, and it is difficult for me to see one developing directly from the other without the addition of external ceramic elements. As Adams (1971: 154) recognized, "relationships between Xe and San Felix ceramic complexes are not particularly close . . . In general terms, the relationships between Xe and Mamom spheres are surprisingly weak, considering the apparent *in situ* development." The ceramic stratigraphy at Altar and Seibal can just as easily be interpreted to indicate a gradual replacement of Xe by early Mamom, with some mixing, as it can to show an evolutionary process.

The relationship between Swasey/Bladen/Bolay and Mamom, on the other hand, is closer. Valdez (1987: 233–39) argues that Mamom develops out of Bolay at Colha, and both Pring (1977: 48–58) and Kosakowsky (1987b: 90) are emphatic that Swasey/Bladen led directly into Lopez Mamom. I agree with this assessment and see a direct developmental relationship between the two complexes, although the early facet of Mamom in the Peten contains a few features that do not appear to derive from Belize, most notably a polished, mottled orange-on-cream, which was identified in small quantities for the first time in northern Belize at Colha (Valdez 1987: 239).

The Xe intrusion into the southern lowlands, then, represents an expansion from eastern Chiapas or the northern highlands of Guatemala into a very sparsely inhabited lowland, riverine terrain. The spread occurred during the time La Venta appears to have been the primary Olmec center. The ceramics of this small group were different from roughly coeval complexes in the Peten and Belize, as well as from the Mamom complex that replaced them about 700–650 B.C., and it is likely that they were absorbed into or replaced by bearers of a Maya ceramic tradition.[12]

**Ethnic Identity of Early Cultures
in Eastern Mesoamerica:
The Greater Isthmian Area,
the Olmec, and the Mixe-Zoque**

The question of the ethnic identity of early cultures in eastern Mesoamerica has long stimulated discussion. If we accept as evidence continuity in material

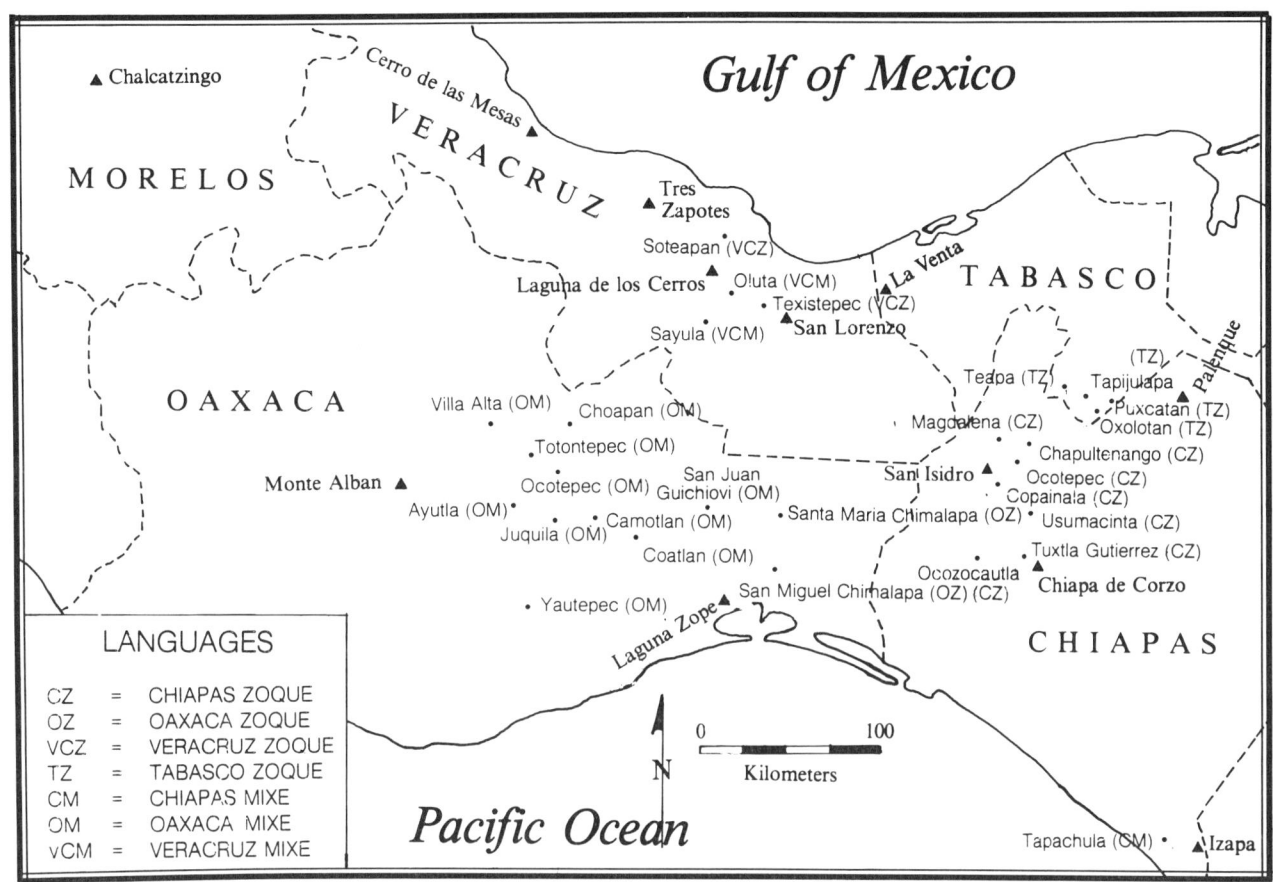

Map 1.2. Olmec-Mixe-Zoque Area. (After Campbell and Kaufman 1976: fig. 1.)

culture, specifically ceramics, Lowland Maya ethnic continuity may be traced back as far as the beginnings of the Swasey, Bolay, Jenney Creek, and Eb phases, or to about 850 or 900 B.C., but not yet beyond this time in the lowlands. The same continuity is apparent in the area comprising southern Veracruz, western Tabasco, and Chiapas, which Gareth Lowe once referred to as the "Olmec Isthmian Block" (Green and Lowe 1967: 71) and the "Greater Isthmian Area" (Lowe 1971: 222), and has more recently called "the Isthmian-Cordilleran mainland" (1978: 351) (Map 1.2).

Lowe has long espoused the views that this area showed cultural continuity from earliest times, that for much of its Formative history the Olmec civilization was its major unifying force, and that it and the Olmec could be linked with the Mixe-Zoque. In 1977 he argued that "the known Zoquean and Mayan cultures represent two branches of an older, originating trunk society, the Isthmian Olmec, and that marked cultural differences over time have resulted from distinctive responses to varied environmental possibilities" (1977: 240). The vast differences between the ceramic traditions of the Maya Lowlands and the greater Isthmian area—seen in decorative modes, firing techniques, vessel forms, pastes, and the nature and colors of slips—provide ample reason for positing ethnic and linguistic differences.

It must be kept in mind when comparing the two that the greater Isthmian ceramic tradition is far older than that of the peninsular Maya, going back at least to the Barra phase on the coast of Chiapas, the beginnings of which date no later than 1800 B.C.

(Lowe 1978: 353).[13] The San Lorenzo Olmec (M. D. Coe and Diehl 1980: 395–96) developed from this Isthmian tradition by 1400 or 1350 B.C., and the first major construction phase at La Venta began before 1000 B.C., perhaps as early as 1200 B.C. (Berger et al. 1967). In the Maya Lowlands no settlements can be dated securely before 800 or 900 B.C. The two earliest dates from the Maya Highlands, for the Xox phase at Sakajut, Alta Verapaz, and the Tok phase at Chalchuapa, El Salvador, suggest occupations one or two hundred years earlier. These early highland manifestations very likely developed from an early Ocos-like stratum on the Pacific Coast, which extended at least as far west as the site of El Carmen, in western El Salvador (Demarest 1987: 336). The gradual divergence of Zoque and Mayan languages and cultures perhaps began in this coastal zone by 1500 B.C.

The linguistic evidence for the ancient ethnic distinction between the Isthmus and the Maya area was presented in 1976 by Lyle Campbell and Terrence Kaufman, who adduced comparative data to support the contention that the Olmec spoke a Mixe-Zoquean language. Their argument rested on evidence that the area in which Olmec civilization arose was occupied in more recent times by speakers of Mixe-Zoquean, and that a large number of Mixe-Zoquean loan words can be found in Mayan and other languages. Many of these loans they considered very old, referring to things that are diagnostic of the mesoamerican culture area and are therefore lexical items that neighboring peoples might have borrowed from the more advanced Olmec, such as the names for cultivated plants, items relating to maize preparation, and certain calendrical and ritual items. Campbell (personal communication 1987) notes that the Late Formative Izapan archaeological horizon must also be recognized as Mixe-Zoquean in speech and therefore as a possible source for loan words into Mayan languages in post-Olmec times.

Early Distribution of Obsidian in Eastern Mesoamerica: Maya, Mixe, and Zoque

The pattern of formative obsidian procurement in eastern Mesoamerica supports the hypothesis of marked cultural differences between the Maya area and the Isthmus and Cordilleran mainland of Chiapas. In the Classic period, the most important obsidian source for the Maya Lowlands was El Chayal, about 25 km northeast of Kaminaljuyu (Hammond 1972; Nelson 1985). El Chayal did not supply obsidian to the lowlands until the Late Formative, however, before which time almost all lowland obsidian, including that from Altar and Seibal (J. A. Graham et al. 1972; Nelson et al. 1978), came from San Martin Jilotepeque, about 25 km northwest of Kaminaljuyu and also near a tributary of the Motagua River (Nelson et al. 1983). The sources are very close to each other, and to explain this difference in distribution patterns it has been argued that during the Late Formative the growing Maya community of Kaminaljuyu took control of the El Chayal outcrop from some other polity or trading network to the west, and that the source remained thereafter in Maya hands (Sidrys and Kimberlin 1979; Nelson et al. 1983; Morley et al. 1983: 28, 67).

El Chayal obsidian was widely distributed, almost always present, and often abundant at Early and early Middle Formative sites in the greater Isthmian area. At sites on the Pacific Coast of Chiapas (Clark and Lee 1984: 243–47), most obsidian was obtained from Tajumulco, closer than El Chayal or San Martin Jilotepeque, but El Chayal obsidian usually exceeded that from San Martin Jilotepeque. At Laguna Zope, Oaxaca, on the southern Isthmus of Tehuantepec (Zeitlin 1978), and at San Lorenzo, Veracruz (Cobean et al. 1971), El Chayal obsidian was common in the Early Formative, and San Martin Jilotepeque obsidian was not.

During the Early Formative of the Central Depression of Chiapas, in contrast, El Chayal and San Martin Jilotepeque obsidian was imported in roughly equal amounts. During the Middle and Late Formative, El Chayal obsidian was rare (Clark and Lee 1984: 259–63), and San Martin Jilotepeque was dominant everywhere. La Venta during the Middle Formative also imported large quantities of obsidian from San Martin Jilotepeque and none from El Chayal (Jack et al. 1972: table 1), also following the Maya pattern. The overall pattern of obsidian distribution, then, could be taken to be in harmony with the suggestion that the greater Isthmian area was ethnically distinct from the Maya Lowlands as far back as the Early Formative, although by the Middle Formative, the Central Depression of Chiapas has become partially realigned with the Maya Lowlands.

Perhaps more striking, however, is the evidence that within the Mixe-Zoque area itself two obsidian distribution systems existed, and that these may have been aligned with ethnic or linguistic boundaries. The first distribution network embraced sites in the Soconusco area of coastal Chiapas that obtained predominantly El Chayal and Tajumulco obsidian, as well as sites to the west in Oaxaca that had El Chayal and Central Mexican obsidian. This first group would also apparently have included San Lorenzo, in the Olmec heartland. Clark and Lee (1984: 246–47) have raised the possibility that the Early Formative El Chayal distribution pattern, extending far up the coast to Oaxaca, resulted from its being tied into a coastal canoe route that allowed obsidian to be traded more widely that it would have through an overland distribution network. The second group of sites lay in the Chiapas Central Depression and included La Venta, where San Martin Jilotepeque obsidian was important in the Early Formative and dominant by the Middle Formative, as it was in the Maya Lowlands until the Late Formative.

These two obsidian networks, if indeed they do form a meaningful pattern, correspond roughly to the distribution of known Mixe- and Zoque-speaking towns in the greater Isthmian area (Campbell and Kaufman 1976: fig. 1; Justeson, personal communication 1987; Kaufman, personal communication 1987; Campbell, personal communication 1987; see also Map 1.2). If this late distribution of Mixe and Zoque speakers indicates the approximate location of these groups in the Formative period, with Mixe-speakers extending east along the Pacific Coast to Izapa and beyond, it would seem that the coastal and Oaxaca Mixe were able to obtain El Chayal and Tajumulco obsidian, whereas the Zoque of Chiapas and Tabasco (including most of the Olmec heartland?) were, like the neighboring Lowland Maya, using San Martin Jilotepeque obsidian. The procurement systems would have developed within preexisting ethnic boundaries, but the eastern network seems to have included both Maya and Zoque by the Middle Formative.

Since this difference in distribution networks appears to have obtained since the beginning of the Early Formative, the suggestion would be compatible with a frequent glottochronological estimate for the divergence of Mixe-Zoquean at 1600 B.C. (Kaufman 1974; 1976: 106; Justeson et al. 1985: table 1).

Late Middle Formative Ceramics on the Pasion River: A Fusion of Maya and Mixe-Zoque?

At Altar de Sacrificios, Adams (1971: 84–86) defined early and late facets of the San Felix Mamom phase. The early facet was characterized by the Mocho Variety of Joventud Red, with a color varying from red to orange to brown, fire-clouding, and a crackled finish. Resist painting and a blotchy, vitrified variety of Pital Cream are also diagnostic. Joventud Red of the late facet (Jolote Variety) is similar to Joventud Red: Joventud Variety at Uaxactun in slip characteristics, having a uniform red color over most of the vessel and being therefore much more like Sierra Red. The Joventud Red: Mocho Variety of early San Felix is also found in Escoba Mamom at Seibal, in both Joventud Red and especially Tierra Mojada Resist (Sabloff 1975: 61–62, 71–74).

This early orange, mottled variety of Joventud Red is closely related, as Adams (1971: 20) noted, to Conchas Orange and other polished orange pottery of the greater Isthmian area. Polished red-orange pottery is often the most obvious diagnostic of the Escalera (Chiapa III) and coeval phases in Chiapas and western Guatemala, serving as a horizon marker for the period from about 700 to 500 B.C. (e.g., Lowe 1978: 366).

Much of this Isthmian polished orange pottery, including a portion of the orange ceramics of the Chiapa de Corzo Escalera complex itself, resembles the early Usulutan resist-decorated, single-slipped or double-slipped orange-on-white pottery of Highland Guatemala and El Salvador far more than it does early Mamom Joventud Red: Mocho Variety of the southern Petén, but some of it shows greater resemblances to early Joventud Red and Tierra Mojada Resist in the southern and northern lowlands. Samples of the orange pottery of Conchas 2 at La Victoria that I have examined, for example, are essentially identical to early Joventud Red: Mocho Variety.

In both Chiapas and the Maya Lowlands this polished, sometimes waxy, mottled orange pottery has no precedent before 650 or 700 B.C. It therefore must ultimately derive, probably by way of Highland Guatemala, from western El Salvador, where the precursors of the Usulutan tradition were present well before 700 B.C. (Demarest and Sharer 1982; Demarest 1986: 140–46). We do not yet know how and where Usulutan ceramics developed into the lowland Tierra Mojada Resist and early Joventud Red or why some sites in the greater Isthmian area retained true highland Usulutan pottery, whereas others have polished oranges that are like lowland Joventud Red.

Tierra Mojada Resist is rare in the eastern portion of the lowlands. It is illustrated from the Eb complex at Tikal (W. R. Coe 1965: Fig. 2a), and Valdez (1987: 87, 239, figs. 14, 15) reports two vessels and several sherds from the Chiwa Mamom complex at Colha, noting that it had not been previously reported from northern Belize. I have not seen it in other Belize collections. In the northern Maya area it is also limited to the western and central portions of the peninsula.

This mottled orange pottery represents continued interaction between the southern Maya Lowlands, the Maya Highlands, and probably the Mixe-Zoquean areas to the west and south. The early Xe settlers along the Pasion River maintained contact with southwestern Guatemala or eastern Chiapas at the same time that they were being incorporated into the larger Maya sphere, and the result is an early Mamom complex that, as Adams (1971: 154) noted, has strong Chiapan links. In the early Mamom phase of the Pasion River we may be looking at the archaeological remains of the fusion of two distinct cultures. By the late Mamom phase, ceramic influence from the greater Isthmian area waned, and the Maya were increasingly the donor culture in contacts between the greater Isthmian area and the Yucatán Peninsula (Demarest 1976; Andrews V 1986).

Spread of the Lowland Maya: Expansion of the Mamom Ceramic Sphere

The expansion of the early Mamom sphere from the southern Peten coincided with a rapidly accelerating spread of the Maya throughout the lowland zone they were to occupy fully by the Late Formative. Mamom-related ceramic complexes appeared from the south to the far north of Yucatán. On the northern plains, as in other areas, Mamom pottery marks the arrival of the first sedentary villages.

Differences within the Mamom sphere suggest that the expansion of lowland Maya population occurred along two major vectors. The earlier appears to have been from the southern Petén rapidly up into the northwestern lowlands, probably by a westerly route.

The Early Nabanche Mamom complex of Yucatan, best known at Komchen, consists of three major slipped groups, the black Chunhinta, the red Joventud, and the cream-to-buff Dzudzuquil; the very minor Muxanal Red-on-cream group, which was an import; and the unslipped Achiotes group (Andrews V 1986; 1988). The complex is similar to early Mamom at Altar and Seibal, especially in the slips. Tierra Mojada Resist at Seibal and the early Mocho Variety of Joventud Red at Altar de Sacrificios are indistinguishable from much of the early Joventud Red in northern Yucatan and also from the common northern Majan Red-and-cream-to-buff, the slip of which is mottled and resist-like. The northern black-slipped pottery and the creams are similar to the Chunhinta Black and Pital Cream of Altar and Seibal, and both areas share a variable, mottled black-and-cream-to-buff that I have not seen in other collections. In short, I see far greater similarity between the late Middle Formative ceramics of the northern lowlands of Yucatán and the Pasion drainage than has been recognized. The ceramics of these zones were more intimately related during the Mamom phase than at any later time.

Given both the absence of remains in northern Yucatan predating about 650 or 700 B.C.[14] and the strong ties to the south visible in our earliest ceramic material, it is probable that northern Yucatan was settled at the beginning of the Nabanche Mamom phase by farmers expanding north from the Peten, probably by way of the Usumacinta zone and the western lowlands, rather than directly north through the central Petén, Rio Bec, and Chenes regions or through Quintana Roo. A western route would explain the absence or rarity in the north of several Middle Formative ceramic traits that were predominant in the southeastern lowlands, such as Mars Orange ware, daub-painted pottery, chamfering, and many composite silhouette vessel forms. This western expansion would also explain certain general ceramic ties in northern Maya vessel forms and slips to southern Chiapas at this time, such as the predominance of the flat-base, flaring-wall dish; a strong emphasis on cream-to-buff slips; and the even greater frequency in the north than in the southern Peten of mottled orange-and-cream resist-like slips (see Andrews V 1986: 32–33 for a more extensive consideration of these southern Petén-Chiapas-Early Nabanche similarities). Despite these Chiapan influences in Early Nabanche, which are stronger in the north than they are in early Mamom of Altar and Seibal, it is nevertheless to the southern Peten that the Early Nabanche complex owes its origin, not to the Olmec or their Mixe-Zoque neighbors in the greater Isthmian area of Chiapas and Tabasco.

The second major route of Maya expansion to the north, at a later date, was a more easterly one, from northern Belize and the northeast Peten, where much of the Classic Maya ritual complex was to develop, up into the areas of Campeche later characterized by the Classic period Rio Bec and Chenes architectural styles, and into Quintana Roo. Many of the areas colonized by this northeastern lowland expansion lacked a significant Middle Formative occupation (e.g., Ball 1977b; Robles Castellanos 1980; Fry 1987: 113), apparently remaining uninhabited by sedentary village farmers until 400 B.C. or later. When the earliest ceramic remains appeared in these areas, they were more like those of northern Belize and the northeast Peten than were early assemblages in the western section of the lowlands.

This dual-pronged colonization of the Maya Lowlands helps provide the historical background that will help us better understand certain persistent features in the northeast and northwest. Throughout the Classic period, cultural ties of the eastern sector remained strongest with the northeast Petén and Belize. Examples are the ceramic complexes and the architectural arrangements of the Rio Bec zone on one hand, and the pottery, architecture, and stone sculpture of Coba, which has often been described as a Peten outpost. In the northwest, the Classic (Early Period and Florescent) ceramic traditions are different from those in the area encompassed by the northeastern expansion, emphasizing slate wares and fine-paste wares with different vessel forms. Architecture of Early Period II and the Pure Florescent (Late and Terminal Classic) at Dzibilchaltún, for example, looks to the west—to Palenque and the Central Mexican highlands—for much of its inspiration (Andrews V 1974; 1979; Andrews IV and Andrews V 1980). Late Puuc architectural arrangements at Uxmal and Merida (Tiho) have close parallels in the Valley of Oaxaca. Some of these stimuli reached the western peninsula precisely because it was the most exposed portion, but the pattern of receptivity to non-Maya traits was an old one here.

Conclusions

A reexamination of the ceramics from a number of early sites in the Maya Lowlands, the Olmec heartland, and Chiapas has led me to several independent suggestions about the early culture history of eastern Mesoamerica. I will attempt to summarize and interrelate them.

The Swasey and Bladen phases at Cuello, in northern Belize, widely if by no means universally accepted since 1975 as evidence of the Early Formative period in the Maya Lowlands, date instead to the Middle Formative. A series of radiocarbon dates from the 1979 excavations at Cuello place the beginning of Swasey/Bladen sometime between 900 and 750 B.C. and suggest that it may have lasted until after 600 B.C., thereby perhaps overlapping the span of the Mamom or equivalent late Middle Formative phase at other southern lowland Maya sites. These dates are consistent with radiocarbon determinations for Bladen ceramics at nearby Colha and also with other dates for settled agricultural villages with pre-Mamom pottery in the southern Maya Lowlands. The shift of the Swasey ceramic tradition from the Early to the Middle Formative forces us to reconsider the origins of the earliest agricultural, pottery-producing groups in the Maya Lowland. Pre-Mamom occupations have been defined at Barton Ramie, Cuello, and Colha in northern Belize, at Tikal and the Yaxha-Sacnab basin in the northeast Peten, and at Seibal and Altar on the Pasion. These complexes, dating between 900 and 600 B.C., seem to divide into three geographic spheres, Xe, Swasey, and Eb, which show varying but limited similarities.

The Xe and Real phase occupations of Altar de Sacrificios and Seibal, on the Pasion River, probably date to about 900 to 700 B.C. Their pottery belongs to the tradition of the Isthmus of Tehuantepec and the Cordilleran mainland that can be traced back to Barra and Ocos and that includes the Early and Middle Formative Olmec. The similarity in ceramic assemblages for more than a thousand years over this large area argues strongly for its ethnic and linguistic unity, for its separation from the Maya Lowlands, and for its identification with the historic Mixe-Zoque, and more specifically with the Zoque, in the state of Chiapas. This view has been accepted by many archaeologists and most linguists for a decade and more and is therefore not particularly startling. The suggestion that the Formative patterns of obsidian distribution might have developed within boundaries corresponding to the Formative location of Mixe and Zoque speakers is somewhat more speculative.

The most likely origin of the early Xe farmers is eastern Chiapas or the northern highlands of Guatemala, rather than the middle Usumacinta drainage of the northwestern lowlands. Xe ceramics are most like those of Chiapas, and this may be their most probable origin. But as the Early and early Middle Formative Xox complex of the Salama Valley and other areas of Alta Verapaz shows a number of typological and modal similarities to Xe, an entry into the lowlands through the Pasion-Sebol River drainage can by no means be ruled out.

The identification of Xe with Mixe-Zoque provides an avenue for the diffusion of Mixe-Zoque vocabulary into Lowland Mayan (Cholan and Yucatecan) at a relatively early date. Justeson et al. (1985: 23–24) state that Mixe-Zoque had a greater impact on Mayan than any other linguistic group. They note a number of "very early" and widespread loans into Mayan and other languages from Mixe-Zoque, including many with calendrical content, as well as loans later in the Formative period.

Lexical diffusion should have been possible from Mixe-Zoque into Highland Mayan during the Early and Middle Formative periods, but such terms would not necessarily have spread rapidly north into the Lowland Mayan group. The postulated Xe movement into the Petén, in contrast, could have provided this opportunity for early diffusion into the lowlands.

The origins of the Swasey and Eb spheres, assuming distinct parent populations, are unknown, but it is in the northern highlands that we are likely to find new traces of the forebears of the Lowland Maya, ultimately derived from ancestral Mixe-Zoque-Maya populations in southeastern Chiapas or on the Pacific Coast of Guatemala. The most widely accepted reconstruction of Mayan linguistic history (Kaufman 1976: 107; Lyle Campbell, personal communication 1987) has the first Mayan (Greater Tzeltalan) groups reaching the lowlands from the Cuchumatanes Mountains, probably down the Usumacinta drainage, about 1000 B.C. This accords remarkably closely with the archaeological pattern we now see, but it is also entirely consistent with an identification of the Xe groups as Maya, rather than Zoque.

The marked differences among these earliest ceramic complexes strongly hint, however, that small groups entered the southern lowlands from more than one area, at different times. It also suggests either that the groups who were to become the Lowland Maya had separate origins and that contact among them before their arrival was minimal, or that substantial ceramic divergence had occurred after they had split from one ancestral group. Low population densities in the lowlands for about another two centuries fostered relatively independent development of ceramic traditions, but sometime between 700 and 600 B.C. there began a rapid population growth and expansion to other parts of the lowlands, accompanied by an increasingly uniform Mamom ceramic complex. The pattern of ceramic change in the early southern lowlands indicates the prominent role of interregional interaction in the development of cultural complexity, a conclusion to which archaeologists studying the highland Maya have been increasingly drawn (Demarest 1986; Sharer and Sedat 1987a).

The postulated Zoque Xe population along the Pasion came into sustained contact with other groups in the southern lowlands about 700 B.C. Whatever the nature of this contact, the Xe ceramic tradition was replaced by or became amalgamated into—how gradually is unknown—the late Middle Formative Maya Mamom complex. Xe and early Mamom are so different that the relationship is not likely to have been ancestral. Relationships with Chiapas and the northern highlands of Guatemala, once started, seem to have been maintained because the new polished orange pottery of early Mamom, found primarily in the area earlier occupied by Xe, shows clear ties to the Usulutan orange-resist tradition that had earlier roots in western El Salvador.

From the southern Petén, this Middle Formative, perhaps hybrid, Maya ceramic complex spread into northwest Yucatán. The earliest Nabanche ceramic complexes in the north are very similar to those that replaced Xe in the southern Petén. In some aspects they approach the point of identity, suggesting rapid movement of entire populations.

The second prong of Middle Formative Maya northward expansion appears to have stemmed from northern Belize and the northeast Petén, moving into the Rio Bec/Chenes area, into Quintana Roo, and along the East Coast. This second expansion followed the first by at least a century and appears to have progressed more slowly.

My discussion of the early settling of the Maya Lowlands has omitted consideration of the contribution indigenous hunter-gatherers are likely to have made to the first settled village farming communities. Small groups, represented in a number of areas by their chipped stone tools, had been scattered throughout the lowlands for millennia. The cultural sequence in Belize extends back into the Archaic period (MacNeish 1982), and the fluted point from the Ladyville site (Hester et al. 1982) indicates a Paleo-Indian occupation. In the deep stratified Holocene and Pleistocene deposits of Loltun Cave in Yucatán (Velázquez 1980; Alvarez 1982) a chipped flint and bone tool industry is reported to be associated directly with remains of extinct fauna, notably *Equus conversidens.* And a radiocarbon date associated with maize pollen from Lake Petenxil, in the Central Petén lakes region, suggests the presence of farmers before 2000 B.C. (Cowgill and Hutchinson 1966). But we do not know what relationship these earlier occupants bore to the early Middle Formative villagers of the Petén.

Our knowledge of the Middle Formative in the Maya Lowlands and adjacent highlands is still tightly circumscribed by the sites that have been excavated and by our ability to infer from the few imperishable material remains. As new windows are opened onto this remote time, we can expect the interplay of human actors over an expanding landscape to appear ever more intricate.

Notes

1. Excavations at Komchen, Yucatan, were conducted in 1980 by the Middle American Research Institute and the Centro Regional del Sureste (now the Centro Regional de Yucatán), Instituto Nacional de Antropología e Historia, and were directed by the author and Norberto González C. Reports on the Komchen project have appeared in Andrews V et al. (1984); Ringle (1985); Andrews V (1986); and Ringle and Andrews V (1988, n.d.). The ceramics that I have studied as part of the Komchen comparative analysis include materials from a large number of sites in Yucatan, Campeche, and Quintana Roo housed in the Centro Regional de Yucatán, INAH, Merida; collections from La Venta, Tres Zapotes, and La Victoria in the National Museum of Natural History, Smithsonian Institution; from Altar de Sacrificios, Seibal, and Uaxactun in the Peabody Museum at Harvard University; the Cuello collection at Douglass College, Rutgers University; materials from Chiapa de Corzo at the Laboratory of Anthropology, Temple University; and the Barton Ramie ceramics on loan from the Peabody Museum at Harvard to Temple University.

2. Many archaeologists in the United States and Mexico have given me unpublished information or opinions, advice, or criticism, and some of these and many others have helped this research by making collections available to me, by allowing me access to their own materials or to collections within their curatorial responsibility, or by sending me type collections of sherds that would allow me to judge relationships not always apparent on the printed or typed page. I am especially grateful to Joseph W. Ball, Sylviane Boucher, Norberto González C., Donald W. Forsyth, David C. Grove, Norman Hammond, George R. Holley, Rosemary A. Joyce, Muriel Kirkpatrick, Laura J. Kosakowsky, Gareth W. Lowe, Una MacDowell, Betty J. Meggers, Robert L. Rands, Robin Robertson, Fernando Robles Castellanos, Jeremy A. Sabloff, Peter J. Schmidt, Ricardo Velásquez Valadéz, Gordon R. Willey, and Deborah A. Wood.

For comments on earlier versions of this paper I thank Richard E. W. Adams, Anthony P. Andrews, Joseph W. Ball, Sylviane Boucher, Victoria R. Bricker, Lyle Campbell, Michael D. Coe, Lester A. Embree, David C. Grove, Norman Hammond, Peter D. Harrison, Dan M. Healan, Thomas R. Hester, Rosemary A. Joyce, John S. Justeson, Terrence Kaufman, Muriel Kirkpatrick, Laura J. Kosakowsky, Joyce Marcus, Lorenzo Ochoa, Robin Robertson, Jeremy A. Sabloff, David W. Sedat, Robert J. Sharer, Fred Valdez, Jr., and Gordon R. Willey. If I have not always heeded their suggestions, I nonetheless truly appreciate their help. This paper was completed, except for minor revisions, in January 1988.

3. Conversations and correspondence with Norman Hammond about his archaeological sequence at Cuello, especially in late 1987, have clarified a number of issues

and have helped me toward the following interpretations. I am grateful for his continued cooperation, help in understanding certain matters, and his unfailing willingness to discuss the data and their possible interpretations.

4. This paper uses the British convention of b.c. for radiocarbon ages and B.C. for calendar dates calibrated using the bristlecone pine curve and for other estimates of true calendar years. Radiocarbon ages, calculated with the 5568-year half-life, have been calibrated using the conversion program CALIB and a 20-year (bidecadal) radiocarbon age dataset (Pearson and Stuiver 1986; Stuiver and Pearson 1986; Stuiver and Reimer 1986). Calibrated dates, with one or more intercepts of the bristlecone pine curve, are given in parentheses between the extremes of the 1–sigma ranges, following the suggestion made by Stuiver and Reimer (1986); e.g., 1009 (976, 965, 933) 905 B.C. is calibrated from 850 b.c. ± 50 (2800 ± 50 b.p.), and B.C. 92 (1) A.D. 59 has been calibrated from 100 b.c. ± 50 (2050 ± 50 b.p.).

5. Ten published radiocarbon ages for the Swasey phase, as it was originally defined, supported the placement of this village in the Early Formative (Hammond et al. 1976, 1977; Pring and Hammond 1982; Hammond 1984). These radiocarbon determinations from the 1975 and 1976 seasons, two run by the University of California at Los Angeles Isotope Laboratory and six by the Cambridge University Radiocarbon Dating Research Laboratory, are generally consistent with their relative stratigraphic positions, increasing in age with increasing depth in the archaeological record. They are, in order of decreasing age

Calibrated Dates	Radiocarbon Ages	Lab. No.
2868 (2564, 2541, 2499) 2330 B.C.	2050 ± 155 b.c.	UCLA-1985e
2471 (2456, 2412, 2408) 2298 B.C.	1945 ± 65 b.c.	Q-1571
2317 (2193, 2159, 2146) 2039 B.C.	1805 ± 85 b.c.	Q-1572
2460 (2133, 2067, 2047) 1787 B.C.	1750 ± 200 b.c.	UCLA-2012d
2176 (2114, 2086, 2039) 1967 B.C.	1720 ± 65 b.c.	Q-1574
2280 (2037) 1829 B.C.	1710 ± 150 b.c.	Q-1576
2034 (1936) 1829 B.C.	1630 ± 70 b.c.	Q-1573
2031 (1895) 1767 B.C.	1600 ± 85 b.c.	Q-1577
1735 (1643) 1527 B.C.	1390 ± 65 b.c.	Q-1578
1670 (1523) 1444 B.C.	1310 ± 80 b.c.	Q-1579

The latest two of these dates (Q-1578 and Q-1579) derived from late Swasey deposits that are now dated to the Bladen phase. Three UCLA radiocarbon ages were judged unacceptable, as they yielded calibrated dates about two thousand years earlier than those listed above, and four other UCLA dates from Formative deposits were rejected because they gave dates in the first millennium A.D.

The one Seibal radiocarbon date for the Real Xe phase came from charcoal in Vessel 2 of the La Venta–style Cache 7; it is 831 (803) 781 B.C. (660 ± 75 b.c., UCLA-1437D). One Altar de Sacrificios determination from human bone in a Xe burial is 1040 (836) 770 B.C. (745 ± 185 b.c., GX-172). The other Altar date, on carbonized beans from a level that contained San Felix Mamom pottery but that Adams (1971: 169) believed should be assigned to Xe, is 1253 (998) 840 B.C. (880 ± 130 b.c., GX-163).

The Early Preclassic Tok phase deposit at Str. E3-1 of E1 Trapiche, Chalchuapa, yielded a radiocarbon date of 1009 (926) 896 B.C. (840 ± 60 b.c., P-1551) (Sharer 1978: 115-116).

6. Four radiocarbon determinations from Middle Formative Bolay phase contexts at Colha (Operation 2012, suboperation 3) have been published (Potter 1982: 100; Potter et al. 1984: 628) and are ordered below from the deepest stratigraphic unit (TX-4060) to the highest (TX-4152).

Calibrated Dates	Radiocarbon Ages	Lab. No.
897 (828) 807 B.C.	730 ± 50 b.c.	TX-4060
801 (777) 536 B.C.	580 ± 70 b.c.	TX-4061
844 (818) 803 B.C.	710 ± 50 b.c.	TX-4062
801 (770) 522 B.C.	570 ± 80 b.c.	TX-4152

7. I am grateful to Norman Hammond for calling these radiocarbon determinations to my attention in November 1987 and for his comments on the unpublished series of dates from the same excavation area run by Cambridge University in 1984. Hammond also provided me with unpublished information on the nature of the 1975, 1976, and 1979 charcoal samples and the techniques used to collect them.

8. The five Swasey and Bladen radiocarbon dates from the 1979 season at Cuello were run by the La Jolla Radiocarbon Laboratory. The youngest, LJ-4917, is from Construction Phase I (Swasey); the others are from Bladen contexts.

Calibrated Dates	Radiocarbon Ages	Lab. No.
799 (770) 529 B.C.	570 ± 70 b.c.	LJ-4922
795 (767) 529 B.C.	560 ± 60 b.c.	LJ-4923
793 (762,678,662,627,600) 422 B.C.	540 ± 70 b.c.	LJ-4919
787 (757,689,651,648,543) 408 B.C.	520 ± 70 b.c.	LJ-4918
760 (484,437,424) 402 B.C.	470 ± 60 b.c.	LJ-4917

9. Thomas R. Hester and Harry J. Shafer (personal communication 1988) say that the placement of Swasey in the Middle Formative would fit the lithic evidence from Colha, as all the Swasey [Swasey/Bladen] lithic artifacts illustrated in Hammond et al. 1979 are compatible with the Middle Preclassic Bolay phase at Colha (Hester 1985: 194–95).

10. Peter D. Harrison (personal communication 1988) reports two radiocarbon samples from K'axob, Pulltrouser Swamp, northern Belize, that were associated with Swasey/Bladen ceramics. Both samples, run in 1982, came from the original ground surface at the bottom of the deepest trench at K'axob. The lower sample, Field No. 4:2A/34, dates to 910 (809) 770 B.C. (690 ± b.c., Beta–5325), which is compatible with the Swasey and Bladen dates from Cuello and Colha. A sample recorded as having been collected a few centimeters above the first dates to 1680 (1512) 1321 B.C. (1260 ± 150 b.c., Beta–5324), although it has been suggested that the two samples were interchanged (McAnany n.d.).

11. My suggestions are based on examination of the large type collection of Xe pottery from Altar de Sacrificios and a smaller collection of Real Xe material from Seibal in the Peabody Museum at Harvard. Richard E. W. Adams (personal communication 1987, 1988) notes that the larger collections of Xe pottery in the Guatemala National Museum, which I have not seen, would provide a better idea of the diversity within types.

12. There are no firm dates for the beginning of San Felix Mamom at Altar or Escoba Mamom at Seibal, but a date of 800 (752, 709, 530) 400 B.C. (500 ± 120 b.c., GX-165) from Altar was associated with a sample of San Felix and Plancha Chicanel pottery. Taking into account the relevant radiocarbon dates from the Maya lowlands, Tabasco, and Chiapas, I would assign a date of about 700–650 B.C. to this transition.

13. The two radiocarbon dates for the late Barra phase at Paso de la Amada, in the Soconusco, Chiapas, are 1852 (1607, 1554, 1544) 1420 B.C. (1350 ± 160 b.c., I-8162), and 1940 (1677) 1420 B.C. (1410 ± 225 b.c., I-8161) (Ceja Tenorio 1985: 34).

14. As I have noted elsewhere (1986: 29–30), small-neck water bottle sherds of Yotolin Pattern-Burnished from Mani Cenote and Loltun Cave, which George Brainerd (1951; 1958: 24–25) originally called Mani Pattern-Burnished ware and which he believed dated to the Early Formative, are associated with Middle and Late Formative ceramics at both Mani and Loltun (Velásquez V. 1980; 1981; Robles C. 1986; cf. Joesink-Mandeville 1976). Our most reliable stratigraphic evidence therefore indicates that the pattern-burnished pottery was a functionally specific part of the Middle Formative Early Nabanche ceramic complex and probably the early Late Formative Late Nabanche complex as well. The unacceptable alternative would be that Yotolin formed a separate and earlier ceramic complex of a single pattern-burnished bottle form that was broken only near water sources.

The dating of this oft-discussed type to the Middle and Late Formative in Yucatan fits well with my proposed redating of the Swasey complex at Cuello to the Middle Formative, since Pring (1977: 95–103) equated pattern-burnished sherds in Swasey deposits with Yotolin Pattern-Burnished from Mani. It should be noted as a further caveat that the Swasey sherds are similar but not identical to Yotolin Pattern-Burnished, that this decorative mode at Cuello is not certain to have been applied to bottles (Pring 1977: 100; N. Hammond, personal communication 1987), and that pattern-burnishing is in any case not rare in Formative nuclear America.

Fernando Robles C. (1986) has tentatively identified three sherds of the northern Belize type Chicago Orange: Variety Unspecified (with the assistance of Daniel R. Potter) and one sherd of the Xe type Huetche White in Edward H. Thompson's unstratified Loltun Cave collection of about 2000 sherds in the Peabody Museum at Harvard. I have not seen them. They are the only candidates I know for an early Middle Formative (Xe-level) occupation in Yucatan, but as Chicago Orange at Cuello continues into the Late Preclassic (Kosakowsky 1987b: 81–83), and as the sherd of Huetche White is listed only as a possible identification, their candidacy is weak.

A radiocarbon date of 2456 (2273, 2245, 2205) 2043 B.C. (1840 ± 105 b.c., I-10,430) from Loltun Cave (Velázquez V. 1980) is from the uppermost preceramic level. Another charcoal sample, taken from a plaster and stone floor of a 40-cm-high late Middle Formative (Early Nabanche) platform, at a depth of 82 cm (Level V), dates to 800 (765, 673, 667, 613, 608) 410 B.C. (2500 ± 100 b.p., UCLA-2195A). This is the only radiocarbon date available for early Nabanche in Yucatán that comes close to the expected age.

Two

A Genealogy for Freestanding Maya Monuments
By Flora S. Clancy

My efforts have been to study monumental forms and the compositional structures that carry the iconographic images. The monuments that come within the concerns of this essay are the boulder, the basalt column, the stela, and the pedestal (altar) (Clancy 1976). In this essay, I try to find and chart the early moments in which the manipulation of certain artistic forms seems to affect the developmental history of the free-standing monument. The continued use of such manipulations is understood as a conscious act and not a random or unique occurrence.

Few if any Preclassic monuments are found in their original contexts, sometimes because of their ancient age and often because of the Precolumbian habits of moving, re-using, and burying old monuments. Without a clear archaeological history, previous efforts to elucidate the origins of Maya art have focused on tracing formative connections through iconographic images (M. Coe 1965; 1977; G. Norman 1976; L. Parsons 1978: 28) or on trying to trace a history of artistic styles (J. Quirarte 1973; 1977; 1979; L. Parsons 1986).

The problems with stylistic assessments are many. The stela from Cerro de la Piedra, Veracruz (Figure 2.1), for example, has been variously dated to from the sixth to ninth century A.D. by Alfonso Medellin (1971: 41), to the first century A.D. by John Scott (1977: 112), and to the eighth to sixth century B.C. by Lee Parsons (1986: 121). The problems inherent in the study of iconographic connections are not so obvious. The relationships between an image (icon) and what it means have been found in other art histories to be protean (E. Panofsky 1960). That such a protean relationship exists in the

Figure 2.1. Stela from Cerro de Piedra, Veracruz. Variously dated between 600 B.C. to 600 A.D. on the basis of style. Drawing by author.

art histories of the New World is the subject of debate (see, for example, G. Kubler 1969; 1973; and G. Willey 1973). Furthermore, iconography has traditionally depended on a knowledge of correlated literary traditions to help elucidate the connotative functions of images. These literary traditions surely existed in Preclassic Mesoamerica, but they are mute as far as any study of the Preclassic period is concerned.

The artistic trait, composition, is a particular arrangement of imagery within a given field. I have found it useful to distinguish between compositional field and compositional mode. A compositional field is the actual shape and extent of the imagery displayed. In Mesoamerica, regardless of monumental type, the compositional field will be one of the following four: *panel, multi-panel, wrap-around, and recto-verso* (Figure 2.2). Compositional modes determine the interrelationships of the images within the field, and range between two complementary poles: a *narrative* mode of asymmetrical arrangements (see Figure 2.5) and a *hieratic* mode of symmetry. The intermediate range, most common to the Classic period but not to the Preclassic, I call the *iconic* (see Figure 2.6). The iconic mode presents a single figure whose only context is costume, emblem, and the monument on which it is carved. Within the iconic mode a narrative may be implied, but is not represented (see Clancy 1985).

I cannot say at this time that studying the fields and modes of monumental compositions produces better results than an iconographic or stylistic analysis. I am sure, however, than in concert with stylistic and iconographic analyses, a better basis is made on which to make assumptions about the history of this art and the Preclassic peoples.

This outline begins with the Middle Preclassic, that is, around 900 B.C., and ends at the beginning of the Classic period around A.D. 200.[1] Geographically, it ranges from the Olmec homeland in Veracruz through the modern Mexican states of Chiapas and Guerrero to the Guatemalan Highlands and Pacific Coast. The appendix, organized by time and monument type, lists the monuments belonging to each type to be discussed here.

Middle Preclassic Monuments

Between 900 and 500 B.C., that is, during the Middle Preclassic, a major artistic change occurs. The Early Preclassic emphasis on sculpture in the round changes to a preoccupation with the quasi-dimensional techniques of relief carving. Along with this change, and positively related to it, is the emergence of specific free-standing monumental forms, the basalt column and the boulder monument, devoted to bearing the new relief work. Only two monumental types, both sculptural, are recognizable from the preceding Early Preclassic: the "altar," which I call the block pedestal (see D. Grove 1973), and the colossal head (R. Heizer 1967: 38). Otherwise, the monuments are the various sculptured forms exemplified by the monuments of San Lorenzo (M. Coe and R. Diehl 1980). During the Middle Preclassic, the block pedestal and the colossal head were only sporadically produced.

Basaltic Columns

In the Middle Preclassic the basaltic column was developed as a new monumental type (L. Parsons 1986: 16, 92). This monument has the smooth surfaces and the prismatic proportions typical of some Classic stelae. Rather than four sides, however, the column usually has five, sometimes more. The volcanic basalts used can be quarried in this shape and generally require little smoothing or shaping. The basaltic columns, almost without exception, employed the wraparound field and a narrative compositional mode. The imagery focuses on one human figure, and this figure is often posed with a particular extroverted gesture where one arm is raised over its head. This gesture can be represented without a clear context, as on Stela 9 of Kaminaljuya (Figure 2.3), with a subordinate figure as seen on the Alvarado stela, or in context with a monstrous animal as represented on La Venta, Monument 63 and San Lorenzo, Monument 56.[2]

Boulder Monuments

During the Middle Preclassic, sometime around 700 B.C., the paneled field was introduced to present relief-carved images on boulder monuments. Most but not all boulder monuments show at least some evidence of being smoothed to make a better surface for the relief images. However, the shaping done to the original boulders to prepare them for images is not so visually impressive as the "naturalness" of the boulders themselves.

The relief-carved boulders dating from the Middle Preclassic seem close in form and appearance to natural rock walls carved with petroglyphs (Figure 2.4). In fact, Proskouriakoff (1968: 121) ar-

A Genealogy for Freestanding Maya Monuments 23

Figure 2.2. The four varieties of compositional fields.

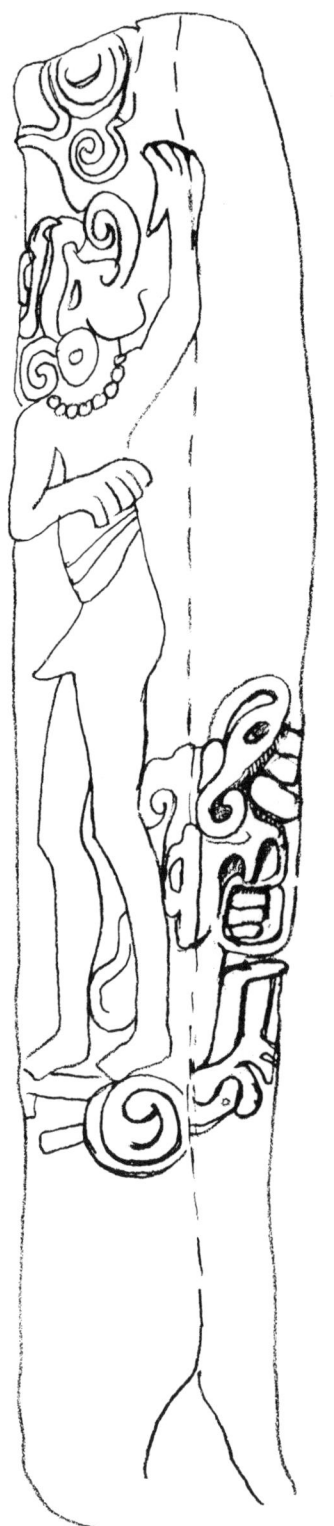

Figure 2.3. Middle Preclassic basaltic columns. Stela 9 from Kaminaljuyu. Drawing by author.

Figure 2.4. Middle Preclassic boulder monuments. Stela 1 from Acotpan, Veracruz. Drawing by author.

gues that "the stela originated in the Olmec habit of recording their presence wherever they went, and that the lack of native rock at La Venta led to the substitution of artificial slabs."

Stela 2 of La Venta, perhaps one of the earlier examples, presents its main figure in high relief which is reminiscent of the relief-carving method used for the block pedestals. The boulder assists or insists in projecting this figure forward into a space perceptually different from its context of six secondary figures carved in low relief as if floating around the main figure. The compositional field is not wraparound because the images are mainly presented on one face of the boulder. However, the images flow over the undressed stone surface with seemingly little regard for creating or respecting the boundary or limits of the field. It is difficult, therefore, to determine whether the paneled field was used as an intentional compositional strategy: the images seem to emerge as suggested by the natural face of the stone. The boulder monument from Las Victorias (S. Boggs 1950) is carved with four figures each on its roughly contoured four faces. Boggs (p. 90) considers the figures to represent one scene. If so, it would be a conscious use of the wraparound field. Like Stela 2 from La Venta, however, the visual evidence is vague as to the original compositional intent.

The paneled imagery presented on Stone 1 from Pijijiapan (Navarette 1974) Monument 1 from El Viejon (de la Fuente 1973: 131, 132), and Monument 1 from Los Mangos (Fuente 1973: 159, 160) appears to be more intentional, but these monuments still evoke strong associations with the petroglyphic traditions observed by Proskouriakoff.

The relief-carved monuments of the Middle Preclassic consistently used natural stone shapes with very little preparation before the addition of the relief carving. The images carved on the natural surfaces do not obscure an awareness of their bearing form. When the "naturalness" of the medium is so intrusive we are allowed or perhaps supposed to think that a particular image has been engendered as much by revelation through the stone as by the intention of the sculptor.

The wraparound field is a conscious compositional strategy convincingly used with the basaltic columns. Although natural in form, the columns have smooth faces and clear angles and are apparently easier to objectify. Importantly, this field, by involving several surfaces of the monument, maintains a referential and perceptual connection to sculpture in the round by its use of the mass and dimensionality of the stone. The images within this field, therefore, derive some of their meaning from the actual shape of the monument as the field wraps around it. The relationship is an active one with strong associations to sculpture in the round: the stone empowers the image, the image empowers the stone.

The panel field may be understood as a continuation of the age-old tradition of carving on natural rock walls, but now under more civil circumstances of the ceremonial center. Its clear, formal distinction from the wraparound field, however, is the main reason for suggesting that its first conscious use dates to the Middle Preclassic.

The Middle Preclassic compositional mode is almost always narrative, utilizing strong asymmetrical arrangements. The boulders with panel fields represent multi-figured narratives usually representing meetings between people of like status. The wraparound fields on the basalt columns display a single elite figure usually portrayed in an extroverted pose, sometimes shown with a captive, sometimes with a monstrous animal. There is not enough visual information to form a clear idea about the meaning of the narratives or to distinguish between historical or allegorical content.

Late Preclassic Monuments

It is during the Late Preclassic (500–200 B.C.) that the stela and the pedestal appear as recognizable monuments. The natural qualities of the stone medium were controlled by a more careful shaping that created smooth surfaces and more regular overall shapes. This allowed the relief-carved images to take on greater visual importance. As a monument type, the basaltic column all but disappears while the boulder continues as a viable monumental form.

Boulder Monuments

The wraparound field is now transferred from the basaltic column to the boulder. The boulder is more regularly dressed but in a way that still retains formal references to the older, more sculptural forms. The wraparound field as it is now used on the boulder monuments enhances the common image of a large head, often with a scene or a figure in its open, niche-like mouth. It is with these monuments that the first hint of the recto-verso field may be detected.

The most impressive image of Monument 2 from Cerro de las Mesas is its allusion to the sculptural tradition of colossal heads. It carries much more iconographic detail than the Early and Middle Preclassic sculptures to which it refers, and it is not truly sculpture in the round. The back of the head is flattened and on this smoothed surface a relief-carved scene depicts two figures, a standing male and a female (with drooping breasts) seated in a slumped posture. What may have been a glyph column divides the space between the two figures. The two images, the face and the scene, are rendered in two very different carving styles. Because the low relief scene was "crudely done," Matthew Stirling

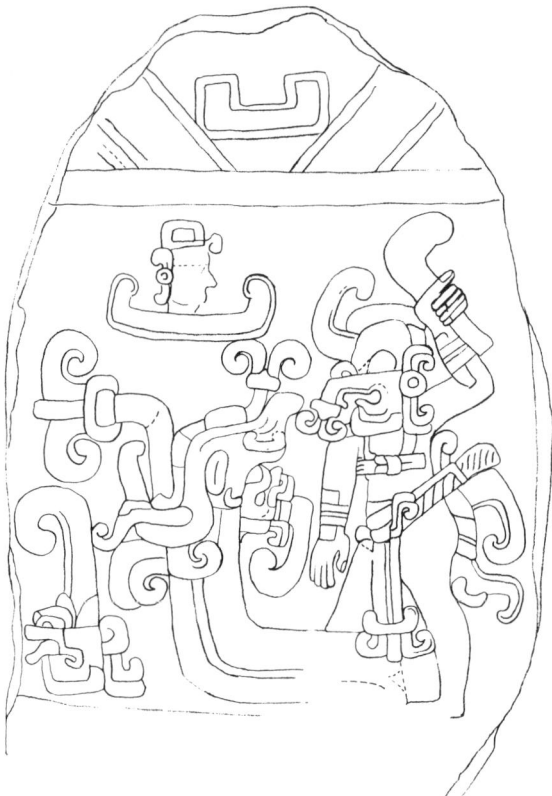

Figure 2.5. a. Stela 3 from Izapa, Late Preclassic period.
b. Stela 4 from Izapa, Terminal Preclassic period.
Drawings by author, after G. Norman 1973.

(1943: 45) thought it might have been carved at a later time than the face, which was carved, according to him (p. 48) during the Early Classic—a much later date than either Lee Parsons (1986: 35) or I would suggest. Whether carved at different times or not, however, Monument 2 would have to be considered as a proto-example in the development of the recto-verso field. (The stela, carved on two faces, reported by Cervantes [1967: 32–35] as from the Gulf Coast, presents the same questions concerning compositional intent as Monument 2 of Cerro de las Mesas.)

Stelae

The paneled field is especially suited to the new stela monument. It presents all the visual information on one plane in an upright, visibly accessible manner. The combination of the panel composition with the stela monument will become a major solution for the Classic requirements of public monuments. During the Late Preclassic, this new monumental combination is most commonly used to present narrative scenes of allegorical imagery and seems to be a formal and stylistic development inspired by the Middle Preclassic boulder monuments with their narrative, multi-figured scenes. The single figure in an iconic composition makes a small but important appearance in what are now considered peripheral areas of the Preclassic.

The stelae presenting narrative and allegorical scenes are from Izapa, Chiapas, and Kaminaljuyu in the southern highlands of Guatemala (Figure. 2.5), and they usually make reference by their supernal and basal motifs to the gigantic heads with open mouths just discussed for the contemporary Late Preclassic boulder monuments. These references, however, are greatly reduced and abstracted, and have been called "signature panels" or the "Izapan signature" by S. Miles (1965). The stelae are not carefully or rigidly shaped into shafts or prisms but their monumental forms are recognizable as manmade whether they carry reliefs or whether they are plain. That "plain stelae" are recognizable monuments in the Late Preclassic (N. Hammond 1982; L. Parsons 1986: 96) rests on the fact that this is when the stela form was configured to be distinct from the natural forms of the boulder or the basalt column.

For a long time the monumental sculpture of Izapa was seen as a link or bridge between the great flowerings of the Olmec culture and the Maya (M. Coe 1962; 1965; J. Quirarte 1977; L. Parsons 1978). Lately, students are more inclined to emphasize its artistic uniqueness in the Preclassic world because when examined closely, its images and iconographies seem elusively undirectional (J. Quirarte 1973; 1979; V. Smith 1984; M. Raish 1984). One can see the imprint of the Olmec, but find very few actual borrowings of images and icons by the Izapan artist. The signature panels are perhaps the clearest connection between the two sets of imagery. Equally, the Izapan narrative mode, with its allegorical iconography and complete lack of glyphs, seems to have had little impact on the incipient Maya monumental tradition that was almost exclusively iconic in mode, glyphic in context, and concerned with regalia and costume of an honored individual. Scenic and narrative imagery like trees, birds, animals, and narrative gesture are to be associated with Late Preclassic concepts of imagery.

The stelae that introduce the single figure composed by the iconic mode are found at sites that are widely spread throughout southern Mesoamerica. They are from seemingly small, peripheral centers that erected few, if any, other monuments save the ones under discussion (Figure 2.6). In this study, these stelae are placed in the Late Preclassic because no convincing evidence suggests that the distinctive monumental stela shape existed before this time. Except for the enormous chronological range cited above for the stela from Cerro de la Piedra, Veracruz, the suggested Late Preclassic date for these particular stelae is often a later date than has been cited by previous students of these monuments. Stela 1 of Cacahoatan, Chiapas is dated between 700 and 500 B.C. by Parsons (1986: 121); the stela from San Miguel Amuco, Guerrero is dated 900–700 B.C. by Grove and Paradis (1971: 95–102); Monument 1 from Padre Piedra, Chiapas is placed in the Dili Phase (700–500 B.C.) by Green and Lowe (1967: 36, 37). The stela from La Angostura, Chiapas (J. Gussinyer 1976: 78) and the so-called stela from Cival, Guatemala (P. Mathews 1985: 7) are generally placed in the Preclassic with no specific phase suggested.

The imagery of the single figure may suggest a continuation of basaltic column imagery, and this

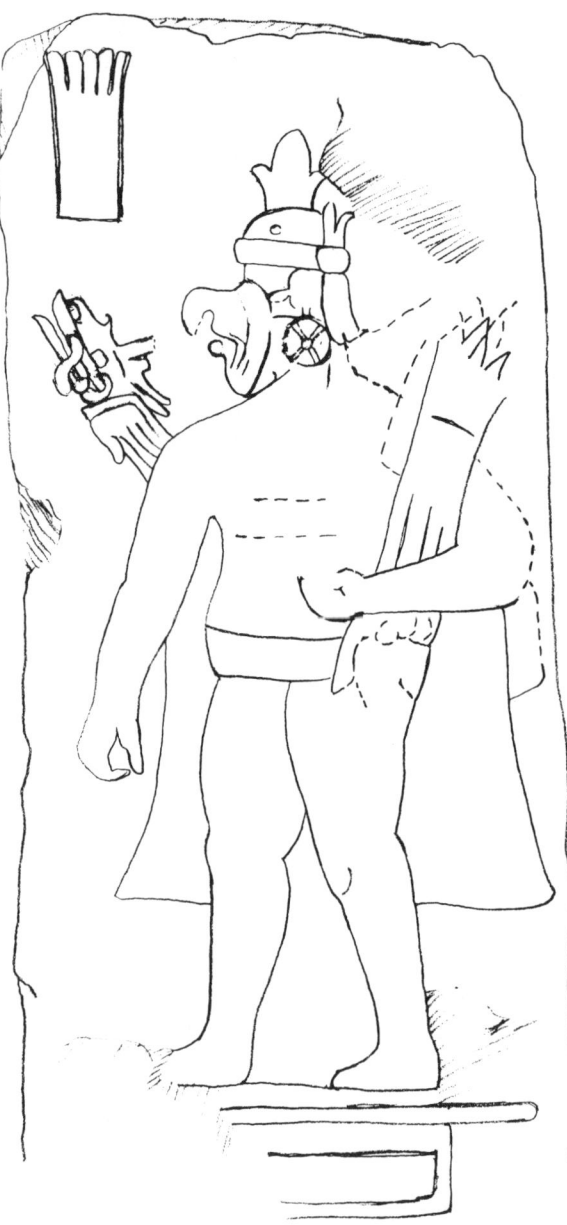

Figure 2.6. Late Preclassic stela using the iconic compositional mode. Stela from San Miguel Amuco, Guerrero. Drawing by author, after Grove and Paradis 1971.

could be supported by the formal congruities between the column and the stela. Such connections, however, do not account for the important differences in compositional field and mode. Besides the depiction of the single figure, however, these monuments share two other distinct artistic traits: a generous amount of negative background space that emphasizes the figure, and the use of the old Olmec graphic style and Olmec iconography. While no student would mistake these monuments as examples of pure Olmec style, the Olmec connection is strong (see Grove and Paradis 1971; J. Scott 1971; I. Bernal 1976: 148, 149). Seemingly, it is the common use of the Olmec graphic style and iconography of these monuments that has suggested dates earlier than their formal properties would permit.

The formal and compositional traits are innovative and prototypical of the Classic Maya stela, but in combination with an old graphic style and iconography, a seeming paradox of innovative and provincial anachronisms is the result. Important to these considerations of historical connections is the use of the neutral background space that evokes, along with the style and iconography, a comparison to engraved Olmec celts. And one cannot forget the stela-like shape of the celt itself. I can think of no easier way to explain these monumental anachronisms of innovation and provinciality than by suggesting the celt as the primary inspiration. Easily transportable and available to provincial peoples, they were apparently saved as heirlooms. Why the peripheral peoples understood them as proper monumental maquettes cannot yet be answered.

Pedestals

The only monuments that can be surely identified as pedestals during the Late Preclassic are the ones shaped like cylinders. There may well have been rectangular pedestals, but without sure contextual information, they are difficult to distinguish from the wall tablets of architectural sculpture. Wall tablets of necessity employ the panel field since, in situ, only one face would be exposed to view. The cylindrical pedestals employ the panel field as a choice, not as a necessity, and it is the top, circular surface that holds the imagery (Figure 2.7). Like the dressed stelae from peripheral areas, these are innovative monumental forms that use the old graphic style of the Olmec. The addition of a frame is an important feature of these monuments. The Late Preclassic frame is figural itself and very likely gives a "frame of reference" for the images contained within it.

The monumental shape, narrative compositional mode, figural frame, and the icons of footprints are shared between several Late Preclassic pedestals (the pedestal from San Antonio, Guatemala, Monument 16 of San Lorenzo, Veracruz, and a pedestal from Las Choapas, Veracrus—see Figure 2.7b).

The San Antonio pedestal represents a remarkable image of a frontal bust with the head turned in profile. The bust is framed by a "contortionist" lying on his belly and holding his two feet with one rather enlarged hand. Shook and Heizer (1976) have interpreted this image to be two interlocking contortionists: one represented in profile as the figural frame, and the bust to be understood as that part of the contorted figure that touches the surface of the stone while the rest of the body invisibly arches back and around so that the soles of the feet rest on the visible surface of the stone on either side of the profiled head.

I think there is some merit to this interpretation of the image. One must remember that the paneled field was a relatively new compositional strategy. Most Late Preclassic sculptors probably would have been familiar with the older and more traditional wraparound field where images extended from one face of the monument to another, and where, without movement on the part of the viewer, the whole image could not be seen at once. I am therefore not surprised to see on early panel compositions evidence of the sculptor's innate sense that the stone could contain hidden or obscured parts of the image.

During the Late Preclassic, the relief-carved monument takes the recognizable shapes of pedestal and stela: conventionalized and tamed forms that could not be mistaken for having occurred naturally. The paneled field becomes increasingly important but is still used for the most part to support narrative, allegorical imagery. The important addition of the iconic compositional mode that focuses on one figure with no overt narrative context seems tentative because it is the product of peripheral sites and is not common at the central, large centers of Izapa and Kaminaljuyu. The non-allegorical image of the iconic single figure leads to the assumption, prob-

Figure 2.7. Late Preclassic Pedestals. a. Pedestal from San Antonio Suchitepequez, Guatemala. Drawing by author after Shook and Heizer, 1976. b. Pedestal from Las Choapas, Veracruz. Drawing by author.

ably correct, that it represents an actual person by a type of portraiture.

The loss of narrative and the growing power of the iconic can be seen on two Izapan stelae, early and late, that display similar figures (Figure 2.5 a and b). The scene depicted on Stela 3, dating from the Late Preclassic, depicts the old narrative image common to the Middle Preclassic basaltic columns, a human-like figure with an extroverted gesture somehow engaged with a large monstrous creature. The compositional mode of Stela 3, strongly asymmetrical and narrative, is arranged as an irregular triangle within the panel. The human leg and upright body of the anthropomorphic figure is the short span, the base line is the long span, and the hypotenuse runs from the grotesque head on the left up through the serpent's head to the figure's head.

On the Terminal Preclassic Stela 4 of Izapa, the human figure is portrayed brandishing a club with the same aggressive gesture. The diving anthropomorph above, the asymmetry of the main gesture, and perhaps the basal and supernal signatures could by connotation signal the narrative aspects of the content. However, the axial alignment of the main figure along the center line of the panelled field no longer allows enough space for the actual, denotative representation of narrative.

Terminal Preclassic Monuments

In monumental, compositional, and even iconographic terms, the stage is almost set for the Early Classic Maya monuments as we know them. Monumental sculpture in the round is latent; the relief-carved monuments of stela and pedestal are common. The panel field predominates and the iconic mode of structuring the image of the single figure has entered the compositional vocabulary.

Two artistic events of the Terminal Preclassic (200 B.C. to A.D. 200), however, need to be discussed: the addition of a glyphic text to the image, and the addition of the plain frame around the image.

On relief-carved monuments of the following Classic period, frames are common and are usually plain bands surrounding the imagery—a plain frame. Infrequently, framing is done by patterned designs of geometric figures—the patterned frame.

The earliest frames, as we have seen, consist themselves of iconographic imagery that is somehow related to the main imagery of the monument—the "frame of reference."

By reifying the monument's edge the plain frame becomes associated with the formal and non-mimetic meanings (M. Schapiro 1969) of the stone and its shape rather than with the iconographic meanings of the image or scene it surrounds. The observer associates the frame, then, with the empirical realities of the monument as a dressed stone set in the ground, and upon which images are carved in relief.

The frame also signals the physical limits of the foreground and background planes by defining the actual depth possible for the relief-carved image. As the frame reifies the shape of the monument and defines the foreground and background planes, it acts, perhaps in a more subtle way, as the boundary between the illusionistic place of the imagery and the actualities of the shape and place of the monument (S. Nodelmann 1967). In this way, we understand the illusionistic image as existing within the real boundaries of the frame.

The frame therefore acts to separate, visually and conceptually, the image from its bearing form—the image from its medium—because the frame simultaneously proclaims the limitations of the illusion and the actualities of the stoney medium. Along with a greater reliance on panelled fields and the use of iconic compositions, the plain frame signals an important conceptual change for the location of the major meaning of the monument; that is, in the image and not the stone.

The inclusion of glyphs is an important addition to monumental imagery and also reflects this conceptual change in monumental presentation and function.[3] The stela in particular begins to function as a monument for the display of a secular human identified by the iconography of its costume and gesture as well as by a text. With the advent of glyphs the narrative mode that utilized strong asymmetries to organize complex compositions is no longer preferred. The visual narrative is lost for the most part or is conventionalized into emblems. The stylistic goals of imagery also change. Certain aesthetic and expressive qualities no longer have as an important role in the function of the monumental imagery as do its didactic and denotative capabilities.

Interestingly enough, with the addition of glyphs the image becomes very detailed and complex, difficult for the Western eye to see. Close attention is required to perceive the body position within the massed details of costume or regalia. The common dictum that says one should first find the distinctively round earflare and from that find the other parts of the human figure is to the point in this discussion. During the late Terminal Preclassic, looking at monument imagery becomes more like the kind of seeing required for reading.

In summary, during the Middle Preclassic period, sculpture in the round, although not entirely replaced, certainly gives way to the relief-carved monument which develops in tandem with a greater reliance on two-dimensional imagery for public or civic contexts. Natural shapes were chosen. The panel field seems tentative because on the natural boulder it looks like a continuation of the ancient tradition of petroglyphs. The wraparound field, employed on the basalt columns, is more clearly a conscious compositional strategy used to evoke some of the dimensional powers of sculpture in the round. Both monument types display narrative imagery.

During the Late Preclassic, the distinctive monument types, the stela and pedestal, are developed, while narrative imagery continues to be the major compositional mode. Nevertheless, it is at this time, in sites peripheral to the major centers, that the iconic compositional mode is developed and the single figure is displayed without the benefit of narrative.

The addition of the plain frame and text during the Terminal Preclassic seems to overwhelm any residual desires for a visual narrative. The great narratives of the Preclassic have been conventionalized and iconicized on passive monument shapes to display within simple panels the costume, regalia, and text of the honored person.

Notes

1. I am following the temporal divisions for the Preclassic period used by Lee Parsons for his exemplary work, *The Origins of Maya Art* (1986).

2. The archaeology and associated ceramics for Monuments 41 and 42 of San Lorenzo are reported by Michael Coe (M. Coe and R. Diehl 1980: 350–52) to be from the end of San Lorenzo B (ca. 900 B.C.) and early San Lorenzo A (ca. 1200 B.C.) respectively. They are of basaltic stone, and have been worked into true columnar shapes with the natural angled edges removed. They may or may not be prototypes for the Middle Preclassic monuments under discussion.

3. The questions about the origins and development of Maya glyphic writing are too complex to be considered in this essay (*see* M. Coe 1957; H. Prem 1971; E. Benson, ed., 1973; J. Marcus 1976b; G. Lowe 1977; 237; P. Mathews 1985: 46–49). I have previously pointed out (1983: 236) that the two Maya graphic systems, imagery and text, come together in the Terminal Preclassic, each fully formed. That is, they do not seem to share formative, developmental histories.

The use of glyph texts with relief-carved images can be dated as early as the Middle Preclassic (see the Alvarado Stela and Monument 2 of Cerro de las Mesas discussed in this essay). It is not until the Terminal Preclassic, however, that the glyphic text becomes the norm and not the odd exception when studying compositional fields and modes of monuments.

Appendix

Preclassic Monuments by Type and Period

The following outline is provisional:
Middle Preclassic Period (900–500 B.C.)
Basaltic Columns: Wraparound Compositional Fields
    Angel R. Cabada, Veracruz, (Ingenio) Monument 1
    La Venta, Veracruz, Monument 63
    San Lorenzo, Veracruz, Monument 56
    El Meson, Veracruz, Monument 1
    Kaminaljuyu, Guatemala, Stela 9
    Alvarado, Veracruz, Stela

Boulder Monuments: Panel Compositional Fields
    Pijijiapan, Chiapas, Stone 1
    Las Victorias, El Salvador, Boulder (wraparound field?)
    La Venta, Veracruz, Stelae 2 and 3
    El Viejon, Veracruz, Monument 1
    Los Mangos, Veracruz, Monument 1

Late Preclassic Period 500–200 B.C.
Basaltic Columns: Wraparound Compositional Field
    Kaminaljuyu, Guatemala, Monument 2

Boulder Monuments: Wraparound Compositional Fields
    Cerro de las Mesas, Veracruz, Monument 2 (recto-verso field?)
    Tres Zapotes, Veracruz, Stelae A and D
    Monument from Veracruz, (see L. Parsons 1986: fig. 184)

The following Boulder Monuments are provisionally placed in the Late Preclassic. They may be earlier, but no earlier than circa 700 B.C.

    Abaj Takalik, Guatemala, Monument 16,
    La Venta, Veracruz, Monument 71
    Tiltipec, Chiapas, Boulder
    Los Cerritos-South, Escuintla Guatemala, Monument 2
    Izapa, Chiapas, Monument 2

Stela: Panel Compositional Fields
    Izapa, Chiapas, Stelae 3, 6, 10, 11, 19, 20, 28, 50, 89(?)
    Kaminaljuyu, Guatemala, Stelae 5, 16?
    Cacahoatan, Chiapas, Stela 1
    Cival, Guatemala, Stela 1

    San Miguel Amuco, Guerrero, Stela
    La Angostura, Chiapas, Stela
    Padre Piedra, Chiapas, Stela
    Cerro de Piedra, Veracruz, Stela
    Stela from Gulf Coast ? (Cervantes 1967: 32–35)

Pedestals: Panel Compositional Fields
    San Antonio, Suchitepequez, "Shook Panel"
    San Lorenzo, Veracruz, Monument 16
    La Venta, Veracruz, Monuments 13, 61
    Laguna de los Cerros, Veracruz, Monument 27
    Monument in Museum of Santiago Tuxtla, Veracruz (see Cervantes 1969: 38)
    Las Choapas, Veracruz, Monument

Terminal Preclassic Period 200 B.C. to A.D. 200
Boulder Monuments
    Kaminaljuyu, Monument 65
    Abaj Takalik, Altar 12, Stela 4

Stelae (does not include fragments)
    Abaj Takalik, Stelae 1, 2, 3, 5 (multi-paneled field), 12, 13, and "Altar" 13
    Izapa, Stelae 1, 2, 4, 5, 8, 9, 12, 14, 18 (wraparound field), 21, 23, 27
    Kaminaljuyu, Stelae 3, 11, 17, 20, 25, 26 (recto-verso field)
    Tres Zapotes, Stela C
    El Meson, Monument 2
    El Baul, Stela 1
    Bilbao, Monument 42
    El Jobo, Stela 1
    La Lagunita, Sculpture 11 (multi-paneled field)
    Cerro de las Mesas, Stelae 9, 14
    Tonala (La Tortuga Ruin), Stela (recto-verso)
    [These last five stelae may be third century]
    Tepatlaxco, Veracruz, Stela
    Tintal, Guatemala, Stela 1
    El Mirador, Guatemala, Stelae 2 (recto-verso), 4
    Uaxactun, Stela 10 (recto-verso)
    Polol, "Altar" 1

Pedestals
    Izapa, Altars 3, 20, and Throne 1
    Kaminaljuyu, Altars 1, 2, 8, 14, and Stela 20

Three

New Perspectives on Old Problems: Dynastic References for the Early Classic at Tikal

By Juan Pedro Laporte and Vilma Fialko C.

This study develops a model which identifies at least two dynastic lineages in the sociopolitical process at Tikal during the Early Classic period. The two lineages evidently were local, and can be recognized through an analysis of the architectural, funerary, and iconographic traditions associated with them, although one of the lineages adopted certain cultural features of a foreign tradition. The differences between the lineages can be established by association with architectural complexes that had specific functions, political or funerary or both. Through such associations, specific functions can be inferred that were probably characteristic of the roles played by the lineages in the political organization of both Tikal and the Maya in general.

Much of the model is based on information recovered during excavation in the three architectural groups known as the North Acropolis, the Mundo Perdido Complex, and Group 6C-XVI (Figure 3.1). The last two groups were explored by the Proyecto Nacional Tikal between 1980 and 1984, when Stela 39, the Ball Court Marker, and numerous Early Classic burials were discovered.[1]

It is well known that since the beginning of the Late Preclassic the villages of the Maya Lowlands evolved into complex centers that incorporated major architectural groups and varieties of sculptured monuments, the result of an elaborate social structure founded on intensified agricultural production and commerce. A collateral aspect of this development was the building of Commemorative Astronomical Complexes which came to be the foremost architectural group for public ceremonies. The structural plan of such complexes is exemplified by Group E at Uaxactun. The buildings evolved into great stages displaying symbolic imagery as explanation for the order of the universe and the structure of society (Schele and Miller 1986: 105).

The Preclassic period manifests a clearly defined political state with respect to the centralization of power, as is indicated by the sequence of rulers wherein kinship bonds regulated political relationships. In this type of early state, rulers sought to legitimize their accession to power by manipulating symbols and beliefs associated with the supernatural (Becker 1983; Matheny 1986).

Evolution of the Mundo Perdido Complex and Its Funerary Implications

Mundo Perdido is a ceremonial area at Tikal with a long history of use that began in the Middle Preclassic period and proceeded uninterrupted until Terminal Classic times. The lengthy sequence of activity can be analyzed in terms of settlement patterns by defining the components that comprise a Commemorative Astronomical Complex and the ritual and propitiary aspects related to it. The ritual nature of the complex is apparent in the orientation of Structures 5C-54 and 5D-86 along a general east-west axis.

Various concentrations of material located in holes carved out of bedrock indicate an occupation at Mundo Perdido from the Early Eb phase (700–600 B.C.), although the first evidence of architecture is probably Late Eb (600–500 B.C.). The Late Eb remains include a radial pyramid (5C-54-1st) situated to the west of a rectangular platform (5D-84/88-1st) across a small plaza. The arrangement ap-

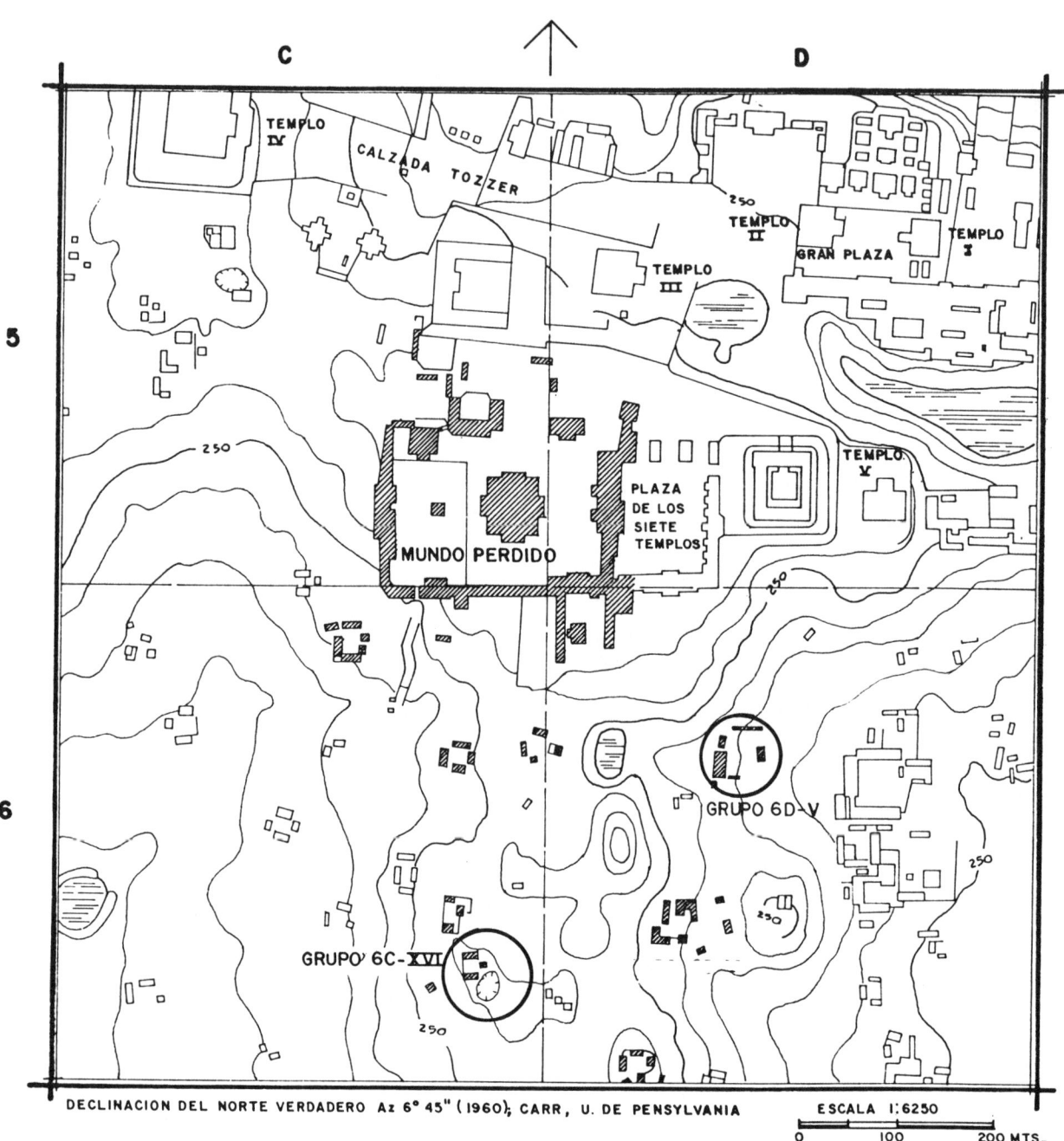

Figure 3.1. Plan. Mundo Perdido and Group 6C-XVI.

pears to be a prototype of the Commemorative Astronomical Complex (like Group E at Uaxactun), which seems to have had its origins in a calendrical ritual.

This architectural concept became formalized during the Tzec phase (500–250 B.C.) when a new version of the radial pyramid (5C-54-2d) and a new East Platform (5D-84/88-2d) were constructed, both of them considerably greater in volume and height. During the renovation of the buildings the east-west axis, which would become the norm for the complex, was ritually established through the deposition of burials without associated offerings (PNT-002 and 003), located below the summit platform of the radial pyramid. They do not appear to be elite burials, although their location had ritual significance.

Further renovation of the pyramid (5C-54-3d) and East Platform (5D-84/88-3d) in the Chuen phase (250–100 B.C.) indicates the completion of a preestablished ritual cycle. The radial pyramid again increased in volume, but it now included monumental masks as decoration, flanked by auxiliary staircases. Within the latter were positioned two burials with offerings, associated with the east-west axis (PNT-001 and 004). It was just after these developments when the causeway which gave access to Mundo Perdido from the northeast was formalized as the principal means of communication with the recently developed area of the North Acropolis.

The enlargement of Mundo Perdido continued during the Cauac phase (100 B.C. to A.D. 250) through the leveling of areas that formed plazas and open spaces, a massive expansion of the radial pyramid (5C-54-4th), and the construction of three temples on top of the East Platform (5D-84/88-4th). The temple in the center (5D-86-4th) had two jaguar masks conforming with the established axis. Deposited along the same axis were a pair of burials without offerings (PNT-020 and 032), their position once more indicating a ritual significance, although without elite-status connotations.

Throughout the Preclassic at Mundo Perdido, burials were regularly aligned with the established axis of the Commemorative Astronomical Complex. Such activity appears more commensurate with dedication ceremonies rather than with elite funerary customs. Nevertheless, the individuals interred evidently had a certain rank, to judge from the presence of intentional cranial deformation as well as dental inlays and modifications.

From the Late Preclassic period differences between the deposition of burials are evident at Mundo Perdido and at the North Acropolis. At Mundo Perdido burials were placed ceremonially in conformance with the established axis. But at the North Acropolis, beginning with the Chuen phase, burials of men, women, and children have an elite connotation related to later vaulted tombs (Burials 122, 123, and 126, as well as Burials 85, 166, and 167 of the Cauac phase; W. Coe 1965; Culbert 1977). The luxury offerings included ceramic vessels, marine materials, and traces of wall paintings; based on the pattern of such elite goods, it is evident that the ruling lineage preferred to inter its members in this location. It is not yet possible to identify the specific lineage to which the persons in the early North Acropolis tombs belonged.

The Jaguar Paw Lineage and the Commemorative Astronomical Complex

Preference for the North Acropolis as a place to receive elite burials evidently changed between A.D. 250 and 378, when no burials can be ascribed to a distinctive dynastic lineage in that location. Not until about A.D. 400 was this preference revived. The inclusion of tombs of the Manik 2 phase in Mundo Perdido, however, marks an important change in the funerary tradition of Preclassic times. The tombs at Mundo Perdido became the only elite funerary representations at this time at Tikal, reflecting as such prevailing ideological concepts of the period that were intimately tied to the traditional characteristics of the Jaguar Paw lineage. The preference for locating its dynastic funerary site in the Commemorative Astronomical Complex may indicate activities descriptive of this lineage.

The Commemorative Astronomical Complex of Mundo Perdido is the only example of this type of architectural group known so far to have associated royal tombs. Indeed, one notable characteristic of this type of group is the usual absence of elite burials. In Group E at Uaxactun, the other well-known example of the complex, the axis was established through commemorative caches that only on occasion included human remains (Ricketson and Ricketson 1937: 150–52). Such deposits do not indicate

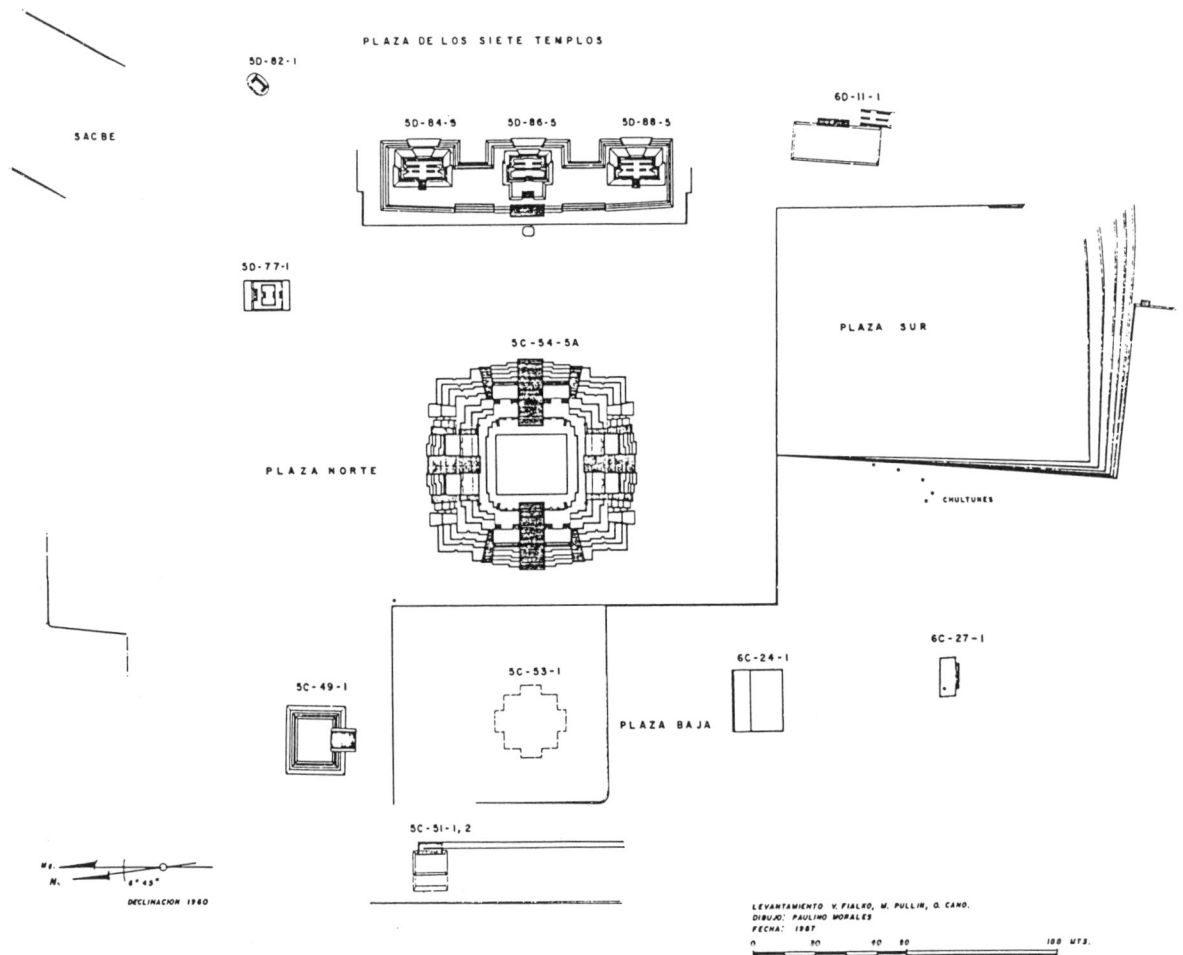

Figure 3.2. Plan. Mundo Perdido, Manik 1 phase.

elite funerary contexts related to the ruling lineages, notwithstanding the fact that rulers erected stelae in this location during the Early Classic period.

The Manik 1 phase can be assigned to the transitional period A.D. 250–300, when characteristics of the Preclassic were changing to those of the Early Classic period. Stratigraphy at Mundo Perdido indicates that all existing structures were again remodeled and new units were added. Moreover, massive leveling operations altered the composition of the group, gradually changing the overall focus of the location itself (Figure 3.2). The access causeway retained the same dimensions and orientation that it had had in the Preclassic period.

Examples of new buildings are Structures 5D-77-1 and 5D-82-1, located in the extreme northeast corner of the complex very close to the causeway. The easternmost of these two buildings had a semicircular substructure that sustained a building with a longitudinal chamber, and whose exterior cornice included a frieze with figures modeled in stucco. The south side of Mundo Perdido underwent considerable alterations that came to define the South Plaza. Adjacent to this new South Plaza, Structures

Figure 3.3. Reconstruction drawing. Mundo Perdido, East sector, Manik 1 phase.

6C-25–1 and 6D-11–1 were built. A later peak of construction in Manik 2 (A.D. 300–378) was an outgrowth of continuous renovations carried out on the South Plaza.

All this took place as work progressed on the Great Pyramid, a fifth version of the radial structure that defined the west side of the Commemorative Astronomical Complex at Tikal (Figure 3.3). In its first stage, Structure 5C-54–5 consisted of eight terraces with sub-aprons, offset with benches, rectangular frames, and recessed panels. The east and west façades were symmetrical, with centrally placed outset staircases that provided access to the summit, while the central staircases on the north and south reached only to the bottom of terrace eight. Other features projecting from the structure, besides terrace aprons, staircases, and staircase outsets, included a variety of niches and largescale masks.

Masks had been featured on the pyramid's façades since Chuen and Cauac times, although they were smaller in scale and located only on the east and west on the upper terraces. The advanced state of erosion prevents determining whether they represented anthropomorphs or zoomorphs, although they resemble the masks found on other Preclassic structures in the central Maya region.

The renovations carried out on the pyramid in Manik 2 (Figure 3.4) included the construction of a ninth terrace (5C-54–5b) and the deposition of two caches in alignment with the established axis (PNT-001 and 002). With the addition of terrace ten (5C-54–5C) in the final part of the phase, the pyramid reached a height of approximately 31 m, becoming for that time the tallest structure at Tikal (Figure 3.5). With respect to later phases, only a few structural adjustments are noticeable. W. Coe and Haviland (1982: 37) suggested that the Mundo Perdido pyramid was the only surviving ediface of a strong Preclassic development of ritual significance, which was finally eclipsed by North Acropolis.

Figure 3.4. Reconstruction drawing. Mundo Perdido, East sector, Early Manik 2 phase.

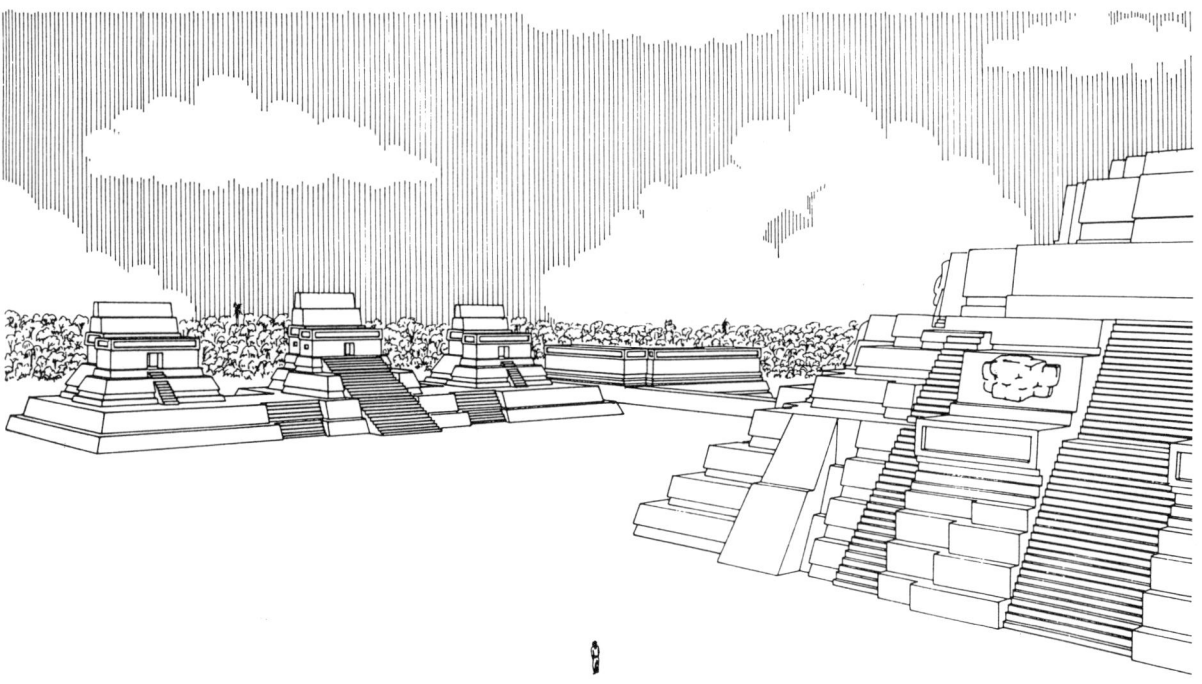

Figure 3.5. Reconstruction drawing. Mundo Perdido, East sector, Late Manik 2 phase.

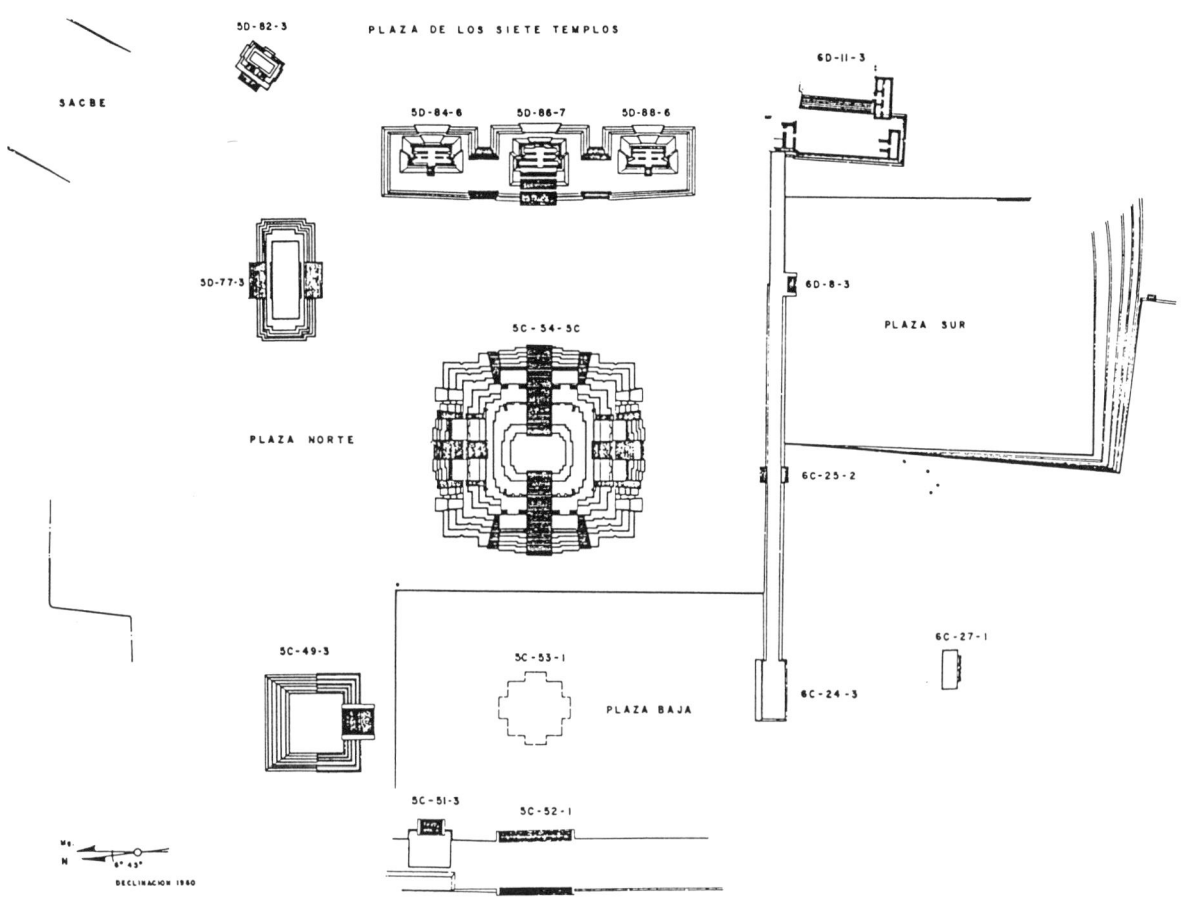

Figure 3.6. Plan. Mundo Perdido, Late Manik 2 phase.

In a manner similar to Structure 5C-54, the East Platform (5D-84/88–5) also underwent regular change. The four recessed terraces that were built during the Cauac phase were partially covered over on the north and south ends during Manik 1 times, with only small intermediate areas reused (Figure 3.2). During the Manik 2 phase, the substructure retained its rectangular plan but increased in length to 99 m from north to south, while it varied in width from 16.5 to 24 m from east to west. The front façade was interrupted by a centrally placed staircase in front of Structure 5D-86–5 (Figure 3.6). The East Platform continued to support the three temples that had characterized this type of complex since the Cauac phase. Principal access was from the upper terrace of the platform they shared. The two outer temples were essentially twins, while the middle temple, straddling the central axis, was constructed somewhat more elaborately. By now the plan of the East Platform closely resembled the corresponding structure in Group E at Uaxactun.

The construction of Structure 5D-86–5 covered

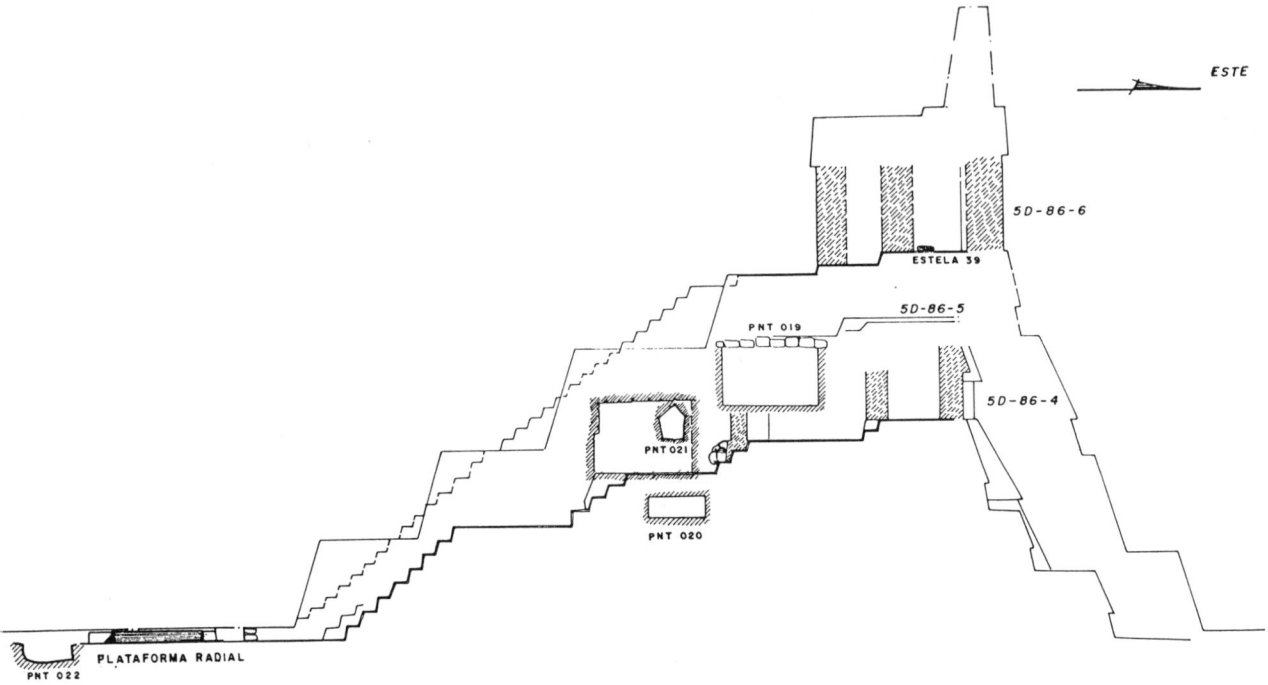

Figure 3.7. Section. Structure 5D-86, Mundo Perdido.

over the transitional burial PNT-021, whose offerings included materials associated with the Protoclassic period (Figure 3.7). The burial was oriented toward the established axis and placed within a pentagonal space in cross section. The tomb was vaulted with stone slabs set at a slight incline, without binding material or capstones, and appears to be the first burial that can be considered a royal tomb at Mundo Perdido because of its elaborate construction technology and sumptuousness. Among the offerings were vessels associated with the Cimi ceramic complex. The tomb was partially destroyed in the Manik 2 phase, so that the only osteological remains encountered during excavation were incomplete fragments. These were found with a tetrapod cylinder vase of the Aguila Group, a small artifact of jade, and a shell. Cache PNT-010, deposited in a later level of Structure 5D-86, included three tetrapod plates with mammiform supports of the type known as Ixcanrio Orange Polychrome and distinguished by complex geometric designs that may have astronomical implications. It is not impossible that these materials derived originally from Burial PNT-021.

The terminal date for the Manik 1 phase may approximate the death date of the protagonist of Stela 29, the first known ruler of the Jaguar Paw lineage, who reigned between Katuns 12 and 14 of Baktun Eight (A.D. 278–317), and leads to the possibility that Burial PNT-021 may be the interment of a member of the Jaguar Paw lineage or the protagonist of Stela 29. But because of the fragmentary state of the osteological remains and the apparent removal of the burial goods, this hypothesis cannot be supported with any certainty.

One interesting feature built on the central axis of the complex at plaza-level in front of Structure 5D-86–5 is a small radial platform about 0.30 m high and 3 m on each side (Figures 3.3 and 3.4). On its top surface is a series of holes, possibly for the support of roof posts or standard-bearers. The platform was associated with and partially covered a mass grave (PNT-022) from Manic 1 times. The burial consisted of 16 or 17 individuals apparently sacri-

Figure 3.8. Comparison between captive figures: a. Left: mural figure 2 from North sector of Structure 5D-86-5. b. Right: relief-carved figure from columnar altar at A-3-Sub-2a, Rio Azul (after G. Stuart 1987:18).

ficed, and included men, women, and children accompanied by offerings of utilitarian objects (Salas and Pijoan 1982), indicating that the grave did not belong to an elite family group but more likely to captives sacrificed during dedication ceremonies for a building or a monument. The affinity for mass sacrifice is exemplified at Cuello, where 26 individuals were sacrificed and dismembered for the dedication of a building around A.D. 400 (Schele 1986), while a mass sacrifice discovered at Miramar, Chiapas, seems of a votive kind, probably propitiatory or for astronomical-calendrical rituals (Agrinier 1978).

The construction of a platform on the central axis just after the mass sacrifice suggests that the function of the platform was to support a stela. For the Manik 1 phase the only monument known at Tikal is Stela 29 (8.12.14.8.15 13 Men 3 Zip, A.D. 292), which was found in an area near Temple III not far from the causeway leading to Mundo Perdido, all of which suggests that originally Stela 29 may have come from this complex. The small platform was covered over in the latter half of Manik 2.

Confirming the significance of the established axis for the Manik 1 phase are two dedicatory caches in Structure 5D-86-5 (PNT-007 and 009, see fig. 3.9). The ceramic pieces that functioned as cache covers have glyphs painted in black on their bottoms in calligraphic style and in a manner similar to that reported for the lid of Cache 144 from North Acropolis (Coggins 1975: 121–22).

During the initial phase of Manik 2 the Maya constructed Structure 5D-86-6 (Figure 3.7). Above a battered section on the back wall of the front room, a frieze about 0.90 m high was incised to represent five nude captives who had been partially mutilated. The figures were posed in a genuflective position, two of them looking south, three of them north, and with their hands bound in front of them with braided rope. The captives appear to be carrying figures on their backs attached by bands tied around their chests. In the examples that can be identified the figures are zoomorphic or anthropomorphic (Figure 3.8). Similar figures have been reported from the site of Rio Azul (Adams 1986).

These are rendered on altar or column tops and are contemporaneous with the frieze at Mundo Perdido.

Below the stairs of Structure 5D-86-6, a vaulted chamber was constructed of tuff with an irregular arch (1.10 m wide, 2.75 m long, and 1.97 m high). This may have been a tomb that was never used or that was emptied during construction activity in the latter part of Manik 2 (Figure 3.7), when the last of the verifiable renovations that adhered to the established axis (5D-86-7) were made.

It is difficult to determine to whose reign the vault and prisoner frieze corresponds. Treating them as features of early Manik 2 (A.D. 300–350) eliminates the possibility that they correspond to Jaguar Paw I. A probable protagonist for this time period is the ruler represented on the Leyden Plaque, named *Balam Ahaw Chan* (Jaguar Lord Sky) (Schele and Miller 1986), or Moon Zero Bird (*see* Stela 31, D6; Mathews 1985). This Leyden protagonist held power beginning at 8.14.13.1.12 (A.D. 320) and may be the second Tikal ruler of the Jaguar Paw lineage, or Jaguar Paw II.

Traditionally, the Leyden Plaque is considered to have originated at Tikal as part of the grave goods in Burial 22 on North Acropolis, before the tomb was looted (Coggins 1975). This remains a tentative and controversial hypothesis (Morley and Morley 1938).

During the latter half of the Manik 2 phase (A.D. 350–378), a number of changes were made to the East Platform of the Commemorative Astronomical Complex (Figures 3.5 and 3.6). The three upper temples were remodeled following the disposition of various elite burials whose characteristic offerings reflect a high social standing. Structure 5D-86-7 covered Burial PNT-019 as well as a cache deposited above. Structure 5D-84-6 included Burials PNT-024, -025, and -026, while Burials PNT-062 and 063 were placed in Structure 5D-88-6 (Figures 3.7 and 3.9).

These tombs were all located on the east-west axis of their respective buildings and were also oriented in this direction, except for two that were oriented north-south. The chambers were covered with flat roofs of large stone slabs. The interiors were coated with stucco and painted an intense red. The tombs were not intrusive but constructed contemporaneously with the renovation of the temples. The burials contained a middle-aged male (PNT-019), a middle-aged female (PNT-024), two young male adults (PNT-025 and 062), a female adolescent (PNT-063), and an infant (PNT-026) (Salas and Pijoan 1982).

Among the burial offerings in these tombs the ceramic pieces exhibit a distinctive elaboration in design but maintain a preference for the stylistically older and more traditional forms of basal flange bowls with dome-shaped lids topped by a handle modeled into effigies of macaws and monkeys (Hammond 1982a). The cylindrical tripod form apparently was not considered, even though these pieces date from the Manik 2 period.

The vessels display complex iconographic images—an amalgam of anthropomorphic, zoomorphic, abstract, geometric, and glyphic motifs—above serpentine forms. The bodies of the images are painted on the vessel's surface while the three-dimensional heads function as the handle of the lid. Many of the zoomorphic motifs include depictions of birds—macaws, herons, turkeys—as well as turtles, monkeys, jaguars, lizards, and insects, due perhaps to a particular liking for these animals by the lineage represented in the burials.

One outstanding artifact from Burial PNT-019 is a tetrapod vessel made of perishable material, of which only the stucco-embellished supports survive. These represent human heads painted with a combination of black, red, green, and white, colors possibly associated with the cardinal directions. An anthropomorphic handle indicates that the vessel had a lid, although the lid's precise form is unknown. The inclusion of stuccoed artifacts supports the probability that we are dealing with the last burial of the Manik 2 series at Mundo Perdido, approximately contemporaneous with Burial 22 in North Acropolis, which is transitional to the Manik 3A phase.

Stela 39 (Figure 3.10) refers to Katun 17 of Cycle 8, which is also its dedicatory date (Ayala 1985). However, because of the erosion of glyph A7 there is a possibility that it refers instead to the completion of Katun 19. Nevertheless, the architectural sequence of structure 5D-86 where the stela was found, and the style and characteristics of the offertory materials of the diverse tombs and caches, favors Katun 17 as the firmer possibility.

The stela was found redeposited in Room 3 of Structure 5D-86-7, a circumstance which amplifies

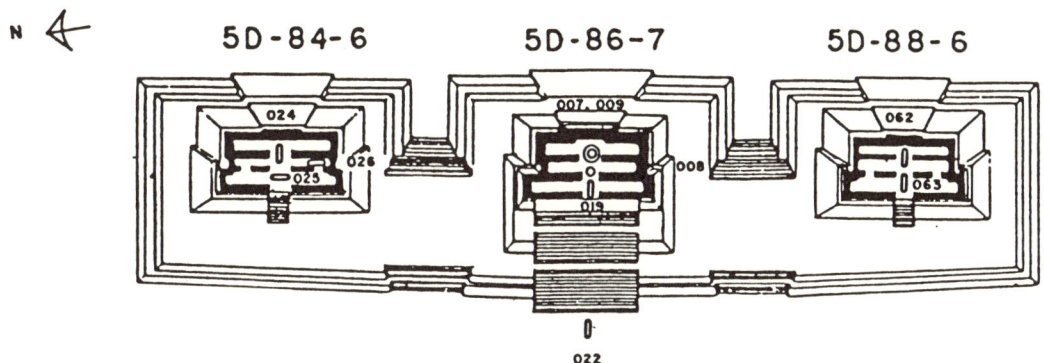
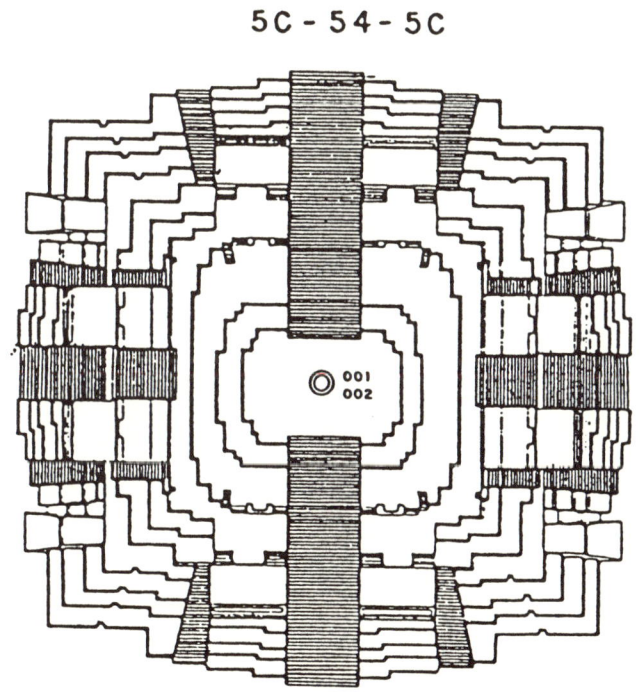

Figure 3.9. Plan, Commemorative Astronomical Complex, Mundo Perdido, Late Manik 2 phase.

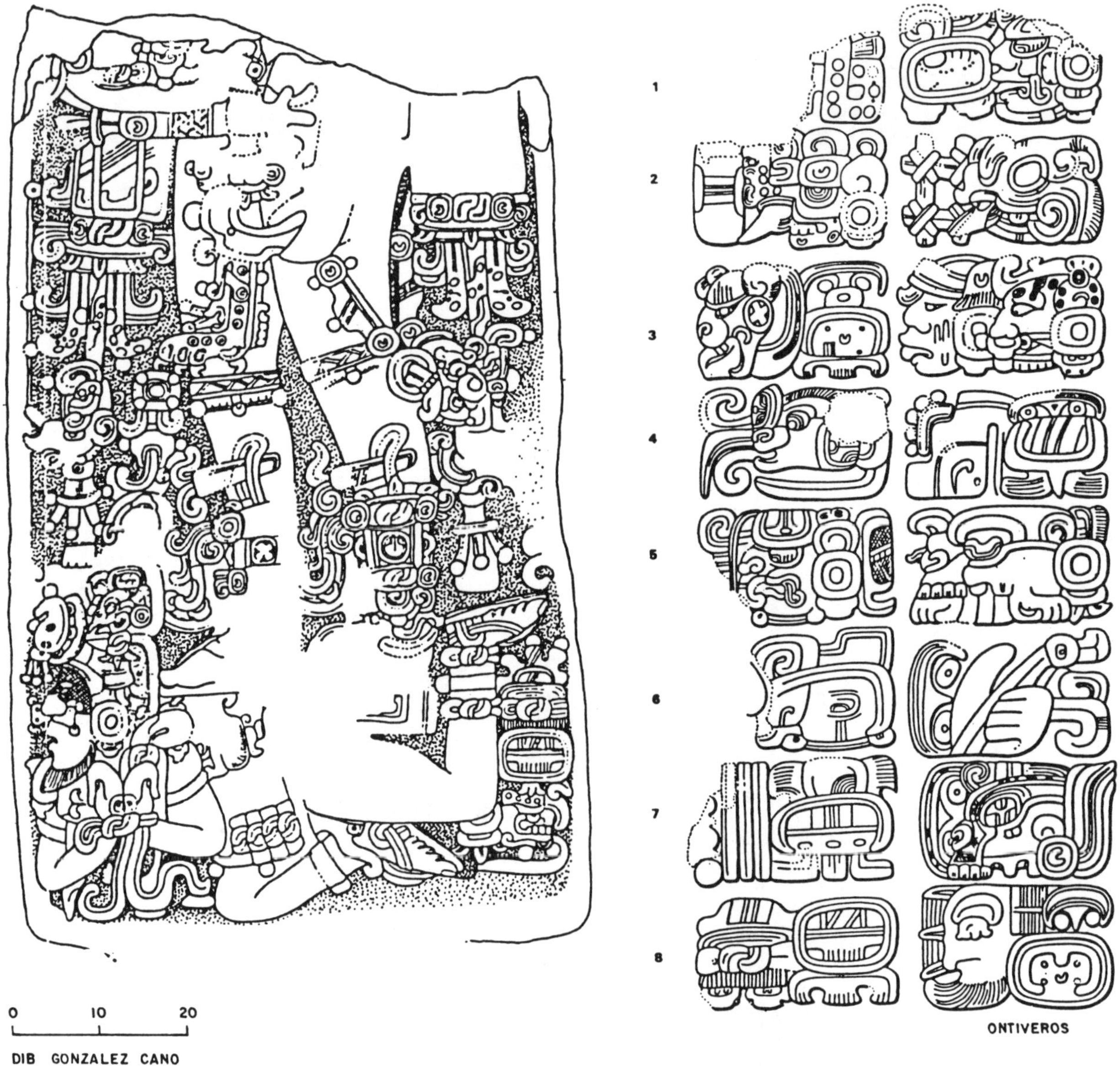

Figure 3.10. Drawing of Stela 39 from Mundo Perdido.

the possible interpretation of Mundo Perdido, and places the previously described burials within a dynastic context. We can assume that the ruler represented on Stela 39 is Jaguar Paw III, known also as Jaguar Paw Skull I (Ayala 1985), who ruled from about A.D. 360 to 378. Following his death a dramatic change occurred in the political, calendrical, and ritual direction of Tikal.

The individual in PNT-019 may correspond to this ruler. The tomb is one of the largest of the previously discussed burial series, and was positioned, significantly, on the established axis of the complex. Supporting this identification is the inclusion of a Kin sign (the day sun) on the ankle support on the ruler's right leg on Stela 39, and an Akbal sign on the left leg (the night sun). These signs regularly appear in other representations of the Jaguar Paw dynasts, as in the case of the Leyden Plaque. Among the ruler's grave gifts in Burial PNT-019 was a jade mask, recovered in multiple fragments, on which these glyphs appeared.

The individuals in the other five tombs found in the East Platform, the materials from which are closely related stylistically and chronologically, therefore correspond to prominent members of the Jaguar Paw dynastic lineage; they may have succumbed during the reign of Jaguar Paw III, or they may have been sacrificial victims who were among the ruler's close relatives dispatched after his death. Other interpretations regarding the death and burial of these persons must await a larger osteological analysis.

Before the discovery of these tombs and Stela 39, which carries the first textual example of the Tikal emblem glyph (A8), there were few references to the Jaguar Paw lineage. The only ruler of this line who had been firmly identified was the protagonist of Stela 29, and then more tentatively, the person represented on the Leyden Plaque. Now it is possible, however, to better document the lineage through characteristic offerings from the known tombs and by physical association with an especially important complex in the sphere of ceremony and ritual at Tikal, the Commemorative Astronomical Complex.

In addition to the astronomical-calendrical functions inferred from its associations with Mundo Perdido, the dynastic lineage must have participated in military activities, judging from the inclusion of captives on its monuments. Captives, at this time, are restricted to three examples: the above-mentioned frieze in Structure 5D-86-5, the captive on the Leyden Plaque who has a "decorated Ahaw" and deer antler on his forehead to designate his status as "lord" (Schele and Miller 1986: 109, 121), and the captive on Stela 39 who appears to have been a nobleman from his apparel and the *hel*-vulture glyph on his headdress.

The capture of these persons of rank suggests a confrontation of lineages that may have occurred both internally and externally. There are no clear references from the archaeological sites adjoining Tikal to support an assumption of external confrontation, except for the recent discovery of captives at Rio Azul (mentioned above), which may indicate expansion by the Jaguar Paw lineage.

In the ceremonial precincts of Tikal, no other Early Classic tombs of the Jaguar Paw lineage are known after those found at Mundo Perdido. Soon after the events surrounding the death of Jaguar Paw III on 8.17.1.4.12 (A.D. 378), a relocation of the lineage to Uolantun may have taken place, since Stela 1 (8.18.13.5.11) from that site represents a person who exhibits Jaguar Paw iconography (see Jones and Satterthwaite 1982; Ayala 1985).

In considering that the hierarchic organization of Tikal may have been centered around three primary lineages, as proposed by Proskouriakoff (Coggins 1979b), the representations of captives at Mundo Perdido may indicate a local struggle among the three lineages for political control over the site. At present, the Jaguar Paw lineage can be identified as one of the competing entities, while another was the lineage associated with the Ma'Cuch title, a dynastic line whose influence peaked in the fifth century A.D. Not enough references survive to speculate about the third lineage.

The Lineage of the Ma'Cuch Title at Tikal

Group 6C-XVI is located about 350 m to the south of Mundo Perdido (Figure 3.1) in the southeastern sector of the Tikal epicenter, and is situated on an elevation associated on the Carr and Hazard map with the 250 m contour line immediately south of Group 6C-XV (Carr and Hazard 1961). The group now consists of some Late Classic residential platforms (Structures 6C-51/53). Below this occupation, however, were ample Early Classic materials that gradually had been covered over during the course of 21 construction stages. The Early Classic construction consisted of pyramidal structures, platforms, and buildings of various rooms, porticoes, patios, and passageways, generally grouped around small plazas; all are characteristic of Early Classic residential groups in Mesoamerica such as at Teotihuacan and Monte Alban.

The sequence of construction at Group 6C-XVI was especially clear in the two most relevant phases of the Early Classic period, Manik 2 and Manik 3. An initial surge is noticeable in the last half of Manik 2 (A.D. 350–378), as inferred from various caches (PNT-37, 45, 67, 71), burials (PNT-160), and problematic deposits (PNT-019 and 032). The associated artifacts are homogeneous and diagnostic for this phase and were sealed below ceramic materials related to the Manik 3A phase, notable for their foreign traits.

The problematic deposits primarily consist of concentrations of refuse sealed under contemporary construction elements that assure their isolation from later cultural episodes such as floors of rooms or of plazas. The deposits derive from ceremonial paraphernalia used briefly then rejected and intentionally deposited. They tend to be found in cavities in the natural rock, a trait known in the Maya area since the Middle Preclassic period (W. Coe 1959: 94–95; Lowe 1960: 50; Ball 1977b: 4).

Among the more remarkable discoveries at Group 6C-XVI is the Ball Court Marker, whose dedication date of 8.17.1.4.12 (A.D. 378) allows its association with a series of dynastic events that were apparently linked to the death of Jaguar Paw III and the inauguration of the ruler Smoking Frog. On the marker, the notation of the date *11 Ahau 3 Uayeb*, emphasizes that on 8.17.1.4.12 11 Eb 15 Mac, Smoking Frog was inaugurated with the title *Ma'Cuch* as ruler Hel 4 of the succession at Tikal.

Diverse discoveries realized in Group 6C-XVI support an association with the lineage of Smoking Frog, which became a dynasty upon his inauguration. A number of collateral functions of the lineage identified by the Ma'Cuch title have been determined, some of them related to the ball game. Significantly, the lineage assumed for itself foreign architectural modes and iconographic elements.

At Group 6C-XVI, the implementation of the *talud-tablero* architectural mode is conspicuous from the first construction stage. At Tikal this feature is an example of eclecticism. As a cultural trait it was widely diffused throughout Mesoamerica during the Terminal Preclassic, receiving greater or lesser acceptance where it came to be used and undergoing modifications through contact with architectural styles prevalent in each place. In the Maya Lowlands, the *talud-tablero* mode has been reported at Becan, Dzibilchaltún, Rio Azul, and possibly Yaxha.

At Tikal certain *talud-tablero* elements found their way into various versions of Structure 5C-54 at Mundo Perdido, where, beginning in the Middle Preclassic period (5C-54–1), *alfardas* were used to delimit the staircases (Figure 3.11), as shown by excavations on its northwest corner. Later versions of the pyramid exhibit variations of this element, although not combined directly with staircases but with the terraces of recessed corners and niches that define the north and south sides of the structure (Figure 3.12).

At Mundo Perdido during Manik 1 (A.D. 250–300), the pyramid 5C-54–5 exhibited *tableros* of great dimension. Close by, Structure 5C-49–1 incorporated *taluds* into three terraces. The upper terrace supported a vertical *tablero* without a frame and painted black; the stairways had alfardas without cornices or *remates* (Fig. 3.12).

From the beginning of Manik 2, the three-terraced Structure 5C-49–2 displayed clearly defined framed *tableros* on the front façade. These continued around the sides, where they united with inclined terraces; otherwise, only the upper terrace had a *tablero* on all four façades (Figure 3.6). It is possible that at Kaminaljuyu the first buildings on the Acropolis had this architectural variant of interrupted *tableros* (see Cheek 1977: 51–53). Other buildings at Mundo Perdido with *talud-tablero* façades at this time were Structures 5C-51–3/4, 5C-52–1/2, and 6C-24–2/3 (Figure 3.6).

At Group 6C-XVI during the latter half of the Manik 2 Phase three *talud-tablero* platforms were constructed (Figure 3.13). Structure Sub-04–1st had elements of this style combined with apron moldings only on one sector of its sides; its staircase did not have alfardas (Figure 3.14). A series of figures modeled in stucco was found in one of the recessed *tableros*, while the front surfaces incorporated large-scale masks representing a deity that has not been identified.

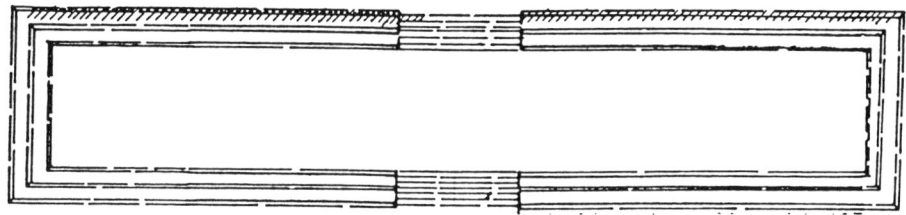

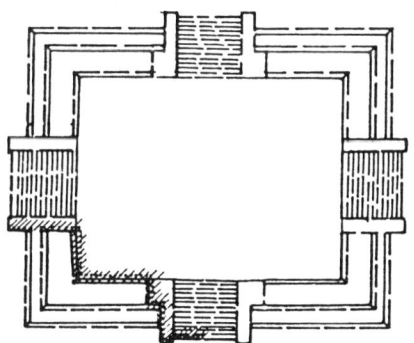

Figure 3.11. Plan, Mundo Perdido, Structures 5D-84/88-1 and 5C-54-1, Late Eb phase.

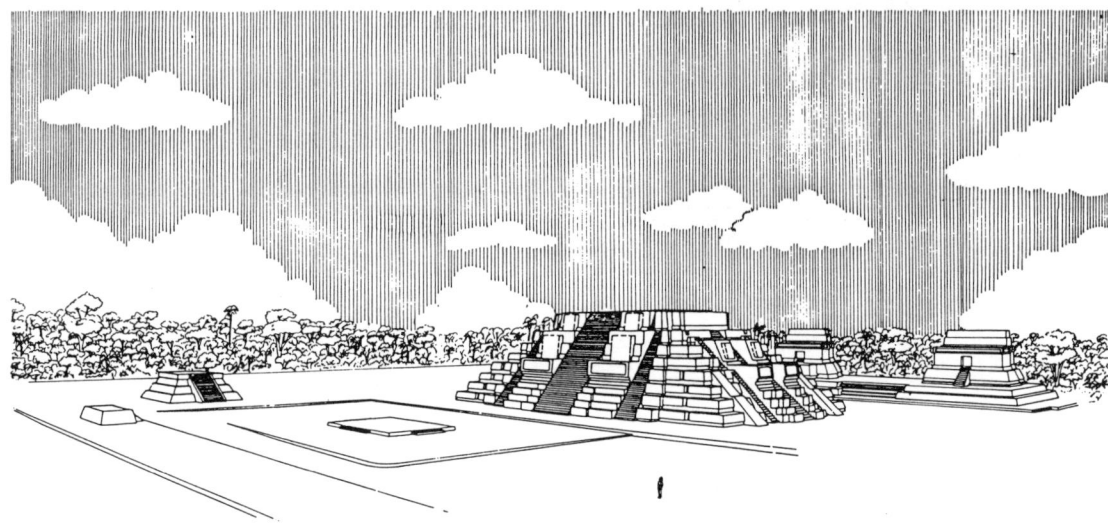

Figure 3.12. Reconstruction drawing, Mundo Perdido, West sector, Manik 1 phase.

Structure Sub-17 exhibited a *talud-tablero* on its front façade and parts of its sides combined with apron moldings, and had a staircase without alfardas (Figures 3.13 and 3.14). The third example, Structure Sub-26, had *talud-tableros* on all of its sides, and the staircase had alfardas with cornices or *remates*, the only example of corniced balustrades at Tikal at this time (Figure 3.15a).

During the Manik 3A Phase, other structures exhibited this architectural style. At Group 6C-XVI another platform was constructed, Structure Sub-57, in whose recessed tablero were located three painted figures in low relief, seated and in profile. Furthermore, at Mundo Perdido, the base of the East Platform of the Commemorative Astronomical Complex was remodeled with huge *talud-tableros*, while other buildings of the group show similar changes (Figure 3.16).

Another example of a *talud-tablero* judged to be of the Manik 3A phase is Altar Sub-48, situated in the center of the north *plazuela* at Group 6C-XVI, where it is assumed the Ball Court Marker was displayed as a public monument for dynastic display from A.D. 378 (Figure 3.15b). The structural pattern of the plazuela continued to be maintained for approximately forty-five years (until about A.D. 425), when it was covered over entirely and the marker deposited as part of a ritual offering (PNT-049) within a perforation in the altar's platform. Placed in the cache beside the Ball Court Marker was a shell and an anthropomorphic head removed from some stucco wall at that time. Two caches (PNT-043 and 051) and a burial (PNT-153) were also deposited on the east side of the altar.

The meter-high Ball Court Marker (PNTE-005) was fashioned from compact limestone (Figure

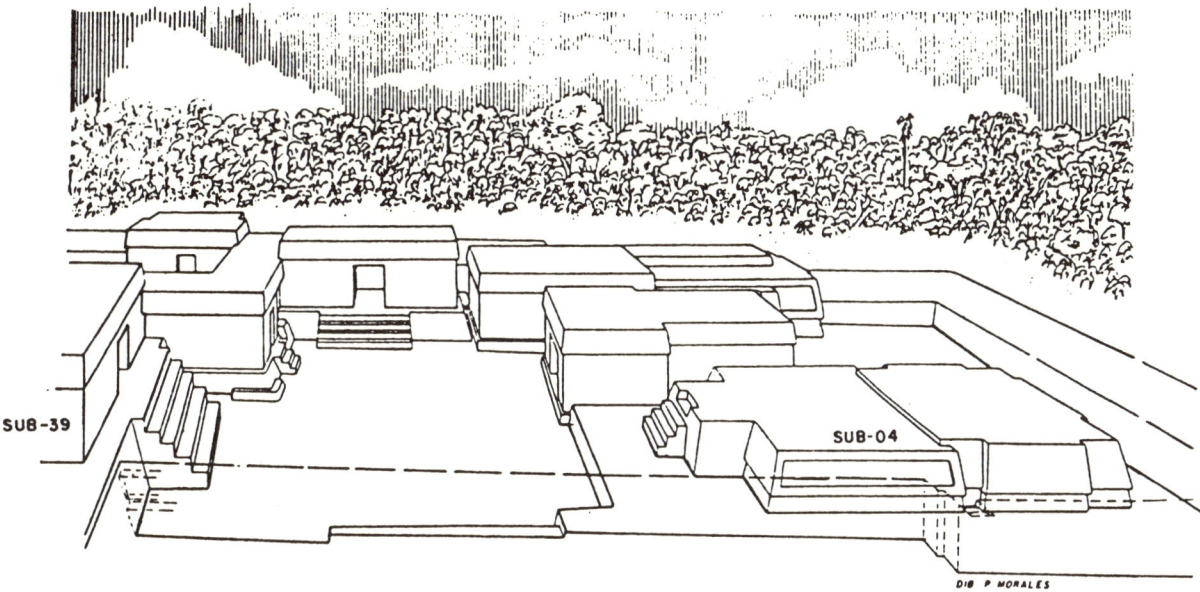

Figure 3.13. Reconstruction drawing, Group 6C-XVI, South Plazuela, 8th stage, Manik 2 phase.

Figure 3.14. Reconstruction drawing, Group 6C-XVI, Southeast Plazuela, 6th stage, Manik 2 phase.

a) ESTADIO 3

b) ESTADIO II

Figure 3.15a. Reconstruction drawing, Group 6C-XVI, North Plazuela, 3d stage. b. 11th stage.

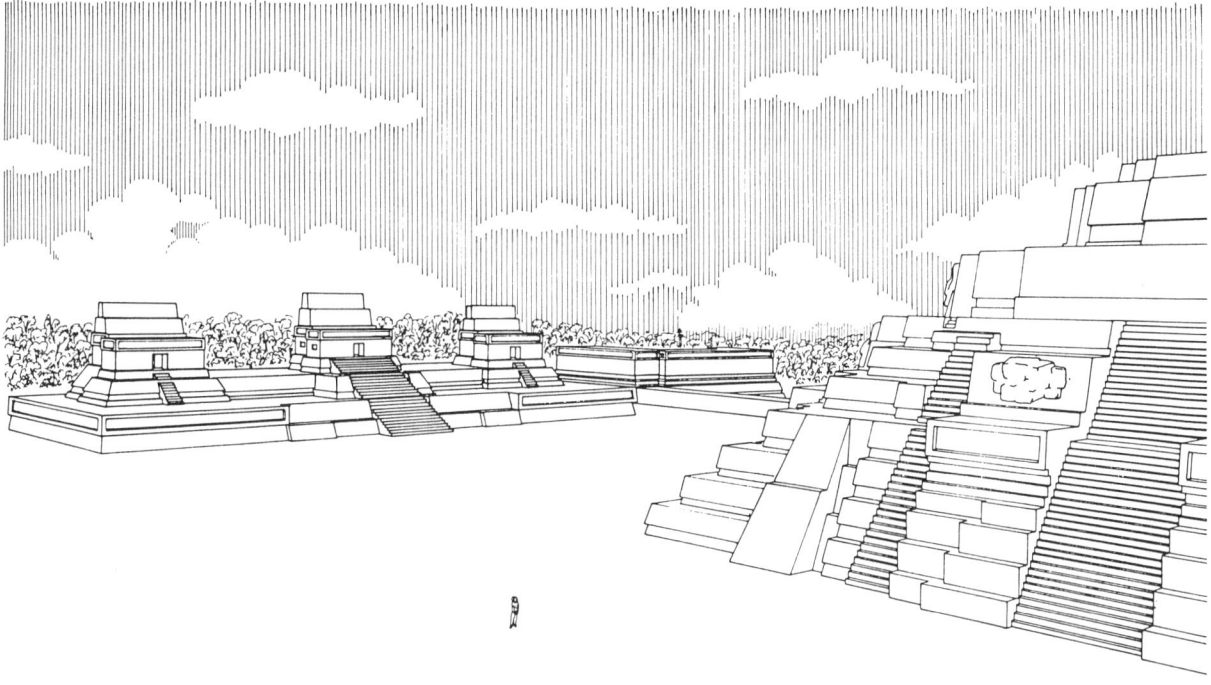

Figure 3.16. Reconstruction drawing, Mundo Perdido, East sector, Manik 3A phase.

3.17). It has a composite silhouette, with an oval upper area; the middle section is an integration of a spherical shape with a truncated cone, while the lower section is cylindrical.

In the marker's upper section, Side A is carved with feather motifs. In the center of this medallion or oval space is a glyphic configuration of a stylized Tlaloc rendered as three dots above a horizontal bar whose ends curve downward—a feature common throughout Mesoamerica at sites such as Teotihuacan and Xochicalco, and on Escuintla tripod vessels (Bernal 1968; Saenz 1975; Hellmuth 1975; Berlo 1980).

In the center of Side B, the upper section displays a profile representation of a bearded owl whose left eye has a trilobe form and who has a "Smoking Ax" (?) in his forehead, iconographic motifs of the Old God. Overlying the profile of the owl, a left hand grasps an *atlatl* or spear-thrower (Figure 3.17).

The middle section's spherical area is enhanced by four ovals. Side B depicts in lower relief than the rest of the marker the faces of two individuals who have headdresses of a foreign style; they are united through one of their ear ornaments and wear as noseplugs a representation of a butterfly. Located below the faces is a stylized trapezoid form of the "Mexican Year Sign"—the earliest example of this symbol at Tikal (Figure 3.17). The truncated conical area, like the uppermost feature of the marker, is decorated with feather motifs.

The lower section includes two panels on each side of the cylinder, each carved with thirty-six glyphs arranged in four columns of nine glyphs. The complete text totals 72 glyph blocks. A particular characteristic of the inscription's syntax is its redundancy, wherein various glyphs that are different in morphology express the same meaning.

Smoking Frog, the first documented ruler of the *Ma'Cuch* lineage, appears to be mentioned three times in the text of the Ball Court Marker (A8, D4, H4), accompanied on two occasions by the lineage title (B8, F4); he also used the title *Owl and Atlatl-in-hand* (C3, E9, F9), boasted the *18 Jog* title (D8, H6), and is mentioned as *Ahpop* (F2, H1, G4).

In at least three cases, Smoking Frog clearly designates his affiliation with the Old God and therefore with an associated ritual mentioned at B7, D1, G3, and G5. The Old God is represented with a "Smoking Ax"(?) and a blood prefix that perhaps functions as a verbal qualifier, perhaps sacrifice, in relation to the nominal that it accompanies, either Smoking Frog (A8, H4) or Two Coyote (H3) (see below).

The Old God ceramic effigy from Burial 10 in North Acropolis has ritual connotations related to sacrifice. His distinctive characteristics are a beard, a three-pointed device that covers the eyes, ear ornaments that are sometimes punctate, and a Kin sign on the head. On the Hauberg Stela (Schele 1985: 136) which refers to a ritual blood sacrifice, a person with a beard and with his eye covered by a three-pointed device emerges from the mouth of the Vision Serpent. The three-pronged element is also characteristic of the glyph that denotes the ruler Kan Boar (*See* Stelae 3, 7, 9, and 13; Jones and Satterthwaite 1982).

The Ball Court Marker also appears to refer to an ancestor of Smoking Frog, an individual represented by the glyph Two Coyote (H3). Two Coyote is associated with the date 8.16.5.1.9 12 Muluc 12 Kankin (A.D. 362) and who establishes the functions of the Ma'Cuch lineage and its dynastic emblems. These signs are the same ones illustrated in the upper oval area of the Ball Court Marker and represented in the text at positions F8, E9, and F9; they seem related to death, sacrifice, and war.

The architectural and stratigraphic evidence at Group 6C-XVI, along with the inclusion of Problematic Deposits PNT-019 and 032, correspond to the Manik 2 phase (La Porte 1974). Stylistically, the Initial Series glyphs on the Ball Court Marker resemble those of Stela 29 and the Leyden Plaque, and likewise support the probability that the marker's chronological record refers to these times.

After Smoking Frog, the Ma'Cuch title was used by Curl Nose on Stela 4, which also mentions Smoking Frog as the former ruler (see also Stela 18). The effigy figurine of the Old God found in Curl Nose's Burial 10 (Coggins 1975) makes more emphatic the close kinship ties between these two rulers.

In the historical narrative on Stela 31, Stormy Sky mentions an event that came to pass on 8.17.1.4.12 11 Eb, of which the protagonists were Smoking Frog and Jaguar Paw (Mathews 1985). Stormy Sky's father, Curl Nose, who uses the *Ma'Cuch* title, is also mentioned. On the front surface of the monument, Stormy Sky poses in all the ostentation of his office, wearing dynastic emblems that include a bearded owl fixed to his left wrist, the same that was illustrated in the oval area of the Ball Court Marker (Side B).

Furthermore, Kan Boar, the ruler of Tikal between A.D. 457 and 488, was of the Ma'Cuch lineage under the tutelage of the Old God and the sacrificial ritual which was apparently associated with that deity. The trilobe device that covers the eye in the Kan Boar glyph is the particular trait that links him to the *Ma'Cuch* titular god (see Stelae 9 and 23).

The *Ma'Cuch* lineage, besides its activities related to the calendar, may have had functions linked to the ball game, to war, and to sacrifices associated with the cult of the Old God. Special plazuelas at Group 6C-XVI, evidently had ball game associations beyond those inferred from the Ball Court Marker.

At Group 6C-XVI the first element related to the ball game is the Ball Game Mural, a painting that decorates the front of Structure Sub-21 in a plazuela on the east side of the group that dates to the terminal part of Manik 2 (Figure 3.18). Although mutilated in its upper part, the mural depicts a ball player in action moving towards a ball which is painted black. The ball has a hieroglyph in the center that may be related to death or to the Underworld (Muan?), but lacks the numerical coefficient often found on representations of balls as discussed by Schele and Miller (1986: 255). This section of the mural may have had its symmetrical counterpart on the opposite side of the staircase, which lamentably was destroyed by later construction.

In the terminal facet of the Manik 2 phase, Struc-

New Perspectives on Old Problems 53

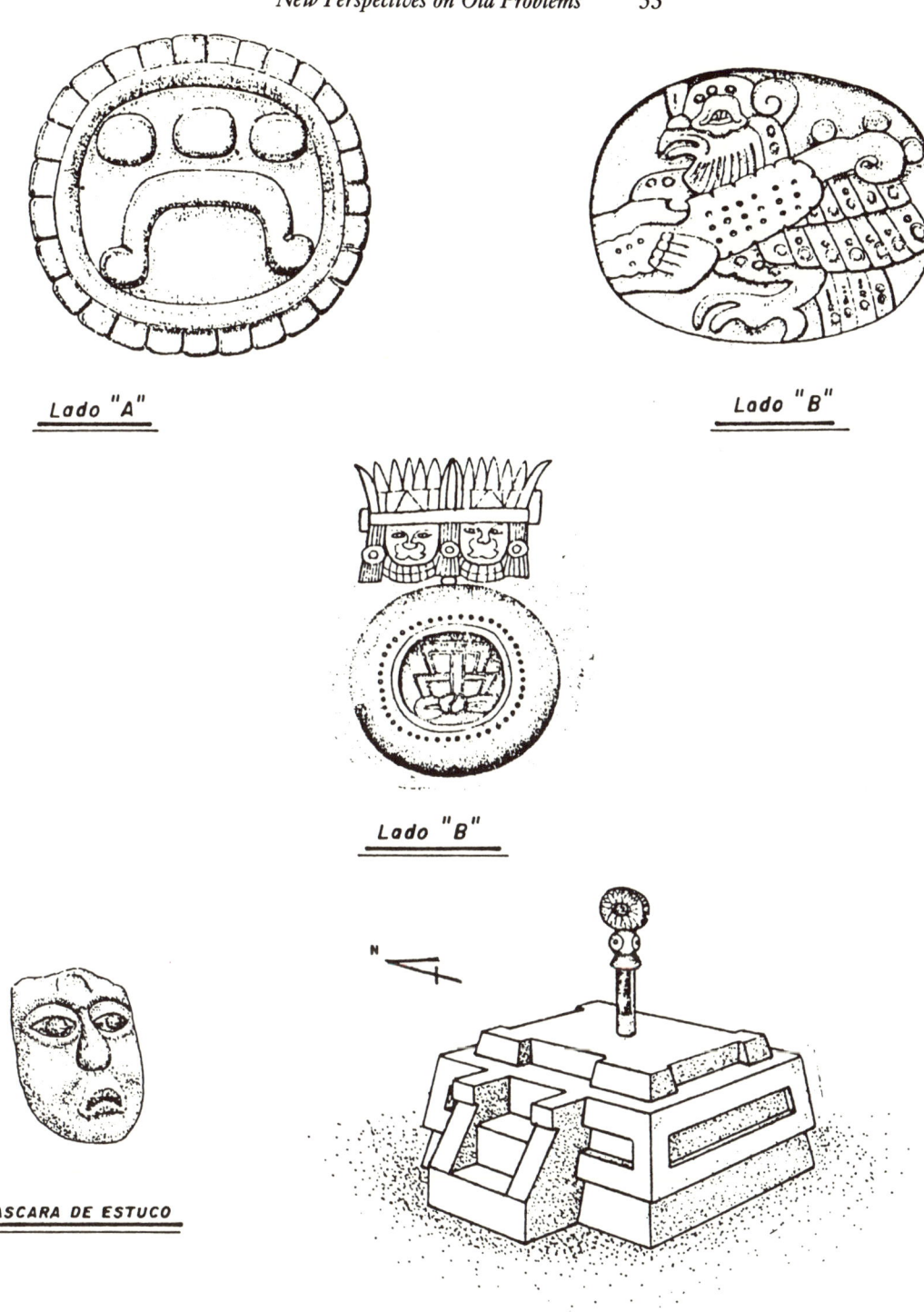

Figure 3.17. Ball Court Marker and stucco mask from Structure Sub-4B, Group 6C-XVI.

Figure 3.18. Ball Game Mural from Structure Sub-21 of Group 6C-XVI, Late Manik 2 phase.

ture Sub-39 was constructed on the north side of the south plazuela. The *talud* of its substructure provided a surface for another painting called *The Mural of the Ball Players*. The mural was divided in two by a centrally placed staircase painted with glyphic elements in red and black (Figure 3.19). The west section of the mural was discovered in good condition, preserved both in its upper and lower zones, and represents a sequence of three persons in profile looking toward the east, each in a pose that denotes movement.

The person closest to the staircase (Person 1) wears a skirt held up by the three-part waist protector characteristic of ball players (Figure 3.20); on his left leg he uses a knee pad with an unidentified glyphic sign. The details associated with his head and headdress present more iconographic complexity; a pectoral of indefinite form but painted red hangs from a collar fastened by a band knotted behind the neck; part of a component of the ear ornament can be identified as a representation of God C. A portion of Person 1's face has been rendered with colored bands, a feature similar to that observed on the captive on Stela 39, and may correspond to some manifestation of the ball game and nobility.

The central person (Person 2) lacks both the skirt and the knee pad, but wears the three-part "ball deflector" around the waist. From his collar hangs a pectoral from which emerges a bifid serpent painted red; the collar itself represents "death eyes" and is fastened to a band knotted at the back of the head. Except for the lips, which are painted red, the face is left uncolored, while the ear ornaments have elements distinct from those of Person 1. One particularly outstanding detail is that Person 2 carries a bloodletter in his left hand.

The figure at the extreme west end is the most destroyed in this section of the mural (Person 3). He has neither a skirt nor a knee pad, but he wears the

New Perspectives on Old Problems 55

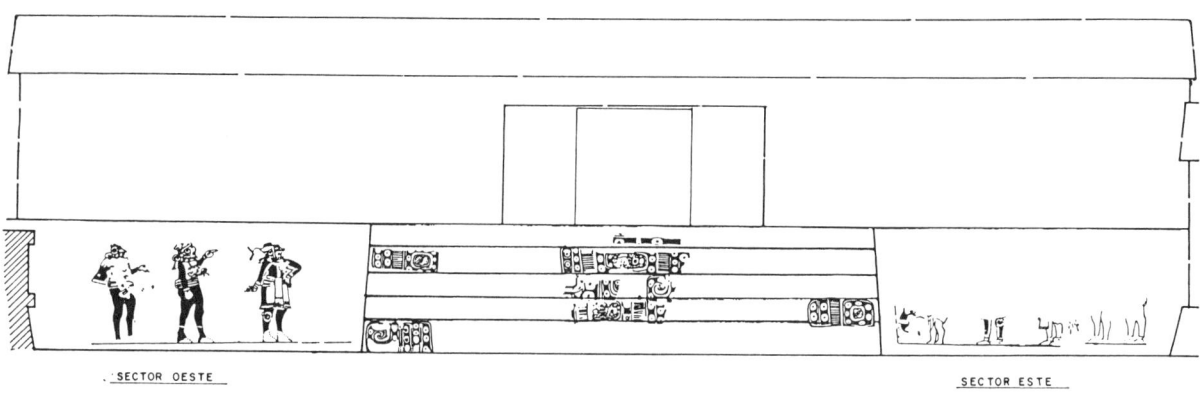

Figure 3.19. Mural of the Ball Players from Structure Sub-39, South façade, Group 6C-XVI.

Figure 3.20. Mural of the Ball Players from Structure Sub-39, South façade, detail of west side.

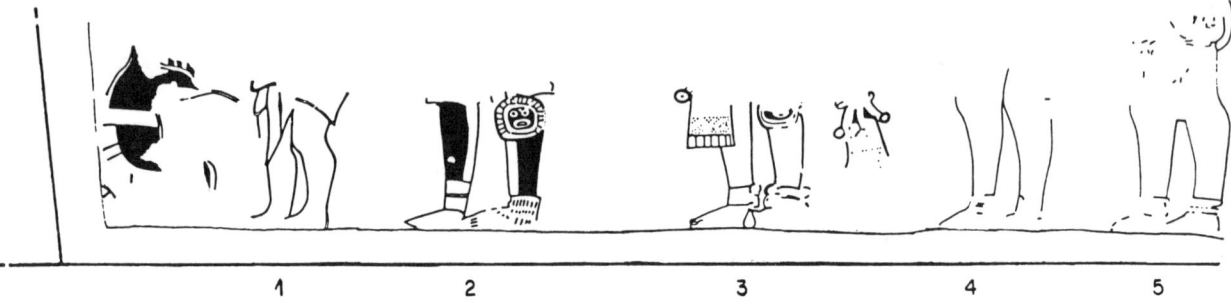

Figure 3.21. Mural of the Ball Players from Structure Sub-39, South façade, detail of east side.

three-part deflector around the waist, down to which reaches some item evidently hanging from the neck (Figure 3.19). He may also have had a pectoral and a collar. The ear ornament differs from the other examples in that something emanates from its central element. The face is painted similarly to that of Person 1.

The five persons depicted on the opposite, or east, side of the mural are destroyed from the knees up (Figures 3.19 and 3.21). They are smaller in dimension and their colors are better preserved than those of the west section. The person nearest the staircase (Person 1), as well as the figures on the extreme eastern end (Persons 4 and 5), exhibit a greater degree of deterioration, conserving only some lines that define their legs. It is possible to make out only certain elements of the two central figures (Persons 2 and 3).

Person 2 is the only figure on this side of the mural whose legs are painted black; his recognizeable features are sandals, the lower edge of a skirt, and on the left leg a knee pad with an Ahaw glyph (Figure 3.21). The identifiable features of Person 3 are the lower end of an apron hanging from his missing waistband and a knee pad worn on the left leg, as well as traces of a set of ankle cuffs. There is an additional element depicted behind him that may be part of his attire.

The risers on the staircase, five in all, had three vertical panels painted red and black in geometric and glyphic forms that have possible bloodletting associations (Figure 3.19). On the central panel there appears to have been represented various gods related to bloodletting rituals, although the bad state of preservation does not allow a discussion of these in greater detail. It is, however, possible to observe in general that glyphs represented on staircases sometimes refer to the deaths of captives and to the day of the "inferior conjunction of Venus" as the most appropriate time for war and sacrificial rituals (Schele and Miller 1986: 250). The staircase of Structure Sub-04, situated in front of the edifice of the Mural of the Ball Players, displays iconographic elements similar to the stairs described above, as well as fragmentary remains of another ball player.

It is possible that the placement of Group 6C-XVI to the south of the Tikal epicenter is an indication of the ball game's significance with respect to death and the Underworld. A connection is therefore conceivable between the group's location and the reference to the direction "south" in the text of the Ball Court Marker (D3), a glyph that in an alternative form has the connotation "death" (Schele 1986, personal communication).

The artistic evidence indicates that a part of the ball game—and perhaps a distinct form of this sport—took place in association with staircases. It came to be an important Early Classic manifestation of the ball game in the Maya Central Area, and for these reasons it was depicted so often on sculptured monuments and polychrome vases. Good examples of sculptured monuments are Altar 8 at Tikal and the carved stairways at Yaxchilan, Dos Pilas, Tamarindito, Ceibal, and La Amelia.

The clear association of Group 6C-XVI with the ball game suggests that this was a group occupied by a segment of the *Ma'Cuch* lineage that was specifically dedicated to this activity, functioning perhaps as a retreat for preparation and initiation rituals, for training in the particulars of the ball game, as well as for promotion of the event.

The Lineage of the Ma'Cuch Title at Uaxactun

Apparently, the *Ma'Cuch* lineage at Tikal was subordinate to the Jaguar Paw dynasty until 8.17.1.4.12 11 Eb (A.D. 378). With the rise to power of Smoking Frog, the *Ma'Cuch* lineage became dynastic with implications of expansionism, as indicated by Stelae 4, 5, and 22 of Uaxactun that name Smoking Frog as a protagonist. In some manner Smoking Frog assumed political control of Uaxactun, becoming the only person to govern contemporaneously at both sites. Upon the death of Smoking Frog, the rulership of Tikal and Uaxactun was assumed by different people aligned with the *Ma'Cuch* lineage: Curl Nose at Tikal, at 8.17.2.16.17 (A.D. 379), and the lord in Burial A-29 at Uaxactun. Respectively, this is signalled by Stela 18 at Tikal and Stela 4 at Uaxactun (see, Mathews 1985).

An important difference between Tikal and Uaxactun is that before the date 8.17.1.4.12 we have no information concerning the dynastic lineage that governed at Uaxactun. This is because no elite tombs have been found for the Chicanel Horizon and the initial part of the Early Classic period, except for Burials A-6 and B-1 (Robert Smith 1937; A. L. Smith 1950).

Discovered east of Group A-V at Uaxactun below the East Plaza is a series of structures of the Tzakol 2 phase, later covered over by Structure A-18, that included various palaces and platforms, some of which were circular (Valdes 1986b). The presence of Altar Sub-9, constructed as three terraces in a circular plan and painted shiny red, allows the possibility that this sector may have been an area where a variant of the ball game was carried out in the Early Classic period, without, however, identifying which lineages were involved in this activity. No other altars like this are known in the Maya area, although a polychrome vase possibly of the Tzakol 3 Phase shows a similar element together with some ball players (Robicsek and Hales 1981: 189).

After the introduction of the *Ma'Cuch* lineage into the dynastic spheres of Tikal and Uaxactun, a strong architectural and functional similarity between North Acropolis at Tikal and Group A-V at Uaxactun becomes apparent. A particular feature of this lineage was the unification within the same complex of ceremonial, ritual, and political functions with those of dynastic burials, thereby placing emphasis on funerary ostentation and on tombs carved from the limestone bedrock. Such burial practices have been recently discovered at Rio Azul.

A sequence of rulers at Uaxactun belonging to the *Ma'Cuch* title lineage can be inferred on the basis of artifacts amply documented from excavations at Group A-V and other complexes (A.L. Smith 1950; Robert Smith 1955; Valdes 1984). The sequence begins with the ruler in Burial A-29, located in the center of the group. Tripod cylinders characteristic of the Tzakol 3 phase appear for the first time, and include ceramics related to Tzakol II, resembling, in this way, Burial 22 at Tikal. The ruler in Burial A-29 must have governed until about A.D. 400, contemporaneously with Curl Nose at Tikal.

The next ruler, the lord in Uaxactun Burial A-31, located on the axis of the earlier tomb, is associated with Stela 26, erected on 9.0.10.0.0 (A.D. 445) a few years before his death. He reigned contemporaneously with Stormy Sky at Tikal (A.D. 426–457) and with the ruler named Lord X at Rio Azul (A.D. 434–463) (Adams 1985).

After a lapse of approximately 20 years at Uaxactun, during which no specific ruler can be identified, the sequence continues with the ruler in Burial A-22, who may have been inaugurated in A.D. 465. Upon his death, Structure H was constructed with Stela 22 in its interior (9.3.10.0.0 [A.D. 504]), which commemorates through a Secondary Series the date 8.17.1.4.12 (Marcus 1976a). The ruler's term in office coincided in part with the reign of Kan Boar at Tikal. Toward the end of the reign of the ruler in Burial A-22 the hegemony of the *Ma'Cuch* lineage at Tikal was broken during a crisis that led to a change of lineages in the dynastic sequence at that site.

Based on the chronological position of Burial A-20, over which Structure I was erected, this situation did not have the same repercussions at Uaxactun, where a member of the *Ma'Cuch* lineage continued to rule until the end of the Early Classic period. The ruler of Burial A-20 may be associated with Stela 25, dating with some uncertainty to A.D. 534 (Morley 1938: 200). Jaguar Paw Skull was ruling at this time at Tikal.

The characteristic cultural elements of the *Ma'Cuch* lineage that are diagnostic of the Manik 3A phase stop being evident at Tikal and give way during the Manik 3B phase, which overlaps the Late Classic period, with a gradual alteration of its diagnostic components. The tradition of elite burials at Tikal continued into Manik 3B with Burials 160 and 162, located in Group 7F-I (Haviland 1981). These burials have associations with another dynastic line that may have been related to the old Jaguar Paw lineage. Uaxactun, by contrast, during all of Tzakol 3 was dominated by members of the *Ma'Cuch* lineage, and so the transition into the Late Classic at that site was relatively more abrupt.

All these events that involved Tikal and Uaxactun were the products of a socio-political dynamism whose basis must be found in the system of kinship structure within Maya social organization. The Maya system traditionally was associated with ties to a legendary ancestor, as in Kirchhoff's conical clan model (1955). Essential to the system's maintenance was the importance of identification symbols and the regular celebration of particular rituals associated with the dominant lineage (Michels 1979: 261–62).

Considering that the kinship and socio-political ties between Tikal and Uaxactun are not well understood before the inauguration of the *Ma'Cuch* lineage at both sites (A.D. 378), such ties can only be assessed after the advent of a common ancestor, in this case Smoking Frog, who raised this lineage to a dynastic level. Smoking Frog ruled only briefly at both Uaxactun and Tikal. After his death the *Ma'Cuch* dynasty continued at both sites but under separate rulership: Curl Nose at Tikal and the ruler in Burial A-29 at Uaxactun. In order to understand this situation, the characteristics of dynastic succession should be considered in terms of kinship relationships.

According to the model of dynastic succession proposed by Fox and Justeson (1984), based on epigraphic evidence from sites in the Usumacinta River zone, the system for succession came to be a matrilateral of parallel cousin descent—a pattern that could be illustrated through the dynastic manifestation and expansion in the Early Classic period of the *Ma'Cuch* lineage in the northeast sector of Petén. Following the death of Smoking Frog—the ancestral figure of his lineage—the rulership of Tikal was retained by Curl Nose, who may have been both his son-in-law and nephew, while at Uaxactun, rulership was carried out by his fraternal nephew, the ruler in Burial A-29, afterwards forming two family lines within the same *Ma'Cuch* lineage.

Through this manner of dynastic succession, it is possible that various members of the lineage came to rule at other sites after marriage and dynastic alliances were made between family lines of the same *Ma'Cuch* lineage, thus forming entities organized at a socio-political and economic level. This model of expansion may have been extended during the Early Classic to such sites as Rio Azul, Yaxha, and El Zapote.

Nevertheless, in political entities organized on the basis of a system of clans, the prosperity of a controlling lineage seems to be relatively short, since the charisma of an ancestral patriarch survives only for three or four generations (Sanders 1974: 111; Rivera 1982: 117). Based on the data actually recovered, the *Ma'Cuch* lineage at Tikal lost its hegemony by about A.D. 488, about 110 years after its introduction, while Uaxactun continued to be administered by this family line for another 50 years. This may be the case at other sites within the *Ma'Cuch* sphere.

Social Implications for the Manik 3A Phase

With respect to the categories of relationships established between Teotihuacan and other Mesoamerican sites, the best fit for the evidence from Petén would seem to be the interaction sphere. This is represented in larger sites that appear to have maintained some sort of ties with Teotihuacan where influences flowed in both directions, manifest in iconography, sculpture, and artifacts, and in other areas as well (Santley 1983).

The equilibrium of these relationships might have resided in what W. Coe (1972) called the "ideological response" to commercial impact. At Teotihuacan, besides aspects of Maya influence at the level of art and ceramic production that have been amply discussed in the literature (Linne 1934; Rattray 1984; R. Millon 1981), another aspect had an ideological impact of cultural importance. This is to be found in the architectural plan of the Ciudadela, an architectural group situated at the epicenter of the site and that, as in the case of Mundo Perdido, includes a massive pyramidal structure, the Temple of Quetzalcoatl, situated to the east of three buildings on a common substructure. This pattern may be a reference to the Commemorative Astronomical Complex from the Central Maya area where it was in use from the Middle Preclassic period, with the most representative examples being Group E at Uaxactun and Mundo Perdido at Tikal.

Furthermore, from the Temple of Quetzalcoatl there has been reported a series of symmetrically placed burials that comprise at least thirty-four primary and secondary inhumations of about sixty individuals, perhaps dedicatory sacrifices, of a type unlike those usually found at Teotihuacan (Sugiyama 1986).

Besides interaction spheres, another category signalling relationships with Teotihuacan is that of the enclave, a form of political interference that is considered to be exemplified in the Maya area by Kaminaljuyu. This site supported a cultural complex that included ceramic, funerary, and architectural affiliations (*talud-tablero*) traditionally considered non-Maya and of Teotihuacan origins. Nevertheless, the idea of a political enclave at Kaminaljuyu does not account for the greater importance these cultural similarities show in the light of the evidence recently found at Tikal during a phase even earlier than would usually be expected. The *talud-tablero* feature, in vogue at Tikal from the Manik 1 phase (A.D. 250–300), was used frequently at Mundo Perdido and other groups, with its popularity continuing until the Late Classic period. This evidence permits the assumption that relationships between Tikal and Kaminaljuyu were more complex and on a level that transcended the purely commercial.

Material Relationships

The Manik 3A phase is defined principally on the basis of its ceramic content and encompasses certain traits that are traditionally considered to be foreign in character, presumably linked to Teotihuacan. These ceramic materials are known at diverse sites in the Maya Lowlands, generally from well-documented funerary contexts, at Altar de Sacrificios, Yaxha, Becan, Altun Ha, Rio Azul, Tikal, and Uaxactun (Adams 1971; Pendergast 1971; Ball 1977b; Matheny 1986). Ball (1983: 125–31) considered it necessary to distinguish between ceramics characterized by similarities and those that are identical. The first refers to vessels from two or more spatially separate locations that imitate or duplicate each other but differ in the technology they employ. Separate and local production is indicated, as in the case of tripod cylinders. The other refers to identical vessels as a genuine flow of ceramics from one location to another, reflecting commercial activity as exemplified by Thin Orange ware.

At Tikal, the ceramic complex of foreign traits is documented by the material originating in the well-known tombs of North Acropolis and in the problematic deposits explored by the University of Pennsylvania (PD-22, 31, 50, 72, 74, 77, and 111; Culbert 1979; Moholy Nagy 1986). Recent discoveries in Group 6C-XVI have expanded the cultural material related to this Manik 3A Phase: Burials PNT-141 and 174, as well as the caches PNT 30, 40, 47, 48, 50, and 70. Problematic Deposit PNT-021 in Group 6D-V is also pertinent.

After the ritual interment of the Ball Court Marker about A.D. 425, the construction process and the dimensions of Group 6C-XVI continued to increase. Buildings of greater proportions were erected, as in the case of Structure Sub-50 into which was intruded Burial PNT-141 (Figure 3.22): the direct, primary and simultaneous interment of two individuals in an extended dorsal position, partially flexed, with the heads directed toward the east end of the tomb. The individuals' apparel included pendants and brooches of shell, earspools and necklaces of shell and jade, as well as jade bracelets. The ceramic offering consisted of 14 vessels of the ceramic groups Aguila, Pucte, and Balanza, and of the types known as Caldero Buff Polychrome and Lucha Incised. Also included was a tripod cylinder of the Urita Gouged-Incised type, with hollow rectangular supports. Two pieces were decorated with the "coffee bean" motif.

After the deposition of the above-mentioned

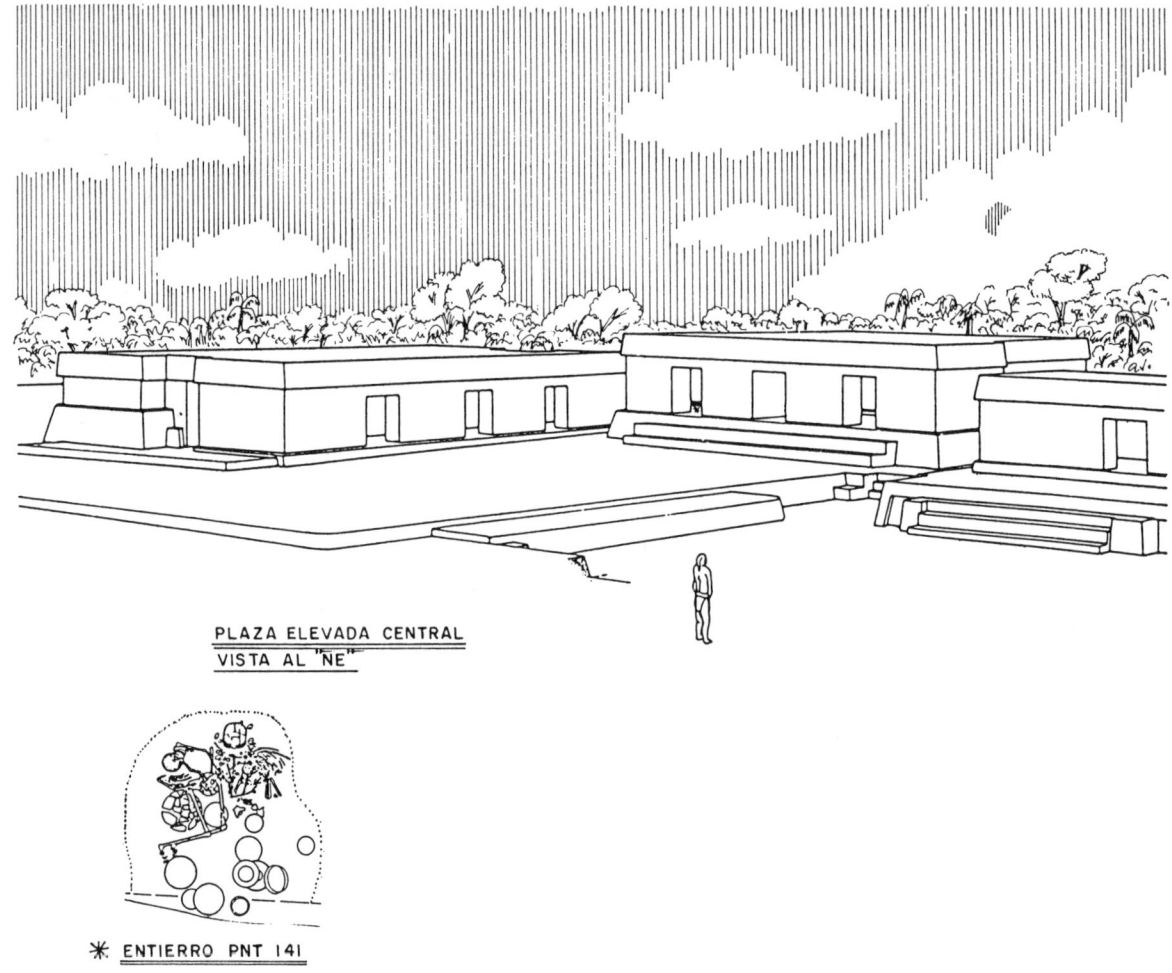

Figure 3.22. Reconstruction drawing. Group 6C-XVI, elevated central plaza, 13th stage, Manik 3A phase. Inset: intruded burial PNT 141.

burial and during the final occupation of the group, a building was constructed that covered all of the architectural evidence of earlier phases (Sub-84). Below the upper platform of this building were constructed in an intrusive manner three stairways leading down into three compartments (Figure 3.23). In the south compartment a concentration of materials was found that included fragments of *incensarios;* the central enclosure contained Burial PNT-179 without associated offerings; and in the north compartment was placed Burial PNT-174. The compartments had flat roofs and may have been completely filled in in order to prevent the collapse of the upper platform of the ediface, or they may have been clogged with debris after the collapse of their wooden roofs. A similar case has been documented at Kaminaljuyu (Kidder et al. 1946: 87; Cheek 1977: 142–43).

Burial PNT-174 was primary, indirect, and multiple, incorporating an adult and an infant who were

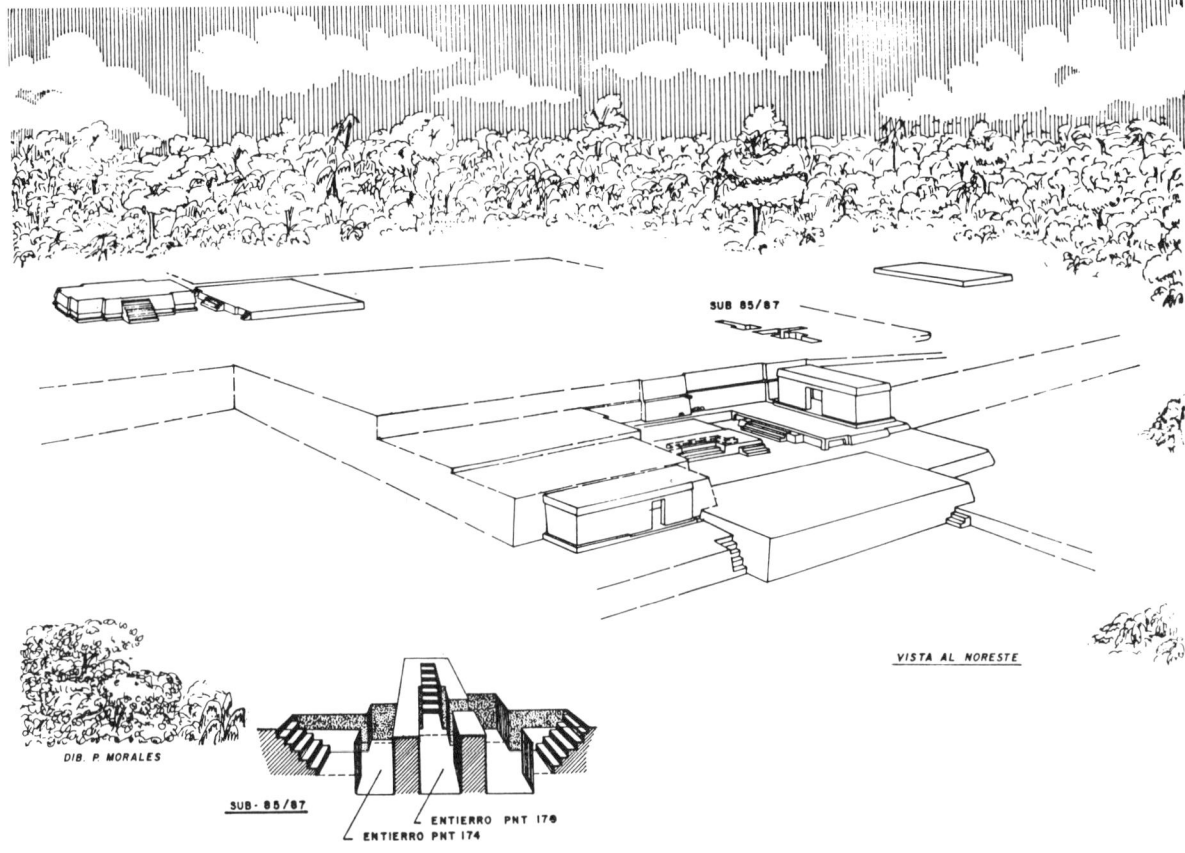

Figure 3.23. Reconstruction drawing, Group 6C-XVI, 19th stage, Manik 3A phase. Inset: Structure-Sub 85/87 with burials PNT 174 and 179.

associated with various skulls that appear to have been part of an offering, all in bad condition. They were found with the following materials: pendants and beads of shell, necklaces of shell and jade, flint tools (chisels, pounders(?), scrapers, blades, polished axes), a diorite grindstone, flint projectile points, green and gray obsidian knives, cube-shaped beads possibly of pyrite, rock crystal, small disks of stone, plaques, and a slate eccentric, as well as a slate disk completely coated in stucco.

Of the ceramic offerings, 21 vessels and 4 lids of the ceramic groups Aguila and Balanza were included, along with the types Lucha Incised, Japon Resist, and Caldero Buff Polychrome. Outstanding were two vessels of the *florero* type belonging to the Ratones Group, an effigy vessel of the Aguila Group representing a parrot or macaw, and an anthropomorphic vessel of the Lucha Incised type. The lids have effigy handles representing turkeys, birds, and turtles, as well as stirrup handles. Also included in the tomb were six more vessels and three more lids of the Aguila and Balanza Groups as well as the Delirio Plano Relief type that had been coated with stucco and painted with designs. The lids have anthropomorphic and stirrup handles.

In the contents of this burial it is possible to observe a tendency by local potters to produce the equivalent of Thin Orange Ware by thinning the local pastes to resemble the imported ceramics represented only by the two florero examples of the Ratones Group.

Burial PNT-174, according to the stratigraphic sequence determined for Group 6C-XVI, appears to date beyond the chronological limits of the Manik 3A phase—that is, after the death of Kan Boar (A.D. 488). This, then, is the last funerary manifestation of individuals of the *Ma'Cuch* lineage, which was by then displaced from rulership. This burial might express likewise a reorientation of the function of Group 6C-XVI toward a funerary one. Related contemporary manifestations in the group are a variety of caches (PNT-23, 26, 42, 53, and 72).

Another related discovery is Problematic Deposit PNT-021, which was found in Group 6D-V (Iglesias 1986) to the southeast of Mundo Perdido (Figure 3.1), and which contained burials and offerings of the Manik 3A Phase that were related to individuals of elite status (PNT-186 and 177). The materials concentrated in the Problematic Deposit 021, however, reach beyond this phase and reflect practically the whole of the ceramic sample that, in general, appear in different contexts of Maya society during this period. The deposit represents the largest concentration of such material from the Early Classic period so far discovered, and includes domestic, funerary, and ceremonial objects: pendants, beads, plaques, and "buttons" of shell; coral, pearls, and spondylus shells; ceramic figurines; and the remains of such animals as deer, peccaries, turtles, rodents, and birds. Objects of pyrite, mica, and rock crystal were also found. The abundance and diversity of stone tools located in this concentration may represent more than one habitational group or several generations, perhaps reflecting the mechanism of the deposition.

A characteristic of Early Classic problematic deposits and of those at the beginning of the Late Classic is the inclusion of human osteological remains, whose haphazard dispersion suggests that these are extensive multiple burials of a secondary nature not necessarily contemporaneous with each other. In deposits PNT-019, 021, and 032 (Manik 2 and 3) various human bones were found to have been used as tools: polishers or burnishers using frontal and parietal bones (Figure 3.24), and awls made out of long bones (Pijoan and Salas 1984). Such tools have never been reported from contemporaneous deposits excavated during earlier projects at Tikal. Sacrifice and dismemberment, which these materials imply, was a custom that was evidently stronger in the Early Classic period than at any other time, and its dynamics can be interpreted only with the study of such additional manifestations. Other finds with implements made from human bones were reported near Group 6C-XVI (Burials PNT-059 and 070).

Social Relationships

To the degree that cultural interrelationships are manifest in the Manik 3A phase, we can consider that the cultures involved share a pattern of historical development that included the exchange of ideas and objects that retained at the same time a regional identity (Parsons 1969: 152). This gave way to a high degree of artistic and architectural innovation through highly eclectic styles and the development of an iconographic syncretism (Pasztory 1978: 8). At any rate, much of the Manik 3A phase symbolism can be considered pan-Mesoamerican since it occurs in diverse artistic styles. Those aspects that referred to military technology and ideology and promoted concepts and implements related to warfare had because of their nature, greater regional mobility and dispersion, and were bellicosely used for ritual purposes or for political control.

Three tombs have been found on North Acropolis that can be assigned confidently to rulers from the *Ma'Cuch* lineage; Burial 10 has been assigned to Curl Nose and Burial 48 to Stormy Sky (Coggins 1975); and it is reasonable to propose that Burial 22 corresponds to Smoking Frog, belonging to the initial part of the Manik 3A phase. Besides additional individuals in these burials, the offerings included vessels of local origin such as cylinder tripods, some of them with stucco decoration and occasionally painted with trapezoid symbols, Tlalocs, and the Kan Cross.

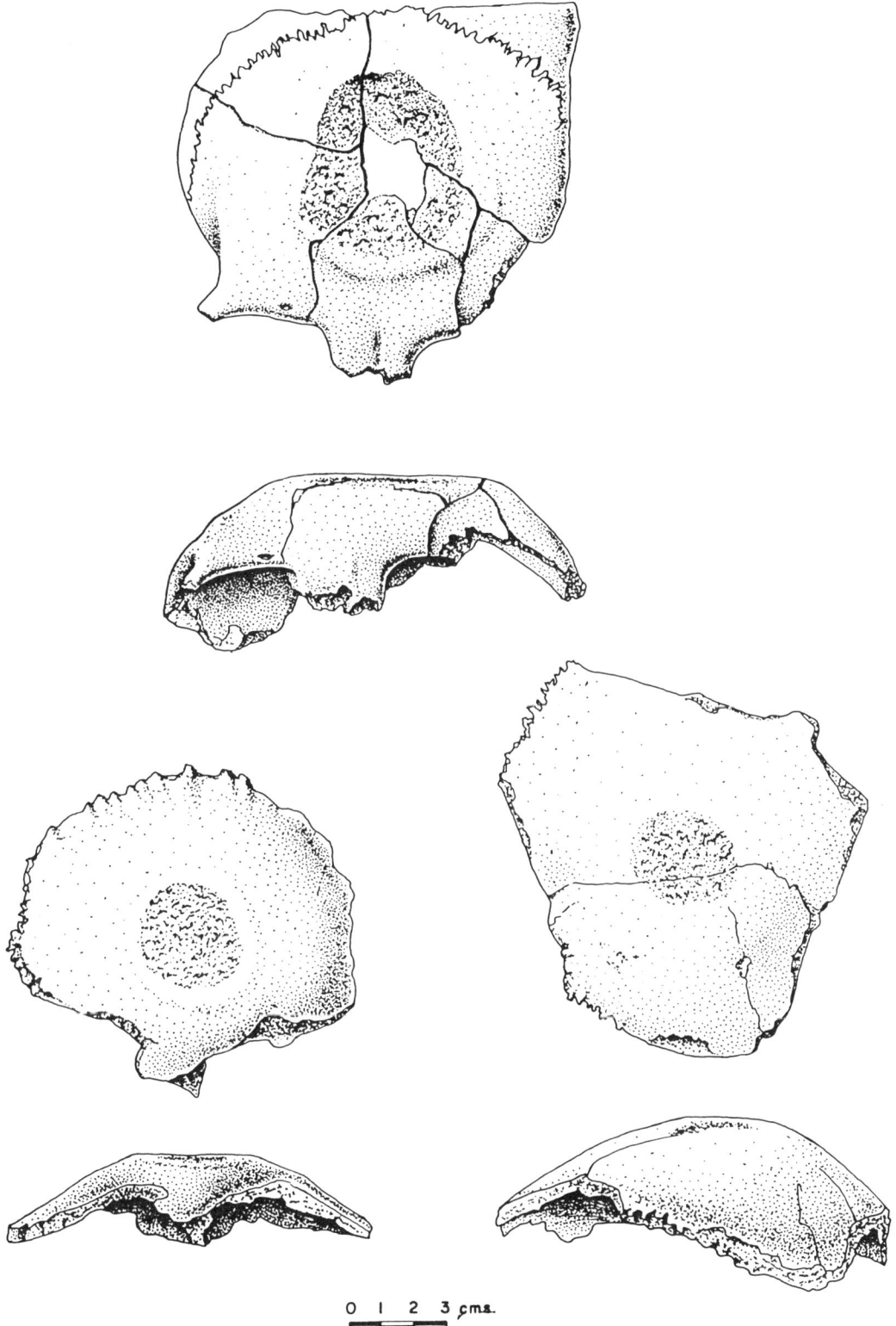

Figure 3.24. Drawing of cranial bones showing evidence of use.

These traits are also found on decorated materials from Burial PNT-174 in Group 6C-XVI. Among the outstanding iconographic elements on the decorated vessels of this interment is the trapezoid-reptile eye-"triple drop of blood" complex, associated with the triumphant warrior theme and used on the murals at Cacaxtla (Foncerrada de Molina 1982; Berlo 1980).

Other developed iconographic motifs are plumed serpents that enclose Tlalocs; owls both in frontal and profile position with their plumes extended in an attitude of predation, with which are associated the "drops of blood" glyph; Serpent X; a procession of jaguars with volutes that have aquatic associations; floral designs; and stars interspersed with marine motifs (Hellmuth 1969), all of which compares to well-known representations in Teotihuacan mural art.

The iconographic material just mentioned, combined with information from the Ball Court Marker, allows the consideration that the uses of this foreign-style regalia—usually thought to be unconventional for the Maya although clearly associated with rulers of Tikal who were members of the *Ma'Cuch* lineage and rulers at other sites—was oriented toward ritualized warfare. The uniform of the victorious warrior includes Tlaloc imagery that appears on shields and sacred bundles. That such uniforms were worn in battle and during ritual bloodletting (Schele and Miller 1986: 213), is corroborated by Lintel 2 of Piedras Negras, Aguateca Stela 2, Copan Stela 6, Yaxha Stela 11, and Dos Pilas Stela 16, to mention but a few examples. From all this it can be deduced that the representations contained on the Ball Court Marker at Tikal are the earliest manifestations of this regalia in the Maya area.

Triadic Pattern Architecture and Commemorative Astronomical Complexes

The two lineages that came to be established within the socio-political scheme at Tikal in the Early Classic period may have been associated with certain specific architectural complexes because of their political implications. These are exhibited by a plan of ceremonial differentiation that is manifest at other sites in the Maya central area after the Preclassic period.

Mundo Perdido and the North Acropolis experienced a parallel architectural evolution, each with a distinctive functional and ceremonial focus. Mundo Perdido had developed its Commemorative Astronomical Complex by the end of the Middle Preclassic period. On the North Acropolis a complex of Triadic Pattern Architecture gradually evolved during the Late Preclassic; its existence was first discussed by Proskouriakoff (Coggins 1979b) as a manifestation of the three principal lineages in the power centers of the central lowlands. These Triadic complexes seem to reflect religious and political themes expressed in a symmetrical pattern of three buildings that leave open one end of a plaza and that, joined with sculptural manifestations, constitute a conscious unification of religious and political beliefs held throughout the Maya Lowlands. These groups have been documented at Palenque, Uaxactun, El Mirador, Nakbe, Edzna, Calakmul, and Tikal (Proskouriakoff 1946; A. L. Smith 1950; Coggins 1979b; Hansen 1984; Gendrop 1984; Matheny 1986).

The developmental sequence of the North Acropolis indicates that the oldest construction is from the Chuen phase. A notable increase of architecture can be seen during the following Cauac phase, in which Structures 5D-Sub-1, Sub-3, and Sub-9 were prominent and decorated with monumental masks. Stylistically and temporally, this version of the complex of Triadic Pattern Architecture compares with Group H of Uaxactun (Valdes 1986b).

In its original form, the platform that supports this complex seems to have been oriented toward the west (W. Coe 1965: 8–9), which allows for the possibility of a functional relationship with the causeway that leads to Mundo Perdido. This in turn suggests a possible interrelationship between the two fundamental architectural expressions of Tikal's socio-political structure.

As an alternative form of the Triadic Pattern Architecture structural plan, the Commemorative Astronomical Complexes reflect a specialized ceremonial function that developed separately and possibly earlier. This complex implicitly denotes its ceremonial and political nature. Preclassic examples of these complexes have been found at Uaxactun and Tikal, and examples at Yaxha and Balakbal may correspond to this period; other reported examples

Figure 3.25. Reconstruction drawing, Mundo Perdido, West sector, Manik 3 phase.

of the complex lack chronological information.

Because of the importance of such complexes within the ritual cycles implemented by the Maya at various early sites, it is possible to distinguish a tendency by the lineages in power to select a specific location for monumental architecture to serve the collateral functions of retaining funerary depositions at a dynastic level and representing the lineage's seat of political authority.

In Group A-V at Uaxactun during the Early Classic phases Tzakol 2 and 3, several collateral functions were combined, becoming the most representative example of the complex of Triadic Pattern Architecture (Proskouriakoff 1946; A. L. Smith 1950). These complexes—at Tikal as well as Uaxactun—seem to have been favored by rulers, associated with the *Ma'Cuch* lineage title, who used the structures for both funerary and political functions.

In the case of Tikal, political and funerary functions were combined in North Acropolis dating from the Preclassic period, but these functions were divided between separate locations at the beginning of the Early Classic period, indicating a change in the socio-political dynamics of the site. Ritual manifestations are to be associated with the Jaguar Paw dynastic lineage, which favored a funerary site at Mundo Perdido, while the locus of political authority continued to be the North Acropolis. This last is supported by the fact that for now no other complex of the Triadic Pattern Architecture kind is known with connotations of political authority at Tikal.

The known references to the Jaguar Paw lineage correspond to its final moments and are clearly related to the Commemorative Astronomical Complex. This is demonstrated by the tombs found in the East Platform that correspond to a temporal moment that coincides with the death of Jaguar Paw III and the inauguration of the first ruler of the *Ma'-Cuch* title, Smoking Frog. The antiquity of these local lineages can be inferred from manifestations of their activities in Mundo Perdido as indicated on the one hand by Stela 39, associated with the Jaguar Paw lineage, and on the other by the use of the *talud-tablero* architectural style, associated with the *Ma'Cuch* lineage and observed initially in Structure 5C-49 from the Manik 1 phase (A.D. 250–300).

The *talud-tablero* continued to be used during the Manik 2 and Manik 3 phases at Mundo Perdido and at Group 6C-XVI (Figure 3.25). In this last group the *Ma'Cuch* lineage assisted in ritual activities related to the ball game, but in an alternate form that includes references to a calendrical function as inferred from its presence at Mundo Perdido. Both activities were deeply rooted in the ritual cycles traditional to the Maya, functions which may have been restricted to the local lineages.

The early development of the *talud-tablero* architectural tradition at Tikal, in a form which was without foreign iconographic traits, occurs during the Manik 1 and Manik 2 phases, a period of political hegemony for the Jaguar Paw lineage, and suggests that there were two distinct instances when this architectonic feature was assimilated. The first instance is when the *talud-tablero* was originally implemented at the site. The limited excavation of Early Classic levels at other sites in the central Maya area makes it impossible to observe this situation in a more regional focus. A second instance of cultural interrelation during the political hegemony of the *Ma'Cuch* lineage occurred along with the adaptation of certain ceramic forms and Tlaloc iconography related to warfare and sacrifice—iconography that continued to be used into the Late Classic period.

Notes

1. This study is a direct outgrowth of the research carried out by *Proyecto Nacional Tikal* in Mundo Perdido (Fialko 1985; Laporte 1985a; Laporte and Fialko 1985, 1986a, 1986b; Laporte and Vega 1986), as well as in Group 6C-XVI (Fialko 1986; Laporte 1985b). The final illustrations were made by Paulino I. Morales based on surveys, plans, and numerous field drawings. They include the numbers allotted to individual discoveries of the Proyecto, which are prefixed with the initials PNT in reference to the catalogue system of the Proyecto Nacional Tikal.

Four

The Jester God. The Beginning and End of a Maya Royal Symbol

By David A. Freidel

One of the most important and enduring emblems of authority among the Lowland Maya is a small image attached to the headbands of rulers, dubbed the Jester God in reference to its characteristic three-pointed cap (Schele and Miller 1983: 47; M. Coe 1978). The glyphic form of the Jester God in Classic texts acts as a semantic determinative of *Ahau* (Schele and Miller 1983: 37), the principal title of lordship, and iconographically it is among the most pervasive and diagnostic attributes of political power during this period.

In light of its importance, it is intriguing that the Jester God image precedes the advent of royal authority among the Lowland Maya, and survives the ninth-century collapse of southern lowland civilization. Antecedent to the Maya usage of this symbol, V. Fields (1982) has made a persuasive case for its presence in Olmec iconography, and it appears as well on Stela 5 at Izapa, a Late Preclassic period monument outside the lowlands. Following its prominence in the Classic southern lowlands, the Jester God remains an emblem of authority among the lords of Terminal Classic/Early Postclassic period Chichen Itzá in the north.

The Late Preclassic period witnesses the abrupt emergence of large public centers and hierarchical authority among the Lowland Maya (Freidel and Schele 1988a; Schele and Miller 1986). The Terminal Classic witnesses an equally profound change in Maya society, the collapse of the southern lowland kingdoms and the rise of large-scale conquest states in the northern lowlands. As an image which iconographically endures both of these major episodes of social and symbolic transformations, the Jester God is candidate for testing hypotheses of continuity and disjunction in the correspondence of form and meaning of central icons through time.

Olmec Antecedents

Building upon David Joralemon's identification of maize associations with his God I of the Olmec (Joralemon 1971), Virginia Fields (1982) has persuasively argued for the presence of a trefoil element in Olmec iconography which represents tasseled or sprouting maize seeds. This element occurs both on large stone monuments and upon portable objects of precious stone. The trefoil element occurs predominantly in the position of a diadem worn on the helmets of human authority figures or over polymorphic face masks. Fields notes that the distribution of the trefoil diadem is extensive in Mesoamerica, and essentially follows the distribution of other Olmec-related iconography of the Middle Preclassic Horizon style. Fields suggests that the Olmec horizon distribution may be due to the concomitant diffusion of both maize seed crop technology and the Olmec ritual complex associated with emerging differential status as hypothesized by Flannery (1968).

Clearly the Olmec examples provide both a formal and a contextual antecedent for the later Lowland Maya Jester God, for this trefoil image also occurs as both an object and as a diadem in the latter case. A major problem in linking the Olmec horizon usage of this image and the Maya Lowland usage is the evident spatial and temporal disjunction between the Middle Preclassic florescence of the former, which ends by 500 B.C., and the Late Preclassic rise of the latter civilization.

There is the possibility that this disjunction is more apparent than real, for E. W. Andrews V (1986) has recently reported on a cache of 17 jades from the site of Chacsinkin in the central northern lowlands. These jades, although not of Classic Olmec iconography in certain respects, are clearly of the Middle Preclassic Horizon style perpetrated by the Olmecs of the Gulf Coast heartland. However, there are no examples of the trefoil image in this collection. Furthermore, only one other cache of such materials is currently known from the lowlands proper, from the site of Seibal (Willey 1978), despite considerable investigation of Middle Preclassic contexts in such sectors of the lowlands as northern Belize (Hammond 1985; Potter et. al 1984) in the last few decades. Nevertheless, as discussed below, there is reason to suspect that one formal source of inspiration for the Maya Jester God was the use of Olmec period heirloom pieces by Late Preclassic authority figures.

Another likely source of inspiration are the many Late Preclassic art styles of the Pacific Slopes and Maya Highland regions which generally show more substantial derivation from Olmec antecedents (Norman 1976; Quirarte 1976; G. Lowe 1977). The trefoil diadem, for example, is worn by a figure on Stela 5 at Izapa (Norman 1976), and the entire complex of elements of the Late Preclassic Jester God headband, which includes a central trefoil flanked by "u" emblems, occurs as a top-line composition at this site. While this is one of many significant correspondences linking the iconography of the southern and northern regions occupied by Maya peoples in the Late Preclassic period, the styles are essentially coeval, the stylistic diffusion no doubt went in both directions. Further, there is no clear association of the trefoil element with maize iconography in the Izapan or related styles. One good reason to suspect, nevertheless, that the Jester God image is possibly derived from the Olmec-inspired cultures of the southern Maya region is that the image is associated in the lowlands, from its earliest occurrence, with expressions in precious greenstone imported from the south.

Whether diffused directly during Middle Preclassic times, or indirectly in Late Preclassic times, the likely mechanism of diffusion of the trefoil image into the Maya Lowlands was on portable objects of precious and exotic stone. This is a demonstrable medium for the image in the Middle Preclassic period, and the same medium is employed by the Lowland Maya. Further, there is essential continuity in the context in which the image occurs, as a diadem and as a grasped, cradled, and otherwise displayed portable object. Insofar as this continuity in form and function holds, the Lowland Maya drew upon familiarity with long-established notions concerning exotic power objects obtained through long-distance trade in the construction of their own distinctive regalia and definitions of hierarchical authority. Such long-distance trade, and trade among the Lowland Maya, played an important role in generating the conditions that precipitated the sudden emergence of kingship in the first century before the present era (Freidel 1979, 1981 and 1986; Freidel and Schele 1988b).

The Late Preclassic Lowland Jester God

The Jester God image occurs in several different contexts and forms in the archaeological record of the Late Preclassic centers of the lowlands. The most explicit display of the Jester as a symbol of royal authority occurs on a quartzite plaque reportedly collected in the northern lowlands and currently housed at Dumbarton Oaks (Figure 4.1; Schele and Miller 1986; Freidel and Schele 1988a). The Dumbarton Oaks plaque is definitely an example of Olmec work of the Middle Preclassic period. The front of the piece displays a snarling were-jaguar image with a bifurcated head. This head is flanked by ear-flare flanges with drilled central holes and incised Saint Andrew Crosses. The rear surface of the piece has an incised seated portrait of a Maya ruler who is wearing an anthropomorphic version of the Jester God as a diadem flanked by "u" emblems. The text accompanying the image has the Jester God as a glyph in its non-personified variant, and it includes an accession, "seating" statement of the lord to the status of ahau. Although this piece is out of context, both the image and the form of the glyphs in the text indicate that it dates to the Late Preclassic period. For example, the ear-flare assemblage worn by the king not only has all of the major conventional elements found on this assemblage in firm Late Preclassic archaeological contexts (decorated buildings), but it still retains the full representation of the flanking profile polymorph as found in imagery of this period. The text makes it clear that the Jester God image is integral to the status of this lord as ahau, and that it is a central concept in the text and image. Finally, it is significant that this piece is pierced for suspension as a pectoral or diadem.

That this image and text should appear on a portable, carved, and precious stone of Olmec vintage is not fortuitous. There are several other known examples of Olmec-style carved stone heads with early Lowland Maya glyphs incised on them. Schele and Miller (1986: pl. 45) illustrate such a piece that has been clearly broken off a larger artifact and pierced for suspension. The image is again the snarling were-jaguar baby, but without the bifurcated head. The rear of this piece has a brief glyphic text which evidently gives titles of the Maya owner as a man of substance (the penis glyph) and with a title which includes the bone element and a head with a mirror in its fontanel. The style of the glyphs is definitely early and Schele and Miller (1986: 151) assign reuse to the Late Preclassic or Proto-Classic period (150 B.C. to A.D. 150). Schele and Miller (1986: pl. 31) illustrate another Olmec-style carved stone face which has been broken off from a larger piece and inscribed with early Lowland Maya glyphs. Although they speculate that this piece was also worn, it is not pierced for suspension.

There is thus an emerging pattern of reuse of Olmec heirloom pieces in the Late Preclassic period of the Maya Lowlands. It may be significant in this regard that the extraordinarily large cache of Olmec jades reported by Andrews V from Chacsinkin shows that 13 of the 17 known pieces have concave depressions and are pierced for suspension, a proportion Andrews V (1986: 25) observes is unusual for Middle Preclassic offerings of such materials. The interest in concave depressions is intriguing, for as discussed below, the Jester God image among the Lowland Maya is particularly associated with mirror surfaces.

A Late Preclassic cache of stone pendants found at the site of Cerros, northern Belize (Figure 4.2; Freidel 1979; Garber 1983, 1986), furthers the hypothesized connection between Olmec heirloom pieces and the Lowland Maya Jester God icon. This dedicatory cache found at the summit of a substantial acropolis is stratigraphically and ceramically firmly anchored in the first century B.C. Five head

Figure 4.1. The lord engraved on the back of the Dumbarton Oaks plaque. Drawing by Linda Schele.

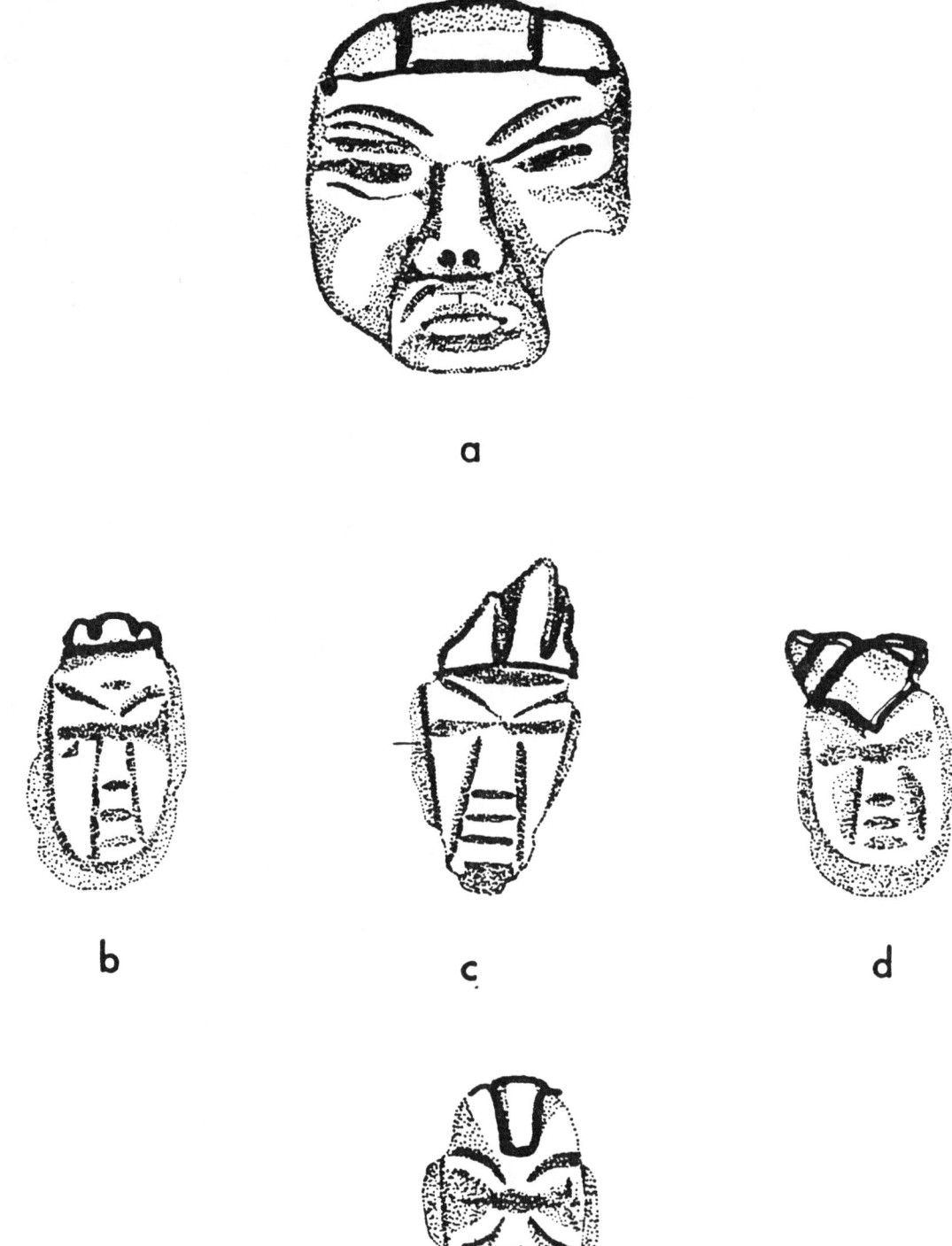

Figure 4.2. Carved greenstone pendants from Cerros, Belize, Cache 1.

pendants of precious stone were discovered in a deliberate arrangement within a large ceramic bucket. The largest head, found in the center of the arrangement face upward, is carved in a style that is clearly related to the conventions of the Middle Preclassic period. It includes such technical diagnostics as drill holes in the corners of the mouth and a pierced septum in the nose along with general adherence to Olmec practices of careful carving and modeling. The iconography of the piece is not "classic" Olmec, however, and relates to a number of other carved stone heads from Late Preclassic Lowland Maya contexts, which appear to register the emergence of a Maya tradition in stone carving that will persist subsequently for more than a millennium. In brief, the piece is apparently a Maya imitation of an Olmec heirloom.

Arranged in four quadrants around this central head were four small head pendants. One of these (Figure 4.2 c), bears the three-pointed cap of the Jester God. The overall iconography of the four small heads taken together has been discussed in detail elsewhere (Freidel and Schele 1988a). Suffice it to say here that this rendering of the Jester God image is clearly not an Olmec heirloom piece but a Late Preclassic Maya carving. A case can be made that these four small pieces together formed a crown of rulership such as worn by the king on the Dumbarton Oaks plaque. Among other things, the "u" emblems which flank the Dumbarton Oaks Jester God diadem are particularly used to denote precious stone objects on Classic Maya royal regalia, suggesting that this crown also employed multiple precious stones.

Although this particular rendering of the Jester God image as a precious stone diadem is unique from Late Preclassic archaeological contexts, a virtually identical piece has been recently discovered by Richard Leventhal (personal communication 1986) in a Classic period tomb from Nim Li Punit in Belize, and a similar assemblage of four small head pendants has been reported by Norman Hammond from Late Preclassic context at the site of Nohmul, also in Belize (Hammond 1985). Furthermore, the fuschite mask from Burial 85, a substantial Late Preclassic burial in the North Acropolis at Tikal (W. Coe 1965), portrays a Maya ruler wearing the non-anthropomorphic form of the Jester God, flanked by "u" emblems as on the Dumbarton Oaks plaque. Like the other stones described here, this one is pierced. There is thus a clear association of the Jester God image with portable carved stones of precious materials, particularly greenstones, in the Late Preclassic period. This association persists into the Classic period, when established examples of the actual diadem are also of this medium and expression, as discussed below.

The Jester God image also occurs on monumental decorated panels adorning pyramidal structures at Uaxactun in Guatemala (Valdes 1986c) and at Cerros in Belize (Freidel 1986; Freidel and Schele 1988a). Among the spectacular newly discovered Late Preclassic façades in Group H at Uaxactun, the Jester God occurs as a human-faced diadem on masks on Structures H-Sub-4 and 5 (Valdes 1986c). The evidence from Group H at Uaxactun shows that already in the Late Preclassic period, when monumental sculptured pyramids occur for the first time in Lowland Maya civilization, the Jester God is a central image of interest.

The Cerros architectural examples of the Jester God are more problematic than those at Uaxactun, but are still worth considering. Firstly, the upper main masks on Structure 5C-2nd are wearing headdresses decorated with three elements compositionally identical to the headdresses worn by the king on the Dumbarton Oaks plaque and on the mask from Burial 85 at Tikal. Unfortunately, the particular designs on these elements were destroyed at the top. While the preserved sections of these elements do conform to the flanking "u" emblems and trefoil central element of the Jester God headdress, this is only a possibility and not a demonstrable identification.

The other example from Cerros occurs on the ear-flare assemblages flanking the main masks on Structure 5C-2nd (Figure 4.3). These elaborate assemblages in modeled stucco and polychrome paint show bundle knots with mirror elements on top of them flanking the central flare above and below. The bundled mirror is an important glyph in accession verbs of the Classic period (Schele and Miller 1983). These bundled mirrors are intimately associated with two major icons, the Jester God (the bright mirror), and God K (the dark mirror). These distinct iconographic references are conveyed in the glyphic forms by the inclusion of a bifurcate scroll surmounting the "dark" mirror, surmised by Schele

72 David A. Freidel

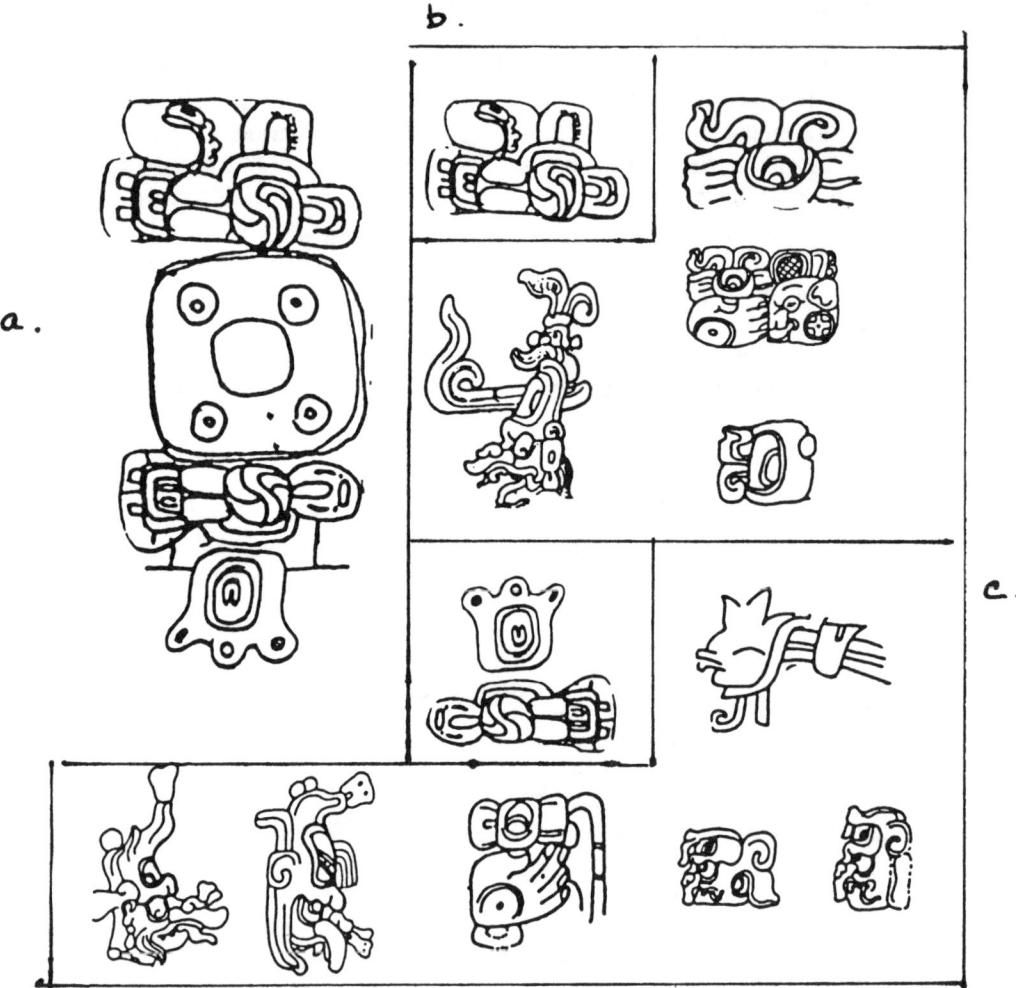

Figure 4.3. a. Ear-plug assemblage from Cerros, Belize, Structure 5C-2nd. b. Upper bundled knot (dark mirror) compared to Late Classic images and glyphs of God K. c. Lower bundled knot (bright mirror) compared diadem from Dumbarton Oaks plaque and Late Classic images and glyphs of the Jester God.

to refer to the homophonic values of *tah*, torch, and *tah*, obsidian, for the God K image, and the absence of this bifurcate scroll on the "bright" mirror. The grasping of these glyphs denotes accession to office, and the objects to which they refer are displayed by Maya kings in accession scenes among others.

There is reason to believe that the bundled mirrors above and below the ear-flare assemblages on Structure 5C-2nd register the "dark" and "bright" mirror dichotomy of Classic inscriptions. The upper bundled mirrors on the ear-flare assemblages carry the same bifurcate scroll used to denote the "dark" mirror in Classic iconography. The lower mirrors have depending from them trefoil elements with rounded terminals that are further decorated with dots. The Jester God of the Proto-Classic period onward often has such dots attached to the three ends of the trefoil element. Although the trefoil element is lacking from the Classic period glyph for the bundled bright mirror, the association of this element with the Jester God is clear and unequivocal. Furthermore, the rounded terminals of the depending element may be an iconographic reference to the bone element. The Jester God image of the Classic period frequently has the bone element attached to the terminals of the trefoil instead of the dot. One word for bone, *bac*, is a major glyphic and conceptual feature of Classic epigraphy, with reference not only to bone, but also to captive (D. Stuart 1985) and possibly to large seed (Freidel and Schele 1985). If the "bright" mirror of the Jester God proves to be associated with *bac*, it is still unlikely that this connotation bears any conceptual continuities with the Olmec connotation of maize kernel, for *bac* as a seed refers to large pits such as that of the avocado, and would pertain to trees rather than to maize.

In addition to the iconographic correspondences between the bundled mirrors on Late Preclassic ear-flare assemblages and their Classic counterparts, it is also clear that the ear-flare position, along with the helmet and chin-strap positions, is the appropriate place in the composition to display objects of power. While on full-figure representations of Maya rulers there are many places to show such objects, these monumental panels are strictly hieratic and focused on face masks. In the absence of full figures, the ear-flare position is loaded with such objects. The objects of the ear-flare position are endowed with intrinsic power, shown by their association with profile polymorphs which, in reduced form, become phonetic *wah*, "power," of the Classic period (Freidel and Schele 1988b).

For the present argument, the most important feature of the ear-flare display of the "bright" and "dark" mirrors as references to the Jester God and to God K is that it shows already in the initial stage of usage of these icons that they are associated with mirrors and with the quality of being "shiny." In the actual objects that convey the Jester God image in the Late Preclassic period, there are no specific elements that convey "shiny" or mirror surfaces (bearing in mind the possibility that the Chacsinkin objects are literal representations of such mirrors in greenstone). Under the circumstances, the quality of "shiny" may refer originally not to mirrors but to the brightly polished surfaces of the portable carved stones. The bundling of such objects, and their unwrapping and display, is commensurate with general Mesoamerican manipulation of such power objects and is documented in Classic Maya depictions of the Jester God (Schele 1979).

Summary of the Late Preclassic Jester God

Present evidence suggests that the Late Preclassic Lowland Maya redefined greenstone power objects of exotic manufacture and material as the Jester God icon of royal authority. Just when the Lowland Maya began circulating such objects is a matter for further investigation, either during the Middle Preclassic Horizon or somewhat later, but it is reasonable to hypothesize that such objects were in circulation for several centuries before the formal definition of the Jester God icon in the first century B.C. That the Maya should build their image of power upon a scarce, exotic and highly exchangeable commodity, in wide circulation in Mesoamerica, is commensurate with the notion that trade and the ritual interaction accompanying it were central sources of power and authority among the Maya prior to, and following, their invention of kingship.

At the same time, there are clues to suggest that the Lowland Maya did not import the meaning of these power objects from their sources of manufacture, but rather redefined such meaning. The association with maize posited by Fields for the Olmec finds no ready counterpart in the Maya usage. The Maya bring out and emphasize an intrinsic quality of the objects, brightly polished surfaces, which is not iconographically important to the Olmec. Insofar as the Jester God can be currently given a specific conceptual referent, it is *ahau*, lordship or power in the abstract. This is not to suggest that such objects had no other conceptual or ritual referents. On the contrary, there are reasons to believe that such small objects of greenstone and other materials were used in complex rituals of magic and divination (Freidel and Schele 1988a) carried out by rulers and other people in authority. Such referents, however, appear to be indigenous to the Maya Lowland region.

The Classic Jester God

Beginning in the Proto-Classic period, the Lowland Maya portray their rulers on carved stone stelae and on bas-reliefs. Several of these early portraits display the Jester God diadem, as on the Loltun bas-relief in Yucatán (Freidel and Andrews in press), and on the Hauberg Stela, dated at ca. A.D. 200 (Schele 1985a). Subsequently, this image becomes one of the most pervasive and diagnostic references to royal power among the Lowland Maya. It continues to be worn as a diadem and displayed as an object. When we have actual objects, they are made of precious greenstone and are not mirrors, although there are mirrors of various materials from Late Preclassic through Classic period contexts which might have been used in conjunction with such objects.

During the Proto-Classic and Early Classic periods, we have no evidence that the Jester God was associated with ranks other than that of *Ahau*, the first rank of rulership. Where there are texts associated with portrayed individuals wearing the Jester God, there is evidence that they carry the *ahau* title. Attached to other images in the glyphic texts, the Jester God headband is a semantic determinative for *ahau*, and the *ahau* glyph can substitute positionally for the Jester God image on such headbands. There is no reason to suppose that the trade and exchange which facilitated the origination of the Jester God was less important institutionally to its maintenance (see Sabloff 1986).

The Late Classic Period: Beginning of the End

During the Late Classic period, the Jester God image participates in some significant structural changes in the symbolic expression of Maya authority, registering changes in southern Lowland Maya political organization. Although the Jester God remains a semantic determinative for *ahau* in this period (see Bonampak, Miscellaneous Stone 1, M.E. Miller 1986: Fig. 42), this icon, along with its God K counterpart, becomes associated with the distinctive and secondary rank of *Cahal* as well. The *cahal* title, identified by David Stuart (n.d., see also Schele and Miller 1986) may mean "principal of the community." Whatever its exact decipherment, *cahal* is a title extensively used throughout the Western Rivers region of the southern Lowlands during the Late Classic period. Individuals of this rank are intimately involved with others of the rank of *ahau*, including the mothers and wives of men carrying the *ahau* title, compatriots in war, councilors and members of the royal court, and rulers of secondary centers under the aegis of the capitals of Maya kingdoms. In general, the individuals who carry the title of *cahal* are not iconographically distinguishable in their regalia from individuals carrying the rank of *ahau*. That is, the same kinds of power objects are displayed and worn by both ranks.

One clear and unequivocal illustration of the dissociation of the Jester God icon from its meaning, *ahau*, is the Tablet of the Slaves at Palenque (Figure 4.4). David Stuart, in his investigation of the *Cahal* title, noted that Chac Zutz, the protagonist of the Tablet and presumably a king of Palenque, was given the title of *cahal* during the reign of his brother Chaacal. Although there are several titles in this text which refer to Chac Zutz as *ahau* using the "Ah Po" form identified by Floyd Lounsbury (1973), it is clear that he is formally acceding to the title of *cahal* in this scene by grasping the "dark" bundled mirror. The "dark" mirror, it may be recalled, refers not to the Jester God but to God K. Chaacal is given accession to the kingship with the "bright" mirror verb in this text. While Chac Zutz is acceding to the *cahal* title, the image shows his father handing him the drum-major crown of kingship, which is decorated with the Jester God. The dislocation is thus two-fold on this monument: (1) the Jester God is the object shown, while *cahal*, not *ahau*, is the title acceded to; and (2) the accession verb is the "dark" mirror, while the object displayed is the referent of the "bright" mirror. No doubt the confusion in this case was deliberate and appropriate, given the fact that Chac Zutz had some claim to the rulership at Palenque. Nevertheless, it was a manipulation of objects and concepts that made sense in light of a general trend to extend the iconography of power to Maya rulers of the second rank throughout the region.

The social dynamics behind the dissociation of the Jester God, God K, and other emblems of power from the status of *ahau* have been discussed by Mary Miller (1986). Generally, insofar as access to titled position was hereditary, there must have been a considerable proliferation of nobility with legitimate claim to such titles, and to the objects which proclaimed them, as Classic Maya civilization progressed. The formal designation of a second rank of rulership would have been one way to im-

Figure 4.4. Tablet of the Slaves from Palenque. Drawing by Linda Schele.

Figure 4.5. Monument 1 from Mopila, Yucatan. Drawing by Karim Sadr after interpretation by David Freidel.

pose some order on this burgeoning elites' relationship to authority and power. Evidently this solution was only partial, for the Classic Maya failed to establish distinctive regalia and symbols to designate this second rank status and instead vulgarized the symbols of *ahau*.

The Terminal Classic Jester God

The Jester God image survives the ninth-century collapse of southern Lowland Maya civilization and occurs as a diadem worn by numerous personages depicted in the Great Ball Court at Chichen Itzá (Robertson, Kurjack, and Maldonado 1985), one of the latest major structures at the site. As these scholars observe, the Jester God diadem is associated with both sacrificers and victims in the bas-reliefs of the Ball Court. Given the many instances of the Jester God at this site, it is unlikely that they all pertain to rulers of the first rank, *ahau*, although the *ahau* title occurs in texts at Chichen Itzá, and there is an "*ahau ahau*" title which might make a claim of superior power over others of the *ahau* title (Kelley 1982, cited in Kowalski 1985).

Recently (Freidel 1987), I found a monument with a text near Chichen Itzá that suggests that the same dissociation of the Jester God title from the rank of *ahau* found in the Late Classic southern lowlands held for the Terminal Classic northern lowlands. Originally, this small bas-relief (Figure 4.5) was set into the back wall of a sixteenth-century church at the site of Mopila, two km from the town of Yaxcaba where it is currently housed in the library. The image shows a individual wearing a polymorphic mask surmounted by a long-beaked bird with the non-anthropomorphic trefoil variant of the Jester God above the beak. The center of the image has been carefully cut out in a shallow circle, the dimensions of which are appropriate for a slate-backed mosaic mirror. The text accompanying the image is an accession statement. Following a date in the 260-day calendar, there is the hand grasping the bundled "bright" mirror accession verb. Following the verb are three titles, the first of which might be 17 Rabbit and the personal name of the individual. After these three titles, the sentence ends with a *cah* title, a known variant of the *cahal* title. This title may have had the *vl* suffix, but the key part of the glyph is not preserved here.

Iconographically, the Mopila monument is part of a distinctive local style of bas-relief carving found at several small sites surrounding Yaxuna, the terminus of the great *sacbe* from Coba and a site showing Terminal Classic occupation and construction in association with its ties to that center. Although it remains to be demonstrated that this local Terminal Classic style is coeval with the carving of the reliefs at Chichen Itza, certainly the Mopila example is close in both space and time. That the *cahal* title was known and used in the Terminal Classic northern lowlands is further substantiated by texts from the Hieroglyphic Group at the Puuc-related site of Xcalumkin in Campeche (Pollock 1980). The South Building of this group is evidently an accession monument to an individual who is taking the title of *cahal*. A bas-relief on the medial wall portrays this individual as a seated lord, accompanied by a sentence which begins with the hand grasping the "bright" mirror verb and which ends with the *cahal* title. Here, as in the Mopila case, the accession verb refers to the mirror associated with the Jester God. The *cahal* title is repeated in the text framing the medial doorway in association with the personal titles of the individual taking it. The size and elaborateness of this monument suggest that the title of *cahal* was of primary importance at this site. The *cahal* title occurs in other texts at Xcalumkin, which further suggests its importance at this site. The glyphic dates at Xcalumkin are thought to be relatively early for the Puuc development (A.D. 730–770, Pollock 1980) and suggest essential contemporaneity with the Western Rivers region development of the *cahal* title. Although the matter of the overlap between the Puuc fluorescence and the Late Classic southern lowland kingdoms is a matter of ongoing controversy, it is at least a distinct possibility that the *cahal* title was adopted in the north during its period of special prominence in the political orders of the neighboring southern kingdoms.

The evidence available from the northern lowland polities which began to flourish at the same time that the southern lowlands underwent collapse suggests that the extension of such icons of power as the Jester God to incorporate other ranks of authority below *ahau* was transmitted and perpetuated in the north. Why this strategy of vulgarizing the emblems and objects of power succeeded in the north while it failed in the south is a matter worth further investigation.

Conclusions

The Jester God illustrates some of the evolutionary dynamics of Lowland Maya society as it underwent successive transformations of political organization and symbolic legitimation of that organization. Beginning as an object of power and wealth, the Jester God was redefined as a diadem expressing the status of *ahau*, divine king. No doubt power and wealth, through command of trade among other means, provided a major antecedent condition for the initial innovation of Maya kingship. While there appear to be significant disjunctions in the meaning attached to the trefoil icon by the Olmec and those assigned by the Late Preclassic Maya, the essential connotations of power and wealth were no doubt carried forward, sanctified and made legitimate by the definition of *ahau*. In the Late Classic period, the Jester God was detached from *ahau*, and, along with other emblems of this central rank, became generalized and accessible to lower ranks of the growing Maya elite. This process surely signals increasing internal competition for access to power and titles of authority, a social and economic upper class outgrowing the organizational potential of the institution of *ahau*. Although diluted, these redefined emblems of authority carry forward the sanctity and legitimation of many centuries of association with central power. While this process of generalization failed in the southern Lowland civilization, it evidently succeeded in the north, or at least was a dimension of the successful redefinition of Lowland Maya political order in that region.

Five

The Birth of the Baktun at Tikal and Seibal
By Clemency Chase Coggins

For the ancient Maya historic time began in the fourth millenium B.C., as do the current Hindu era and the Judaic calendar. Dates written out in the uniquely Maya Long Count counted from this early date and calculated time on a vigesimal base in which the largest unit of time was the *baktun*, consisting of twenty times twenty, or 400, tuns. The word *baktun* is a modern reconstruction that means "400 *tun*"; a *tun* is a year of 360 days.

The earliest known Classic period Long Count date comes from the southern Maya Lowlands; found on Stela 29 at Tikal, this is 8.12.14.8.15, early in the second half of Baktun Eight (A.D. 292). Like the dedicatory dates on all known Maya stelae before 8.16.0.0.0 this commemorates an event, not the culmination of a calendric cycle. The completion of the preceding Baktun Seven and beginning of Baktun Eight, at about A.D. 40, is not known to have been recorded at Tikal or anywhere else, although Tikal was an important site during the Preclassic period and continued to be so throughout the Early Classic—at least 24 carved stelae were erected in the 150 years between A.D. 378 and 525. During the Late Classic only 11 more stelae are known to have been erected in the 285 years until A.D. 810, and a solitary last one 3 katuns later at 870 (Jones and Satterthwaite 1982, table 3).

Southwest of Tikal at the Pasion River site of Siebal the major Classic period occupation was late, A.D. 700 to 900. Siebal's first carved stela was erected at 771, just as Tikal was tapering off, with a concentration of monuments at 850 when Tikal had none and was virtually abandoned.

I argue here that these different trajectories and apparently idiosyncratic commemorative practices at the two sites had a common religious and political rationale that expressed the basic structure of Maya belief. Maya belief rested on a historic framework that was expressed in the recurring completion of periods of time; my study is concerned with the 400 tun baktun cycle and, more important for the history of Tikal and Seibal, with the birth of each following baktun. A repeated historical pattern at these two sites, in which similar and parallel events were associated with sequential baktun endings, provides startling evidence for the often noted Maya perception of time, and consequently of life, as cyclic (Roys 1933: 182–87).

At Tikal, just before the completion of Baktun Eight, a warrior wearing the uniform of the city of Teotihuacan became ruler of Tikal by marrying into the local ruling lineage and deposing(?) the Maya ruler Jaguar Paw (Coggins 1975: 140–46; 1979a).[1] This foreigner had a Venus name and wore the Venus warrior headdress (on Stela 4, Jones and Satterthwaite 1982, fig. 5—all Tikal monuments are illustrated in this work; and see Figure 5.1a of Stela 31, left figure). No monument was erected at the completion of Baktun Eight (9.0.0.0.0 8 Ahau 8 Uo), but the termination date was commemorated ten tuns later on Stela 31 at the Venus-associated date of 7 Ahau, 3 Yax. Stela 31 was the monument of the son of this Teotihuacan-affiliated ruler and he also had a Venus name, but his reign was legitimized through a combination of his mother's previously ruling lineage and the power and authority of his father's intrusive foreign persona.

At Seibal toward the end of the next baktun another ruler named Jaguar Paw was captured and Seibal lost its autonomy to the Tikal-associated site

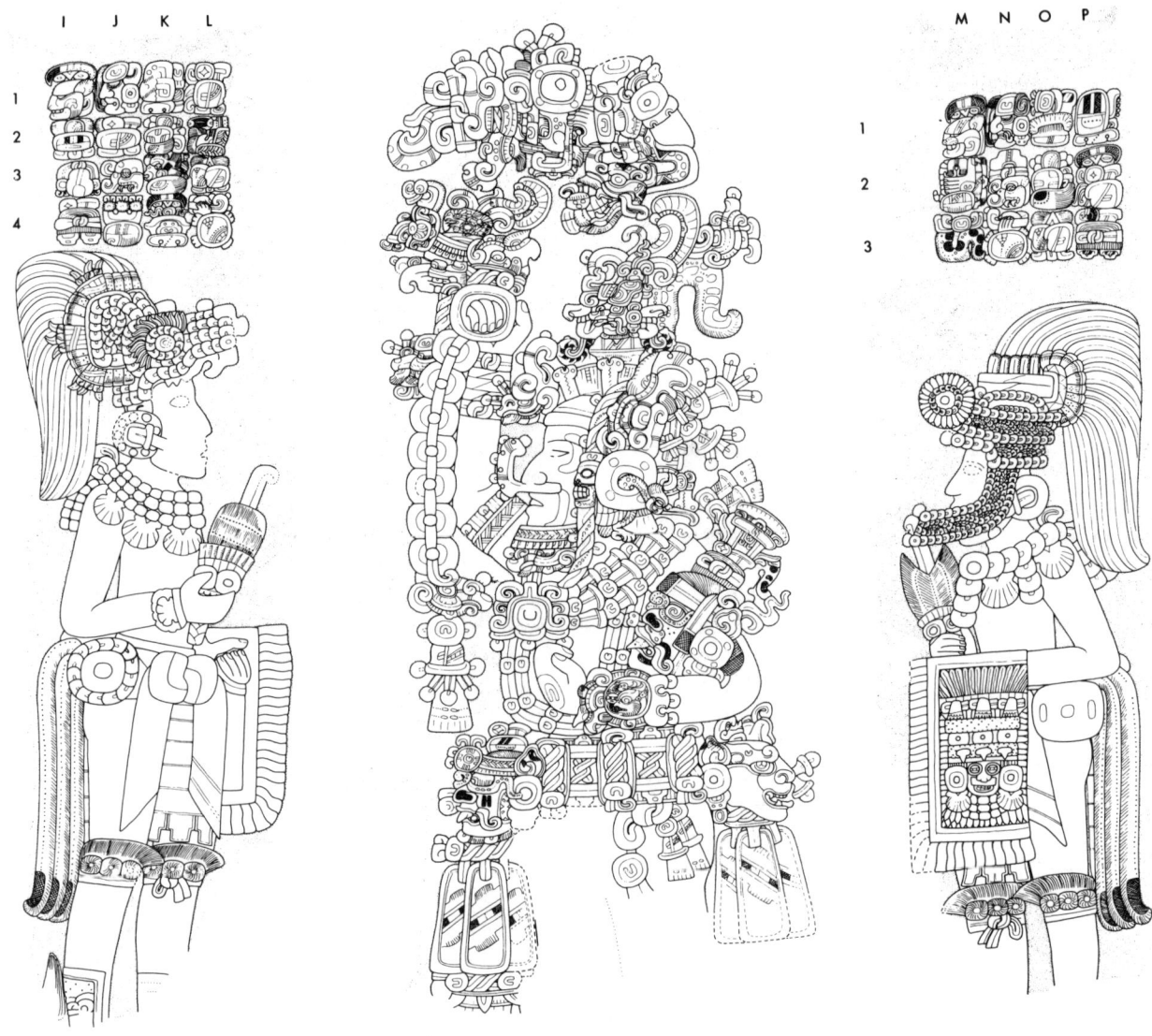

Figure 5.1. Tikal Stela 31. (Courtesy of the Tikal Project, University Museum, University of Pennsylvania.) a. Face and sides. b. Top of inscription on back.

b

of Dos Pilas. However, closer to the end of Baktun Nine, Teotihuacan-affiliated warriors also came to rule Seibal. Instead of erecting a stela, they built a structure to commemorate the completion of the baktun at the Venus date of 10.0.0.0.0 7 Ahau 18 Zip, and one katun later, five stelae commemorating the baktun completion were erected at 5 Ahau 3 Kayab. And, as at Tikal a baktun earlier, the man who was ruler at the beginning of the new baktun combined the regalia of the local ruling dynasty with more Teotihuacan-derived insignia.

The Baktun

On stelae the Maya recorded events in the Long Count in order to fix rulers and their births and accessions in relation to the beginning of time. A notation of the number of baktuns completed begins most of these Initial Series Inscriptions (Figure 5.1b: A5). The baktun glyph usually consists of the head of a mythological bird, which has a hand in place of its lower jaw (Figure 5.2a); alternatively it may, however, consist of two Cauac elements, each

Figure 5.2. Baktun glyphs (from Thompson 1960: figs. 26, 27). a. Head form. b. Cauac form.

one signifying a cycle, and read *k'u* (Thompson 1970),[2] meaning godly or divine, so that together two of them, *k'u k'u,* may be read *k'uk'(u)* (Figure 5.1b, A5; Figure 5.2b).[3] Other time periods use this Cauac cycle element in their name, but I postulate that the baktun represents the divine cycle, or *k'uk'*.[4] *K'uk'* is the name of the symbolically charged quetzal bird as well as, by substitution, for *k'uk'* (divine cycle); it is thus one of the names of the mythological serpent-bird that represents the major time periods in the inscriptions.[5]

An extraordinary facet of the Maya commemoration of period endings is the lack of monuments dedicated to the end of baktuns—the largest and most important periods of historic time—even though smaller period endings are regularly observed.[6] I suggest that the ends of baktuns inspired a millenarian terror—a fear that time would come to an end as was believed in medieval Europe at the year 1000 (in reference to the apocalyptyic Biblical predictions of Revelation 20: 1–7)—and as happened elsewhere in Mesoamerica at the end of each 52-year period. Thus it may have been considered unpropitious to carve baktun endings in stone; Maya ritual was instead devoted to surviving these dates, of which there were only two during the Classic period: 9.0.0.0.0 (A.D. 435) and 10.0.0.0.0 (A.D. 830), the two dates considered here.

The *K'atun* and Toltec Warriors

The next, smaller, period of time in the Maya Long Count is the katun, or *k'atun,* composed of twenty tuns. Commemoration of katun period endings was, in contrast to baktun, the most common reason for Classic Maya stela erection. I have suggested that the celebration of katun completion was a Maya practice that was inaugurated under the influence of Teotihuacan-affiliated foreigners toward the end of Baktun Eight (Coggins 1979b, 1980). Recently I have revived the old idea that Teotihuacan was the original Tula, and by extension proposed that all Teotihuacanos abroad were by definition Toltec, as were their mostly Maya descendants (1987a, 1988a, 1989).[7]

Thus it was Toltec men who were depicted carrying Teotihuacan-style weapons, and who had settled at Uaxactun and at Tikal, at least as early as the Long Count Date of 8.16.0.0.0 (A.D. 357) when the first katun commemoration monument was erected at Uaxactun, or perhaps even by 8.14.0.0.0 (A.D. 317), the earliest date on Stela 31 (see Laporte and Fialko, this volume). They intermarried with the ruling Maya at Uaxactun and Tikal as they did at their southern highland base of Kaminaljuyu. The Yucatec Mayan word for warrior is *k'atun,* and after one of these military men became ruler of Tikal, katun-marking monuments were erected there. Tikal (*Tik'al*) thus became known as the place of katun (*k'atun*) commemoration.[8]

The emphasis on katun completion for the dedication of monuments tended to shift attention, structurally, from idiosyncratic historic events in the life of the local ruling dynasty to the more predictable and neutral events of cyclic completion (Coggins 1980).

A Toltec Ruler of Tikal

The Toltec warrior who became ruler at Tikal is known in the literature as "Curl Nose" after the form of his name glyph (Coggins 1975: 140). This name was probably actually read *Yax K'an,* Blue-green, First or Venus "Serpent" (Figures 5.1a and b).[9] *Yax K'an* denotes Quetzalcoatl or *K'uk'ulkan,* which, as the blue-green celestial crocodilian, was Venus the Evening Star (Coggins 1988a; n.d. a, b).[10] On his inaugural Stela 4 *Yax K'an* wears the frontal jaguar-crocodilian-bird *K'uk'ulkan* headdress often worn by Toltec warriors when they were represented in Mesoamerica. *Yax K'an* wears two variations on this headdress in his portraits on Stela 31, where he is shown standing both in front of and behind his son (Figure 5.1a). From this dual portrait it is clear that these headdresses were constructed of small perforated plaques or spangles; seventy-eight such spangles were found near his head in his tomb (Hattula Moholy-Nagy, personal communication; Coggins 1975: fig. 45a). Spondylus shell spangles are *k'an* in Maya, and Toltec warrior headdresses were still constructed of them centuries later at Tikal and Piedras Negras, and finally at Seibal (Figure 5.6).[11] While the name of this Tikal ruler, *Yax K'an,* meant Venus Crocodile-Serpent, it also referred specifically to the precious disc Toltec headdress that he wore (Coggins n.d., a,b).

Recent excavations in the southwestern sector of Tikal have demonstrated that Teotihuacan-style architecture and imported goods were present at Tikal centuries before *Yax K'an* became ruler (Laporte and Fialko, this volume), and from his burial assemblage it is clear that he represented the culture of Teotihuacan at Tikal (Coggins 1975, 1979a, b).[12] It is not known if *Yax K'an* became ruler by capturing and possibly sacrificing his predecessor, but from the inscription on Stela 31 it is clear that the name of this previous ruler was Jaguar Paw. Laporte and Fialko postulate that the Jaguar Paw lineage controlled the astronomical ritual carried out in the Mundo Perdido group at Tikal, and thus imply the lineage was associated with the early Teotihuacan-style architecture found there, and in Group 6C-XVI (this volume).

I suggest that the foreign *Yax K'an* may have managed to marry the daughter of the ruler Jaguar Paw and to become ruler of Tikal precisely because of the Tikal Jaguar Paw lineage's ancient connection with Teotihuacan, although I believe *Yax K'an* himself probably came from Kaminaljuyu or the south coast, by way of Uaxactun (Coggins 1979b, 1983).[13] William Coe probably best described the relationship with Teotihuacan when he remarked that "[w]hile perhaps three cultural *entradas* of Petén life can be discerned over eight-odd centuries, we cannot be sure that we have not uselessly segmented a continuous though changing Mexican infusion of Petén life" (1972: 258).

The Completion of Baktun Eight

Yax K'an probably died between ten and thirty years before the end of Baktun Eight. After a political struggle that is reflected in the final burials in the eastern structures of Mundo Perdido (Laporte and Fialko, this volume), his son and successor, known as Stormy Sky, acceded to the rule at 8.19.10.0.0. Four-hundred tuns earlier, at the end of the preceding baktun, no monuments were being erected in the Maya Lowlands, so the beginning of Baktun Nine, at 9.0.0.0.0, was the first opportunity for the Lowland Maya to have commemorated a baktun ending in stone. At that time the recording of katun endings had recently been institutionalized at Uaxactun and at Tikal, but no monument was erected at either site at the supreme period ending 9.0.0.0.0. Instead, the Tikal ruler Stormy Sky, son of *Yax K'an,* erected Stela 31, (Figure 5.1) one-half katun after the end of the baktun.

On the back of Stela 31 a long inscription summarized the preceding six-katun history, identified Stormy Sky's own parentage, and commemorated both the one-katun anniversary of his accession and the apotheosis of his father *Yax K'an* in the sky—while adding, only toward the end of the inscription, an Initial Series date that recorded the completion of the baktun. Stela 31 was, however, dedicated to the doubly Venus-associated date 7 Ahau 3 Yax that occurred ten tuns later. Seven Ahau is a day name that may correspond to Venus as Evening Star,[14] while the Venus serpent-crocodile was patron of the month Yax, as can be seen from the month indicator at the top of the oversized Initial Series Introducing Glyph that begins the long historical inscription on the back of Stela 31 (Figure 5.1b). At the top of the face of the stela, immediately behind this introducing Venus "serpent" on the back, the former ruler, *Yax K'an*, is shown in the sky as Stormy Sky's ancestor (Figure 5.1a), thus relating their two celestial Venus identities. *Yax K'an* is also shown twice more on the sides of the monument as two smaller figures mirroring each other while flanking his son—a form in which he represents the Venus twins (Morning and Evening Star) (Clancy 1980: 44–53). All three of these portraits of *Yax K'an* on Stela 31 are identified by his name glyph, and the three Venus ruler images are further evoked by the 3 Yax month day.

In addition to wearing the identifying *Yax K'an* Venus name in his headdress, the figure in the sky on Stela 31 displays the features of the Sun God, while a hand replacing the lower jaw signifies the baktun itself (See Figure 5.2a). Such a combination of baktun, solar, and Venus cyclic symbolism is inherent in the concept of the *k'uk'*, or cycle.

In this celestial figure, the completed baktun cycle is identified with the sun and Venus and with the apotheosized ancestor-predecessor who legitimized the reign of his son from above when the new Baktun nine was already one-half katun under way. The actual moment of baktun completion had been safely negotiated, and this monument with its venus date celebrated the beginning of a new cycle and epoch.

The Tikal Ruler "Stormy Sky"

At the beginning, the new baktun had a number of interesting characteristics that are evident on Stela 31 itself (Figure 5.1a). Particularly important was Stormy Sky's declaration of his Maya dynastic heritage in his own regalia which, instead of including the foreign elements worn by his father, adopted the heraldry of an earlier katun ruler (depicted on Stela 29), apparently thus emphasizing his legitimacy through his mother's local Jaguar lineage. Elements of costume that identify maternal lineage can often be identified by how the ruler wears them. Maternal and female symbolism tend to be associated with the left hand and with the west and underworld directions, whereas paternal symbolism is found more often on the right hand and associated with the east and the sky (Coggins 1975: 17–19, 54, 55, 203–207; 1980: 728–29; 1985: 55–56). Stormy Sky's belt summarizes his legitimacy by showing the symbols associated with his father in the right hand (celestial, solar) head on his belt, which is just below the chain of discs that he holds up in his right hand toward his sun-eyed father in the sky. The head at the proper left side of Stormy Sky's belt represents a nocturnal or underworld (terrestrial, solar) jaguar. In the crook of his left arm Stormy Sky holds the nocturnal head of the sun with a topknot of hair that was an early form (pre-9.0.0.0.0) of the Tikal Emblem Glyph, and which has a lineage(?) temple and the jaguar tail of his maternal lineage on top of it.

The Name of Stormy Sky

Another aspect of Stormy Sky's declaration of his parentage is his personal name, displayed in his headdress (Figure 5.1a). This consists of a long-nosed supernatural (often called God K) emerging from a cleft sky with an axe hafted in its forehead (signifying a stormy sky). This creature adopts an unusual posture, with arms upraised, and elbows sticking out. The Yucatec Mayan word for elbow is either *k'uk'* or *kuk*, and I suggest that this figure which emerges from the split sky was called *K'uk' Ka'an*, a pun for *K'uk'kan*, bird-serpent, in turn a variation of *K'uk'ukulkan*, Venus bird-serpent. Verification of this reading is found in the name of the Quirigua ruler known as "Cauac Sky" (Kelley 1962; Jones and Sharer 1980, fig. 10, glyph no. 22). This man's name glyph consists of a sky glyph superfixed by upraised arms with projecting elbows that flank a Cauac glyph substituting for the head. The Cauac sign may be read *k'u*, and thus serves as a phonetic indicator for the *K'uk' Ka'an* reading of this Venus name.

The "God K" Motif

Stela 31 is the first known example of formal portraiture that associates the "God K" motif with a living ruler, although an analogous form was shown in the sky—in ancestor position above *Yax K'an* on his inaugural Stela 4. Stormy Sky's "God K" name, which may be read *K'uk' Ka'an* (a Venus name), is thus associated with this paternal lineage. David Kelley long ago pointed out that at Palenque, God K (or GII) was an aspect of Venus (1965). In Late Classic times the God K figure with hafted axe in the forehead became the manikin scepter held by rulers who, like Stormy Sky, claimed Toltec ancestry, however diluted it may have been by generations of pure Maya intermarriage. The long-nosed storm and sky deity cast lightning downward to men and thus made the connection between sky and earth: with this serpentine lightning the divine seed of the ancestor in the sky was sent down to his descendant, who was the ruler below (Coggins 1988b). On Stela 31, Stormy Sky himself personifies this manikin through his personal name, while during the Late Classic period the connection is symbolized by the ruler carrying the manikin scepter.

The Tikal Emblem Glyph

Another important concept first embodied in Stela 31 is the complete emblem glyph (Figure 5.3a), although the complete glyph with affixes is not present in the inscription on the monument. Emblem glyphs consist of a main, iconic sign that has prefixes (on the left) known collectively as "the water group" (Berlin 1958) and superfixes usually read as *Ahau*, meaning *Lord* or *supreme* (Lounsbury 1973). These emblem glyphs refer to places, and the Tikal emblem symbolizes the role of Tikal as the place where the commemoration of the katun, or the count of twenty (*k'al*), was celebrated (Coggins 1987b). The water group prefix, which usually consists of drops of liquid falling from a *k'an* element,[15] has been described as representing water or blood (D. Stuart 1984), though when it is in its equivalent ritual form known as "the scattering gesture," it has also been identified as corn (Kelley 1976: 51–52) or

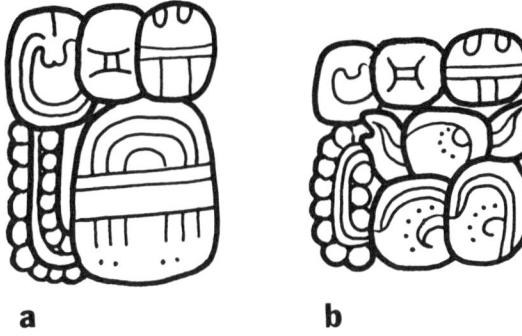

Figure 5.3. Emblem glyphs. a. Tikal (on Seibal Stela 10, D3). b. Seibal (on Seibal Stela 10, C2).

copal (pellets of copal resemble corn; *see* Hammond 1982b; Love 1987).

I believe this "liquid" is indeed intended as seed (like corn), but that in this context it is human seed, or semen, that is symbolized, and that the water group prefix may be read *eel*, *yel* or *hel*, meaning eggs or semen. With the prefixing *K'an* Cross and its interchangeable elements, this prefix may thus be read *k'an hel*, which is also a name for the manikin scepter—whose role is that of metaphorical conduit between the deified ancestors and man (Coggins 1988b), as was literally true of semen. At the time of Stela 31, early in Baktun Nine, the water group prefix and the Ben Ich superfix had not been added together to the Tikal emblem in the inscriptions (Figures 5.1a, I4, P3).[16] I suggest that the stela image of Stormy Sky himself was the equivalent of a complete emblem glyph, and perhaps the earliest conjunction of the component elements. In the crook of his arm Stormy Sky holds the earlier form of the Tikal emblem that resembled a bound topknot of hair, while above him in the sky his father, conflated with the sun, symbolized the Ahau (Ben Ich) superfix of the emblem glyph (Lounsbury 1973). In this imagery the water group prefix is equivalent to the chain of *k'an* discs; these are the drilled jade or spondylus discs with which Stormy Sky reaches up toward his ancestor in the sky. Such drilled precious discs represent precious liquid (as does the analogous Mexican *chalchihuitl*), and in this context they signify the divine semen that connects Stormy Sky to his ancestor in the sky. After this date emblem glyphs are regularly coupled with the "water group" prefix.

Thus at Tikal just before the completion of the baktun a man of Teotihuacan affiliation who had come to power at Tikal brought Toltec cultural traits to the rulership, including costume, ceramic imagery, and certain architectural forms, although some of these traits may already have been displayed by people living in the southwestern part of Tikal (Laporte and Fialko, this volume). The commemoration of the end of the baktun in stone was underplayed, but once the new baktun had begun the ruler chose a Venus date to celebrate his combined ancestry, to recount the history of his predecessors by katuns in the monumental inscription, and to portray himself flanked by his young father in the guise of the Venus twins. He is surveyed by this same father who, aged and dead, looks down from the sky above while he maintains lineage contact with his son through his precious seed, as symbolized by a chain of *k'an* discs.

Twin Pyramid Complexes

At Late Classic Tikal ceremonial groups, known as twin pyramid complexes, were built expressly for the commemoration of katun completion (Jones 1969; Coggins 1979b, 1980), a periodic ritual that I have suggested was inaugurated at Tikal by Stormy Sky's foreign father, and that became Tikal's ritual focus and the reason for the name *Tik'al* (Coggins 1987b). Twin pyramid groups have square plazas that are characterized by their eastern and western pyramidal substructures, each with four stairways—an equilateral or radial plan that resembles the Maya sign for the completion of a cycle (Figure 5.4). There is no evidence at Tikal that a single radial pyramidal structure was erected in commemoration of the completion of baktun eight, although it is very possible that the great Preclassic Structure 5C-54, which served as a solar observatory and was constructed on this radial plan, was reconstructed at the baktun-ending date (Laporte and Fialko this volume). Structure 5C-54 was the largest pyramidal structure at Tikal and it was probably associated with certain ancient ruling dynasties (Laporte and Fialko this volume). I have postulated that the new ritual of katun celebration introduced by the Toltec (*k'atun*) warriors was intended to revise the focus of calendric celebration (Coggins 1979b, 1980, 1984), and that the later reconstruction of this observatory, along with the eclipse of its Jaguar Paw lineage (Laporte and Fialko, this volume), may have served this purpose.

After the reign of Stormy Sky, Tikal continued to be powerful, with some vicissitudes, until near the end of the baktun that he had inaugurated (Coggins 1979b). Then, as at most Classic Maya sites, the rulers of Tikal stopped erecting monuments. The single site that continued to erect monuments beyond the end of Baktun Nine and that prominently observed the baktun completion was Seibal.

Seibal and the Baktun

Three quarters of the way through Baktun Nine the ruler of Seibal, Jaguar Paw, was captured and sacrificed by the Lord of nearby Dos Pilas (Houston and Mathews 1985: 17). After this, Seibal continued within the sphere of the site of Dos Pilas (which had a little-understood relationship with Tikal that involved sharing an emblem glyph) until about 9.18.10.0.0, when Seibal apparently regained its independence. Then, as at Tikal a baktun before, a militaristic Toltec took control of Seibal, introducing foreign ceramics and architectural forms (Willey et al. 1975; 31, 32, 36, 42). At the end of the baktun the ruler of Seibal represented both the local Maya dynasty of the earlier, sacrificed ruler, Jaguar Paw, and that of his father(?) whose non-Maya facial features he shared. Both men had relatively short, heavy noses and the square-cut hair and mustaches of foreigners (Figures 5.6 and 5.7). Although at this time, about a century after the end of Teotihuacan, such Toltec may have traced their ancestry to Teotihuacan, they probably actually came from the western periphery of the southern Classic Maya Lowlands.

As at Tikal, no stela was erected to commemorate the end of Baktun Nine; instead, on the culminating Venus day of 7 Ahau (the same as the Venus dedica-

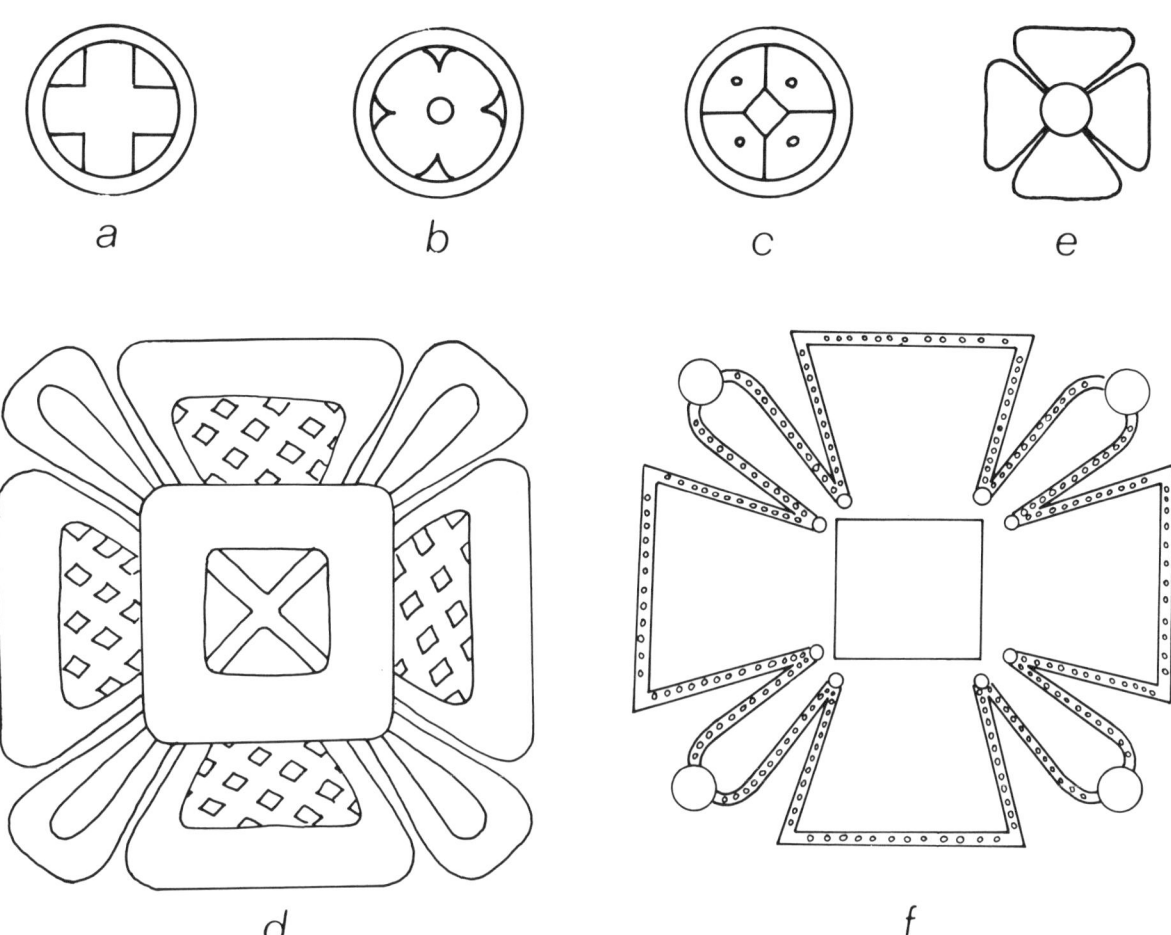

Figure 5.4. Cyclic completion signs. a. Kan Cross. b. Kin glyph. c. Lamat (Venus) glyph. d. Maya completion sign. e. Teotihuacan flower emblem (possibly signifying completion). f. Fejervary Mayor calendar form.

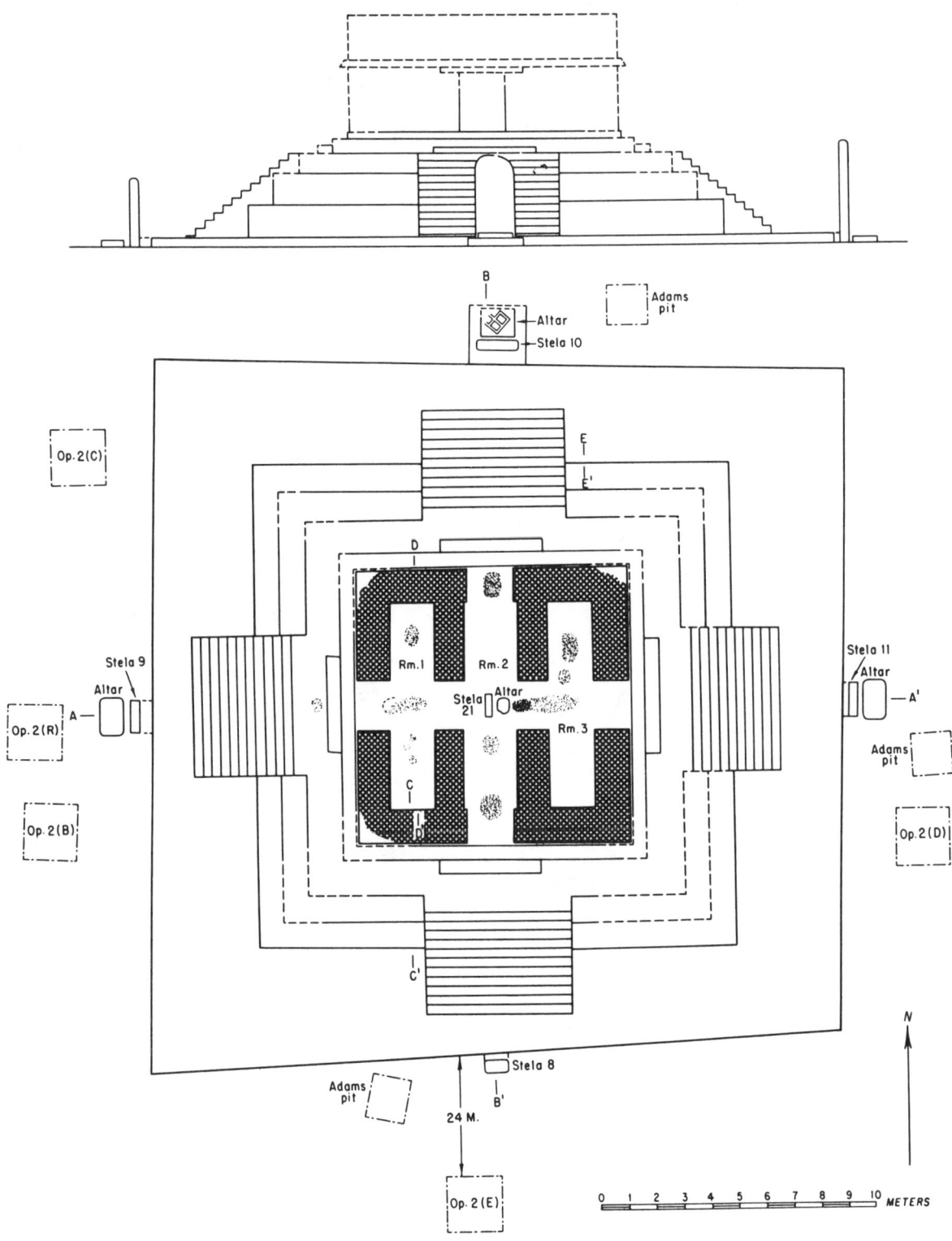

Figure 5.5. Plan and north elevation of Seibal Structure A-3 (from A. L. Smith 1982: fig. 17).

tory day of Tikal Stela 31), a four-stairway radial structure was constructed in the shape of the cyclic completion sign (Figure 5.5; Smith 1982; 47, 55). Such radial structures were probably also built at the same baktun completion at Chichen Itzá and at Dzibilchaltún (Coggins 1983: 55–57; 1989). And as at Tikal was was not until the new baktun was under way that stelae were erected, although at Seibal five were dedicated to the next katun ending 10.1.0.0.0 5 Ahau 3 Kayab.[17] Anthony Aveni has recently explained that five is the quintessential Venus number, that "fiveness" epitomizes Venus, partly because there are five Venus cycles in the combined Venus and solar cycle (Aveni 1990). The five-part form of the Venus glyph (Figure 5.3c), and of the analogous baktun completion Structure A-3 itself (Figure 5.5), the five stelae erected, and the 5 Ahau date all restate this theme.

The 7 Ahau Venus date of the completion of Baktun Nine also announced and prefigured the completion of at least two more major cycles. The end of the baktun occurred March 13, 830, and once this date was safely past priestly attention turned to two more imminent climactic events that were critical to survival in the new baktun. These were the end of the 52-year Calendar Round in November, followed by the heliacal rise of Venus on the day 1 Ahau at the winter solstice (Coggins 1989).

The Seibal Stelae

The five stelae represent four or, more likely, five different rulers of Seibal. Four of these men appear at the foot of each of the four cardinally-oriented stairways, and perhaps in the sequence of a counterclockwise ceremonial circuit around the equilateral structure (Figure 5.5). As with most Maya ceremony, the circuit probably began in the east where the sun came up and where the current ruler was shown on the tallest stela in the act of "scattering" (Figure 5.6). As on Stormy Sky's monument, both the post-baktun dedicatory date and the baktun completion date are noted in the inscription on Stela 11, and, like Stormy Sky, this man wore regalia of local Maya and of Toltec character. Most notably adopted from what may have been his Maya matriline is the diagonal headdress bar with a "God C" finial and a "shell-winged dragon" (Schele 1979: 65) riding on top. He also wears the Toltec shell spangle *yax k'an* warrior headdress first seen in the Maya Lowlands worn by the ruler *Yax K'an* at Tikal, on Stela 31—the preceding baktun monument. Finally, only the man on Stela 11 wears the fish and water lily headdress. This motif, which may be read *ka(y)-nab* (fish-water lily), is a pun for sea, *K'anaab;* it evokes the primordial sea in which *k'uk'ulkan* swam (Coggins 1988c, 1987b) and, like the *yax k'an* headdress, associates the ruler with *K'ukúlkan* and Venus.

I postulate that the counterclockwise ceremonial circuit took the celebrant backward in historic time, just as did the inscription on Stela 31 that began with the current ruler and went backward in time. Thus it would be the predecessor, probably the father, of the man on Stela 11 who he closely resembles, who is portrayed posthumously on Stela 10 at the foot of the north stairway (Figure 5.7). The man on Stela 10 appears to be named *Ah Bolon Tun* at B5 (bottom right glyph in upper group). Seibal Stela 10 was apparently dedicated by *Ah Bolon Tun* at 9.18.0.0.0 (Graham 1967: 101–02) who, if he was the father of the man on Stela 11, would have the same relationship to him as did *Yax K'an* to *K'uk-'Ka'an* (Curl Nose to Stormy Sky) a baktun earlier. The former in each case erected an eighteen *k'atun* monument and the latter a belated baktun marker.

I assume *Ah Bolon Tun* is dead because he holds the bicephalic sky bar with differentiated heads, because a smoking tube in his headdress suggests his personal identification with the lineage deity "God K" in the sky (as also displayed by the dead Pacal on his sarcophagus lid at Palenque), and because north is the direction associated with the sky and the ancestors (Coggins 1980, 1982). I suggest that it is the sacrificed ruler, Jaguar Paw, who is portrayed on Stela 8 on the south side of Structure A-3, or, by his placement in the circuit, farthest in the past (Figure 5.9). In traditional Maya symbolism south is associated with the underworld, a link that is most clearly made in the nine-doorway structures on the south side of the twin pyramid groups at Tikal (Guillemin 1968; Coggins 1980, 1982). Jaguar traits may also be associated with death and the night sun in the underworld and, as was noted in Stormy Sky's regalia, with a Maya matriline. The man on the southern Stela 8 is thus shown in the Underworld wearing a complete set of four jaguar paws. Below his ribcage a large hole in the stone probably

Figure 5.6. Seibal Stela 11, east. (Courtesy of Peabody Museum, Harvard University).

Figure 5.7. Seibal Stela 10, north. (Courtesy of Peabody Museum, Harvard University).

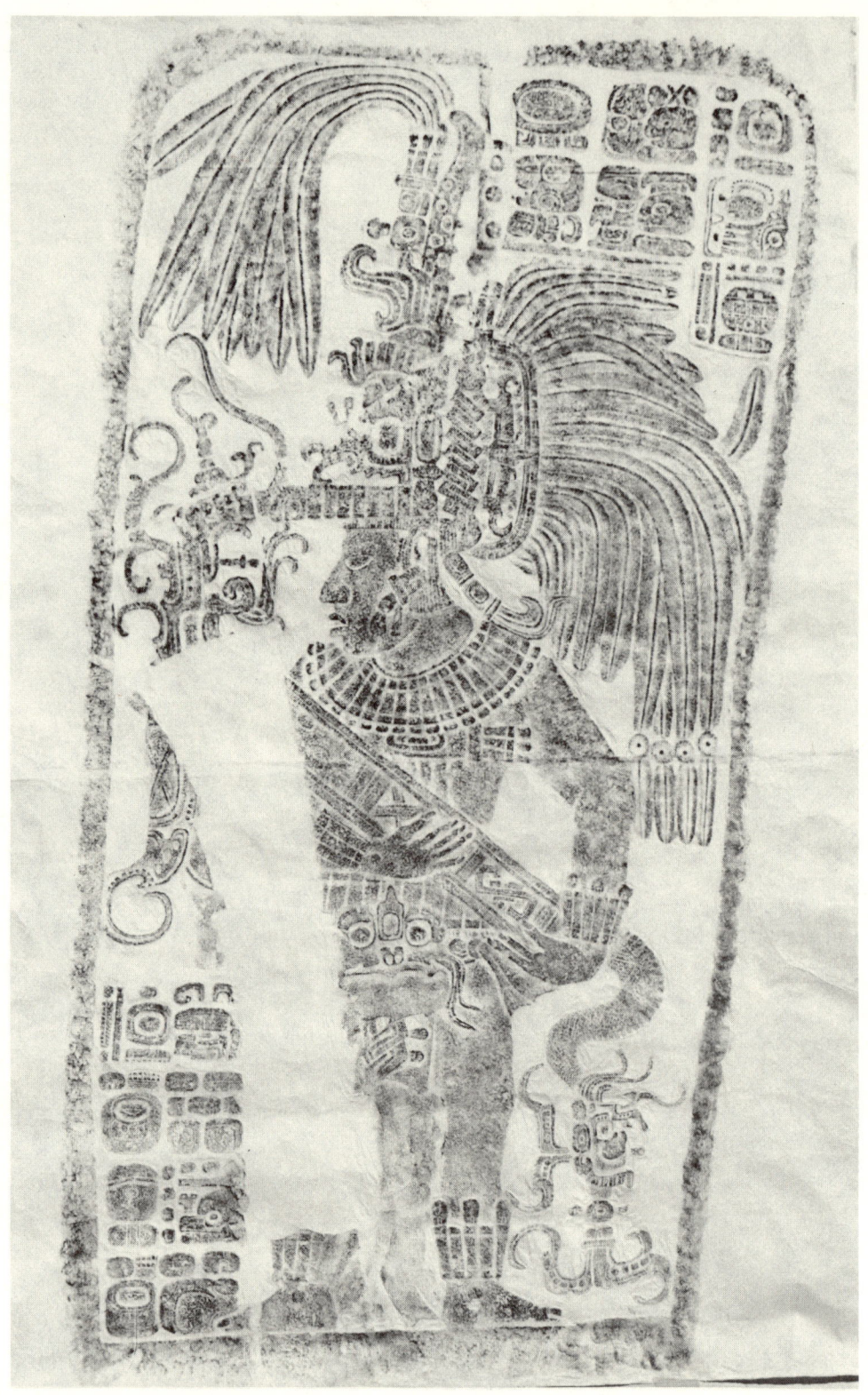

Figure 5.8. Seibal Stela 9, west. (Courtesy of Peabody Museum, Harvard University).

signifies his death by heart sacrifice.[18] He also wears at wrists and anklets the sets of three knotted bands that connote sacrifice (Joralemon 1974) while in his right paw he holds up the decapitated head of the lineage deity "God K"; this may symbolize the royal lineage at Seibal that was interrupted by this ruler's death.

The man on Stela 8 may be Jaguar Paw, the Seibal ruler who was captured and sacrificed by the ruler of Dos Pilas at 9.15.4.6.11 2 Chuen 4 Pax, after which Dos Pilas and the nearby site of Aguateca ruled the region for about three katuns. This man's personal insignia included the diagonal bar with a God C finial and a "shell wing dragon" on top that are also worn by the man on Stela 11 who was probably his matrilineal descendant. It is interesting to note the final glyph in the inscription of the southern Stela 8 (Figure 5.9). It is a cross; this is emblematic of the form of Structure A-3, as well as of cyclic completion (Figure 5.4), and of the ritual circuit that would have been completed on the south side of the temple, at this stela.

On the west side of Structure A-3 the ruler on Stela 9 has a Maya profile like the Jaguar Paw ruler on the south (Figure 5.8). Because of the western position, and the differentiated bicephalic sky bar like the one carried by the man on the north, I judge this to be the third posthumous portrait of a previous ruler. Like Jaguar Paw this man wears the *xoc* monster head (here as an apron) that is ordinarily worn by women; these two men may represent the original ruling dynasty of Seibal and the legitimizing maternal lineage into which the rulers on Stelae 10 and 11 married. However, the bicephalic bar is just like the one carried by the man on the north, and he also seems to be described as the son of the man on the north in the inscription (second and third glyphs last row, above). It is possible that this dead man on the west was the brother of the living ruler on the east. If the "Toltec" man on the north (Stela 10, Figure 5.7) is father of the Mayoid man on the west who declares his kinship, as well as father of the "Toltec" man on the east who he resembles, then his role again would have been parallel to the Toltec *Yax K'an* at Tikal, since *Ah Bolon Tun* had probably also married into the local Jaguar lineage.

The fifth monument, Stela 21 (Figure 5.10), was erected in the center of the central room at the top of the cruciform Structure A-3. This ruler holds a manikin scepter and his east-facing portrait would have been visible above and beyond that of the current Seibal ruler on Stela 11. He might be the same man as the current ruler, but he resembles the sharp-nosed ball player on the earlier Seibal Stelae 5 and 7 (Willey et al. 1975: fig. 29), and he is likely a lineal ancestor because of the higher position of his portrait. In any case the two east-facing stelae (Figures 5.6 and 5.10) together display the combined motif that is found in the portrait of Stormy Sky on Stela 31 at Tikal. There the manikin scepter is represented above in Stormy Sky's headdress (Figure 5.4), while here it is carried by the figure who is above on the raised stela at the center of Structure A-3. At Tikal the scattering act is performed symbolically by Stormy Sky, who holds up the *k'an* discs, while scattering is carried out more literally by the Seibal ruler on Stela 11, at the lower level. The man above, on Seibal Stela 21, may thus correspond to the ancestor in the sky above Stormy Sky and also to the sky figure above the ruler who makes the scattering gesture on Tikal Stela 22, in the twin pyramid group constructed for the completion of the katun 9.17.0.0.0.

The Baktun and the Seibal Emblem Glyph

The "scattering" ritual is implicit in the water group prefix of all emblem glyphs—and as with the Tikal emblem glyph the name of Seibal in its emblem signifies the role of the site as a cyclic completion center (Figure 5.3b). At Tikal, katun completion was celebrated from 8.18.0.0.0, whereas Seibal calendric ritual was apparently focused on the completion of Baktun Nine, or 10.0.0.0.0., although 8.19.0.0.0 (just before 9.0.0.0.0) was recorded on the Late Classic hieroglyphic stairway at Seibal (Mathews 1985: table 2). The Seibal emblem glyph reflects this site's specialization since it consists of three *k'u* elements like the two that comprise the baktun glyph and signify *k'uk'*, or cycle (Figure 5.2b). With three of these *k'u* elements the emblem glyph of Seibal might be read as *k'uk'uk'(u)*, meaning godly or divine cycle. This reading is probably phonetically reinforced by the leaves at either side of the emblem glyph that might be read as *k'uk'*, sprout or shoot. Thus in its emblem glyph Seibal always referred specifically to a baktun that was to end at Seibal, and to the new one that was to be born there.

Figure 5.9. Seibal Stela 8, south. (Courtesy of Peabody Museum, Harvard University).

Figure 5.10. Seibel Stela 21, center. (Courtesy of Peabody Museum, Harvard University).

Conclusions

Tikal and Seibal, each with an emblem glyph with calendric significance, followed parallel historical patterns as they approached the end of a baktun, 400 tuns apart, just as the Maya who believed in the cyclic nature of history would have expected. Both places experienced Toltec intrusion and intermarriage and the loss of a local ruler named Jaguar Paw. Both avoided erecting stone monuments at the completion of the new baktun, although soon after, both erected monuments that displayed *K'uk'ulkan* heraldry and Venus dates and recorded aspects of the recent history of the site, particularly concerning predecessors. And at both sites the rulers who inaugurated the new baktun emphasized local Maya and Toltec ancestry, while employing the combined symbolism of the manikin scepter (God K) and "scattering," which together linked the ruler with the divine ancestor in the sky. These similarities between Tikal and Seibal cannot be either coincidental or universal traits. The parallels were deliberately constructed, whether before or after the fact. The Maya of Tikal and Seibal were following the same prophecy, the same divine script that shaped human events and was designed to protect the Maya from the terrible hazards of the unforeseen.

Notes

1. These Early Classic men were dressed as Teotihuacan warriors, and they apparently gained temporary political control in several parts of Maya territory (Kaminaljuyu, Uaxactun, Tikal, Tres Islas), but it is important to note that there is no evidence of large-scale military conquest at any of these sites; while at Copan with the contemporary installation of a Teotihuacan affiliated ruler, there is no apparent warrior component (Coggins 1988a).

2. The orthography used is that of the Cordemex Dictionary (Barrera Vasquez, ed., 1980) because I postulate that Yucatec Mayan was spoken at Tikal and that the hieroglyphic inscriptions were legible in that language.

3. Although the Bishop de Landa read this as *ku* (See Fox and Justeson 1984; 48;), J.E.S. Thompson argues Landa did not always recognize glottalized consonants and that the inscriptional context of the Cauac glyph indicates it had godly or divine connotations and could be read phonetically as *k'u* (1970).

4. In Yucatec Mayan *K'uk'* may mean Maya patronymic, quetzal (bird), shoot or sprout, renewal, descent, or elbow.

5. David Kelley (1976: 175) and Victoria Bricker (1985) read the "double Cauac" as *kuk*, cycle, while David Stuart suggests it is read *yi* (1987: 11–13). As part of his argument Stuart shows that the baktun bird head (a substitute for the "double Cauac"), also substitutes for the "Smoke Squirrel" name at Copan. However, this substitution corroborates the *kuk* reading, since squirrel is *ku'uk* in Yucatecan. However, I argue that the "double Cauac" and the baktun bird may be read as both *k'uk'* (as a kind of pun), referring both to the baktun cycle, and to the mythical bird. *K'uk'*, in its various loosely homonymous forms, is the basis for many Maya *K'uk'ulkan* (or Quetzalcoatl) titles. Another example is the name of the Late Classic ruler of Quirigua "Cauac Sky" whose name was actually *Kuk'ka'an* (as noted below in the text). Stephen Houston has remarked on another such *K'uk'ka'an* name on a vessel excavated at Uaxactun (1984: 799–800), while another name he publishes but does not read is a "Two-legged Sky" name at Altun Ha, which, like the formally analogous "Cauac Sky" at Quirigua, may also be read *K'uk'ka'an*.

6. The baktun completion at 9.0.0.0.0 is recorded on El Zapote Stela 5, but this monument is unusual in that on one side it portrays a woman who is apparently involved in the correlation of a Maya date with a non-Maya one (Coggins 1984: fig. 8). An allusion to baktun completion at 10.0.0.0.0 is made on Machaquila Stela 7 but the monument is not dedicated to it (Graham 1967: fig. 57); there is, however, one known initial series 10.0.0.0.0, found on Stela 8 at Xultun (Von Euw 1978).

7. If Teotihuacan was the original Tula then Teotihuacanos who emigrated and intermarried with other cultural groups, at any period of the Central highland city's history, would have introduced "Toltec" blood into those lineages. If this was considered desirable, as the Aztec clearly thought, then the Maya or others with such ancestry might describe themselves as "Toltec" indefinitely.

8. The name of Tikal (*Tik'al*), which was probably used only after the completion of Baktun Eight, means "at the place of the count of twenty," since *ti* means at, and *k'al* means count of twenty. The most common Tikal emblem glyph depicts the burden, or *kuch*, of time (Figure 5.3a) that was set down symbolically at Tikal at the end of each period of twenty tuns, or of each katun (Coggins 1987b). While the emblem glyph actually depicts the *kuch*, or burden of the *K'atun*, it is read *k'al*, count of twenty, in all of its stela variations. This reading is determined by the knot prefix (T60) which is read *k'a*, from *k'ax*, to tie.

9. On Stela 31 this name glyph consists of *yax* and

knot prefixes to a serpent head (Figure 5.1a 13-J3 T60:16 844, N2 T16:60:844; Figure 5.1b: F6 T16:60:844). As with the *k'al* of the Tikal emblem glyph this knot (T60) is read *k'a* (from *k'ax* to tie or knot), and acts as a phonetic determinative in this personal name that is read *Yax K'an* (See Coggins 1989 for other glyphic occurrences of this *K'a*). *K'an* is a pun with *kan*, serpent, and *Ka'an*, sky. The month Yax has Venus as patron, thus endowing the word with Venus connotations.

10. Linda Schele has also identified this name glyph with Quetzalcoatl (n.d.).

11. Such uniforms are shown at Teotihuacan, Becan, Xochicalco, Piedras Negras, Chichen Itzá and Tula (see Kubler 1972 for a different interpretation).

12. Until recent excavations in the Mundo Perdido and 6C-XVI groups (Laporte and Fialko, this volume, for bibliography), evidence for Teotihuacan presence at Tikal has rested on a cluster of Early Classic burials, caches, "problematical deposits," and two stelae (see W. R. Coe 1972; Coggins 1975); now all of this excavated material must be taken into consideration in any reevaluation of the nature of this puzzling foreign manifestation.

13. Peter Mathews has read the name "Smoking Frog" on stelae at Uaxactun and Tikal in association with "Curl Nose" (*Yax K'an*) and a date common to both sites (1985: 44). He concludes Smoking Frog was ruler of Uaxactun, and that Uaxactun dominated Tikal at this time. I believe, however, that this name, which has the same main sign as the birth glyph (T740), was actually "Smoking Toad," and denoted the daughter of Jaguar Paw, wife of "Curl Nose" (*Yax K'an*) and mother of Stormy Sky (*K'uk'ka'an*), who had married "Curl Nose" while he was briefly ruler of Uaxactun (portrayed on Stela 5) and before he took over at Tikal. The date that is repeated at Uaxactun (Stela 5) and at Tikal (Stela 31 and Ball Court Marker (Laporte and Fialko, this volume)) probably records the marriage of the Tikal princess "Smoking Toad" and the Toltec officer "Curl Nose," whereas the *Ma'kuch* title that Laporte and Fialko view as dynastic (this volume) may refer to "Smoking Toad" as someone who was "not, or was almost (*ma'*) Governor (*kuch*)" (Coggins 1987b: note 10).

14. One Ahau is a name of Venus as Morning Star and one and seven Ahau when associated (as in the highland Quiche *Popol Vuh*) denote Venus, while they also refer to the completed 260-day divinatory cycle (Tedlock in press). Seven Ahau may thus denote Venus as Evening Star, and also cyclic completion. Anthony Aveni (1990) has also shown that the 260-day ritual calendar itself may reflect the mean interval of appearance of either of the Morning or Evening Star phases of the Venus cycle.

15. In inscriptions the *K'an* cross prefix (T36) is interchangeable (both homonymous and synonymous) with a shell (T38, Figure 5.3), and sometimes with a perforated disc (as on Copan Stela A:G6); all three may be read *k'an*.

16. A Tikal emblem glyph on the face of Stela 39 from the Mundo Perdido group (Laporte and Fialko, this volume) may have an early form of the "water group" prefix.

17. Victoria Bricker (1985) has suggested that the Gods (specifically G1, G2, and G3 at Palenque) celebrated baktuns that were 21 rather than 20 katuns long, or 1/20th longer than those of mortals. The Seibal stelae at Str. A-3, dedicated at 10.1.0.0.0, might be understood as commemorating such a 21 katun "great baktun" since 9.0.0.0.0.

18. This hole in the solar plexus of the figure on Stela 8, suggestive of heart sacrifice, is probably where a ball of chert was embedded in the limestone at the time of the carving and later removed. It was, no doubt, significant to the Maya that sacrificial knives were made from such chert.

Six

The Revolution in Ancient Maya Subsistence

By Peter D. Harrison[1]

Ancient Populations and Food Supply: the Problem

The portion of the geographic zone occupied by the ancient Maya civilization known as the "lowlands" comprises an area measuring approximately 70,000 square miles, or 182,000 square kilometers. This area is roughly equal to the size of the state of Oklahoma. Within this area, many primary centers are known to exist, perhaps in excess of one hundred. These major sites are distinguished by their size and surviving monumental architecture. Such sites are scattered from northern Yucatán to eastern Chiapas and southwards through the Petén in Guatemala to northern Honduras. A variety of studies conducted from the 1960s to the present have shown that the monumental cores of these major settlements represent a small fraction of the settlement that surrounded them during the peak periods of population (Puleston 1983; Kurjack 1978; Sabloff 1986; Folan et al. 1983). These studies draw a sharp contrast between the restricted zone of the ceremonial centers seen by the tourist, and the actual terrain surrounding those centers, occupied in Classic times. The image that emerges is one of large populations diminishing in density concentrically from the center (*see* Ford 1986), combined with smaller, dense satellite sites.

Attempts at estimation of the peak populations for such major settlements have exhibited an upward curve over the decades in response to new ideas concerning the range of food-getting techniques exploited by the Maya. For example, the earliest estimates for the population of Tikal were in the range of 10,000 (W. Coe 1967), while the updated revision of this estimate quickly reached 100,000 (Haviland 1969). The foremost factor leading to conservative population estimates has been the assumption that milpa agriculture, with its demonstrably limited carrying capacity (77 persons per sq. km), provided the primary food source. As mapping and survey work gradually revealed the true density and extent of architectural remains, the assumption of limited populations became ever more unrealistic. The problem, therefore, was one of disagreement between the expanding results of concrete survey data and the assumptions about food production (Sanders 1972).

Students of demography in the Maya Lowlands tried to explain this discrepancy in terms of ever-increasing sizes of the sustaining areas that were utilized around the site center, on the grounds that larger populations could still be supported by swidden agriculture if enough of the "empty" terrain between major centers had been used for this purpose. However, there is only so much arable land in the lowlands, and over the years more and more "large" sites have been discovered to exist, or recognized as more significant than previously thought. For example, the site of El Zotz west of Tikal was only discovered in the late 1970s; its presence decreases the amount of "empty" terrain surrounding Tikal that theoretically would have been available for milpa agriculture. Also, the sites of Rio Azul and El Peru, both of the Petén, have been found upon investigation to be much larger than perceived. The notion that all sites of this magnitude are still not known, even today, has had to be accepted. This recognition meant that even when considering only the major sites, the amount of terrain available for milpa agriculture was shrinking in the face of discovery of more and more such large sites.

Other surveys in the lowlands turned their attention toward the zones that lie between major sites (Puleston 1974; Ashmore 1981; Ford 1986). The most current orthodoxy recognizes that the regions between major sites are occupied by secondary and tertiary ceremonial centers, each with their own surrounding settlements and many hundreds of smaller hamlets. Only a small portion of the well-drained ground in the lowlands is totally unoccupied. Bullard was the first to report on this condition of continuous settlement as early as 1960, but more recent studies have verified his observation outside the Petén. A large portion of the 182,000 sq. km remains unexplored by organized study, but enough surveys have been accomplished to suggest that this nearly continuous settlement is the rule rather than the exception.

As the degree of the imbalance between the obvious size of Classic period population and the low capability of support available from milpa agriculture became clearer, other explanations of food sources were sought, all bearing their own validity. These explanations were a response to recognition of a problem within the economic model in which milpa agriculture, supplemented by hunting and gathering, was credited with support of the entire population of the Classic Maya. This model greatly oversimplified an environment that offered many other resources and possibilities. By now these explanations are well known. They include the exploitation of marine foods (Lange 1971), root crops (Bronson 1966), *ramon* cropping (Puleston 1968), and low levels of intensification, such as fertilization and cultivation in the swamps (Sanders 1972).

While these explanations recognized that the economy was indeed more complex than previously conceived, they still fell short of accommodating the extraordinarily high populations indicated by intensive settlement studies. Thus, well into the 1970s the large size of perceived populations could not be reconciled with a low-yield economic model. That this problem continued to plague understanding of Maya demography was demonstrated by new population estimates that were forced sharply upward in light of the settlement data, but without an accompanying explanation of the supportive economy. While the extensive milpa system was capable of supporting only 77 individuals per sq. km (Cowgill 1962), population estimates for large portions of the Lowlands ranged between 100 and 700 individuals per sq. km (Rice and Puleston 1981), at least for the core zones of the major sites.

The Bajo Zone

Settlement can only occur on high ground that is permanently dry. A significant portion of the lowlands does not fit this description, but is seasonally or permanently inundated. These geographic features are the bajos (*akalche* in Yucatec Maya; *swamp* in English). Bajos are shallow karstic basins with a suite of ecologic characteristics. The areal distribution of bajos was defined by Miranda (1959) within specific geographic limits: bajos extend from the northern Yucatan peninsula throughout the Petén in Guatemala. A few portions of the lowlands lie outside the zone of bajo distribution, specifically, the northern and east coastal littorals of the peninsula and, of course, the southern mountainous regions. Informal and undocumented estimates of the proportion of land occupied by bajos have been made (Sanders, personnal communication 1984). Roughly one-third of the terrain in the Mexican portion of the bajo zone is seasonally inundated, and almost one-half of the Petén zone is comprised of bajos. Given these admittedly rough estimates, it is perhaps not surprising that all major sites are located on or close to the borders of bajos. On the surface, this choice of settlement location for major sites does not appear logical given the relatively hostile ecological characteristics of the bajos.

My personal observations in southern Quintana Roo indicate that the geological basins collectively referred to as bajos include a broad range of hydrological activity. Many retain water year-round and of these some are overgrown with sedge grasses such that, to the naked eye, they appear dry. Others exhibit a border of sedges with open water at the center in the manner of a shallow lake. However, the most commonly known hydrological state is one of seasonal inundation. Often a seasonally flowing river drainage passes through the low points of the basin. The Bajo Santa Fe in the Petén and the Bajo Morocoy in southern Quintana Roo both exhibit this feature.

Maya Use of Bajos: A Brief History

Elsewhere, I have reviewed the history of archaeological interpretation of ancient use of bajos (1977), but a brief recapitulation is in order here. In 1931 Cooke first suggested that the bajos had been permanently wet, shallow lakes in Classic times, and that a millennium of milpa agriculture had led to their gradual siltation and to permanent alteration of the hydrological regime. There is growing evidence today to support this position. Ricketson and Ricketson (1937) added the notion that bajos may have been used by the Maya for intensive forms of agriculture, but did not elaborate on the forms which such agriculture might have displayed. In 1957 Palerm and Wolf introduced the idea that the form of intensive agriculture in bajos might have been analogous to *chinampa* agriculture as known from the Mexican Highlands. Sanders (1972) reversed this opinion, holding that the physical characteristics, specifically the hydrological regime, had remained unchanged since Classic times. In 1974 Turner reported on his aerial observations of vegetational patterns in the Bajo Morocoy (southern Quintana Roo) and revived the analogy of raised field (modified chinampa) agriculture in bajos. Independently, this author observed the same patterns at the same time in the same bajo. Subsequent collaboration between Turner and myself resulted in publication of *Prehispanic Maya Agriculture* (Harrison and Turner 1978) in which the presence of intensive agriculture in bajos was strongly supported by several different lines of evidence. Up to this point there had been no ground proof for this interpretation.

The importance of bajo use derives from several factors. Milpa agriculture is highly limited in its food production. Thus, models of Maya agriculture relying solely on milpa techniques are plagued by the imbalance between a low long-term yield on the one hand, and the growing knowledge of settlement density in the lowlands on the other. By contrast, intensive agriculture as exemplified in use of raised fields is not as subject to fluctuations in rainfall and is capable of a much higher food yield. A minimum of two crops per year is possible and the area of land use is restricted, converting otherwise unusable land into a zone of production more efficacious than upland milpa. As an explanation for the correction of the imbalance, it was very attractive, if proven factual.

By 1978 a specific group of questions had coalesced and remained unanswered. Were bajos indeed used by the Maya for agriculture? Has the hydrological regime altered since Classic times, or not? Do all of the karstic basins which lie within Miranda's Bajo Zone exhibit similar features, and hence offer the same possibilities for intensive exploitation? How extensive within the Bajo Zone was this exploitation? What effect would use of the bajos for food production have had upon political organization?

Unlike the milpa system, raised field agriculture requires a high manpower input, not just for initial construction but for maintenance and crop care as well. A society investing in such a system could have a quite different configuration from one that relied solely on the family-oriented milpa system. At the lowest level of exploitation and effectiveness, the use of bajos for intensive agriculture could mean that a few localized communities removed themselves from the uncertainties and restrictions of the milpa system by producing more food than they could consume. At the highest level, it is only possible to imagine the effects wrought upon the society. If some or all of the largest bajos were exploited from edge to edge, a high degree of central organization would be required to maintain the work force that would be permanently deployed in the fields. At this level the limit to the size of population that could have inhabited the lowlands would be extraordinarily high. In the absence of precise figures for areas and methods utilized, speculation on upper limits of population is not helpful, other than to say that there would be no problems of accommodation for the density of settlement that has been abundantly recorded.

The Program of Investigation

In 1979, Turner and I gained funding to conduct an investigation to address some of these questions. The original intent was to investigate the Bajo Morocoy in Quintana Roo because this bajo exhibited 246 sq. km of vegetational patterning that was visible in aerial photographs.[2] As the largest area of such patterning yet observed, the location would have been ideal. However, insurmount-

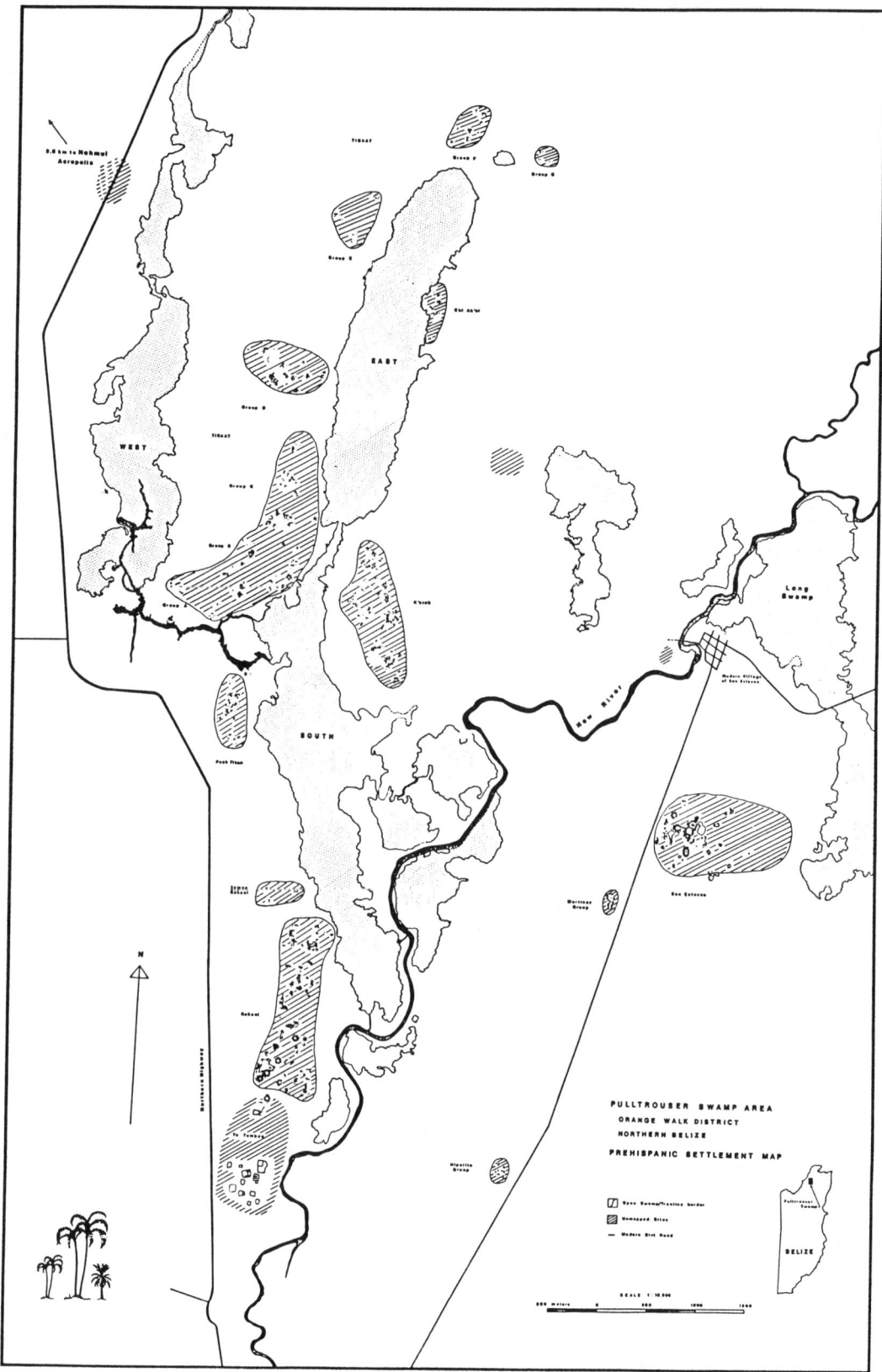

Map 6.1. Prehispanic Settlement, Pulltrouser Swamp Area, Orange Walk District, Northern Belize.

able bureaucratic complications resulted in a shifting of the investigation out of Mexico. A comparable example of visual patterning in a bajo was sought in the adjacent country of Belize. Pulltrouser Swamp in Orange Walk district lay a mere 60 km from Bajo Morocoy and, although smaller in size, the patterns visible within the bajo were even more clearly delineated than those in Morocoy.

The results of the first season of investigations have been reported in the volume *Pulltrouser Swamp, Ancient Maya Habitat, Agriculture, and Settlement in Northern Belize* (Turner and Harrison 1983). These results provided answers to some of the questions posed above, but also raised new questions. Pulltrouser Swamp is a type of bajo with which we were not previously familiar. It is comprised of three oblong, interconnected basins; the southernmost basin is contiguous with, and at least seasonally connected to, the New River (Map 6.1). Only the western arm goes completely dry, the water levels in the eastern and southern arms rise and fall in accordance with the fluctuations of the nearby New River. The visual patterns were located on the ground and tested. They were found to be artificial in construction. Two types of raised fields were identified during the first season: channelized raised fields that were only partly artificial, located along the borders of the bajo, and artificial island fields completely detached from the shoreline. Ceramic and lithic artifacts were found in the artificial fill (see Turner 1983 for a full description) as well as on the surface. The abundance of bifacial ovates found both in the fields themselves and in nearby settlements has been persuasively argued to have been associated with agricultural practices (Shafer 1983; McAnany 1986). The settlement of Kokeal, a small ceremonial and residential center adjacent to the border of the south arm, was investigated. I have estimated that it supported a population during the Classic period of approximately 350 individuals (1983). The characteristics of architecture and artifactual yield suggest a rural group of considerable wealth whose occupants nevertheless did not construct nonperishable walled or vaulted architecture, even though these features are present at nearby larger ceremonial centers (e.g., San Estevan to the east and Nohmul to the northwest).

Thus far, it was established that the visual patterns seen from aerial photos did indeed represent raised fields of human construction and of agricultural use associated with a small population with "unusual" characteristics. The analysis of recovered macrofossils established that corn (*zea mays*), chaya (*Cnidoscolus*), and beans (*Phaseolus* spp.) were present both in the raised fields and at the settlement of Kokeal. The possible presence of cotton (*Gossypium* spp.) pollen and a fragment of cacao wood (*Theobroma*) are tantalizing because of the implication of commercial crops comingled with food sources, but their specific identification remains problematic (Miksicek 1983).

At the termination of the first season, knowledge of the extent of associated settlement with the bajo complex was incomplete, and further investigation of both the extent and variety of raised fields was needed in order to interpret the relationships between ancient settlements and bajo uses.

Objectives of the second season were multifaceted and included (1) expanded investigation of raised fields through mapping and excavation; (2) definition of the variety of field types; (3) dating of both the fields and adjacent settlement; (4) mapping the entire associated settlement and test excavations in both random and non-random programs; (5) estimation of the total population size in direct association with the bajo complex; and finally, (6) estimation of the total production that the raised fields could yield.

Field work was carried through two programs of research: the ecological program and the settlement program. The ecological program surveyed the modern botanical regime and analyzed ancient pollen. It recovered and analyzed microfossils from archaeological contexts, surveyed fresh water and land snails, both ancient and modern, and examined water patterns within the swamp and soil patterns in the adjacent region. Excavation of raised fields also fell within the ecological program.

The settlement program surveyed the entire boundary of the swamp complex, mapping all structures. It test-excavated ten percent of these structures randomly, and conducted strip excavations of two residential buildings for functional analysis. The program engaged in a test study for nonmounded and buried structures (i.e., structures having no visible vertical dimension).

Modern Land Use

Due to the long history of occupation in the Pulltrouser Swamp region there is no remaining virgin forest. The bulk of terrain in northern Belize was being used to grow sugar cane at the time of this investigation. The western boundaries of both the western and southern arms of the swamp were planted in sugar cane, except for a small amount of pasture land in the north. The "peninsula" formed by the eastern and western arms was also used as pasture. The eastern boundary has undergone a lengthy period of nonexploitation and supports a high secondary growth, with rented portions used for milpa agriculture. This eastern side is also characterized by a high sandy ridge which lies between Pulltrouser Swamp and the New River and forms a higher swamp-upland embankment than is found on the western boundary.

Ecological Program

It is not within the scope of this study to report extensively on these results before their formal publication. However, for the sake of the argument presented here, some comments are appropriate.

The high, sandy ridge between the swamp complex and the New River provides a micro-niche that is distinctive from the swamp boundaries elsewhere. The interface of high ground with swamp edge is more vertically pronounced in this area than elsewhere in the swamp complex. The ridge is most pronounced near the north end of Pulltrouser South, on its eastern side, adjacent to the site of K'axob (Map 6.1). This zone of high embankment produced yet another type of raised field not discovered during the first season. This third type was produced by digging a canal through the natural terrain of the swamp boundary, thus creating an island of natural ground. To this a horizontal, artificial addition was made. This method of producing a raised island field, which is part natural and part artificial, was not found at other locations investigated around the swamp. In other respects, this third form of raised field exhibits similar characteristics: surface artifacts, particularly on the side slopes, and artifactual content in the fill of the artificial portion. Channelized fields and wholly artificial fields of the types known from the earlier season were also located in the same region, but all types of field are larger in scale here than elsewhere around the swamp.

Along the western boundary of the eastern arm of the swamp (Map 6.1) it was established that artificial islands were constructed in rows outward from the swamp littoral for up to six ranks. It was not feasible to conduct an underwater program to determine if other ranks of islands exist farther out from the shore in deeper water. Such islands could be eroded and now inundated. However, it is not established whether raised fields once extended to the center of the swamp where the water is deepest. In certain locales, where the arms of the swamp complex meet and narrow to riverine proportions, raised fields do fill the shallow waters from swamp edge to swamp edge.

An earth drill providing a broad core (width: 6–7 cm) was used to test sedimentation below several of the raised fields. The maximum drill length available was two meters. Cores extracted in this program showed fine layers of sedimentation to the limits of the drill's capability. The bottom of such sedimentary layers was not reached. These deep sedimentation cores were extracted through raised fields close to the well marked drop-off at the edge of the swamp. During the dry season, the ancient canals separating such fields from the upland shore have dried up, although the center of the swamp here remained inundated to an unknown depth. Therefore, the portion of the swamp edge which now supports raised fields is underlain by more than two meters of sedimentation, while at the same time standing water is retained throughout the year in the center of the swamp basins.[3] The clear implication is that the basins of Pulltrouser Swamp were interconnected deepwater lakes in pre-Maya times. Only when these lakes had sedimentated to a viable level was it possible to build raised fields atop the sediments in shallow water. The slope of the sedimentary base may have determined the distance from shore that was usable for raised field construction. In addition to the implications for the long-term hydrology of the swamp basin, the cores extracted are being analyzed for pollen content and concomitant changes through time. At the moment no geological or biologically based dating can be provided for the rate of this process, excepting that the raised fields were constructed on top of the deep sedimentation levels. It is hoped that eventually pollen analyses may allow a rough dating in the form of a *terminus post quem* for raised field construction. New questions are raised by this research program. For example, what effect did the fluctuating water level of the New River, and hence of the connected swamp levels, have upon the agricultural fields in the swamp complex? Did the Maya control these fluctuation levels within the swamp by means of check dams at the connecting points? These questions remain unanswered.

Dating of the fields remains problematic largely due to the lack of sealed lots by the very nature of the constructs. Nearly 80 percent of all excavated lots contained Preclassic ceramics, but since they were unsealed these could well have been transported from elsewhere as part of the construction fill. Surface ceramics date largely to the Late Classic, particularly on the side slopes. These are interpreted as depositions contemporary with usage, but this interpretation does not preclude an earlier date for original construction of some of the fields. That at least some fields date to the Late Preclassic is supported by a C14 date of A.D. 150 ± 150 from the fill of a field at site 2, if indeed this dated material was not re-deposited, a perpetual hazard in artificial construction. Further support for a Late Preclassic origin of raised fields is found in the abundant presence of Cocas Chicanel ceramics (400 B.C. to A.D. 250) within the artificial fill of the fields. Again, these deposits may or may not be contemporaneous. Nodes of water lilies retrieved in excavation from artificial fill indicate that the hydrological regime at the time of construction was not unlike that which exists today.

Water levels in parts of the swamp fluctuate with the levels of the New River. This fluctuation leaves many fields dry during the low water season. As described above, the sedimentation process in Pulltrouser Swamp has been demonstrated through the earth cores. Fields could not be constructed until such time when the sedimentation provided shallow off-shore waters. This timing clearly occurred during Maya occupation of the uplands. However, the sedimentation process not only did not stop at the time of Maya use of bajo waters, but rather, the use of adjacent uplands for milpa agriculture would surely have accelerated the rate of run-off and hence of sedimentation. Also, the sedimentation process has continued since the area was abandoned by the ancient Maya. As a result, the cycle of flooding and drying of artificial canals witnessed today is not likely to coincide with either the conditions with which the Maya began use of the swamp, nor the conditions under which they were abandoned. Since run-off and sedimentation are not reversible, the depth of the swamp basin and of the artificial canals can only have decreased over the years. Many canals, visible by contour today, remain dry throughout the year. Excavation revealed that the water table in such canals lies below the surface of present-day soil line but above the bottom of the ancient canal, thus demonstrating the principle of continued sedimentation.

In all, eight separate locations of raised fields were tested and partially mapped. Once the man-made or man-modified character of the fields had been established it was possible to use the aerial photographs to estimate the total surface area available for agricultural purposes within the three arms of the complex.

The inundated swamp area covers approximately 8.5 sq. km. The combined surfaces of distinct and indistinct surface patterns, as interpreted from aerial photographs, totals 668 ha. (Turner and Harrison 1981). Turner (Turner and Harrison 1983: 261) has calculated that this amount of garden surface is sufficient to feed 3500 individuals with a single crop, or 5200 individuals with a double crop. In studies of productivity of wet raised field intensive agriculture elsewhere, this system has been demonstrated to be used for multiple cropping (Sanders 1976). Therefore, an assumption of double cropping at the Pulltrouser swamp complex remains conservative.

Settlement Program

When the survey and mapping program was completed the overall pattern of settlement appeared dispersed. It is possible, however, to distinguish groupings or hamlet-like communities separated by apparently open space. There are two seminucleated communities with probable ceremonial structures reaching a present height no greater than 13 m. These two communities, Kokeal and K'axob, are linear. Kokeal, on the west bank of Pulltrouser South follows an embankment of high ground along the swamp edge, and has a ceremonial center located at the southern boundary of the site. Its earliest known construction dates to Cocos Chicanel (Late Preclassic). The site expanded toward the north in the Late Classic period; during this later expansion platforms were constructed adjacent to a major cluster of raised fields. It is from this northern portion of Kokeal that the late Preclassic date for a raised field was recovered. K'axob is located on the east side of Pulltrouser South, close to its confluence with Pulltrouser East and adjacent to a large cluster of elevated raised fields described above as the locus of the third field type. The site occupies the crest of the high sandy ridge also described above and, like Kokeal, its ceremonial complex is located near the southern boundary of occupation. The largest architecture associated with the swamp was documented at this site, as well as the longest time span. Deep excavation in the platform of "B Group" recovered sealed strata containing ceramics of Swasey phase probably compatible with the Bladen complex defined at Colha (Kosakowski 1987b). A C14 date of 1228 B.C. ± 150 (Beta–5324) from the same stratum agrees with the ceramic identification. This sample calibrates to 1680 (1512) 1321 B.C. (See Andrews V, this volume).[4] Site occupation continued through the normal sequent phases up to a strong presence in the Terminal Classic, although continuous occupation through all time periods is not to be found at a single locus.

The site of Tibaat occupies an arc spreading from the base of the peninsula between the east and west arms northward along the west edge of Pulltrouser East. The settlement pattern is definitely dispersed with a group of possibly ceremonial structures occupying the highest ground close to the boundary of Pulltrouser East.

As well as the larger sites of Kokeal, K'axob and Tibaat, there are seven groupings of structures of varying size that might be classified as hamlets. Several have structures that could be ceremonial. In all, there are ten distinguishable communities included in our definition of the settlement of Pulltrouser Swamp with a total of over 400 mapped structures.

An important component of the settlement program included test excavations in "empty space" between platforms. A number of buried platforms showing no vertical surface dimension were discovered. These structures had crushed limestone floors edged with small stones and less well-defined floors outside the house platform. Such structures in modern ethnography have a variety of uses. This form of structure, with perishable pole and thatch walls and roofs, is used for residences, storage houses, and workshops in modern Belize. Discovery of the presence of this type of buried structure suggested that buildings serving as residences, and thus affecting the population, as well as special activity structures associated with the agricultural orientation of the settlements, might occur in large numbers. The lack of surface indication of these structures called for a special program of investigation. Over 500 test excavations, the locations of which were selected through both random and nonrandom techniques, uncovered five examples of this kind of structure in the adjacent high ground surrounding the swamp complex. It was concluded that the presence of these "invisible housemounds" was not a significant factor in calculating the populations of the zone, or in determining special function areas, at least not in this study area.

The chronological sequence for settlement of the swamp zone emerged from excavations in the structures that were carried out under two sampling programs: one random and the other selective. There was a small and scattered population during the Middle Preclassic, present on both sides of Pulltrouser South. Evidence of this occupation from sealed context is present only at the site of K'axob.[5] The population expanded during the Late Preclassic, with sealed lots recovered at both K'axob and Kokeal, but an extensive presence in unsealed lots emerged from five sites. Proto-Classic ceramics were recovered from a looted tomb and an off-platform midden, both in Group B at K'axob, a single locus for recovery of this rare assemblage. Expansion during the Early Classic is firmly documented, mainly at the site of Tibaat. The usual great expansion of population as documented throughout the Maya Lowlands, is represented both by the agricultural and ceramic record in the Late Classic. Terminal Classic occupation is strong, with ceramic materials recovered throughout the settlement zone and architectural construction evident at both K'axob and Tibaat for this period. Postclassic phases, both Early and Late, are sparsely represented, although presented. The scattered representation is more suggestive of passersby and campers rather than of a permanent settlement.

Throughout the communities of Pulltrouser Swamp certain architectural characteristics prevailed. The use of stone and mortar in construction of walls or vaulting was completely absent, even in the cases of temple platforms. For example, the main temple of Group A at K'axob reached a height of 13 m and yet there was no evidence that a stone structure was built at the summit. Ceremonial platforms of temple (pyramidal) configuration of 9 m high at Kokeal in the southeast sector, similarly were devoid of permanent architecture at the summit. House platforms designed to support multiple structures reached a height of over 2 m at K'axob and Tibaat, but supported only crude house platforms without wall foundations. These platforms were constructed of solid masonry using stone blocks, earth fill and mortar: traditional materials for elite construction in other parts of the lowlands. Ability to construct platforms by traditional techniques suggests access to some wealth. Construction of the superstructures with only perishable materials, therefore, must be interpreted as cultural choice, or appropriateness to function, rather than lack of wealth. Trade pieces including some greenstone adornments and Petén-style ceramics support the presence of this wealth. In other words, the population around Pulltrouser Swamp did not consist wholly of the peasant class. Many households were able to afford trade items and to elevate their house compounds on masonry platforms. Social stratification is therefore evident, but there is no evidence of an elite stratum as they are known from larger ceremonial centers.

A total peak population estimate was achieved by using the traditional 5.6 individuals per residence and deducting 10 percent each for non-contemporaneity and nonresidential function. The final population estimate for the swamp zone is roughly 1500 individuals for the peak of the Late Classic period.

Vicinity Settlement Matrix

There are eleven known sites in the "district" or vicinity of Pulltrouser Swamp that qualify by right of their size and architecture as minor or major ceremonial centers. These sites are outside the immediate zone of Pulltrouser Swamp and are not associated directly with the swamp. These sites are Buena Vista, Nohmul, San Luis, San Lorenzo, San Antonio (Albion Island), Yo Creek, San Lazaro, Cuello, Yo Tumben,[6] San Estevan, and Chawacol (Map 6.2). There exist several patterns of equidistant or near equidistant spacing between these sites. The subject of regularity of inter-site spacing has been commented upon by several authors (Hammond 1974; Marcus 1976a; Harrison 1981). On one hand, Marcus viewed the distribution of sites over the landscape in politico-economic terms. On the other hand, Hammond noted that while the general location of a site might be influenced by geographic and economic factors, the *specific* location seemed to have been determined by other factors. In this view, despite geographic and economic factors, there remained a degree of flexibility in the precise selection of site location, and this flexibility made available to the Maya some choice in satisfying other criteria. For whatever reasons, the maintenance of regularity of inter-site spacing appears to have been a result of this choice.

Thus far, the topic of settlement matrix and its features of near equidistant spacing, have not been examined in depth, nor has the nature of the factors that might cause such regularity to occur. Because the settlement matrix of the neighboring sites is in contrast with those settlements on the borders of the swamp, a brief discussion of these factors is in order here.

There appear to be a limited number of factors that might influence the initial selection of a particular locus for settlement. In the case of most sites, such selection would have occurred in the Preclassic period, while subsequent histories of site development served to determine the final expansion or areal development at any given site. It is the initial choice that is of concern here. Primary or *practical* motives should include economics, defense, and communication. Religion, however, is a non practical motive that may also have played a causative role in selecting specific site location. The economic motives would include proximity to good agricultural lands as perceived in the context of a variety of food-producing sources, for example, fertile land for milpa use and, later on, swamp land for intensive use. Access to transportation is another economic motive that can lead to choice of settlement on river, lake, sea, and even possibly swamp littoral locations. Defense motives would likely lead to choice of high

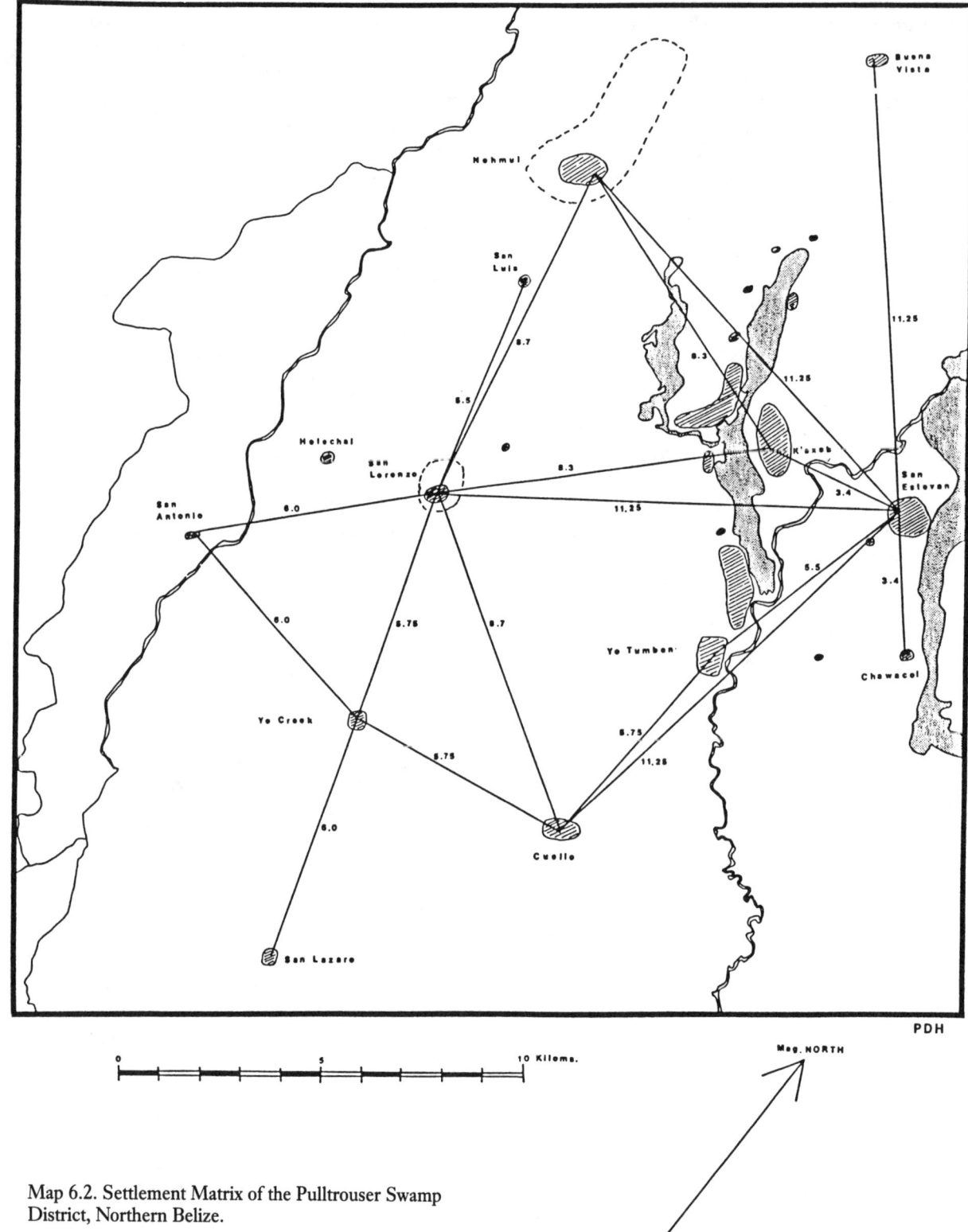

Map 6.2. Settlement Matrix of the Pulltrouser Swamp District, Northern Belize.

ground with long-distance views. Choice of elevated locations might not be exclusively governed by military considerations but could also be motivated by the ability to communicate with the nearest neighbors. Techniques of communication such as heliograph (sun reflection by mirror) are considerably more efficient from high ground. The two factors of economy and defense and their related factors of access to transportation and communication are all practical motives. Non-practical, or religious motivations are more difficult to define.

It is not argued here that a single motive normally determined the choice of location. Specific locales undoubtedly involved multiple considerations. In the vicinity of Pulltrouser Swamp, the north-south string of sites from Nohmul to San Lazaro occupy the crest of high ground between the New and Hondo rivers. It is relatively easy to speculate that the east-west location of each of these sites was determined by the crest location, serving economic, defensive and communication needs alike. However, the selection of the north-south spacing of these sites is less easily extrapolated. A major factor governing this latter choice could also be economic, in terms of trade and communication—the distance easily traveled on foot in one day, for example. If this were so, the sites should all be the same distance apart, and they are not. The spacing relationships are more complex than that. When one adds to the sample those ceremonial centers that do not lie on the crest of the ridge, patterning begins to emerge. This patterning contains a number of either exactly equidistant or nearly equidistant spaces that repeat themselves within this relatively small zone.

In an earlier publication (1981) I reported upon regularity of site spacing in Quintana Roo. Here a distance of 26 km appeared to be a spacing of "primary" significance, while a distance of 13 km related to "secondary" sites. From this I extrapolated a basal distance of 6.5 km for separation of smallest sites and proposed a model of site spacing based upon this lowest common denominator in a paper presented at the fiftieth annual meeting of the SAA (Denver 1985). In this latter paper I developed a concept of site spacing based upon Primary (26 km), Secondary (13 km), and Tertiary (6.5 km) site spacings. Here, this earlier concept of regularity of site spacing is refined.

In the Pulltrouser swamp "vicinity" some regularities of distance can be observed. It is proposed here that these regularities, while not exactly the same as those observed in earlier reportage for Quintana Roo, *are* analogous to those earlier observations and that from these new observations we can not only learn something significant about the site distribution in the Pulltrouser Swamp region, but also something about the generality of site spacing in the Maya Lowlands.

The relationships illustrated in Map 6.2 are a distillation of the analysis, showing only those relative distances that occur repeatedly. Distances occurring in a single instance between sites are not illustrated.

San Estevan is equidistant (11.2 km) to Buena Vista, Nohmul, San Lorenzo and Cuello.[7] This distance of 11.2 km is roughly the same as the 13 km distance discussed for southern Quintana Roo—a "secondary" distance (Harrison 1981). Further, San Lorenzo is nearly equidistant (5.5–6.0 km) from San Luis, San Antonio, and Yo Creek. This distance represents a tertiary relationship. The same tertiary relationship exists between Yo Creek and San Antonio, San Lazaro and Cuello, from which the same relationship exists between Yo Tumben and hence onward to San Estevan. These sites surround and are adjacent to Pulltrouser Swamp. The only site that is situated on Pulltrouser swamp and that seems to participate in this system of relationships in K'axob, which had an established population by the Middle Preclassic period. K'axob, in turn, is equidistant (8.3 km) to San Lorenzo and Nohmul. K'axob also has a separate spacial relationship (3.4 km) to San Estevan, shared with the site of Chawacol to the south. This smallest distance might be termed "quaternery."

At least two interpretations emerge from these observations of repeated distances. (1) Nohmul, the largest site in the vicinity, appears to participate in the local spatial arrangements in a secondary rank. In other words, Nohmul shares a distance with other smaller, sites in the neighborhood. The apparent explanation of this unexpected circumstance could be that as a primary site, the spatial distancing for Nohmul is of the primary order (26 ± km) with other surrounding *major* sites outside the immediate locale. This would account for the apparent secondary role in closer relationships. (2) Of all the swamp-associated settlements only K'axob, with a

Classic period ceremonial center and early beginnings, participates at all in the surrounding system of site spacing. Thus the majority of the swamp-associated settlements, excluding K'axob, do not participate in the settlement matrix of the vicinity. This observation further supports other lines of evidence that the inhabitants on the littorals of the swamp had a special function, a function that excludes them from the spatial matrix of the surrounding locale. A single factor determined the choice of swamp-edge settlement locus: the economic proximity of the swamp and its exploitation. This overriding factor causes them to be excluded from the observed neighborhood matrix of site spacing.

The classification of spacing derived herein from the Pulltrouser locale is the following:

Quaternary	3.4 kilometers
Tertiary	5.5–6.0 kilometers
Secondary	11.25 kilometers
Primary[8]	26 ± kilometers

The Secondary, Tertiary and Quarternary distances are the repeating distances illustrated in Map 6.2. Primary distance does not occur within this limited vicinity, but the site of Nohmul would be expected to be in Primary relationship with more distant sites.

Discussion

The population surrounding the swamp complex lived in close proximity to the raised fields. They were the builders and caretakers of these fields. A peak population of 1500 was producing a food yield capable of supporting 3500 with a single crop and 5200 with a double crop, both conservative estimates. That this group was producing food sufficient for more than twice their own number at least, is a unique example so far of food production as an industry. In order to answer the question of who were the recipients of this planned food surplus, we have to look at the broader vicinity. The major centers of San Estevan to the east and Nohmul to the northwest are located at distances of 3.5 and 3.0 km respectively from the nearest swamp edge. However, Nohmul may be considered to extend to the very edge of Pulltrouser West if its larger settlement is considered. On the other hand, Pulltrouser Swamp is not the only basin showing the presence of raised fields in the area. Long Swamp to the east is filled with the distinctive ground patterns that identify raised fields and it lies a mere 750 m from the site center of San Estevan. The peripheral settlement of San Estevan extends very near to the edge of Long Swamp, which would therefore be a closer source of intensively produced food than would be Pulltrouser Swamp, further to the west. In the case of Nohmul, despite being one of the largest ceremonial centers in northern Belize, there are a number of smaller-scale swamps with visible fields within and adjacent to the boundaries of the site. Some of the resources from Pulltrouser Swamp might have been distributed to Nohmul, but that site, like San Estevan, has other and closer sources for intensive agriculture. This viewpoint, however, only considers *need* for food supply. It may be that food from Pulltrouser Swamp was provided to Nohmul in a system of taxation or tribute. Conversely, the inhabitants of Pulltrouser Swamp may in fact have been participants of the Nohmul hierarchy, expressly settled on the swamp littorals for the purpose of supplying surplus food for redistribution by the major "mother" site. This explication visualizes Nohmul as the dominant site of the vicinity, with Pulltrouser Swamp settlers serving it by providing the economic means for maintaining its dominance.

Such a scenario, however, ignores the presence of the other minor centers that occupy the ridge. If indeed need for food supply was the real motivation (rather than dominance by Nohmul) there are other settlements in the vicinity within close distribution distance to Pulltrouser Swamp. Because of their elevation, the series of small, regional ceremonial centers that range along the high ground dividing the New and Hondo rivers do not have immediate access to wetland intensive agriculture. The exception is Cuello, which borders a small, shallow wetland. It could be argued, therefore, that the surplus food production of Pulltrouser Swamp was destined for these sites, if indeed their own extensive milpa systems were insufficient to supply their resident populations, a probability that is far from established. If, for example, Yo Creek was one recipient of Pulltrouser Swamp produce, the transport distance is minimally 10 km. The important argument is that one population was producing sustenance for another at some distance, although the significance of the argument increases directly with the distance that produce was transported. If food produce was transported for long distances, say equal to the distance between "primary" sites (26 ± km) or more, the economic impact for Maya organization is far greater than if such produce were only transported a few kilometers from source to consumer. In this argument, agricultural products serve as a trade item, leaving the community of their production to be consumed by another, distant community. Just how far this concept can be legitimately extended remains a matter of future debate and research.

It has been argued that food cannot be carried long distances for trade, as the carrier would have to consume his burden and thus limit the distance that such a burden could be transported (Sanders 1976). I do not accept the view that a Maya carrier had the right to distinguish between the natures of the burdens carried. If carrying a burden of jade, the carrier would have his established means of procuring food and water along the route. To consume the burden or part of it would undoubtedly be considered theft meriting capital punishment. I see no reason why a burden of consumable produce would be regarded any differently, once such produce was established by the society as a viable trade item. However, I do recognize that the economics of caloric consumption impose certain limits on the distance that such products could be moved, unless, of course, tribute is involved.

The Pulltrouser Swamp Project has established the veracity of wetland raised field agriculture in bajos, as opposed to riverine edges; it has established that the production in such wetlands is considerable, at a scale that is not comparable to similar systems on riverine littorals. It has also established that raised fields were constructed in a variety of forms, and it may be anticipated that further varieties, not just of raised fields, per se, but of other methods of manipulation of wetland conditions, are yet to be discovered. The project has established that Cooke, the Ricketsons, Palerm, and Wolfe were correct in principle about the exploitation of bajos. The scope of influence this exploitation had upon the fabric of Maya economy, the extent of this influence throughout Miranda's Bajo Zone, the time span of this influence, and the possible causative relationship to the Maya collapse, remain to be demonstrated. Siemens has demonstrated the broad and even common use of bajos in northern Belize for agricultural purposes (1981) and also quite far to the west in a different environment in central Veracruz (1983a). At Pulltrouser Swamp several lines of evidence indicate a presence of intensive agriculture as early as the late Preclassic, but the evidence is not irrefutably conclusive. This date is supported, however, from conclusive evidence for raised field use at the site of Cerros a short distance to the north (Scarborough 1983, 1986).

Due to the efforts of Steve Gleissman et al. (1983) it is now known that the vegetational patterning originally seen in the Bajo Morocoy of Quintana Roo *does* reflect the presence of raised fields. Furthermore, the fields at Morocoy are similar in construction to those of Pulltrouser Swamp. However, Bajo Morocoy differs from Pulltrouser swamp in two major respects: (1) Morocoy is a seasonally inundated swamp containing the drainage of a seasonally flowing or relic river, whereas Pulltrouser Swamp is permanently wet with sedge grass borders, a different *type* of bajo; and (2) Morocoy is 29 times larger than Pulltrouser. From this evidence, it can be concluded that both seasonally and permanently wet bajos, of both small and large scale, were used for intensive agriculture in this part of the lowlands. If it were conservatively estimated that no more than one-half of the visible area of 246 sq. km in Bajo Morocoy was used as growing surface, the result is 123 sq. km or 12,300 ha. of productive field surface. Using the same methods for calculation as at Pulltrouser Swamp, then Bajo Morocoy was capable of feeding 64,400 individuals with one crop, or more than 96,000 with two crops. From this calculation we could conclude that either the uplands surrounding the bajo were extremely densely populated, or else the produce was transported for considerable distances for distribution. Excavation at Pulltrouser Swamp has shown that the produce could not all be consumed locally. Furthermore, in the vicinity of Bajo Morocoy, there are other, unconnected bajos that also display traces of raised fields, further increasing the potential production for that vicinity, and decreasing the likelihood of local consumption.

The scale of the figures calculated from the zone of Bajo Morocoy demand that we revise our notions about quantities of regional food production in ancient times. Raised fields have been ground proofed in northern Belize, Quintana Roo, Veracruz and the western Petén, near the Pasion River (Adams, Brown, and Culbert 1981). It is clear that ground proofing is not always simple, even in the face of clearly visible patterns from the air. For example ground evidence in Bajo de Santa Fe adjacent to Tikal, and Bajo Mirador, has thus far been elusive (Dahlin et al. 1980). Based upon excavation evidence at Cerros, Scarborough commented upon the rapidity with which the ditches and canals infilled due to the lateral slumpage of soils from the flanking high ground (1986: 82). Such infilling may well account for the difficulties of ground proofing in the central Petén. With confirmed evidence of intensive agriculture at Rio Azul (Culbert et al, this volume) and from the western Petén (Adams, Brown, and Culbert 1981), it seems highly unlikely that the region between would not have utilized such a productive system in the seasonally inundated bajos that comprise nearly one-half of the Petén. It seems reasonable to assume that the well-documented vegetational patterning that has been positively ground proofed elsewhere, should also represent some form of ancient manipulation in the Bajo de Santa Fe and Bajo Mirador, despite the difficulties of ground-proofing that have plagued investigations to date.

The Pulltrouser Swamp project has demonstrated that food was produced for consumers at some distance from the source of production. In other zones, such as Morocoy, the enormous levels of food production deduced could mean either that the populations in an area thought to be rural were in fact very dense, or else, as at Pulltrouser, the produce was exported. When investigations into the phenomenon of bajo use have progressed further, it is likely that the ultimate answer will shown regional variation between these two effects of intensive food production, that is, both larger populations over the landscape than heretofore anticipated, as well as long-distance trade of food, wherein some vicinities served as "breadbaskets," regularly providing food to less fortunate areas.

With reference to raised fields at Cerros, Scarborough also commented that the speed of slumpage underscored the communal organization necessary, both for the construction and repair of these fields. The surface areas of raised fields are relatively limited at Cerros, but the need for organization to maintain them is correctly observed. In the context of the gigantic scale of Bajo Morocoy, the relative requirement of organization is so much greater compared to the situation at Cerros we must rethink our ideas of the relationship of agriculture to the family, and consider instead comparison to levels of central organization of hydraulic societies found elsewhere, such as in the Middle East. The groundwork has been laid to approach the Classic period Maya as a society that practiced agriculture at an industrial level for the export of either edible produce or other trade crops such as cotton or cacao. When the Maya began to exploit bajos, this revolution in agriculture modified the fabric of the lowland economy. Such a move meant not only that a much larger population could be supported but also that a larger portion of it had to be devoted to building and maintaining the system. A whole new class of specialists was required: the organizers and overseers of these fertile "plantations." Such specialization in turn heralded new vulnerability, since even slight change in the hydraulic regimes of the bajos could lead to decreased production and crisis in the system. Industrialization of agriculture, with its dependency on stable conditions in an unpredictable environment, probably established the basis for collapse.

Notes

1. I wish to thank B.L. Turner II for his reading and commentary, Patricia McAnany for her very thoughtful, thorough, and helpful reading, and E. Wyllys Andrews V for an extensive commentary and for calibrating the dates for the Pulltrouser Swamp Project. Errors, opinions, and faults of style are, of course, my own.

2. This figure was erroneously printed as 2,460 sq. km in Harrison 1978.

3. The exception is Pulltrouser West, which dries up almost completely during the dry season.

4. Another dated sample derived from amalgamated carbon fragments in the "A" horizon, *below* the cited sample Beta–5324 analyzed to a later date. Stratigraphically lower, Beta–5325 calibrates to 910 (809)770 .. This discrepancy of date inversion has not been explained. However, the earlier but stratigraphically higher date was sealed between floors.

5. Sherds of Swazey/Bladen complex were recovered from the disturbed surface at the sites of Pech Titon and the western edge of Tibaat.

6. This site was partially mapped during the Pulltrouser Project, but lies to the south of the swamp basin. It appears to have been Preclassic in date and abandoned during the Preclassic period.

7. Since sites do not occupy a single point, but occupy a widely ranging area, the distances are taken from the most significant ceremonial plaza exhibiting the largest architecture at each site. While this method arguably has fallacies, it allows a means of comparing inter-site distances.

8. Not used in this discussion, but derived from observations in southern Quintana Roo, Mexico.

Seven

Lowland Maya Wetland Agriculture: The Rio Azul Agronomy Program

By T. Patrick Culbert, Laura J. Levi, and Luís Cruz

As Peter Harrison demonstrates in the previous chapter, archaeological research since the 1960s has revolutionized ideas about Maya Lowland population and agriculture. Rather than a scattered, low density population supported entirely by swidden agriculture, the Maya had a Classic period population numbering in the millions (Culbert and Rice n.d.) that depended upon a variety of intensive agricultural techniques.

The use of the wetlands that comprise as much as half the terrain in the most densely populated parts of the lowlands was a critical factor in increasing support capacity. Although some researchers (Sanders 1979; Ford 1986) remain skeptical about wetland agriculture, most find the kinds of evidence noted by Harrison to be irrefutable. Research in the Maya wetlands is still in its infancy and each new project contributes more information about the flexibility and sophistication of Maya adaptation to a zone of great ecological and hydrological complexity. This study concerns the variability of wetland adaptations and presents results of two seasons of field research in wetlands near Rio Azul, Guatemala.[1]

Wetland Ecology

A series of variables including the regime of inundation, slope and drainage characteristics, proximity to rivers, soil, and natural vegetation affected the nature and potential utilization of wetlands. The regime of inundation was perhaps the most important variable. Wetlands that were inundated permanently (i.e., for too long each year to permit even a dry season crop) could have been utilized only if reclamation was undertaken. Seasonally inundated wetlands might have been farmed during the dry season without modification as is done today in Belize (Wilk 1981), the Peten (local informants), and Tabasco (Orozco-Segovia and Gliessman 1986). Since seasonally inundated areas were frequently modified by the ancient Maya, however, one must presume that modification improved agricultural conditions sufficiently to repay the labor investment. In the Maya Lowlands today, seasonally inundated areas far outnumber those of permanent inundation, although one must remember Harrison's (1977) still-debated suggestion that most low-lying areas were shallow lakes in prehistoric times.

Slope and drainage are closely related to the regime of inundation. Although few data are available, the 2.0 percent slope for *escoba bajo* at Rio Azul reported here must have different implications for drainage than the 0.3 percent slope of the Bajo Morocoy that makes even modern drainage systems ineffective (Gliessman et al. 1983). Whether wetlands are directly connected with rivers must also be considered. Wetland modifications in Belize (Turner and Harrison 1983; Siemens 1982; Bloom et al. 1983; Lambert et al. 1984), Veracruz (Siemens 1983) and along the Rio Candelaria (Siemens and Puleston 1972) are all on flood plains or levee backslopes, where they would have been affected by river regimes. As Siemens (1978) notes, all these river systems involved are karstic and buffered against drastic seasonal variations of water level. The large interior bajos of the Peten and Quintana Roo may be partly drained by seasonal streams that eventually empty into rivers, but their hydrology is poorly understood (Siemens 1978) and it is likely that each bajo is a unique system.

Soil characteristics of wetlands were a critical variable for agricultural use, but would probably have been very different while wetlands were in use than they are today. There is general agreement that the soil structure of wetlands would have retained moisture through or well into the dry season (Gliessman et al. 1983; Lambert and Arnason 1983; Richard Smith 1983; Lambert et al. 1984), and that wetlands under cultivation would have maintained a good balance of soil nutrients. Canal-cleaning would have added nitrogenous materials to the fields, and fields that were still inundated for part of the year would receive nutrients with deposited sediments. But these general comments about wetland soils neglect the great variety that must have existed. Visible soil differences occurred even in the restricted zone of wetlands around Rio Azul.

The natural vegetation of wetlands serves as a clue to microecology. The traditional division of bajos into escoba bajo and tintal bajo (Lundell 1934, 1937) is a vegetation-based scheme of classification that is thought to represent bajos of different relative elevations. We will later propose a subdivision of tintal bajo, and we believe that further studies of interior bajos will provide additional microzones relevant to agricultural use of wetlands.

Wetland Utilization

Following Lambert, Siemens, and Arnason (1984), we distinguish raised fields from drained fields. Raised fields involved both canals and a significant build-up of planting surfaces, while drained fields were created by canalization alone. Early discussions of wetland agriculture after Siemens and Puleston's (1972) discovery of field patterns stressed raised fields. Turner and Harrison's (1981) research at Pulltrouser Swamp—which supplied the first solid demonstration of raised fields—also showed drained fields at the edges of the swamp. Since that time, most of the modifications revealed by archaeological research are drained rather than raised fields. The Albion Island fields now are interpreted to be drained fields (Bloom et al. 1983; Antoine et al. 1982) as are those at Lamanai (Lambert et al. 1984) and in Veracruz (Siemens 1983b). Our own research at Rio Azul, Guatemala, has discovered a drained field system—the first wetland modification demonstrated in the Peten. Only in the Bajo Morocoy in Quintana Roo have additional raised fields been documented (Gliessman et al. 1983).

Raised fields were probably the most productive form of wetland agriculture. If canals contained water throughout the year, continuous cropping would have been possible, as well as the raising of fish (Thompson 1974). Raised fields were also the most labor-intensive wetland adaptation and the most prone to disastrous damage from unusually heavy rain (Gomez-Pompa et al. 1982). In permanently inundated areas such as the deeper parts of Pulltrouser Swamp, the Maya would have found cropping impossible without the investment in raised fields. The reason for raised fields in the Bajo Morocoy, which today is only seasonally inundated, is not clear to us. Nevertheless, the infrequency with which true raised fields have been demonstrated archaeologically suggests to us that the Maya avoided commitment to such a labor-intensive adaptation unless conditions made it a necessity.

Drained field systems must have functioned differently from raised fields. Their association with river floodplains, levee backslopes and interior bajos suggests that they were an adaptation to seasonal inundation. Drained fields probably did not eliminate inundation completely. Indeed, the benefits of annual flooding such as destruction of weeds and insects and addition of nutrient-rich sediments were probably too desirable to forego. Drainage canals may have served to extend the period during which seasonal wetlands could be farmed. As several authors have suggested (Siemens 1983b; Gliessman et al. 1983; Lambert et al. 1984), the juxtaposition of rainy season crops on ridges and slopes with dry season crops in wetlands would have made Maya agriculture productive year round. Agricultural routines may have varied annually in response to local conditions. When the rainy season was long, two crops might have been planted in upland fields in some areas. In drier years, drained fields in wetlands probably dried out early enough to permit two wetland crops.

Wetland Agriculture at Rio Azul, Guatemala

Rio Azul is a major site, at 42 courtyards the fourth largest Maya Lowland site currently recognized. The site was occupied from the beginning of the

Middle Preclassic (900 BC) until the end of the Terminal Classic (AD 1000), but the majority of construction centered in three periods of intense activity during the Late Preclassic (150 BC–AD 250), Early Classic (AD 325–534) and Late Classic (AD 700–830). Rio Azul has fewer small mounds than are encountered at such major sites as Tikal, but has an unusually large number of medium-size groups with masonry "palaces." In architecture, iconography, and ceramics, Rio Azul is closely related to sites in the Peten heartland of the Maya Lowlands, but its geographic location at the far northeast corner of Guatemala (Map 7.1) places it close to sites in Mexico and Belize that are parts of other cultural subtraditions. Adams (Adams 1984: 13) believes that Rio Azul served as a frontier administrative center at the borders of a Tikal regional state, a fact that would account for its unusual concentration of elite architecture and abundant tombs.

The Rio Azul Project under the direction of Richard E. W. Adams (1984, 1986, 1987) completed five field seasons between 1983 and 1987. No specific research on prehistoric agriculture was done during the first two seasons, but in 1984 a possible system of canals was noted by Adams and tested by Stephen L. Black to demonstrate the intentional cutting of canals into underlying bedrock (1987; Black and Suhler 1986). In the 1986 season, the authors began full-scale investigation of agricultural features in the Rio Azul region.

The Ecology of Bajo

The area of Rio Azul consists of a series of limestone ridges separated by swales. Rio Azul itself occupies a large ridge, bounded on the north and west by the river. Relatively little bajo occurs in close proximity to the site, although there are small strips along the river and south of the site. About one km northeast of Rio Azul, the subsidiary site of BA-20, El Pedernal (see Map 7.2), occupies three low ridges separated by strips of escoba bajo that drain westward into the river. It was in one of these stretches of bajo that canals were detected and tested in the 1984 season (Black and Suhler 1986). Larger areas of both escoba and tintal bajo occur south of Rio Azul at distances between 5 and 10 km. None of the bajos near Rio Azul are as large as the major-named bajos of the Peten, but the sum total of wetland accounts for a substantial portion of the terrain. Our research program included survey and excavation in areas of escoba and tintal bajo. The work discovered canal systems in escoba bajo and habitation and other sites at the margins and in the interiors of both bajo types.

The first task of wetland agricultural research was to define precisely the ecological zone under consideration. The term "bajo" has been loosely used by Mayanists, with topography, inundation, and vegetation in some unspecified combination as the defining characteristics. We consider inundation the key characteristic and define bajo as *low-lying flat land so situated in the local topography that it is subject to seasonal inundation.* Although inundation cannot be observed during the dry season, delineation of bajo did not prove difficult once we had become familiar with the local terrain. Bajos are noticeably flat in relation to surrounding land and the rise at the edge of bajo can be easily detected by the practiced eye. Our own judgments matched those of our workmen, who are very conscious of the same phenomenon and point unhesitatingly to what they refer to as the "shore" of bajo.

Escoba Bajo

Many of the natural drainage systems that empty into the Rio Azul are lined with long narrow strips of the vegetational association that is known as *escoba bajo* (Lundell 1934). This type of bajo is characterized by a profusion of palms, among which is the vicious escoba palm (*Crysophila argentea*) with its three-inch spines. Escoba bajo frequently occupies a location bordering tintal bajo as one moves out of bajo toward higher land, but our research suggests that relative local elevation is not the sole determiner of vegetational types. It seems probable that escoba bajo occupies areas with better drainage than tintal bajo—a factor that would be partly elevational—but there also may be soil differences between the two associations.

Our work with escoba bajo took place in a long, narrow bajo that separates two ridges on which the site of El Pedernal (BA-20) is located. There is no tintal bajo in this location, and at the upper edge the escoba vegetational formation blends gradually into upland vegetation. Initial inspection in 1986 revealed a multitude of small surface depressions that

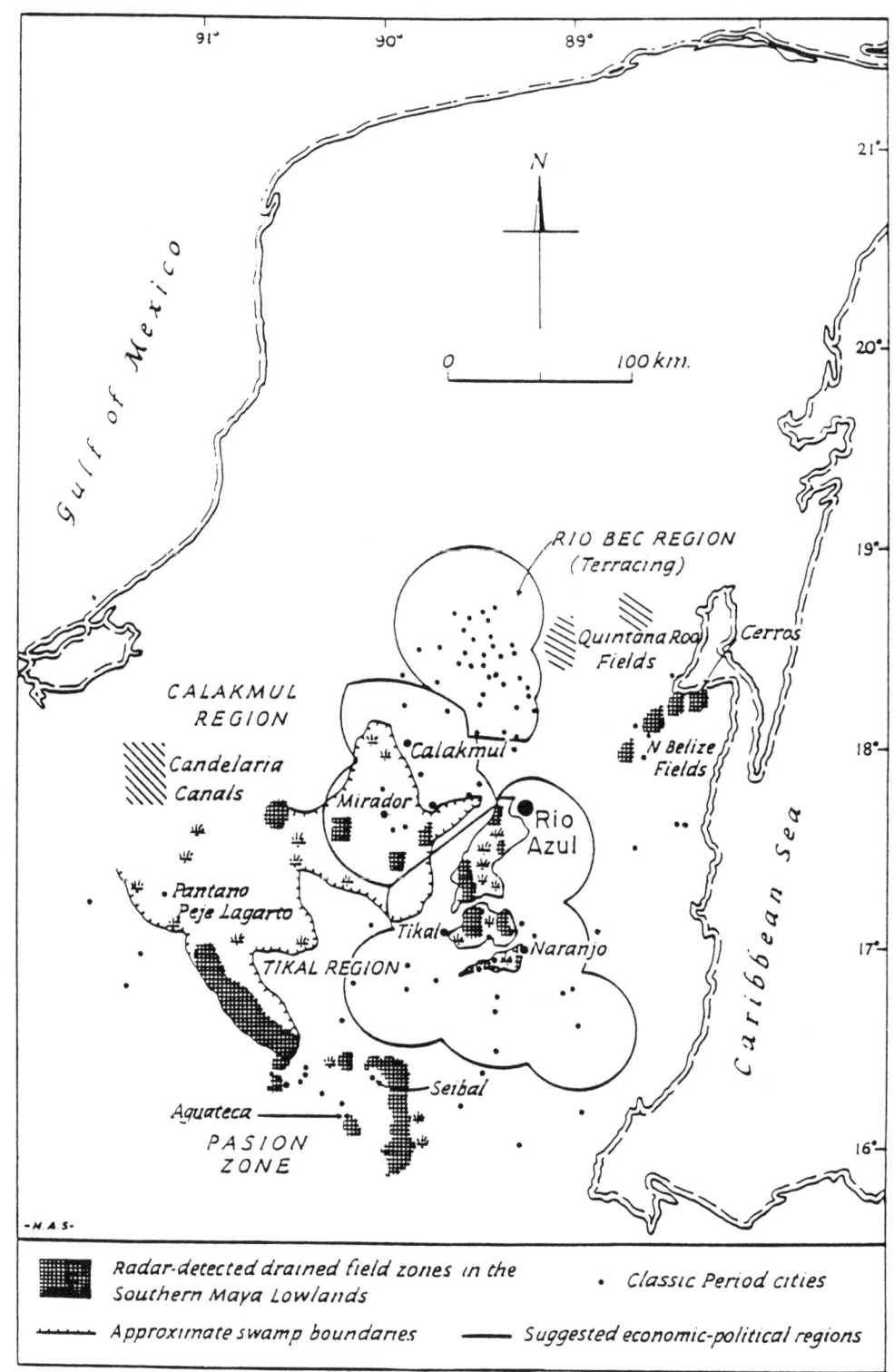

Map 7.1. Areas of Maya Wetland Agriculture.

were rarely more than 30 cm in depth. Some of the depressions were linear and could be followed for distances of 20 to 40 m. The patterns, however, were very complex. Few depressions could be followed for any distance and many were just holes that seemed likely to be the result of recent tree falls or the rotting of dead escoba stumps.

We devised a system of mapping depressions along trails 10 m apart that ran perpendicular to the slope of bajo. The resulting map showed that many depressions were local, appearing on one trail and nowhere else. Others, however, appeared at about the same location in a whole series of trails. With these locations as a guide, it was then usually possible to trace the depressions from one trail to another. A section of the El Pedernal bajo 270 m in length by 100 m in width was mapped. The northern end of the mapped section is close to the point at which the land rises and the bajo ends. To the south, the bajo continues for another 1.6 km before emptying into the Rio Azul. A slope of 2.0 percent exists between the beginning of the bajo and Rio Azul.

Figure 7.1 shows the depressions along our trails (omitting those that were strictly local) and the pattern of linear "canals." Several linear depressions run parallel to the direction of drainage. The pattern is dendritic, with short side depressions angling off at intervals. Cross-cutting east-west depressions were sought by cutting north-south trails and by a 50 m backhoe trench, but there was no indication that they existed.

Surface evidence could not prove that the depressions were of human origin. The proof, however, was easily obtained by excavation. The canal excavation program had started in 1984 (Black and Suhler 1986; Black 1987) with several hand-dug trenches. The north profile of the most successful trench was cleaned at the start of the 1986 season. It clearly showed that canals with rounded bottoms had been excavated into the bajo, reaching depths of 1.5 m below the present surface and penetrating the sterile yellow marl that underlies bajo. In the central section of the profile, three separate episodes of canal-cutting could be detected: an original canal 1.5 m deep; a second canal of equal depth that cut into the edge of the already-filled first canal; and a third shallower canal excavated into the soil that had filled the earlier two. At the western edge of the

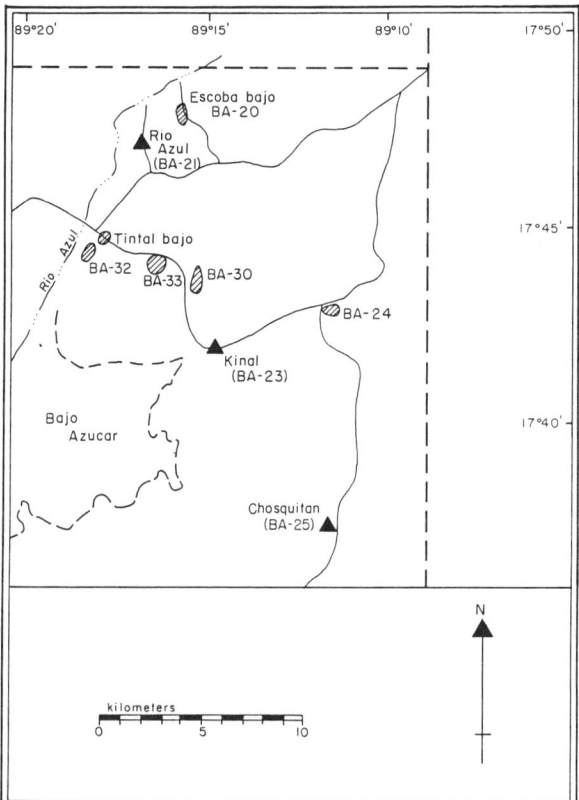

Map 7.2. The Rio Azul Region.

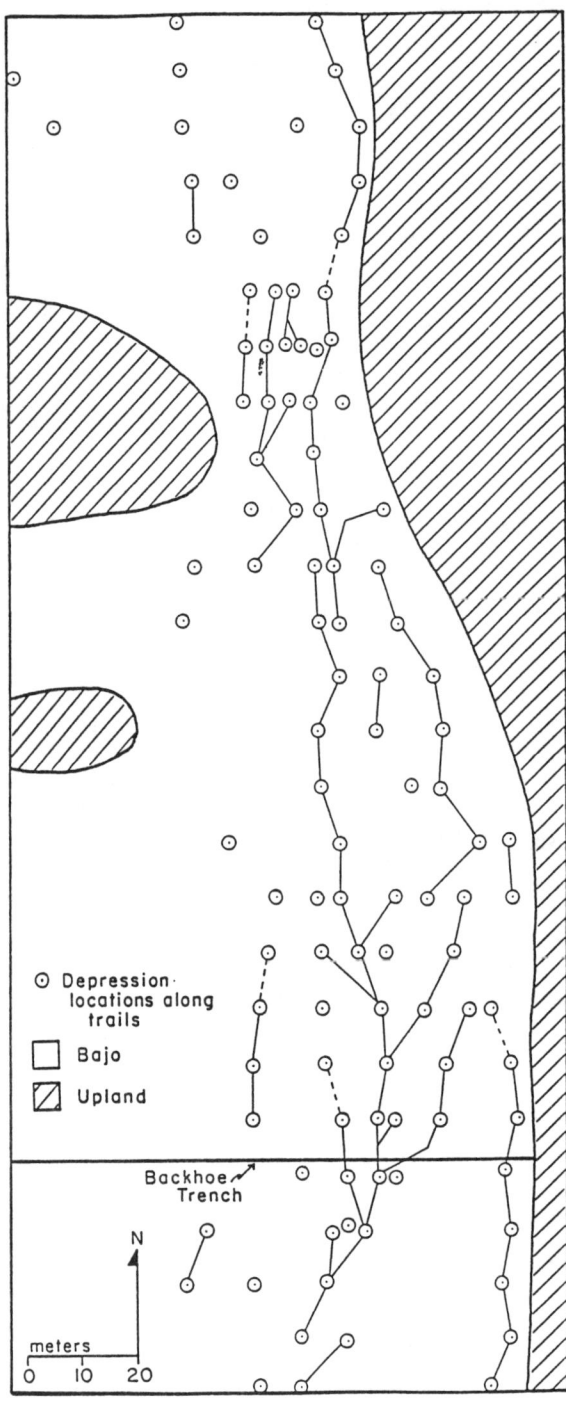

Figure 7.1. Surface depressions at El Pedernal (BA-20).

profile, two or three additional cutting episodes were visible.

The availability of a backhoe at Rio Azul made possible a 100 m trench that sectioned the bajo from one edge to the other, providing information that could never have been obtained by the laborious task of hand excavation. At the point where the section was cut, the surface map indicates five canal-like depressions. All of these depressions were verified as canals in the trench, and two additional canals that had left no surface indications were discovered. These results suggest that surface indicators are a reliable guide to prehistoric canals, but that they do not reveal all canals that were once present.

In the soil profiles revealed by excavation, there is a clear contrast between the fill of canals in which a black, organic-rich clayey soil predominates and the surrounding areas in which a gray, very sticky clay is the primary component. The profiles through canals reveal some of the details of canal construction and filling. The canals show a rounded (U-shaped to parabolic) cross section. A layer of beige clay, almost certainly intentionally placed, lined the bottoms and sides of canals in many places. This layer may have served to seal canals or to prevent erosion of the sides. Canal fill, in addition to the black clay, include a few thin swirly layers that might have been water-laid deposits, but more frequently shows large lumps of gray clay or sascab, the yellow marl that is the basal layer of the bajo. These large lumps of material give the impression that the canals may have been intentionally filled. If so, the canals must in some manner have become obsolete, although what made them so cannot be determined.

Between the canals, the soil profile of undisturbed escoba bajo is relatively simple. A thin (less than 50 cm) layer of brownish black topsoil overlies a deeper (50–100 cm) layer of sticky gray clay that in turn surmounts the yellow sascab that is probably the weathered upper surface of limestone bedrock. Although the gray clay contains pockets of black soil and occasional chunks of sascab, these added materials are too infrequent to indicate the kind of mixing that occurs when field surfaces are intentionally raised. In addition, the lack of east-west canals to create the island-like character of raised fields suggests a relatively unmodified bajo surface between canals at Rio Azul.

In summary, we reconstruct the El Pedernal bajo as having north-south canals, paralleling drainage, excavated into a bajo surface that was not substantially raised above its pre-canal level. Although a series of canals can be detected in the sections, we suspect that most of them were sequent rather than contemporaneous. At any single moment only a limited number of canals—perhaps no more than one or two—were open and in operation.

Survey along the edges of the escoba bajo at El Pedernal revealed a number of low eminences too enigmatic to have been included on the site map, but nonetheless suggestive of human origin. Four of these features were tested by excavation. One proved to have been a quite substantial plastered substructure of cut stone masonry that had originally stood to a height of 1.5 m. No traces of a superstructure were found, but a residential function seems likely. Surprisingly, both major construction phases of the substructure dated to the Terminal Classic Tepeu 3 period, a time interval not strongly represented at Rio Azul. The location of the structure directly at the edge of bajo suggests some kind of continuing use of wetlands during the last phase of occupation of the area. The second test revealed another low substructure located on a ridge that jutted out into bajo. This platform lacked cut stone masonry and was surfaced by a layer of packed limestone cobbles without identifiable plaster flooring, but also seems likely to have been for residential use.

The final two test excavations at the border of the El Pedernal bajo were in locations characterized by densely packed limestone cobbles. Both areas are barely visible at the level of the modern land surface and both are situated less than 10 m from prehistoric habitation sites, at the base of the juncture between bajo land and the limestone ridges rising out of bajo. Full exposure of the cobble zones was not attempted and thus their areal extent remains unknown. Both excavated areas revealed a level of packed limestone cobbles through which a gray-brown soil was thinly distributed. Sherds, and chert flakes and debitage appeared with high frequency in this soil matrix. Neither area offered evidence of a plaster surface overlying the cobbles. In one test, the cobble layer rested directly upon bedrock. In the other, it rested upon a layer of larger limestone boulders that had been placed upon bedrock.

The absence of a sterile soil zone (i.e., an ancient land surface) beneath the low cobble platforms provides an important clue in aid of understanding the primary function of these roughly constructed features. The clay soil of escoba bajo is nearly impermeable. Limestone, on the other hand, is a porous substance through which water drains easily. Undoubtedly, the first construction stage of both platforms was the removal of bajo soils to expose underlying bedrock. Limestone cobbles or boulders were then deposited into the excavated area. Finally a capping of densely packed cobbles finished platform construction. These cobble platforms, then, reflect an effort to extend dry, well-drained land surfaces out into bajo. In effect, the excavations provide a rare glimpse into the technology involved in prehistoric land reclamation. The activities performed on these reclaimed surfaces remains unknown but were probably related to use of the bajo.

After the work in the El Pedernal bajo, several other areas of escoba bajo in the vicinity of Rio Azul were investigated for surface evidence of canal systems. These additional areas included bajos to the east and north of the site of El Pedernal, a bajo on the banks of the Rio Azul just southeast of the main site, and a section of escoba bajo near a newly discovered aguada east of Ixcanrio on the Kinal road. In all of these locations, traces of canals were quite clear, an indication that modification of escoba bajo was very widespread in the vicinity of Rio Azul.

We interpret the canalization in the escoba bajos of Rio Azul as a variant of the drained field modifications I noted earlier. The extent of the canal system seems too small to have prevented inundation completely, a result that would probably not have been desirable anyway. But since the Rio Azul bajos are water-free for nine months of a normal year, a short extension of the dry period at either end of the rainy season would have made it possible to plant two crops annually in escoba bajo. A local informant indicates that modern Peten cultivators plant a March crop in bajo that is subject to the hazard of an early start of the rainy season that inundates the area before the crop is mature. We believe that one of the functions of drainage systems may have been to lessen chances of such early inundation, a function not mentioned by previous researchers who have focused upon draining fields more quickly at the end of rainy season to permit planting. Our surface survey shows that almost all escoba bajo near Rio Azul was drained, a practice that would have added a significant amount of land suitable for dry season cultivation.

Tintal Bajo in the Rio Azul Area

The agrarian potential of tintal bajo is a highly debated issue in many discussions of ancient Maya wetland modification. As is true of lowland swamps and escoba bajos, linear and grid-like vegetal patterns can be detected in the aerial and radar imagery of the Peten's tintal bajos (Adams et al. 1981). In contrast to the former, ground confirmation in tintal has been severely impeded by dense, inhospitable vegetation, and by a disconcertingly dissected microtopography. Where modern clearance of tintal vegetation has eased archaeological exploration in Quintana Roo (Gliessman et al. 1983), ready proof of wetland modifications is available. Most probes into the Peten's tintal bajos, however, have yielded disheartening results (e.g., Dahlin 1976) due to the absence of such extensive ground-surface exposures.

Forewarned by these earlier efforts in the Peten, we adopted a cautious, labor-intensive research design for our preliminary study of the tintal bajos in the Rio Azul region. Since even subtle differences in contemporary soils, vegetation, drainage and hydrology might provide clues to ancient agrarian exploitation of tintal, we considered the documentation of such variation to be a primary goal. An understanding of the distribution of ancient settlement in the vicinity of tintal was also a matter of major concern. The diversity of agrarian techniques employed by the ancient Maya (Harrison, this volume) points to a dynamic and complicated interplay between settlement and modes of agricultural production. Knowledge of the settlement remains associated with tintal bajo would add greatly to our appreciation of the range of Maya settlement systems incorporating wetland areas.

Lundell's (1934, 1937) classic description of tintal bajo (and the well-informed *chiclero*) guided our initial identification of this wetland zone. There is no tintal bajo in the immediate vicinity of the sites of Rio Azul and El Pedernal. The agronomy project therefore shifted its research to an area east of the project camp at Ixcanrio, where the 12 km road from Ixcanrio to the site of Kinal (BA-23) frequently traverses zones of tintal. Along this road, 3 km east of Ixcanrio, a steeply embanked aguada sits at the southeastern margins of a tintal bajo. Two kilometers further east, a low linear mound composed of chert nodules and flakes is surrounded by a second zone of tintal.

Most of our attention focused upon the kilometer stretch of tintal bajo due west of, and incorporating, the aguada. Here, the road to Kinal just skirts the outer shores of bajo. The interior of bajo lies to the north of the road and a higher canopied, upland forest rises to the south. Using the road as our baseline, four *brechas,* spaced approximately 225 m apart, were cut into bajo for a minimum of 500 m to the north. Each of these brechas also extended an additional 200 m to the south of the road into the upland forest. A fifth brecha began 500 m within the bajo interior and ran from east to west for a kilometer, intercepting our four north-south brechas. The brechas were surveyed with a brunton and handheld metric tape. Ancient settlement remains, possible drainage canals, and changes in vegetation and microtopography were plotted along each. Transit measurements documenting fluctuations in land surface elevations were made along two of our northerly brechas and for 500 m in the bajo interior along our principal east-west brecha.

Limited trenching into the bajo adjacent to the aguada revealed that tintal vegetation in this area is supported by a compact, gray clayey subsoil. Our brief examination of the second tintal bajo in the immediate vicinity to the chert mount, however, showed a different soil morphology. In this instance, tintal vegetation is supported by poorly developed topsoils and a subsoil characterized by coarse sands. Siliceous deposits are prevalent and nodules of chert litter the ground surface. The effects upon land use of this geomorphological diversity in tintal wetlands must be resolved by future research.

We have found it useful to partition tintal into two variants on the basis of vegetational associations. Our first variant, "sedge tintal," is always located in the lowest and most poorly drained zones of the tintal bajo (usually the bajo interior). The ground surface in sedge tintal is heavily dissected by deep, narrow channels that create a rough microtopography of hummocks, known locally as *bombolales.* The tree canopy in this zone seldom exceeds 4 m. Vegetation is characterized by many vines, epiphytes, and a dense scrub of thin, frequently thorned trees. Sedges of less than a meter in height comprise the principal ground cover. The tinta, or logwood tree, for which tintal bajo is named, also achieves its highest frequencies in sedge tintal.

We have called the second variant, "herbaceous tintal." Characterized by comparatively high elevation, the ground surface of this bajo zone tends to be fairly level, although wide, shallow depressions create a slightly undulating microrelief (Wright et al. 1959: 59, 295, refer to this phenomenon as "hog wallows"). The forest canopy rises roughly five to eight meters above the ground. The identifying characteristic of this bajo zone is a low, herbaceous forest floor plant. Herbaceous tintal is located along the shores of tintal bajo, as well as in the bajo interior where the occurrence of small elevational rises of as little as 10 cm provides higher ground that is accompanied by a resurgence of herbaceous tintal vegetation and microtopography.

Elevation and, consequently, length of periodic inundation seem to determine the presence of sedge tintal vegetation as opposed to herbaceous tintal. We are forced, however, to discard the traditional view that escoba wetlands complete a continuum of bajo vegetation that depends strictly upon relative elevation (Lundell 1937: 29–30). Although small escoba palms form an integral component of tintal, the margins of tintal are not consistently bordered by a higher, better drained escoba wetland. In one particular instance we found escoba bajo at one of the lowest elevations of our study area, separated from tintal by a narrow arc of ridgeland. Here, the wetland soils support a high, luxuriant palm-forest canopy of escoba type that inhibits the growth of forest floor vegetation. Hydrologically separated from the tintal bajo, this escoba wetland is geomorphologically distinct as well. Elevation, alone, therefore may be an imperfect predictor of escoba bajo vegetation, and the determining factors may relate more to drainage and the drainage properties of certain wetland soils.

Our search for agrarian features in tintal bajo was hindered by an unexpectedly short 1987 season. The large area covered by our exploratory brechas (almost one sq. km) militated against the finer-grained strategy of pattern detection that we employed in El Pedernal's small escoba bajo. Our brechas, however, did expose the curious interlacing of sedge and herbaceous vegetation in the interior of tintal bajo. The slightly elevated patches of herbaceous tintal that are circumscribed by zones of sedge look suspiciously like a remnant agricultural system of higher, eroding field platforms and collapsed drainage canals.

Our brecha system also revealed an impressive sample of ancient settlement remains both in the bajo interior and along its southern margins. Within the bajo, we encountered several low platforms situated atop small, apparently natural rises. Our test pitting operations concentrated upon one larger platform group strategically centered along the arc of ridgeland partitioning tintal from the low-lying escoba bajo. The group consists of four principal platforms and several ancillary mounds bordering a square plaza. Excavations exposed a well-preserved series of plaza surfaces dating to the Early Classic, with each episode of reflooring accompanied by a remodeling of the adjoining platforms.

The care given to the construction of this group argues against the suggestion that Peten bajo zones were subject to only the most ephemeral of occupations (Ford 1986). Our findings south of the bajo shore provide additional evidence of the substantial nature of bajo edge settlement. Here at the site of BA-33, several kilometers of low walls criss-cross the upland zone, incorporating six large platform groups and several small and informally arranged plazuela groups. Each of the large platform groups includes impressive range structures along the plaza perimeters. Excavations into a portion of the wall and at one of the larger platform groups suggest a Late Classic occupation.

At present, we can only guess at the functions of the low walls. Some create large enclosures around the major platform groups, but others lead into areas away from mound groups and down to the bajo shore. Elsewhere in the Maya Lowlands, similar features have been interpreted as field boundary markers (Rathje and Sabloff 1973; Eaton 1975). The site of Colha in northern Belize offers evidence of walled enclosures *within* tintal bajo (Hester and Shafer 1984: 161). The wall segments in our study area that descend to the bajo shore, however, could not be traced to the bajo interior.

Although we do not dismiss the possibility of field enclosures within the bajo, many of the linear walls descending to the bajo shore may have functioned to channel upland waters into the bajo zone. Two of the upland walls descend toward the aguada and their placement suggests that they may have served to direct the flow of runoff into the aguada basin. The aguada possesses two drainage channels, one to the northwest and the other to the southwest. Elsewhere along the aguada rim a mounded embankment blocks the flow of water to and from the catchment pool. Excavations into the aguada floor and drainages exposed a complex layering of sands and silts, overlying a lining of impermeable gray clay. The presence of sands indicates that rapidly moving water periodically flowed into the aguada carrying deposits from canals cut through an as yet unlocated zone of sandy tintal soils. The thin lenses of silts mark interludes characterized by slower moving water. An uppermost deposit of black fine-grained soil represents the era of sediment accumulation subsequent to the abandonment of the system, when open canals no longer channeled water into the aguada.

The relevance of the aguada to wetland agriculture is difficult to reconstruct in the absence of a more thorough investigation of the aguada's two drainage channels. Certainly, upland runoff was directed into the aguada through its southeast channel. Impounded water may then have been released through the northwest channel to irrigate a limited number of adjacent dry season fields within the bajo.

We suspect that the water in the aguada was related to agricultural practices rather than to domestic consumption because of the dearth of ceramic materials recovered from the aguada basin. The quantities of utilitarian ceramics found in the sediments of the aguadas at Tikal speak to the role that these aguadas played in household water consumption, and to the many small mishaps associated with water collection for domestic use. The only ceramics associated with our aguada, however, came from the construction fill of the aguada's embankments rather than from the catchment pool. We have identified numerous small aguadas in association with most of our habitation sites and these probably filled household needs.

Our interpretations of the aguada, the walls descending to bajo, and the significance of the vegetational patterns within tintal bajo are necessarily tentative. We believe, nevertheless, that they supply a compelling justification for further archaeological study of the Peten's tintal bajos. If, as we suspect, the Maya performed subtle and sophisticated feats of engineering to transform tintal bajo into agriculturally productive land, then future archaeological research in tintal must achieve a sophistication equal to its subject matter.

Notes

1. Investigation and research of the varied forms of intensive agriculture (including raised fields) in South America is already much more advanced than in Central America. Early date of appearance and broad usage of such techniques are well established to the south. For a review of this research see William M. Denevan, "Latin America," in *World Systems of Traditional Resource Management*, ed. Gary A. Klee (John Wiley & Sons, 1980), 217–44.

Eight

Southern Belize: An Ancient Maya Region

By Richard M. Leventhal

Our understanding of the cultures and civilizations of the ancient world continues to change with the expansion of data bases and new models with which to interpret this data. In the past 25 years, Maya archaeologists have almost completely shifted their view of this civilization. No longer do we perceive the ancient sites as empty ceremonial centers. No longer are the Maya seen solely as extensive swidden agriculturalists. No longer are the Maya hieroglyphs unintelligible. This process of change continues today with ongoing research in the area.

The pendulum of interpretive models constantly shifts within any research area. Within Mesoamerica, Willey (1977a) has recently argued that one of the pronounced shifts has been between an emphasis on large, widespread cultures or horizons identifiable throughout Mesoamerica, and regional developments limited to smaller geographic areas. Several problems have gradually emerged in Maya archaeology, bringing the regional perspective into new light and importance. Both political and economic models begin to demand an explanation for the dominance of regions rather than individual centers during the Late Classic period of the Maya Lowlands.

Sanders's regional study within the Valley of Mexico presents us with a good picture of what happens when one city dominates a huge region politically and economically (Sanders, Parsons, and Santley 1979). Teotihuacan, when it gained dominance within central Mexico, became the focal point for all activities: economic (such as production and distribution), religious, and social. In fact, Sanders, Parsons, and Santley found that with this incredible centralization of activities, the population of the region followed suit. Between 100 .. and .. 100, the population of Teotihuacan jumped from about 20,000 to more than 100,000 (Sanders et al. 1979). This is too swift a jump to have been entirely internal to the city. Rather, people were gradually abandoning the outlying centers and moving into Teotihuacan for the economic, social, political, and religious activities.

Within the Maya area there is no single center that would have been able to exert a central force sufficient to control the Maya Lowland population and its resources. There were too many cities of approximately the same size in close proximity during the Late Classic period, and probably also during the Early Classic and Preclassic periods, for any one to have been clearly dominant. Why did such centralization not occur? I will argue that a single site within the Maya area did not dominate because small separate regions were the primary political and economic focus for the ancient Maya people.

If the primary economic, social, and political unit for the Maya was the region, then a new, more complex model of this ancient Maya world must be developed. This is not to argue that it is not essential to consider larger units of interaction, including the entire Maya Lowland area or all of Mesoamerica, along with smaller units such as an individual site, village, or hamlet.

Archaeologists working within the Maya area have, until recently (Harrison 1985), focused upon either the microperspective or the macroperspective (C. Smith 1976). These two viewpoints are closely interrelated. As individual sites are continually excavated, analyzed, and published (the microperspective), they are presented in terms of an overarching model for the entire Maya area (the macroperspective). This macroperspective is a continuity of the culture area concept of the early twentieth century as applied to both Mesoamerica and specifically to the Maya area. This overarching model encompasses the entire Maya Lowland area of more than 250,000 sq. km and examines it as a single cultural and ethnic entity. This macroperspective has produced a model that emphasizes the similarities or uniformity of culture throughout the area (Morley and Brainerd 1956). It is based upon the assumed importance of long-distance trade as a prime unifying factor, not only economically, but also politically and socially. Maya culture provided a certain uniform cultural integrity throughout the entire Maya Lowlands based upon the ancient Maya writing system, the generalized form of architecture and plaza organization, a world view, and a series of symbols and iconographic elements that commonly symbolize aspects of this world view to all members of the lowlands. Because this model attempts to identify the similarities in culture it tends to gloss over the differences. But these cultural differences can no longer be ignored. Within some parts of the lowlands, these differences have recently been identified as indicators of ethnic or separate cultural groups. (See specifically the studies within the southeast area by E. Schortman [1982] of the settlement within the Lower Motagua Valley and the recent studies within the Copan Valley by Leventhal, Willey, and Demarest [1987].) Variability has been identified among such entities as architectural form, design and construction (Pollock 1965), plaza group organization, hieroglyphic form and phrasing, along with differences in iconographic grammar (Kelley 1976). This variability can no longer be dismissed as slight variation among various cities. Rather, I believe that this variability indicates distinct regions among the ancient Maya social, political, and economic universe.

This is not to argue that the Maya culture did not exist and should be viewed purely as regional. Rather, I believe that the macroperspective, the overarching model, has been overemphasized in the past at the expense of regional variation. The regional perspective presented here should not be viewed as being a more important model, but rather, one that will provide us with a new and different vantage point from which to examine the Maya. There is little question that long-distance trade and political connections among the elite at all the Maya sites provided the basic macrostructure for the Lowland Maya culture. However, this structure should be seen as a strong façade which binds the area together culturally and which covers the regional and ethnic variability evident throughout the lowland area.

Models

When examining the development of economic and political systems archaeologically, two broad models are currently used for explanation. The first might be seen as a formalist model and is based upon scarcity and control of specific resources. This model is developed from western economic theories where the concept of energy input and output is the basic operating principle. This model has been used in Sanders's interpretations of the development of dominant cities within Central Mexico (Sanders et al. 1979). The control and movement of scarce, important items over a long distance is one of the primary forces of this model.

Another model becoming prominent in archaeological interpretations is based upon Wallerstein's World System Model (1974a, b). Wallerstein's development of this model is based upon his attempt to explain the rise of capitalism as one of the dominant forces within the world today. He argues that beginning with the sixteenth century, there is a gradual development of an economic system encompassing the entire world. He sees the development of a core, periphery, and semi-periphery zones, which allows for the development of a structured production and exploitative system throughout the world. Within this system Wallerstein sees important scarce resources acquired within peripheral areas and then exported to core areas for final production and then final distribution. One of his important concepts is that of the semi-periphery which, to a large extent, forms a buffer between the core and the periphery. This semi-periphery or buffer is both exploited and exploitative—exploited by the core and exploitative toward the periphery. Most recently, Blanton and Feinman (1984) use the Wallerstein model to examine the ancient cultures of Middle America, incorporating the broad Wallerstein model of a core and a periphery into their framework. Blanton and Feinman argue for the movement of "preciosities" from the periphery to the core as a prime mover in the cultural development of Middle America, noting that "controlling the flow of this material [preciosities] was so important that it provided the major motivation for external conquest" (1984: 677).

When attempting to examine ancient Mesoamerica, specifically the ancient Maya world, neither model should be used exclusively, since portions of both can be synthesized into a new, more flexible, model. Long-distance trade, emphasized by many archaeologists and anthropologists as part of the formalist approach, must be combined with Wallerstein's concept of preciosities and regional interaction to form a new model.

It is my contention that all these factors play a crucial role in the development and maintenance of the economic, political, social, and religious system of the Maya. Long-distance trade of precious items allowed for the maintenance of the elite social system and the broad Lowland Maya culture. Localized regional trade, on the other hand, provided for the primary economic stability within regions throughout the Maya Lowlands.

This concept of region is a Maya construct that can be seen in many aspects of both the archaeological and ethnohistoric record. In fact, Grant Jones has argued for the existence of political and economic regions during the Colonial period in the Maya Lowlands (1982, 1983).

It has been recently well demonstrated (Sanders and Santley 1983) that it was difficult in ancient Mesoamerica to move basic food stuffs over a long distance due to the type of transport available. Therefore, regions became particularly important for the survival of any population, whether in the Valley of Mexico or the Maya Lowlands. The major difference, however, between the Valley of Mexico and the Maya Lowlands is that the Valley of Mexico was continually controlled and dominated by a single-center culture: Teotihuacan, Tula-Toltecs, and finally Tenochtitlan-Mexica Aztecs. The question is why this form of city domination does not occur within the lowlands.

Within each region of the Maya Lowlands, it is likely that all the existing large centers had equal access to the surrounding resources. The various centers did not rely upon control of a scarce resource for their existence, as might be argued by the formalist model, because they were part of an internal regional network. This is not to say there was no competition between centers, but competition was secondary to the centers' economic, social, and political survival, which depended first on constant interaction.

Although Maya culture, as demonstrated in architectural form and style, ceramics, and the hieroglyphic writing system, exists as an overarching framework in the lowland area, more detailed study of ancient Maya sites has gradually brought regional variation within these categories to light. Examples are numerous. The unity of the Maya architectural style has often been emphasized. This unity is based upon the existence of the corbelled arch, open plaza areas, large flat-topped pyramids generally facing one direction, long-range structures, and often large acropolis areas demarcated by the largest structures (Morley and Brainerd 1956; Pollock 1965). As a general statement for the unity of architecture within the Maya area, the previous statement does hold together. But details of the architecture clearly show regional variation. Within the southern Yucatan area, for example, three architectural styles have long been defined and generally seem to be located within specific regions. Puuc, Chenes and Rio Bec architecture are all considered to be pure Maya but are quite different in their form and emphasis. An examination of these three architectural styles clearly indicates that these are three regional styles. All three architectural styles are similar in that they emphasize the façades of buildings. The architectural style found in the Rio Bec region focuses upon several large false pyramids. Architecture of the Chenes region focuses upon the façades of buildings, often representing serpents, some of which are false façades. Finally, architecture from the Puuc region emphasizes well-cut veneer masonry with elaborate stone ornamentation (Pollock 1965). Although these three architectural styles overlap greatly in their geographic distribution, I would still argue that these were three separate, individual regional styles that gradually spread throughout the southern Yucatan area. How can all three styles be considered Maya and yet be so different in their emphasis? The answer is that they are all regional styles with a certain similarity in their attempt to present the same overarching themes through different styles and emphases.

Hieroglyphs and sculptural iconography have also

been shown to vary from region to region (Kelley 1976). Various ceramic types and artifact types are also clearly regional in their scope—examples include *candeleros,* found primarily within the southeast region of the lowlands. Ceramic types including Copador, Belize Red, and others are centered within specific regions of the lowlands.

Long-distance trade between centers within the Maya area and between centers throughout Middle America had a major impact upon social, political, and economic unity and organization. Bulk items, however, were not being traded from one region to another; instead, small quantities of elite items formed the basis for this long-distance trade. These items were of great import on several levels. Some may have been raw material of precious resources, such as jade as it moved from its source to the production area. Similarly, finished items with important symbolic iconography moved throughout the system. This long-distance trade moved horizontally throughout the Mesoamerican and Maya system, that is, it remained within the elite sphere of influence in its movement over long distance. Within the Maya area itself, it was this trade of elite items or preciosities that formed the core of Maya culture. These materials did sometimes move vertically through the system. In fact, many of these preciosities like jade, obsidian, and feathers were not immediately consumed, but were hoarded and controlled by the elite. In order to maintain their power position within society, many of these items were then passed on as gifts or payment to second and third levels of individuals. All of these precious items entered the system at the top and gradually worked their way down through the society.

On the other hand, the region was the focus of most of the economic and social interaction between centers within the Maya area. Bulk goods moved within regions and probably included, among other things, foodstuffs, pottery, local stone for artifacts, and locally produced cloth. Tight political and social alliances among elite and non-elite existed within regions, and regional markets that helped economic, social, and political interchange probably also existed. Intermarriage among ruling and elite families probably occurred more frequently within regions than between regions.

This model of the importance of regions helps begin to explain the cultural diversity detailed above. The existence of many centers of nearly the same size, occupied at nearly the same time and at close proximity to one another, along with the lack of dominant centers during the Late Classic, forces the interpretive focus away from individual centers toward regions.

At this point, it is important to differentiate between the concept of regionalism along with the impact of this model of political, social, and ecomic interaction upon our concept of the Maya world and the regional studies of archaeological regions and sites. Regionalism as a concept presents a new and different view of the ancient Maya as it emphasizes the importance of regions as primary interaction zones from the Preclassic to the collapse. Regional studies, on the other hand, have and will test the existence of regions within the Maya Lowlands and will be used as the foundation for the importance of regionalism as a model of the ancient Maya world.

Regional Studies in the Maya Area

There have been several attempts at regional studies in the Maya area, some explicit in their regional scope, others implicit. Regional studies date back to Willey's original settlement pattern program in the Belize Valley (Willey et al. 1965) and Bullard's work in the Petén (1960).

Only a few projects in the 1970s and 1980s have attempted to continue regional studies. A project conducted by Donald and Prudence Rice has examined the lake region in the Peten (D. Rice 1976; Rice and Rice 1980). Two other projects might be considered regional in their perspective, the first a survey conducted by Dennis Puleston between the sites of Tikal and Uaxactun (1974). He attempted to examine the potential relationship between these two sites by locating and mapping the settlement along brechas connecting the centers. A second program, conducted by Anabel Ford, is similar to Puleston's work. This is a transect and survey program between the sites of Tikal and Yaxha (Ford 1986). Together these two studies constitute what might best be considered the beginnings of a true regional analysis, although the examination of the settlement between sites is only the first step in a long, detailed process. Excavation, artifact and ceramic studies, more surveys, and scientific studies must also be utilized to create a detailed regional picture.

Several projects have been started with this regional perspective as the primary goal. Two of the best include Robert Rands's work around Palenque (1974, 1977) and the preliminary survey of the Lower Motagua Valley by Edward Schortman (1982).

Many projects have begun as site-specific work and then, after the completion of the field work, the archaeologists have attempted to put that single site into a regional perspective. This can certainly be seen in the southeastern region of the Maya Lowlands. Site-specific work has, for the past 10 years, focused upon the two major centers within this region: Quirigua, which was excavated by a crew from the University of Pennsylvania (Sharer and Ashmore 1979), and Copan, the focus of research first by the Harvard University–Copan Valley Settlement Project (Willey and Leventhal 1979; Willey et al. 1978) and later by the Proyecto Arqueologico Copan. Following the completion of most of the work, there was a preliminary attempt to put these two sites in proper relation to one another (Willey et al. 1980; Bishop et al. 1980). Many questions developed from this post–field work, some of which may be answered by the recent far-reaching survey around Copan being conducted by David Webster of the Proyecto Arqueologico Copan (David Webster, personal communication 1983).

Finally, hieroglyphic studies have led us closer to a regional perspective. Most often, epigraphic studies have remained focused on either the microperspective or the macroperspective; however, Marcus's study of the emblem glyphs and their distribution throughout the Lowlands is one of the few attempts to define regions in the Maya area. Marcus identified and focused upon what she termed the major "capitals" and their regions. There was no attempt to test the existence of these regions or their possible organizational significance other than political (Marcus 1976).

Regional studies have been, therefore, only a peripheral part of research in the Maya area. Seldom has a project set out to focus on the region. Most often, it is a late, secondary decision that unfortunately leaves many questions asked but unanswered. This clearly diminishes the breadth of the final interpretations and emphasizes the need for some initial regional studies to be developed.

Southern Belize

From 1983 to 1987, southern Belize has been the focus of an intensive regional study. This region is a perfect laboratory in which to examine the concept of regional interaction and organization. It is suitable for many reasons.

At present, five known centers are located within the proposed research zone of southern Belize. From west to east, these sites include Pusilha, Uxbenka, Lubaantun, Xnaheb, and Nim Li Punit (Map 8.1). At least two secondary centers have thus far been identified within the region. These are Uxbentun, near Lubaantun, and Silver Creek, located about 4 km to the west of Xnaheb. It is quite likely that there are numerous more secondary centers throughout the region that will be discovered in the course of the survey program.

During the past four field seasons an extensive mapping program has focused upon the eastern sites of the southern Belize region. Preliminary excavations at Nim Li Punit and Xnaheb were initiated in 1985, and an intersite survey program has been initiated between Nim Li Punit and Xnaheb and the surrounding terrain. Finally, a new major center, Uxbenka, was discovered.

The intersite survey program has focused upon the area between and around Nim Li Punit and Xnaheb. Two transects, one 4.5 km in length and the other 3 km, both 400 m wide, have been surveyed between Nim Li Punit and Xnahcb. Similarly, the areas around these two sites have been surveyed. From Xnaheb, two additional transects have been examined. One runs directly south of the site and examines the settlement within the lower foothills and the flat coastal plain. The second continues to the west within the foothills toward the secondary center of Silver Creek and onward to the center of Lubaantun.

Southern Belize has not been the focus of a great quantity of archaeological research during the past century. Some research was initiated within the region before the 1970s. Hammond (1975b) reviewed this research in rather extensive detail in the appendices of his Lubaantun monograph. Therefore, it is not necessary to review the work before 1970.

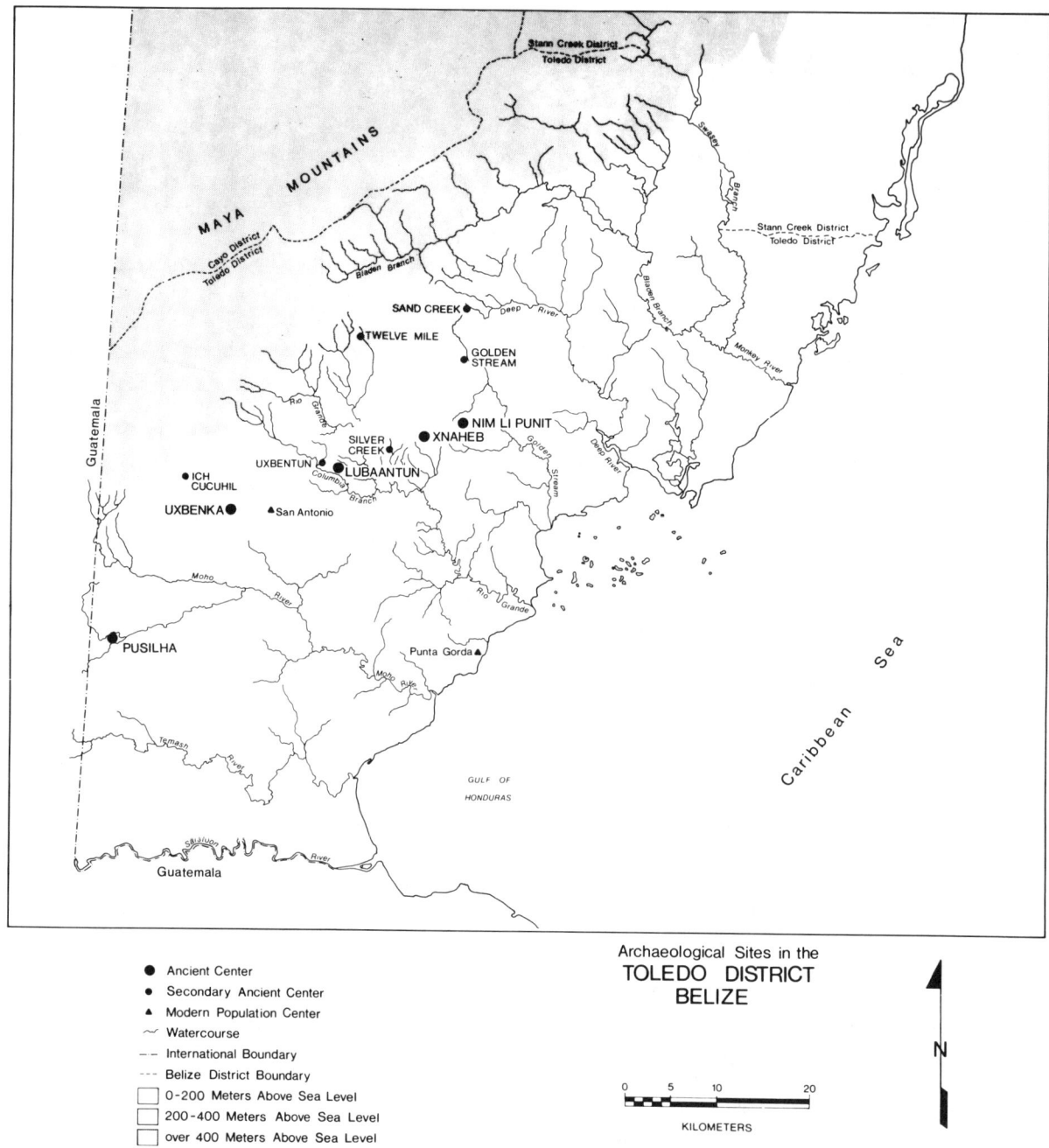

Map 8.1. Archaeological sites in the Toledo District, Belize, C.A.

Lubaantun

In 1970, Norman Hammond directed a six-month excavation at Lubaantun, which has presented us with a very solid base of information upon which we can begin to build many of our ideas and models (1975b).

First, Hammond established that Lubaantun was mainly occupied during the Late Classic period (A.D. 580–800). Hammond also completed a rough ceramic study of the material recovered from the excavations. Hammond and his crew mapped a one sq. km area around and including the main center at Lubaantun. This map, along with Hammond's interpretations of the time and pace of development of Lubaantun, give us a good preliminary picture of this site, one of the most important within southern Belize and which is part of the base upon which this regional study rests.

Hammond returned to southern Belize in 1971 but did not continue his excavation program. Instead, he conducted a rough survey of the southern Belize region, identifying 33 sites from reports in published and unpublished material and from his own previous work within the area. Of these 33 sites, 22 are confirmed, the other 11 reported but unsubstantiated. Again, Hammond has provided a good preliminary picture of the prehistory of the Toledo District. He developed a model of riverine resource utilization but did not have the data to test such a settlement system.

At the end of his work, Hammond produced a major monograph published by the Peabody Museum, Harvard University (1975b). Much of the report is based upon his attempt to view Lubaantun within what he calls a "Maya Realm," an important effort to place a major Maya center within a settlement perspective. He views Lubaantun as a place that draws upon many resources and many people from the surrounding area for its power base. This concept of a "Maya Realm" is an innovative one, although untested. Hammond's interpretation of the Lubaantun center, its internal traffic patterns, its growth and development, and its possible connections to the immediately surrounding terrain are all important results of his work.

Pusilha (Figure 8.1)

In 1979 I initiated archaeological work at Pusilha. A complete review of the two seasons of work at Pusilha is not possible within this space (see Leventhal 1983 for details); however, a brief summary is worthwhile. The two seasons of work at Pusilha were focused primarily upon two major tasks—survey and excavation. The survey of this site examined both the central areas and outlying settlement distribution of the site. This survey program consisted of a series of four transects that ran outward from the central part of Pusilha. The central and outlying settlements of the site were mapped.

In the end, it is clear that the site of Pusilha had two main focal points—the north side of the Pusila River with the Stela Plaza and one of the ball courts, and the south side with Gateway Hill and the second ball court. The north side is characterized by rather small architecture with great quantities of ritual or ceremonial features including 23 monuments located within the stela plaza. In contrast, the architectural appearance of Gateway Hill to the south is enormous. The images of pyramids upward of 30 m high, rising above the top of Gateway Hill (which is 75 meters above the river), creates a sharp contrast with the architecture on the northern side of the Pusila River.

Nim Li Punit (Figure 8.2)

In 1976 a new major center, Nim Li Punit, was accidentally discovered (as was Pusilha by loggers in the early twentieth century) by oil company workers who were cutting a brecha north from the southern highway. The main attraction to the site was the great quantity of stelae located within the central plaza area. The discovery of this site made it apparent that southern Belize remained a portion of the Maya Lowlands little explored and little understood.

Following the discovery of Nim Li Punit, Hammond, at the invitation of then Archaeological Commissioner of Belize, Joseph Palacio, initiated a three-day investigation of the main plaza. A preliminary map was produced, a couple of test excavations were placed within the plaza, and several monuments were turned over in order to examine their hieroglyphic inscriptions and iconography (Wilk and Hammond 1976). At least 25 monuments were identified in this short initial survey of the site. Six monuments have been identified as having the remains of inscriptions or some sort of carving. The mapping of Nim Li Punit during this brief 1976 ex-

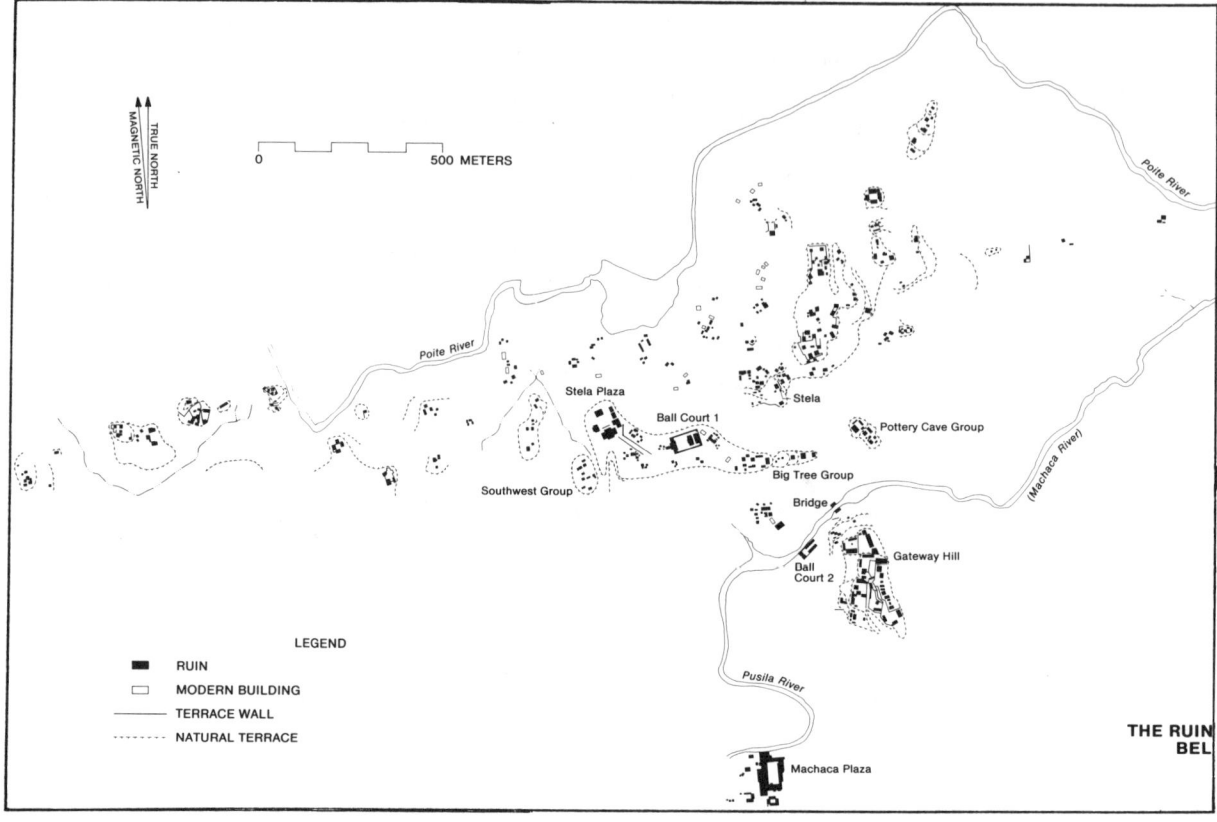

Figure 8.1. Map of Pusilha

amination consisted of a preliminary transit map of the stela plaza, the secondary raised plaza to the west, and a ball court (with marker) to the north. Hammond's three-day survey and preliminary interpretations were the extent of work at Nim Li Punit until 1983, when more extensive research was started by the Southern Belize Archaeological Project.

Nim Li Punit is larger than the original map by Wilk and Hammond (1976) indicates. The central area of the site (see Figure 8.2) is made up of three major groups. The south group is the original stela plaza with associated mounds and monuments that initially drew the attention of the archaeological world. The architecture of this group is fairly extensive, with the largest mound rising 10 to 12 m. The focus of attention has been on the great number of stelae within this central courtyard.

Excavation in this stela group revealed a large tomb within the upper plaza area. The remains of five individuals were recovered along with 40 ceramic vessels and numerous other artifacts. This is clearly an elite tomb, perhaps of the ruling family at Nim Li Punit.

Work at the site in 1983 revealed two other major architectural groups within this central area: the East and West Groups.

The East Group is larger and more extensive than the other two groups. It is a complex series of terraces and plazas arranged on the slope of a gradually rising hill. There are four main plaza levels with structures on each level, culminating in a medium-sized, complex plaza grouping at the top of the hill. The West Group is the smallest of the central architectural clusters, although still impressive in its scale. It consists of only two terraces, with

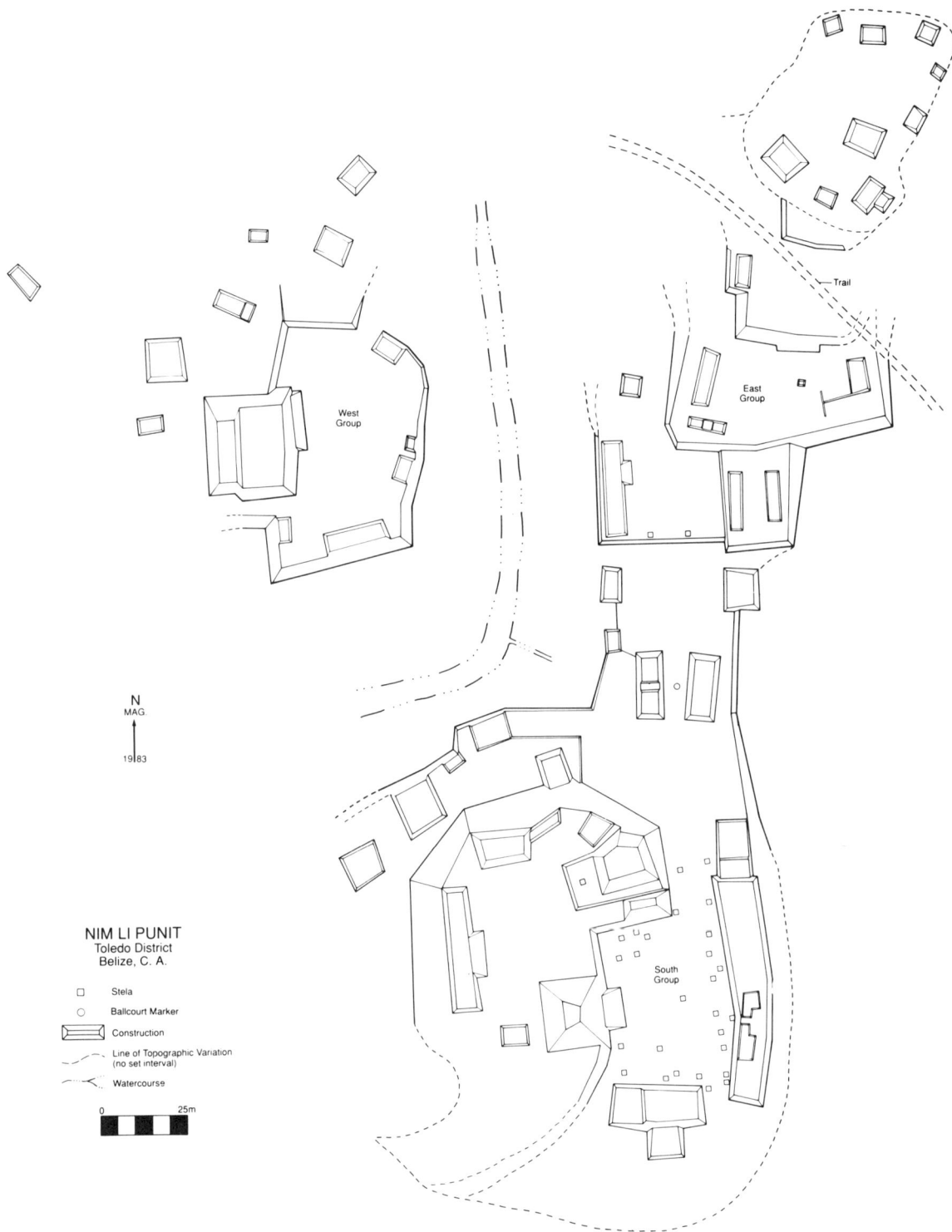

Figure 8.2. Map of Nim Li Punit

structures grouped around plaza areas on each terrace. The main structure is located on the western side and rises about six m.

Nim Li Punit is located on a high ridge about .75 km north of the southern highway and on the edge of the foothills of the Maya Mountains. Settlement was identified all around the site but appears, in preliminary analysis, to be more extensive and larger in areas to the west of the center along the line of the Maya Mountains.

Xnaheb (Figure 8.3)

Located 4.4 km southwest of Nim Li Punit, Xnaheb sits atop a narrow foothill ridge running south from the Maya Mountains. During the 1984 field season, we cleared and transit-mapped almost all of the central area of the site. The site consists of a central plaza group with corresponding smaller groups to the north and south. It incorporates the terrain into the form and organization of the site center, which is marked by the edges of the ridge.

The Xnaheb central plaza measures approximately 50 by 40 m and is enclosed on the east and west by low range-type structures. To the north is the main structure rising 12 m above the plaza floor; this is a natural hill that has been faced, terraced, and altered to create the impression of an artificial construction of great height and magnitude. At the summit, two irregularly shaped plaza areas are evident. The first small one is located nearly on the medial axis of the structure. The second plaza, much larger than the first, measures about 23 by 20 m; it commands the summit but is located off the structure axis to the east. Its location is related to the form of the natural ridgetop. Below this summit plaza both to the northeast and southeast are a series of small structures and terraces built upon the natural contours of the hill. To the north of the summit, a small plaza group lies cradled between the main structure and another group to the north. This north group consists of a series of terraces and small structures situated along the face of another natural hill.

The Xnaheb south group is located at the edge of the main site ridge and offers a spectacular view of the floodplain and Caribbean ocean to the south. Another group of structures, called the Southeast Group, is located to the east of the South Group and consists of three plaza areas attached to one another, running in a north-south line. The largest building is located on the north side and is about three or four m in height. The group is connected to the main stela plaza by means of a small *sacbe* running northwest. The large size of the buildings and plazas of the South Group, along with the existence of the connecting *sacbe,* clearly indicate its importance in Xnaheb's organization.

Six stelae have been located at Xnaheb. Only one monument, dated 9.17.10 (0).0.0, has preserved carving. This preliminary picture of the Xnaheb center begins to place the site in its proper context within the southern Belize region. Most importantly, it can no longer be identified merely as a secondary center due to its small size. In overall extent, it is almost as large as the neighboring Nim Li Punit.

Uxbenka (Figure 8.4)

The newly discovered center of Uxbenka was visited during the 1984 field season. It is located in the western part of the southern Belize region within the modern village of Santa Cruz, about 10 km west of San Antonio. Outlying sections of the site had been noted by previous researchers (Hammond 1975b); however, the newly discovered stela plaza and associated structures are the only sections of the site that have been systematically surveyed and mapped.

The central part of Uxbenka is fairly small, consisting of a large plaza area demarcated by five structures. The main structure, about 12 m high, is located on the north side of the plaza in which eighteen stelae are located. Twelve of the stelae were lined up in front of the central structure, the other six in front of the structure on the west side. This plaza is situated on a small flat-topped knoll whose front or southern side was shaped and faced to create the image of a constructed pyramid. A central stairway runs up this southern face, broken only by a small medial terrace. Of the two remaining monuments located at the site, one is situated on this medial terrace and the second at the base of the stairs.

Only four monuments at the site retain definable iconography and hieroglyphs. The two earliest monuments at the site, Stelae 11 and 21, date stylistically to the Early Classic, approximately 8.18.0.0.0 (Linda Schele, personal communication

Southern Belize 135

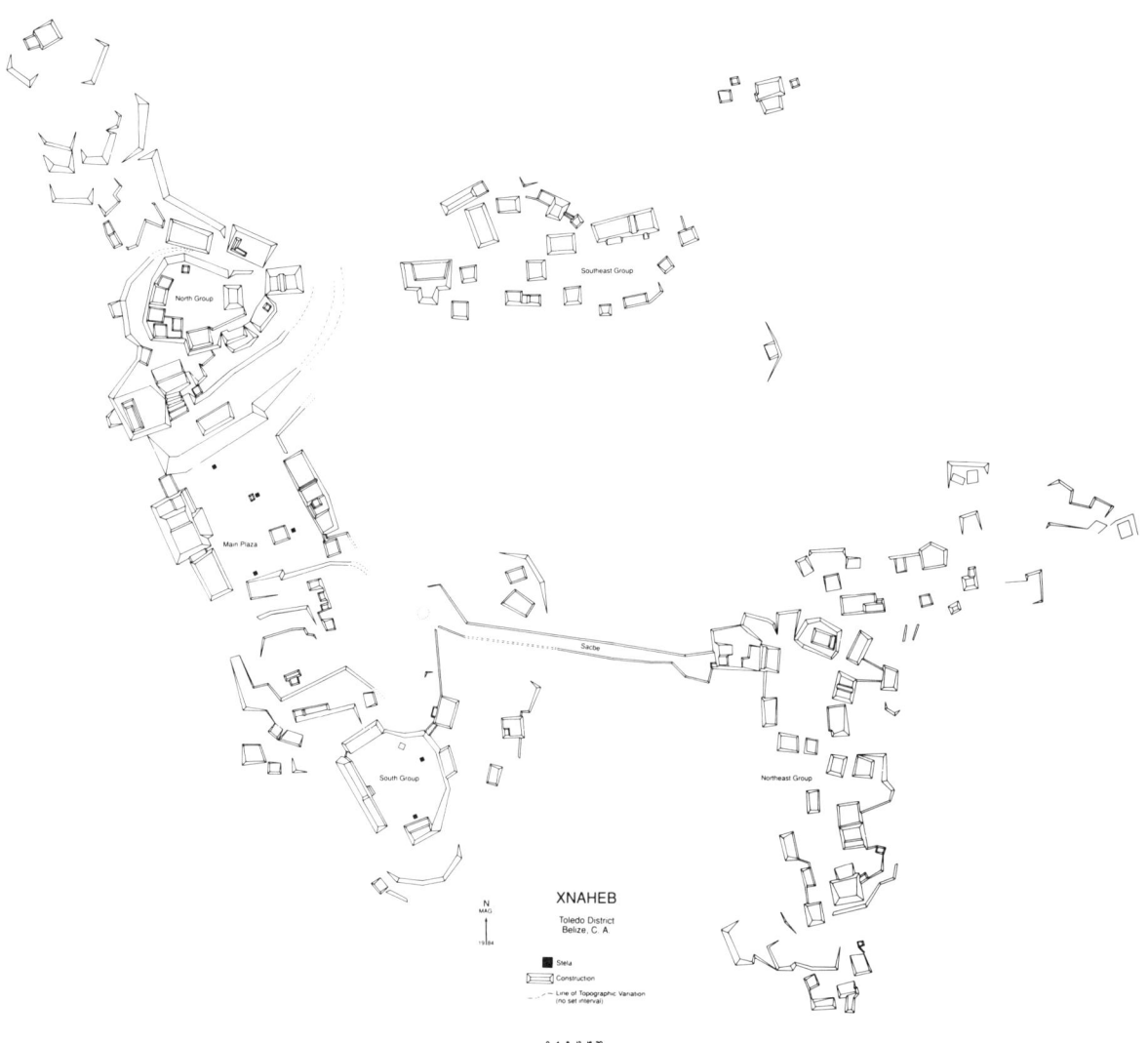

Figure 8.3. Map of Xnaheb

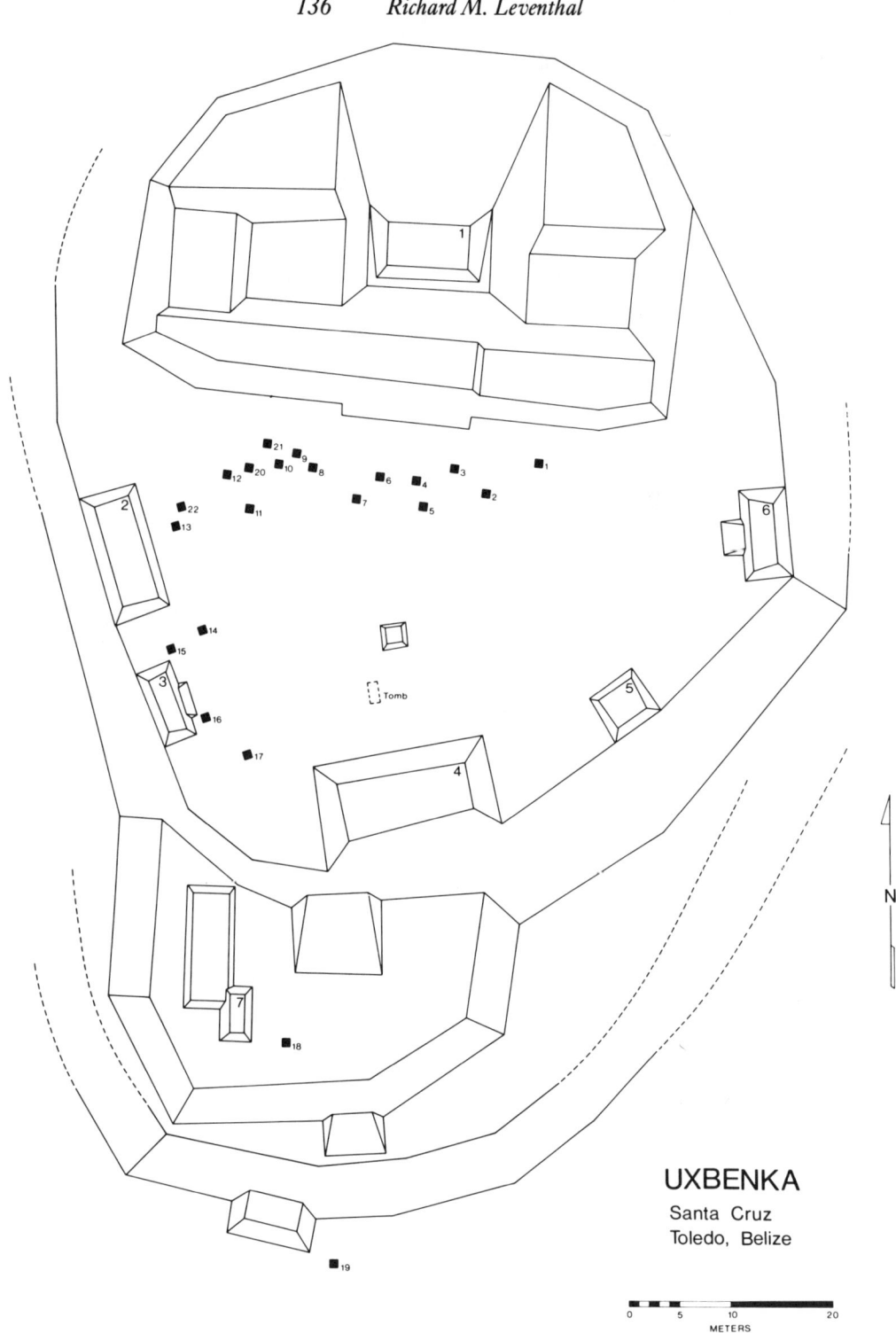

Figure 8.4. Map of Uxbenka

1983). These are the earliest dated monuments within the region and within Belize. The other two monuments date to the Late Classic: Stela 15 (9.17.10.0.0.) and Stela 19 (9.17.10.0.0).

The surrounding site has not been carefully examined although rough preliminary investigations indicate the existence of a fairly extensive settlement.

Until the project described here, southern Belize had not been the focus of extensive archaeological research. We are just beginning to analyze the survey and excavation data from the research of the past several seasons within this southern Belize region. With this analysis, we hope to begin to develop a good picture of the relationships and interactions of Maya sites within a single region. The process is slow but has been started.

The Southern Belize Laboratory

One of the most important aspects of southern Belize and the reason it was chosen for this study is that it can be delimited geographically, culturally, and temporally as a region. The geographic boundaries of southern Belize are fairly clear. The southern Toledo district of Belize is a roughly triangular-shaped area, bounded by the Maya Mountains to the north and west, the Caribbean Ocean to the east, and two major river systems (separated by a large swampy area) to the south—first the Temash River and then, further south and marking the border between Belize and Guatemala, the Sarstoon River. This is an area of the Toledo beds (Wright et al. 1959), which are wedged between the Maya Mountains and the major river drainage of the Motagua to the south.

The key question is whether it is possible to argue that this same geographic area has any meaning within the cultural sphere. For this region, the geographic boundaries appear to clearly relate to the cultural boundaries. The Maya Mountains, to the north, were little occupied during the time of the ancient Maya, evident from various surveys of the area by Thompson (1930, 1931). Therefore, they provide a good northern boundary for our region.

The mountains remain a boundary on the western side of southern Belize. It is to the southwest that southern Belize was probably connected with the rest of the Maya Lowlands. This area to the west, in Guatemala, remains largely unexplored. There have been several recent finds in Guatemala indicating that this zone was occupied during the Late Classic. Such finds include the cave of Naj Tunich, recently discovered and examined by a team from the National Geographic Society (G. Stuart 1981). Generally, there appears to be a lessening of sites to the west in Guatemala, as any movement of goods and people would have to be funneled through a rather small opening in the Maya Mountains. This is the way modern traders, Cobaneros, travel from the central Kekchi area to the outlying villages in Belize.

To the south, the fairly large swampy area between the Temash and Sarstoon rivers marks off a good boundary both geographically and culturally. Further to the south, one moves into the Lake Izabal and Lower Motagua drainage. Between the Lower Motagua and the Sarstoon, there was little occupation evident from the survey conducted by Barbara Voorhies (1969). Only one settlement of any size, San Felipe, was discovered, and this dates primarily to the Preclassic.

To the east, the Caribbean Ocean marks another good cultural and geographic boundary, although it also acted as an entry point into the southern Belize region, as evidenced by contacts with both the southeastern area and the highlands. Hammond did uncover some evidence of small occupation on some of the small islands (cays) off the coast of southern Belize (Hammond 1975b); however there is little present evidence of a direct connection between these small settlements and the major sites lined up along the edge of the Maya Mountains.

The physical and cultural boundaries of southern Belize provide part of the rationale for this regional study, although the model being presented is not diachronic in its scope. Rather, this is an attempt to examine regional interaction and organization within a single time period. Admittedly, the Late Classic is several hundred years long, but this is still short in archaeological terms for Mesoamerica.

Stelae dates throughout the region indicate a predominantly Late Classic occupation. All the dates from Nim Li Punit and Xnaheb fall within the Late Classic. The ball court markers from Lubaantun are clearly Late Classic in their style. Stela O from Pusilha dates to 9.7.0.0.0 or the beginning of the Late Classic. In fact, the only monuments in southern

Belize that clearly predate the Late Classic are Stelae 11 and 21 at Uxbenka. With the dates and styles of the other monuments, however, it seems likely that the preponderance of occupation is during the Late Classic.

Ceramics recovered during the excavations at these sites also confirm the Late Classic occupation. Excavations have been conducted at four of the sites within the region: Pusilha, Lubaantun, Xnaheb, and Nim Li Punit. Except for a very small number of sherds that may date to the Preclassic or Early Classic, almost all the material indicates a dense Late Classic occupation.

The chronology, thus far, seems to allow us to argue for a fairly tight chronological placement of the occupation of this region, helping to define the region for this synchronic study.

The Southern Belize Region

The model of regional importance I have presented argues for a certain amount of internal homogeneity within the region. The broad test implication of this model is that there should be greater homogeneity of cultural features among the centers within the region than among the centers outside the region.

This test of internal homogeneity and external heterogeneity is still undergoing study and analysis, although more and more specific features are being identified that appear to support this broad test implication.

Some of those archaeological features that serve as a demonstration of the initial test of this model will be examined briefly. The features to be identified are found not only within this southern Belize region. Many of them are found at other sites throughout the lowlands, perhaps even at neighboring sites; but it is the intersecting of these features within southern Belize that defines the region from this material perspective.

The ball courts discovered within this southern Belize region provide perhaps the best picture of regional homogeneity and external heterogeneity. Ball courts have been found at three of the major sites in the region—Nim Li Punit, Pusilha, and Lubaantun. All these ball courts are centrally located and mediate between two sections of the different sites. Such location, however, is common at many other Maya centers.

Recent excavations and examination of the ball courts at Pusilha and Nim Li Punit (Figure 8.5a and b) have revealed a sharply distinctive set of features. All three ball courts (two at Pusilha and one at Nim Li Punit) are located within walled enclosures; the walls are free-standing, with the basal sections constructed of several courses of stones. The upper sections were probably of perishable material, perhaps wood. These walls do not simply demarcate the end zones of the courts but are separate walls extending around and behind the ball court structures.

Such walled enclosures were identified around both ball courts at Pusilha in 1980 and have recently been identified around the ball court at Nim Li Punit. Hammond's map of the ball courts at Lubaantun do not indicate such walls or enclosures, but recent preliminary surface investigations indicate the possible if not probable existence of such walls at Lubaantun. If they exist there as well, this would create a tight regional homogeneity of an architectural feature probably relating to the religious and ritual activity associated with ball courts. The basic function of the ball court and the ball game at these sites was probably the same as at most other Maya centers. These walls are a locally imposed feature on the broader Maya sphere. Similar enclosures have not been identified at any other site within the Maya Lowlands or anywhere within Mesoamerica where ball courts are found.

Another architectural feature common to all the sites within this southern Belize region is the use of the natural terrain for terraces and pyramid-like construction. At all the sites, much of the major architecture actually consists of a natural hill or terrace slightly modified and then faced with a façade of cut stone masonry. Gateway Hill at Pusilha is one of the most dramatic examples. The top 30 meters of the hill appear to be a set of large pyramids with several medial terraces. However, examination of the back of Gateway Hill and excavations within the medial terraces clearly reveal the "Hollywood set" type of construction. There is no facing at all on the back of the hill and the excavations within the medial terraces extended only .30 to .50 m in depth before reaching the natural bedrock. The shape of the natural terrain was slightly modified and flattened in places. This slight modification along with the façade created the impression of massive construction.

Façade-natural construction is evident at every

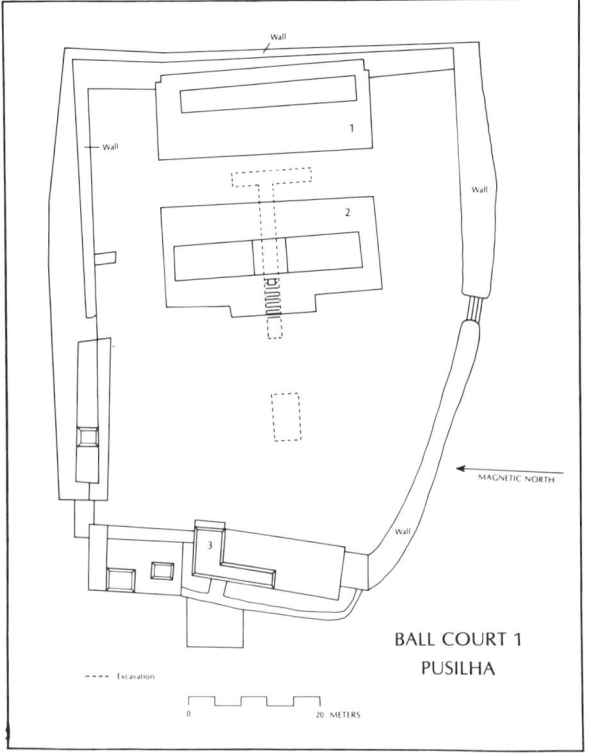
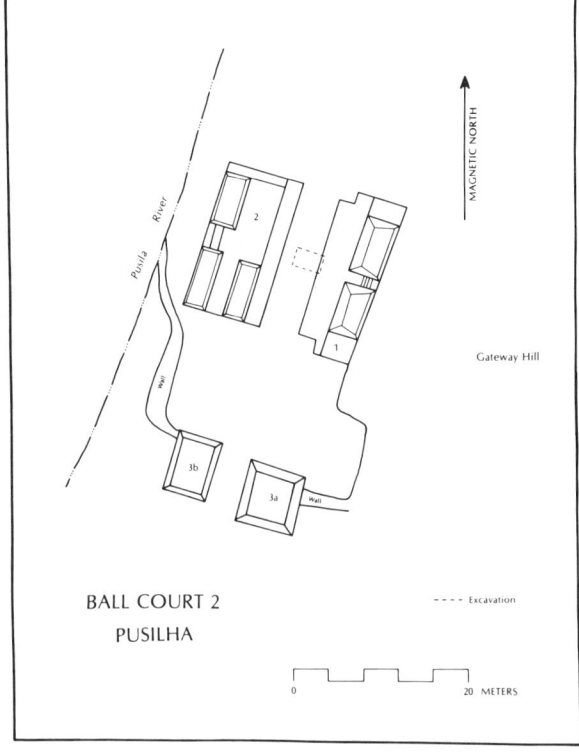

Figure 8.5a. Pusilha Ballcourts 1,2

site and is one of many interesting features that define this particular region; its hilly topography lends itself to such land modification. A second dramatic example is the northern or primary structure at Xnaheb, found on careful examination to be all natural. Unlike the unique ball court walls, façade-natural construction is found at other places within the Maya Lowlands, although not at any of the sites immediately beyond the southern Belize region.

Sequentially used tombs found within southern Belize also may indicate the existence of a southern Belize region. Although such tombs are not found exclusively within this region, they are strong markers of the regional definition. One tomb found within the southern group at Nim Li Punit was used sequentially for five individuals. A similar family tomb, probably also sequential, was discovered by Hammond near Lubaantun. It was in such poor condition, however, it could not be properly examined (Hammond 1975b).

Tombs used for sequential burials are not common throughout the lowlands although they have been found at nearby Caracol, located on the northern edge of the Maya Mountains. Although this specific feature appears to extend into this northern area, Caracol does not fit into the southern Belize region for many reasons, one of which is that its monumental architecture and stelae iconography are much more similar to the architecture and iconography from the central Petén. Also, the Maya Moun-

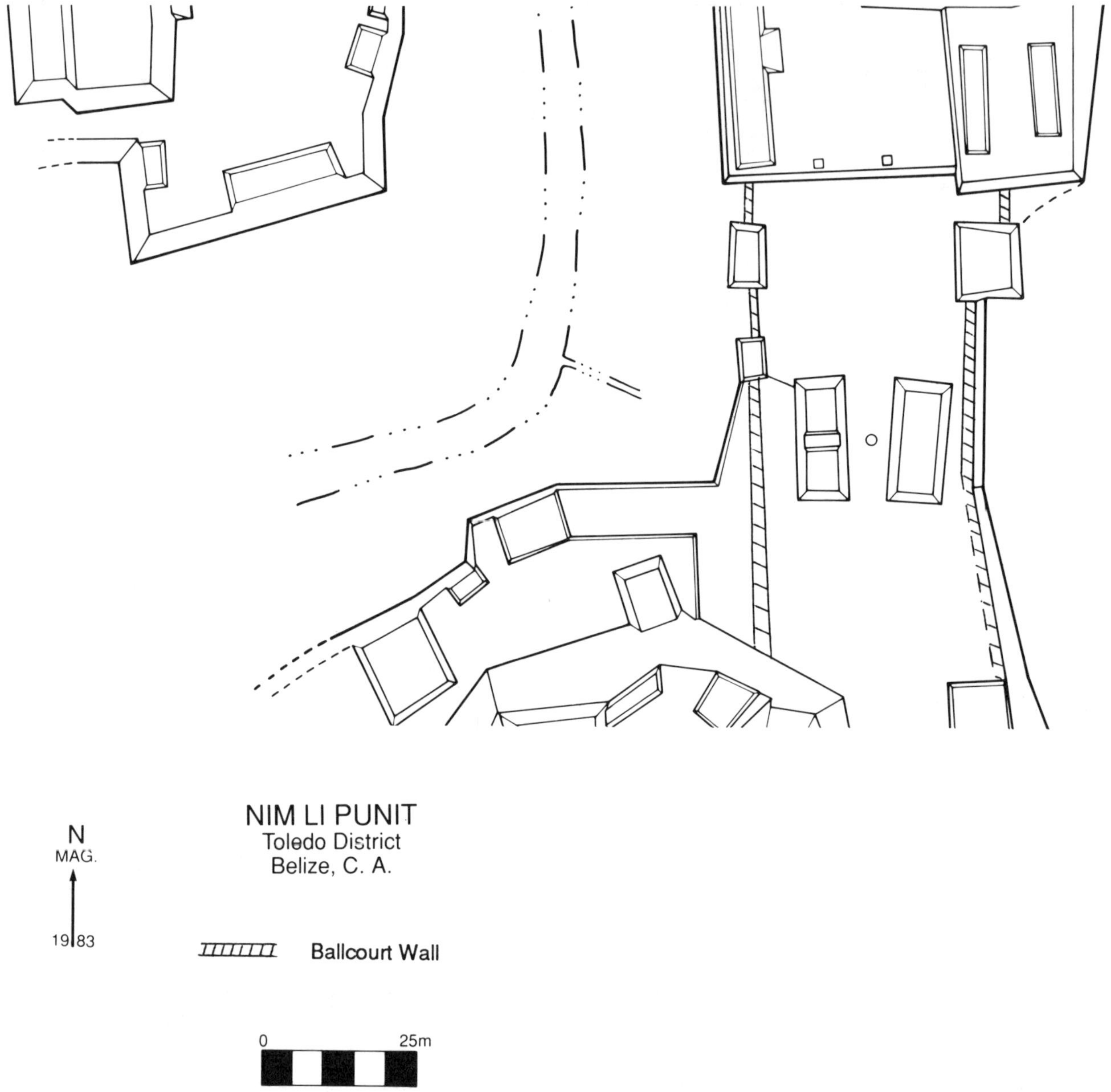

NIM LI PUNIT
Toledo District
Belize, C. A.

Figure 8.5b. Nim Li Punit Ballcourt

tains create what appears to be a clear geographic divide with little habitation evident within the central upper sections of the mountains.

We are currently examining several other features of these southern Belize sites for their internal regional homogeneity and external heterogeneity. Such studies include a detailed examination of architectural form and structure, ceramic types and forms, and settlement density and organization.

Conclusion

The culture area concept of the early twentieth century remains dominant in much of the research and analysis within Mesoamerica and within the Maya area. With this perspective, archaeologists have in the past emphasized the similarities that bind the Maya Lowland area together (the macroperspective), while glossing over the numerous differences. It is important to begin to break out of this culture area construct and examine some of these differences as indications of a regional organization for the ancient Lowland Maya culture.

The lack of a single dominant center and the large number of Maya centers scattered throughout the lowlands can only be explained by a regional structure. Each of these centers (the microperspective) is unique in its own right. But the region should become another important focal point of study and analysis and help mediate between the micro- and macroperspectives. Maya culture clearly exists with an overarching cohesion but this can no longer remain the dominant view. Regional variation and differences of style create a more complex and perhaps complete picture of ancient Maya civilization.

Although still in the preliminary stages, we have attempted to use southern Belize as a testing ground for such a regional model. It surely has long-distance connections with the rest of the outside Maya world and the entire Mesoamerican world, but more importantly, there are numerous features that clearly indicate the internal homogeneity of this region. Future work on the material from southern Belize and from future regional projects should provide us with a more complete analysis of this regional model. Any region defined archaeologically should not be seen as existing in stasis for several hundred if not thousand years. In fact, one of the difficulties in utilizing this model is that these regions were dynamic, constantly changing their structure and boundaries. Still, an analysis of the Maya Lowlands in terms of regions will provide a new perspective on the ancient Maya world.

Nine

 *House Names and Dedication Rituals at Palenque*

By Linda Schele

Images from the Group of the Cross were among the first Maya art published in the modern world, and since Maudslay (1889–1902) published the first accurate photographs and drawings, the many relief-carved panels mounted in this group have figured prominently in the study of iconography and glyphic decipherment.[1]

Each of the three temples in the Group (the Temple of the Cross, hereafter TC; the Temple of the Foliated Cross, TFC; the Temple of the Sun, TS) housed a set of stone and stucco texts and images, including the following:

(1) a large panel on the rear wall of the inner sanctuary recording the main text and central image of each temple;
(2) a panel mounted on the outer wall on either side of the entrance to the sanctuary;
(3) panels mounted on the inside of the doorjamb of the sanctuary;
(4) a single line text running at lintel height across the front of each sanctuary;
(5) a continuous stucco text mounted on the end piers of each temple front;
(6) balustrade panels mounted on either side of the stairs about halfway up the pyramidal base.

The three main texts on the large panels of the sanctuaries record interlocked information using a repeated composition and discourse pattern, although there is significant variation in each temple program. In all cases, the left side of the text records mythological information while the right concerns historical events. The panel of the TC, which records the births and accessions of Palenque's Early Classic dynasty through Chan-Bahlum I, is most distant from the formula used in the two companion temples. Nevertheless, these highly redundant texts concern a very limited number of events. The pattern of the mythological events is as follow:

TC: the births of the mother and father of the gods; a sky event by the father of the gods shortly after the beginning of this era; the birth of GI (God I of the Palenque Triad [Berlin 1963; Kelley 1965]); and the accession of his mother.

TFC: birth of GII of the Triad and the first bloodletting rite by the mother of the gods.

TS: birth of GIII of the Triad and oblique indication of a Jupiter hierophany associated with the 819-day Count clause.

The historical events are the major political and ritual events in the life of the Late Classic Ruler, Chan-Bahlum II (who commissioned the group). These include his birth, his designation as heir, his accession, and two events we have hitherto not been able to understand, although we have discovered much more about the historical contexts in which they occurred. The first of these began on 9.12.16.5.16 2 Cib 14 Mol and continued for three days culminating in a bloodletting rite. The second occurred on 9.12.19.14.12 5 Eb 5 Kayab, which was also the eighth tropical year anniversary of Chan-Bahlum's accession. Recent work by David Stuart (1986) on the Primary Standard Sequence and by Stuart and myself on the inscriptions of Copan have given us the keys to understanding these events at Palenque, which turned out to be the dedication rituals for the temples and inner sanctuaries of the Cross Group.

The 2 Cib 14 Mol Series

The 2 Cib 14 Mol event series (Figures 9.1–9.3) is

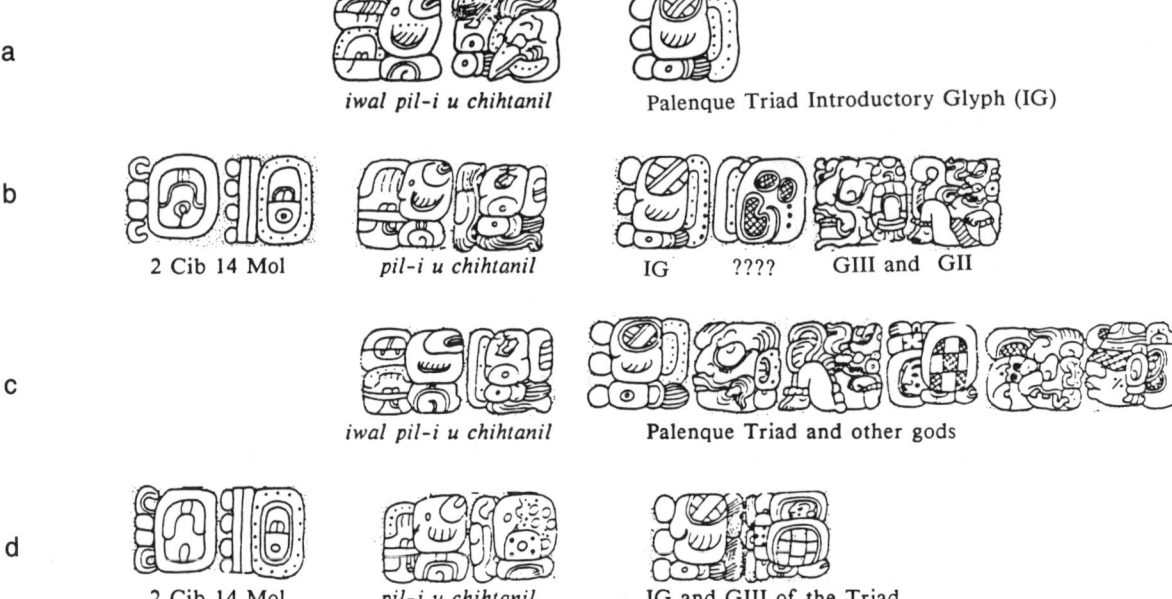

Figure 9.1. The 2 Cib 14 Mol Passages at Palenque. a. Temple of the Cross, O5–O7; b., c. Temple of the Foliated Cross, L1–M4, N8–N12; d. Temple of the Sun, N4–D6.

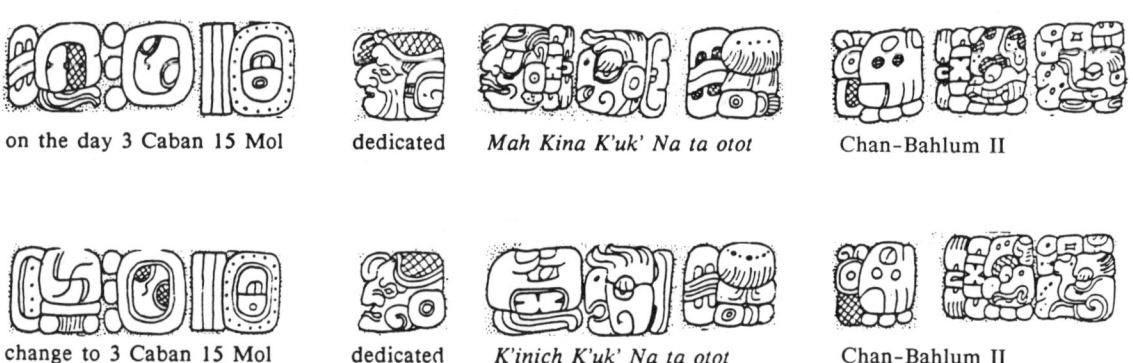

Figure 9.2. The 3 Caban Mol Passages at Palenque. *top.* Temple of the Foliated Cross, L5–M9; *bottom.* Temple of the Sun, N7–O12.

Figure 9.3. The 5 Imix 17 Mol Bloodletting Passages at Palenque. a. Temple of the Cross; b. Temple of the Foliated Cross; c. Temple of the Sun.

recorded on all three panels: in the secondary text behind the image of Chan-Bahlum on the TC, in the first two columns of the right half of the text on the TFC and TS, and in the final clause of the TFC. On the TC and TFC, the 2 Cib event is linked by Distance Number (6.11.6) to the date of Chan-Bahlum's accession and, most significantly, on the TFC and TS, it is linked directly to the births of GII and GIII, perhaps as a declaration of a causal relationship between the two events. This ritual was apparently composed of three consecutive events occurring over a four day period: the first on 2 Cib, the second one day later on 3 Caban, and the third two days later on 5 Cauac. The first and third events are recorded in all three temples, but the middle event (3 Caban) only occurs on the TFC and TS.

Two primary associations for the first event on 2 Cib 14 Mol (Figure 9.1), both resulting from insights by Floyd Lounsbury, have emerged over the years of research. The first association concerns tropical year anniversaries. By 1975, Lounsbury had noted the occurrence of a glyphic expression T79-*te naab-chaan*[2] on the Tableritos (from the Subterranean Corridors of the Palace) in association with the thirteen *haab* anniversary of Chan-Bahlum's heir designation event. Since the same phrase also occurred with the 5 Eb 5 Kayab event on the alfardas and doorjambs, and since this date is the eighth tropical year anniversary of his accession, the anniversary link seemed more than coincidental, although we had no specific evidence then or now that this expression meant "anniversary." Since this same expression closes the 2 Cib episode on the TFC and TS, it seemed possible that those rites were also associated with an anniversary. In checking this date, I found it is indeed very close to a tropical year anniversary of Pacal's accession,[3] as seen in the following dates:

9. 9. 2.4.8	5 Lamat	1 Mol	(29 July 615)	accession of Pacal
9.12.18.5.16	2 Cib	14 Mol	(23 July 690)	anniversary event
3.16.1.8	= 75 (365) + 13 days			

+ 13 days	(23 July 690)	2 Cib 14 Mol	1st event of the series
+ 14 days	(24 July 690)	3 Caban 15 Mol	2d event of the series
+ 15 days	***skipped (this is the 7th tun anniversary of Pacal's death)		
+ 16 days	(26 July 690)	5 Cauac 17 Mol	3d event of the series
+ 19 days	(29 July 690)	true tropical year anniversary	

Although we have no direct evidence that the rites recorded in this episode were specifically designed to be anniversary celebrations, it seems likely that proximity of the Pacal anniversary was considered in the selection of these particular dates.

However, Lounsbury has also shown that this ritual sequence was also timed by an astronomical hierophany as well.[4] On 2 Cib 14 Mol, which corresponds to July 20, 690 in the Julian calendar, Jupiter was at 221.48 and Saturn at 225.51, 4.03° apart in the sky.[5] Furthermore, both planets were frozen at their stationary points, unmoving for over forty days. On this day, first movement from the stationary point could be detected by the unaided human eye. Lounsbury proposed that this Jupiter-Saturn hierophany was the trigger for the 2 Cib 14 Mol series of rituals.

At first, I did not believe the Maya would have paid attention to this type of heavenly event for it did not seem that impressive to me. But over the years I have checked potential Jupiter associations with the occurrences of the same verb in other inscriptions (for example the ear-flares from Tortuguero) and with different events, such as the bloodletting on Lintel 24 of Yaxchilan. The Jupiter associations are consistent enough to convince me that the Maya were indeed preoccupied with the stationary points of Jupiter and with Jupiter and Saturn as a pair.

Both the anniversary and Jupiter-Saturn associations with this event appear to be real, but until recently we had no clues as to how to read the verb itself. New readings proposed recently by Fox, Justeson, and Stuart for various components of the verbal phrase have yielded the following possibility: *pil-i u chitanil* (*pil-i* "to be one of a pair," "to accompany" and *u chitanil* "their awaited prey") (Figure 9.1).[6] Certainly, the freezing of Jupiter and Saturn at their stationary points is adequately described as a "pairing." While the identification of "awaited prey" is as yet unknown, the concepts of warfare and the hunt are associated with astronomical phenomena in the Venus pages of the Dresden Codex. I presume one of the planets was the "awaited prey" of the other. Regardless of the reading or interpretation of the verb, the Jupiter hierophany identified by Lounsbury was surely the trigger event for the ritual sequence that followed.

The 3 Caban 15 Mol Event

In the TFC and TS, the "Jupiter companion" event is followed on the next day by a God N event (Figure 9.2), but this second event is conspicuously absent in the texts of the TC. Our understanding of this second event has also changed over the years with a slow and steady accumulation of information. The first clue came when Peter Mathews (n.d.) recognized that the so-called "west" glyph that follows the God N glyph on the TS is, in fact, a substitution for the *Mah K'ina* title that occupies the same position on the TFC clause. Before this discovery, we had believed these glyphs to be directionals marking the event for "east" (TFC) and "west" (TS). Mathews's substitution clearly demonstrated that the *chi* variant in the TS is not a direction; just as importantly, the glyph for "west" is never written with the T671 during the Classic period. Accepting the equivalency between these two forms, David Stuart (personal communication 1985) read the T671 version of the title as *k'in-ni-chi* (T544: 166: 671) or *k'inich*, "sun-faced" or "sun-eyed." The *Mah K'ina*

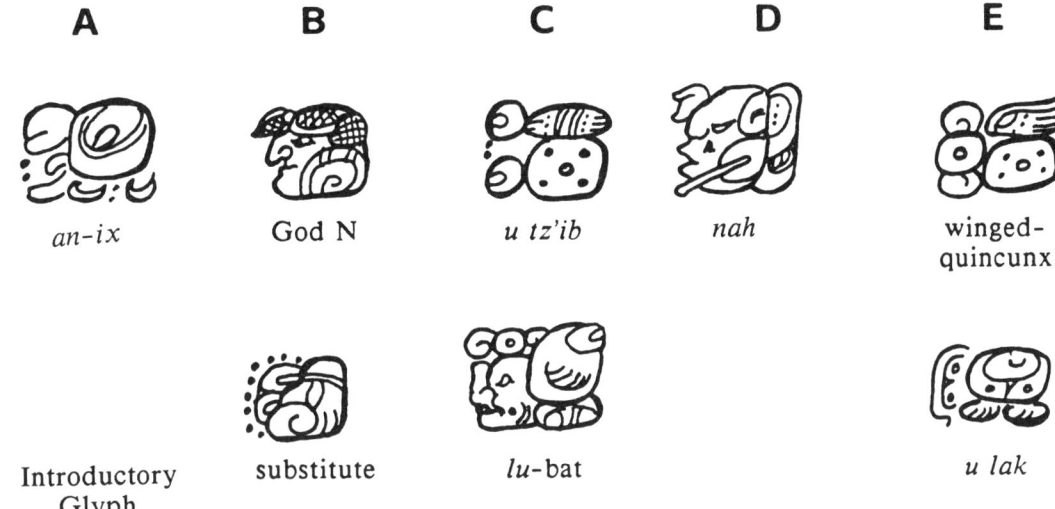

Figure 9.4. The Primary Standard Sequence Substitutions.

and *K'inich* glyphs are different ways of spelling the same title.

Using the Mathews's substitution, Floyd Lounsbury (personal communication 1978) suggested that the *Mah K'ina K'uk'* and *K'inich K'uk'* glyphs following the verb, in fact, name the actor of the clause as the first historical ancestor recorded in the lineage history on the TC (Schele 1978–87). Originally, I found his suggestion problematic for the following reasons:

(1) Since K'uk's name is followed by a "house" glyph, it has always seemed to me that the *Mah K'ina* and *K'uk'* glyphs are part of the verbal phrase. A "house" glyph can serve as a second verb, but I know of no examples where such a "house" verb is also preceded by a locative preposition as we have in this text. The verb concerns something done "in the house."

(2) Since Chan-Bahlum II's name closes this clause, it seemed likely to me that he is the agent. Possibly K'uk' could be recorded as an indirect object, but I found this explanation unlikely because of the "house" (*ta otot*) glyph between the two names.

(3) Both examples of the quetzal (*k'uk'*) name have a *na* sign attached to them; since no other examples of the royal name have this *na*, I felt the identification of this name phrase with the first ancestor's name was not securely proven.

Recent work at Copan and on the Primary Standard Sequence (hereafter PSS) by David Stuart (1986) and Ruth Krochock (in press) has given us a key to this Palenque event. David Stuart's long interest in the PSS came to fruition in the summer of 1986 as he worked on the inscriptions of Copan. He sees the PSS as a limited set of glyphs recording the artistic execution, type, function, and patronage of the pot. The following analysis (Figure 9.4) summarizes his identifications, although other glyphs can be inserted into this sequence and parts of it can be eliminated. The constants are as follows:

(A) The PSS begins with an Introductory Glyph, composed of T228 *a*, a mirror sign *nen* or *ne*, and T126 *ya* or *ix*. Together, they form the term *an-i* or *an-ix*, from the existential stem *an*. T126 is either a clitic meaning "ago" or a *plus cuam perfective*, giving the meaning "it had existed." The glyph is much like "once upon a time" in our own oral tradition.

(B) God N, the second glyph in the PSS, usually has a T575 shell infixed in the cheek or suffixed to it. The most normal suffix is T18 or one of its substitutes. Houston (personal communication 1982) was the first epigrapher to identify T45.843, a glyph resembling a pyramidal platform with an attached footprint, as a substitute for this God N.

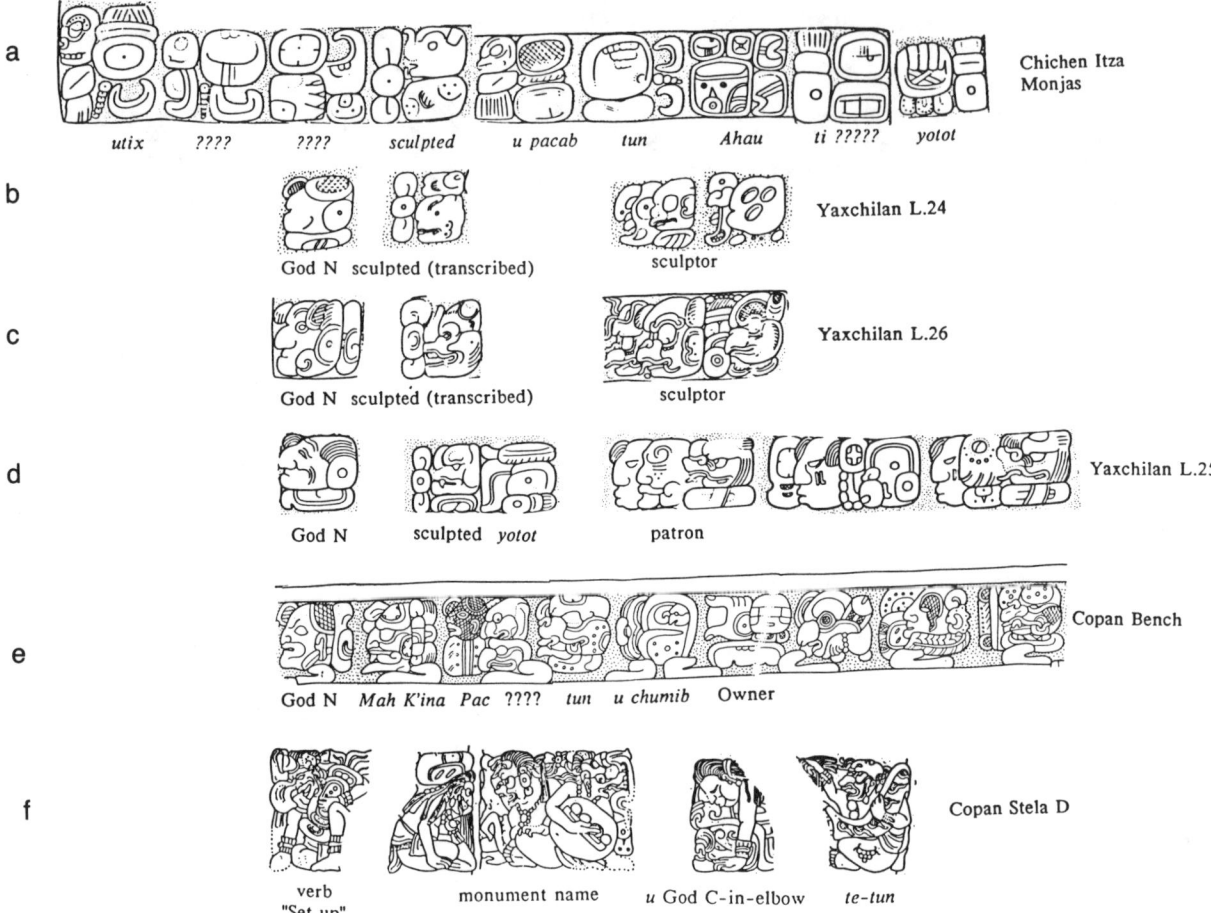

Figure 9.5. "Lu-Bat" Expressions and Monument Dedications. Drawings a–d by Ian Graham; e–f by Barbara Fash.

(C) The third component of the PSS has been identified by David Stuart as *u tz'ib* (Stuart 1988: 1–11), "its painting" or "its inscribing." Stuart (1986) also noted that when a pot is sculpted in relief rather than painted, the "lu-bat" replaces *u tz'ib;* he has proposed that the "lu-bat" is a word for "to sculpt" or some equivalent action concerning carved art.

(D) *U tz'ib* can be followed optionally by either phonetic *nah* or *nahal*. We do not yet understand its function, although Barbara MacLeod and Ruth Krochock have suggested it functions as a verbal ending.

(E) *U tz'ib nahal* is followed by one of two glyphs designating the type of ceramic vessel. Houston and Taube (n.d.) identified one of these as *u lak,* "his plate," and suggested the other, "winged-quincunx," as the glyph for other types of vessel, such as cylindrical vases.

The PSS constants conclude with a series of glyphs (not illustrated) tentatively identified by Stuart as naming the substance, usually blood or some form of cacao, used in the vessel. The name phrase of the patron finishes the PSS text in many examples, followed more rarely by the name of the painter or sculptor.

Based on Stuart's insights into ceramic texts, Ruth Krochock (in press) has suggested that dedication phrases on the lintels of Chichen Itza used the same basic clause sequence, specialized for that context. In these texts, the "*lu*-bat" begins each of these dedication phrases, as in Figure 9.5a, in which it is followed by *u pacab tun ahau ti ???? yotot*, "the stone *ahau* lintel of his house." Here the God N verb is missing, but note that the object carved, a lintel, is used instead of the glyphs for a plate or cylindrical vessel. Stuart has suggested a meaning "to sculpt" for the "*lu*-bat," while Krochock proposes *u tz'il* "to transcribe writing from one media to another." "*Lu*-bat," also occurs on several of the lintels of Yaxchilan, preceded by the God N verb and followed by the sculptor's name (Figure 9.5b, c). On Lintel 26 (Figure 9.5d), it is followed by *yotot* and the name of the patron in a text I suspect records the dedication of the stucco sculpture of Structure 23 at Yaxchilan.

The God N verb also appears as the dedication event on a bench from Copan (Figure 9.5e) as it appears in a variety of phrases on pottery, lintels, buildings, and stela that record the dedication, erection, or decoration of these objects. On Copan stelae, the God N verb is replaced by one specialized to stone monuments (Figure 9.5f) and in an expression that also includes the proper name of the object dedicated. Thus, we have a consistent pattern found on many different kinds of objects composed of the following: a verb meaning something like "to dedicate" or "to erect"; sometimes the glyph for "to write" or "to sculpt (or transcribe)"; the proper name of the object, and the type of object (plate, house, stela, altar) to which the text refers.

At Copan, Stuart has also noted patterns in which the proper name of the monument is followed by a God C-in-elbow glyph (Figures 9.5f and 9.6i).[7] This same naming pattern is associated with yet another "dedication" verb, consisting of the tail of a rattlesnake prefixed to a "fire" glyph and showing up with house events at several sites (Figure 9.6). This "fire" verb is usually followed by the proper name of the building, sometimes a God C-in-elbow glyph, and the glyph *yotot* (Figure 9.6b–h). This pattern closely matches the naming pattern of Copan stelae, although a different verb is used and the object named is a *te-tun*, or "stone-tree." The rite and the object dedicated can thus change in these clauses, but the information is basically the same.

Stuart (personal communication 1986) is also the first to recognize that a phrase equivalent to our 3 Caban 15 Mol event is recorded at Copan. In drawing the Early Classic step under Temple 11, he recognized the same "fire" dedication event that we have seen at Palenque and Yaxchilan, but here the building is clearly named, thus providing the key to our Palenque text. The "fire" verb is followed by a special form of the Copan Emblem glyph (Figure 9.6a), in which the standard *ahau* title (T168 or an equivalent) is replaced by T4 *na*, the word for "structure" or "building." This glyph reads "blood Copan building" or "Copan lineage house." It is followed by *yotot*, "the house of," and *Mah K'ina Yax-K'uk'-Mo'*, the name of the founder of Copan's lineage. The "building of the Copan Lineage" and "the house of the founder" are different ways of saying the same thing. For us, it is important that one of Yax-K'uk'-Mo's successors named a temple after the founder of his lineage.

At Palenque, we have the God N verb in place of the "fire" rite, but the building is named in the same way. The verb is followed by *Mah K'ina K'uk' Na*, "the Mah K'ina K'uk' house," and, like Yax-K'uk'-Mo', K'uk' of Palenque is the first historical ruler in the dynasty listed in the main text of the TC: he is the founder. The 3 Caban 15 Mol event (Figure 9.2) is the dedication of the Group of the Cross as the house of the lineage founder and his successors.

The final event in this ritual sequence occurred two days later with a "fish-in-hand" bloodletting rite by Chan-Bahlum II (Figure. 9.3). This bloodletting is recorded in all three temples with a complex expression which appears to specify ritual context as well as action. The expressions of this rite in the TS and TFC include the *te-naab-chaan* phrase that Lounsbury had associated with anniversaries.

These sections of the Group of the Cross then record the dedication of the Group of the Cross as the *Mah K'ina K'uk' Na*, the "house of the lineage founder." The ritual sequence was timed in two ways: it was near the 75th tropical year anniversary of the accession of Chan-Bahlum's father, and it was the first day that motion could be detected as Jupiter moved out of its second stationary point and a spectacular alignment with Saturn. This last event appears to have been directly recorded as *pil-?? u chihtanil*. On the next day the group was dedicated and given its name as the house of the founder; two days later Chan-Bahlum let blood. The association

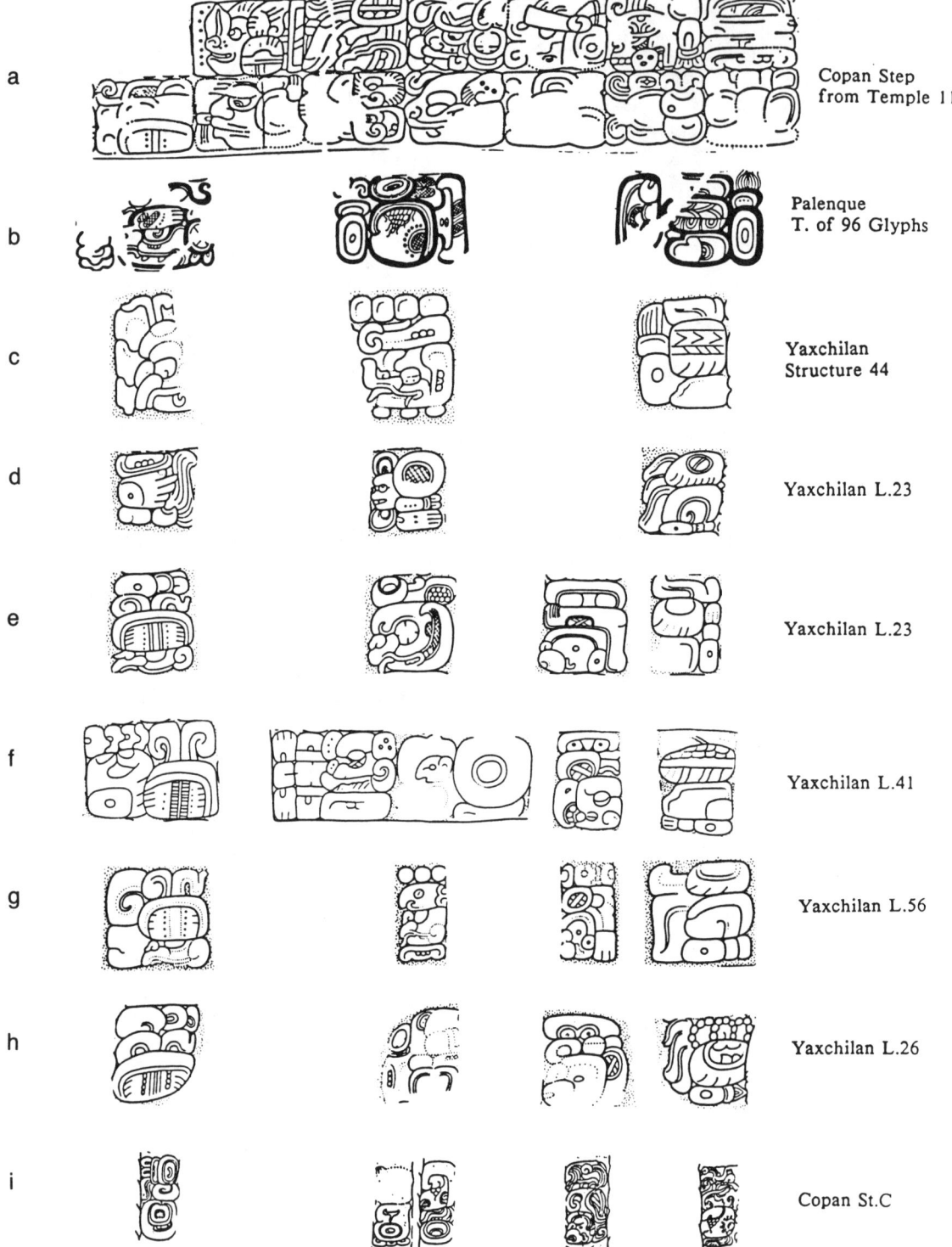

Figure 9.6. Copan, Temple 11 and the "Fire" Dedication Events. Drawings a by David Stuart; b by Linda Schele; c–h by Ian Graham; i by Barbara Fash.

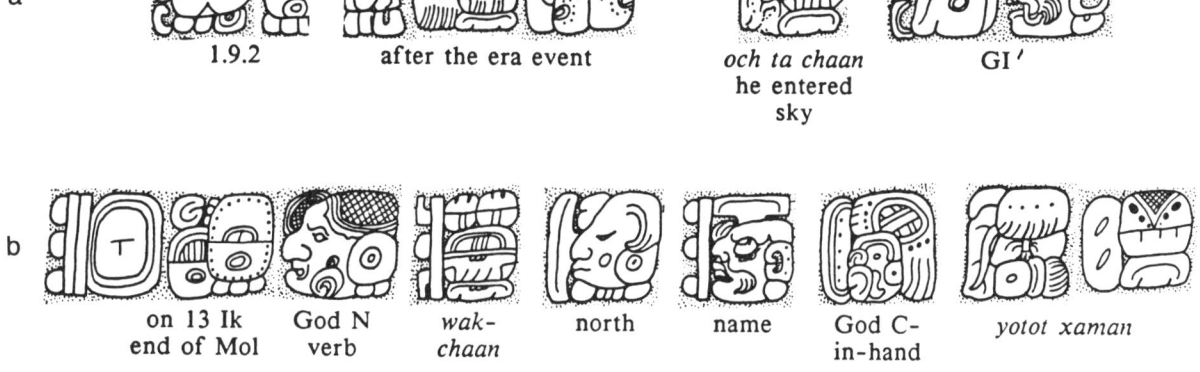

Figure 9.7. House of G1 and the Sky Event.

of this kind of house dedication event with timely astronomical alignments has been noted by Tate (1986) for Yaxchilan.

The House of GI and the Creation of the Sky

The dedication of the Group of the Cross by Chan-Bahlum is set in a careful composition linking it with the birth of the gods of the Palenque Triad and the actions of the gods before and just after the creation of the New Era on 4 Ahau 8 Cumku. Of these mythological events, a house dedication by the father of the Palenque Triad, GI' (prime), is deliberately established as the model for the king's actions in historical time. The record of these events occurs in the second episode of the TC, following the birth episode for the mother of the gods (see Lounsbury 1976, 1980, 1985; Schele 1984, 1987).

Taking place on 13 Ik end of Mol, 1.9.2 after the era date, this mythological event is recorded in a couplet construction (Lounsbury 1980: 99–106). The first statement of the action (Figure 9.7a) is recorded as *och ta chaan* "he entered the sky" (Schele 1987). This same event is shown on a codex-style pot (Robiscek and Hales 1981: 83, 85–86) and interestingly enough the scene is directly related to the central image of the TC. The Hero Twin Hun Ahau aims a blowgun at the Principal Bird Deity, who is flying in to land in the branches of the World Tree. The day of this action is 1 Ahau 3 Kankin and agent of the *och chaan* event is named with the portrait head of the bird. On the TC, the actor is clearly GI', but the correlation of this scene to the imagery of the World Tree on the TC suggests the event generated the tree itself and involved the Principal Bird Deity.

In its second manifestation (Figure 9.7b), this event is recorded with the God N verb, here followed by *wak-ah-chaan* ("six-sky"), the glyph for north, a name-variant of GI', with the number eight and phonetic *na* prefixed to his portrait, and the God C-in-elbow that we have seen as the closing glyphs of proper names. The next glyph designates the type of object dedicated as *y-otot xaman*, "house north." Nicholas Hopkins long ago suggested to me that *wak-ah* might refer to the verbal stem *wak* with a verbal ending. Barrera-Vasquez (1980: 906) glosses *wak* as *cosa enhiesta* ("something set up or raised on high"). In the Motul dictionary (Martinez 1929: 884), *wakab* appears as *cosa que está en pie o enhiesta delante de otro. (De aqui selen los cuatro* **vacab** *o* **bacabes,** *dioses benéficos tutelares, regentes de los años*

Temple of the Cross

u pib nail

Temple of the Foliated Cross

u pib nail

Temple of the Sun

u pib nail

Figure 9.8. 5 Eb 5 Kayab Events on the Temple Alfardas of Cross Group, Palenque.

que son **Kan, Muluc, Hix,** *y* **Cauac,** *enhiestos en los cuatro puntos cardinales . . .*). Both of these entries suggest a house made of the sky raised up on high as described for the atlantean *bacabs.* Perhaps even more relevant is the creation sequence from the Mixtec Vienna Codex in which the supernatural, 9 Wind, lifts up the sky in a scene analogous both to the myth of the bacabs and to the name of this house as *wakah chaan xaman,* "raised up sky of the north."

This 13 Ik end of Mol event is characterized, then, as "entering or becoming the sky" in the first half of the couplet and as the establishment of a north house named *wakah-chaan,* which may mean to lift up the sky from the sea; "north," suggesting that the house corresponds to the pivoting of the sky around the polar star; and *waxac na* GI', a unique variant of GI', as if this part of the sky is being named for the god who structured its order. In the final part of the name, it is called *yotot xaman,* "house of the north." This divine event is deliberately presented as the prototype of the second house event on 2 Cib. The verbs are the same (God N) and the houses are named in phrases with the same structure.

The 5 Eb Event and the Inner Sanctuaries

The inscriptions recording the latest event in the Group of the Cross, 5 Eb 5 Kayab, were displayed on the alfardas[8] (Figure 9.8), on the doorjambs of the interior sanctuaries (Fig. 9.9), and on the first and fourth piers on each temple façade (not illustrated).[9] In each of these inscriptions, the verb is composed of the T221 fist that also appears in the "west" glyph, a piece of cloth that may represent the curtains in a Maya building, and a variant of T518. This last sign has been taken by many of us to be a

Temple of the Cross   Temple of the Foliated Cross   Temple of the Sun

Figure 9.9. 5 Eb 5 Kayab Events on the Sanctuary Door Jambs, Cross Group, Palenque.

Classic version of the *chu* glyph, but David Stuart has recently suggested that here and in the *otot* house glyph, it represents a pyramidal platform. The best demonstration of this idea is a "house" glyph on MT 140 (Figure 9.10b) from Tikal, in which the thatch, walls, and platform of the house are clearly distinguishable. Both here and in the regular house glyph, this sign is simply part of the pictorial representation of the house.

Long ago, Floyd Lounsbury suggested this 5 Eb event is a version of the "house" glyph, a proposal I had previously resisted because I could not produce a reading of T221 that would support this meaning. However, the new insights provided by the dedication events described above have changed my mind. Further, Lounsbury and others had noted that a probable 5 Eb 5 Kayab date is also found on a fragment from the Palace at Palenque, and here it clearly occurs with a "house" verb—*na otot-ah* (Schele and Mathews 1979:#40). This use of a standard house glyph with the 5 Eb 5 Kayab date confirms the nature of the event and very probably the meaning of the T221 verb.

In the TC and TFC, this "house" verb is followed by a glyph specifically tied to the Triad god associated with each temple. In the TC, this is the *wakah-chaan* glyph we discussed with the God N event of the first GI. In the TFC, two different glyphs are used but they must be analogous. On the TFC alfarda (Figure 9.8, middle), we have a glyph consisting of a *na* sign prefixed to a *k'an*-cross with the leaves of the sarcophagus tree superfixed to it. I believe this is a metaphor of the maize tree at the center of the TFC scene and a reference to GII. On the TFC doorjamb (Figure 9.9, middle), the *k'an* glyph is replaced by a sign consisting of the number nine, a personified variant of the *muluc* glyph in the form that appears in the Yaxchilan Emblem glyph—a jade disk; and phonetic *na*. In the TS, we have only one example from this position since only the lunar series of the doorjamb panels survive. The glyph is written with a *Mah K'ina* title, prefixed to a hand and an unknown sign over an earth glyph. We have no other contexts in which this glyph is associated with the TS or GIII, but it bears remarkable resemblance to one of the variants of the Copan name *Yax-Pac*. If this is in fact the same glyph, then the reference is to the sun at dawn, and, interestingly enough, the winter solstice sunrise lights the interior of this sanctuary.

On the doorjambs, these name glyphs are followed by the God C-in-hand glyph that we have identified as a closure for proper names, although this glyph is missing on the alfardas. In all of these texts, the final glyph in the phrase is composed of a third-person pronoun preceding *pi-bi-na-vl* (GI on the alfardas), a glyph that most likely records the category of object being discussed. In other dedication texts, for example, this slot would be filled by *y-otot*, *te-tun*, or the type of pot. I have not been able to find an entry for *pib* in the Cholan languages, but in Yucatec, it is the root for *pibil*, the cooking done in a pit, and for stream baths as used for the sick and for women who have recently given birth. *Nail* is the word for "house," marked by the *-vl* suffix for possession. *Nal* can also be used in terms like *zihnal*, meaning "place of birth or origin." Since this noun is possessed, the *nail* reading seems the most likely one, but I am not sure how the *pib* relates to the house term. On the doorjamb of the TFC, *pib-nail* is replaced by a glyph consisting of a cauac over a belt ornament. Since *pibnail* occurs in the position where the object should be designated, it should be the term for some part of the architecture of each temple. Since the proper name specific to each temple appears to refer to some component of its main panel, I think it likely that *pibnail* is the term for the inner sanctuary itself.

That these phrases name the interior sanctuaries seems to be confirmed by the lintel text surviving in the TC sanctuary. The text ran across the tops of the outer panels onto the wooden lintel that once spanned the door (Figure 9.10a). Although we do not have the middle section of the text, the remaining sections give us enough information to understand what it recorded. Beginning without a verb, the text starts over the west panel with *Wakah Chaan*, the God C-in-hand glyph, and the cauac variant of the "sanctuary" glyph discussed above. This is the exact name recorded on the alfardas and the doorjamb of the sample temple. The text ends over the west panel with "GI, the child of *Mah K'ina* Chan-Bahlum, Blood Palenque *ahau*," reproducing exactly the conclusion of the doorjamb text. The analogous texts from the TFC have not survived, but the TS text ends with the blood glyph used on the alfardas and Chan-Bahlum's name. Since no date or verb introduces these texts, we may presume they name the building, much as verbless texts name actors in narrative scenes.

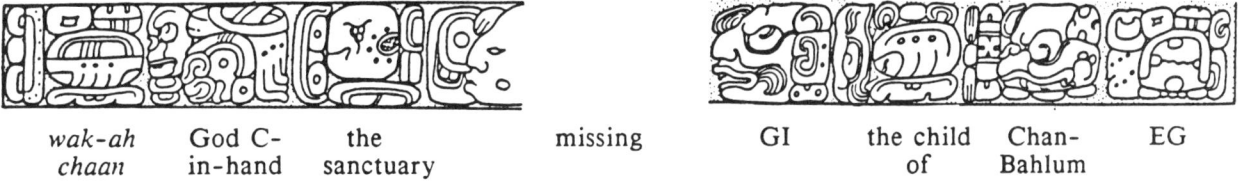

| wak-ah chaan | God C-in-hand | the sanctuary | missing | GI | the child of | Chan-Bahlum | EG |

a

b

Figure 9.10. a. Lintel text from the Temple of the Cross, Palenque. b. Miscellaneous Text 140 from Tikal (after Kubler, 1969: fig. 53.)

This latest event of the Group of the Cross is the dedication or "housing" of the Triad gods in the sanctuaries of the Group, for the actors are the gods themselves. On the alfardas, this action is directly linked to the birth of each Triad god, and on the doorjambs of the sanctuaries the actors are the gods themselves, not the king, where the actors are clearly identified as the gods, rather than Chan-Bahlum. Chan-Bahlum's name occurs on the doorjamb and main tablet in a statement calling him the "mother of the gods" (Schele 1984, 1987). Each sanctuary is named for some quality of its patron god, and perhaps the names relate to the central image of the scene depicted on each tablet. The TC is named *Wakah Chaan*, the same name given to the house created by GI', the father of the Triad. Most interestingly, the central image is the World Tree with a Serpent Bar and the Quadripartite Badge, an imagery complex persistently associated with the Vision Serpent (Schele and M. Miller 1986: 105–16, 282–85, 310–12). Furthermore, David Stuart (1984b) has suggested that the Double-Headed Serpent Bar is structurally related, if not equivalent, to the Vision Serpent, which is named on several pots and the Hauberg Stela as *Wak-Chaan*, "Six-Sky." *Wak-ah-chaan* may, then, be the name of this cosmic structure, which in turn may be related to the house dedicated by the first GI on 13 Ik end of Mol.

Summary

These house dedication events are recorded at many Classic sites and represent a fairly large percentage of the undeciphered portion of the corpus. The dedication of the Group of the Cross at Palenque was triggered by the Jupiter-Saturn hierophany. This association of house dedications with celestial events is also present at Yaxchilan (Tate 1986). The texts of the Group of the Cross, however, offer us insight into the religious foundation of these temple dedication rituals in that they deliberately compare the dedication of the historical temple group with the setting up of a cosmic house 1.9.2 after the beginning of this era. This cosmic house can be associated with the World Tree at the center of the world and with the path traveled by the Vision Serpent (Schele and Miller 1986: 105–16, 282–85, 310–12). The erection and dedication of temples was seen then by the Maya as a replication of the ordering of the universe at the beginning of this era.

Perhaps most importantly, the dedication of the Group of the Cross can be tied to very specific archaeology. Miguel Angel Fernandez and other archaeologists (García Moll 1985: 166–226 and Ruz Lhuillier 1958) investigated the caches deposited under the floors of the temples and in the outer terraces and courtyard. Similar dedication and termination caches are documented at almost all Maya sites. These include the lip-to-lip caches found at Tikal, Uaxactun, and the northeastern Peten and Belize. Perhaps one of the most interesting of these dedication caches is MT 140, deposited in the Central Acropolis at Tikal. The image shows an anthropomorphic figure holding a double-headed bar emitting the Paddler Gods[10] and with the end head specified for each Paddler. A Quadripartite God sits isolated as a separate image at the end of the double-headed bar. The text begins with the *anix* and the substitute for the God N verb. These two glyphs are followed by "house" and a God C "blood" glyph, and the name Jaguar Paw of Tikal. This vessel was found in a dedication cache, confirming a linkage between the function of the vessel as described in its text and its archaeological context. This linkage may be extended to include the "house dedication" texts at many sites and the archaeological remains of the rituals these texts record.

Notes

1. These panels have been part of studies focusing on calendric, religious, iconographic, syntactical discourse, and decipherment research. Some of the most important studies include the following: Berlin (1963, 1965), Freidel and Schele (1985), Kelley (1965), Lounsbury (1976, 1980, 1985), Mathews and Schele (1974), Schele (1974, 1976, 1979, 1981, 1985b, 1978–87), Schele and Freidel (1985), Seler (1902), and Teeple (1930).

2. Capital T refers to J. E. S. Thompson's numbering system in his *Catalog of Maya Hieroglyphs* (1962).

3. The first Late Classic ruler of Palenque and father of Chan-Bahlum II.

4. For many years, the 819-day Count date of the TS had puzzled us because it is not the correct station for the Initial Series date. Furthermore, the Distance Number introducing that section of the text leads not to the recorded date, 1 Ik 10 Zec, but to a nonsense date that cannot possibly be an 819-day Count station.

Given these errors, we had tried to generate the most useful and logical explanations of the texts. For example, the recorded 819-day Count date, 1 Ik 10 Zec, is correct for the 2 Cib 14 Mol event discussed above. I had assumed that the erroneous record simply referred to this later date. After all, the 819-day Count in the TFC is the correct station for the IS dates of both the TFC and TS (they are only 14 days apart); logically the Maya could have used this slot to record the 819-day Count for another important date. Lounsbury, however, is not one to admit that the Maya made an error unless he can find no other explanation; after years of working with this 819-day Count and the odd Distance Number that introduces it, he discovered that the time between one of the possible 1 Ik 10 Zec stations and the CR reached by the odd Distance Number was evenly divisible by the Jupiter cycle. The arithmetic is as follows:

1.18. 5. 3. 6	13 Cimi	19 Ceh	(25 October, 2360 ..)
1. 2.11			
1.18. 4. 0.15	5 Men	13 Yax	(9 September, 2361 ..)
1. 6.14.11. 2	1 Ik	10 Zec	(24 July, 2587 ..) 819-DC
11. 9. 7.13		(207 Jupiter cycles)	
1.18. 4. 0.15	5 Men	13 Yax	(9 September, 2361 ..)

Lounsbury considered that the 5 Men 13 Yax and 1 Ik to 10 Zec positions were intended to signal the presence of a Jupiter hierophany somewhere in the chronology of the Group of the Cross. He decided to check the 2 Cib 14 Mol date first, since the 1 Ik 10 Zec is also the 819-day Count for that date as well (9.12.16.2.2). Using this 819-day Count as the prompt, he discovered that a spectacular hierophany between Saturn and Jupiter occurred on this day.

5. Building on Lounsbury's discovery of the Jupiter-Saturn hierophany, Dütting and Aveni (1982) noted that Mars and the Moon were also in close conjunction with Saturn and Jupiter on this night. They have suggested

that the three planets were seen as the Palenque Triad with the moon representing the mother of the gods. Since the birth dates of the GII and GIII are tied to this 2 Cib 14 Mol event in the TFC and TS, their suggestion seems a good one.

6. See *Notebook for the Maya Hieroglyphic Writing Workshop* (Schele 1987: 128–30) for a detailed explanation of these readings.

7. Judy Maxwell and David Stuart have independently suggested that the God C-in-elbow reads *u k'aba*, "it is its names" or "the name of." These reading have phonetic evidence supporting them, for instance, the frequent occurrence of T501 *ba* inside the elbow and T229 *a* as the final sign, and the meaning is very productive. I accept this reading as the most probable reading of this glyph.

8. Balustrades located half way up the pyramidal platform.

9. This text has survived in fragmentary form only on the Temple of the Sun (Thompson 1954), but each of the three temples repeat the same essential information in the same relative position. Presuming that this pattern held true for the stucco texts and images on the outer piers, the 5 Eb 5 Kayab event should have been depicted on the front of each temple.

10. These are the gods who paddle the canoe on the bones (MT 38a—d) from Burial 116 from Tikal. See Schele and Miller (1986: 52, 270) for descriptions and drawings.

Ten

The Role of Trading Ports in Maya Civilization

By Anthony P. Andrews[1]

Ever since John Lloyd Stephens visited the ruins of coastal Quintana Roo in 1842, archaeologists have been fascinated by the Maya coasts and their past cultural remains. Decades of exploration have led to the discovery of hundreds of sites along the coasts and offshore islands of Yucatán and Belize, and historians have assembled a large corpus of information on Maya maritime activities at the time of the Spanish conquest. The combined information from these sources has presented us with a vision of the coastal Maya that continuously grows in complexity.

The origins of a coastal way of life among the Maya go back to Archaic, and possibly, Paleo-Indian times. The oldest known settlements along the Lowland Maya coastline date to Preclassic times; from that time onward we can trace the development of a Maya maritime tradition involving the exploitation of coastal resources and growing networks of trade that culminated in the complex seafaring world the Spanish encountered in the sixteenth century.

Many of the small fishing hamlets that appeared on the Maya coast during the Preclassic and Classic periods evolved into highly specialized communities performing a variety of functions vital to Maya subsistence, commerce, and communication. While the exploration and excavation of Maya coastal communities has been going on for over a century, few studies have focused on the ports themselves as a major structural component of Maya civilization. This paper addresses this issue; through a comparative synthesis of the available data, I intend to explore the multiple functions of Maya ports and propose a typology of major types.

The Archaeology of the Lowland Maya Coasts

Research on Maya ports began in the mid and late nineteenth century with the initial coastal explorations of Stephens, Le Plongeon, and Holmes on the northern Quintana Roo coast, Charnay's exploration of Jaina on the Campeche coast, and Gann's excavations at Santa Rita in northern Belize. Subsequent work has led to sporadic explorations of sites all along the lowland coastline from Tabasco to Honduras. In the last 75 years, several large-scale regional surveys have been undertaken, numerous sites have been tested, and a handful have been excavated (for summaries and histories of this research see Lothrop 1924; Piña Chan 1968; Ruz Lhuillier 1969; Ball 1974, 1977a; Andrews IV and Andrews 1975; Sabloff and Rathje 1975; Andrews 1977, 1978a, 1978b, 1983b, 1985; Eaton 1978; Benavides Castillo and Andrews 1979; A. Miller 1982; Hammond 1983; Sidrys 1983; Robles and Andrews 1986; Vail 1987).

To date, over 320 sites have been reported along the coasts of Campeche, Yucatán, Quintana Roo, and Belize. Information on the history of occupation of these sites is limited, as it is based mostly on surveys, surface collections and limited test-pitting. Still, due to erosion processes at coastal sites, surface collections have proven to be unusually rich, enabling archaeologists to identify different periods of occupation at many localities. The survey and test-pitting data have been supplemented by large-scale excavations at a few prominent sites, such as Aguacatal (Matheny 1970), Jaina (Piña Chan 1968), Isla Cerritos (Andrews and Gallareta 1986), El

Meco (Andrews and Robles, in press), Cancún (Mayer Guala 1977; Vargas Pacheco 1978), Playa del Cármen (González de la Mata 1984), San Gervasio, Cozumel Island (Sabloff and Rathje 1975; Freidel and Sabloff 1984; Robles 1981a), Xelhá (Robles 1981b), Tancah (A. Miller 1982), Santa Rita (Gann 1900; D. Chase 1981, 1986) and Cerros (Freidel, Robertson, and Cliff 1982; Robertson and Freidel 1986). Tulúm, the most famous of Maya coastal sites, has never been subjected to large-scale excavations (but see Sanders 1960 and Barrera Rubio 1985 for the results of limited testing). Altogether, less than .5 percent of all known coastal sites have been subjected to extensive excavation.

Despite the fragmentary nature of the data, it is possible to offer a preliminary sketch of the history of occupation of the coasts, and to outline the major features of the growth of a maritime economy through time. A synopsis of these patterns follows.

Late Preclassic Period (300 B.C.–A.D. 250)

Late Preclassic occupations have been documented at approximately 55 sites on the coasts of the Maya Lowlands. Except for Cerros, a major population center on the north coast of Belize, most of these sites appear to be small fishing camps and hamlets; many may have been seasonal outposts, and most were probably supplying interior sites with marine resources. There is scattered evidence from this period of trade between the coast and the interior, as ceramics and stone artifacts were most likely traded for marine resources. At Dzibilchaltún and Komchén, several hundred marine shells from Preclassic deposits attest to close ties to sites on the nearby north coast. Smaller quantities of marine shells have also been found in Preclassic contexts as far inland as Tikal, Mirador, Altar de Sacrificios and Seibal. Moreover, evidence of long-distance trade has been reported from Cerros, Belize, and several sites on the north coast of Yucatán. It appears that at least 15 sites along the north coast were involved in salt making, which suggests that by the end of the period long-distance trade of this commodity to the south had begun. The presence of Cerros at the mouth of the New River in Chetumal Bay, and of numerous sites with pronounced Late Preclassic occupations in the Laguna de Términos area, clearly suggests the existence of coastal trade networks at this time.

Classic Period (A.D. 250–750)

Early and Late Classic (Early Period I and II) occupations have been identified at more than 100 coastal sites. While many of these sites are fishing hamlets, a fair number exhibit major public architecture and extended residential zones. The larger settlements include Jaina on the west coast, Xcambó, San Crisanto II, La Providencia, Emal, and Chiquilá on the north coast, and San Gervasio, Xelhá, and Tancah on the east coast. During this period, salt production became a large-scale affair on the north coast, as major complexes of salt pans and associated administrative centers appeared at several locations: at Xtampu, San Crisanto, La Providencia, Las Coloradas and El Cuyo. There is widespread documentation of coast-inland trade during this period throughout the lowlands, and solid evidence of long-distance coastal trade between the north and south.

A major pattern that emerges during the Classic period is the appearance of large settlements of urban proportions within 20 km of the coast. Examples include Chunchucmil, Tzemé, Dzibilchaltún, Yalcihóm, San Fernando, San Gervasio, Chunyaxché, and Altun Ha. Several of these may have been the capitals of small classic polities, and all those that have been excavated—Dzibilchaltún, San Gervasio and Altun Ha—evince close ties to the sea. At Dzibilchaltún, the evidence appears in the form of marine faunal remains, worked shell artifacts, art work depicting marine scenes (the north façade of the Temple of the Seven Dolls), and a large inventory of long-distance trade goods, undoubtedly imported through channels of coastal trade. As scholars have suggested, these goods were most likely acquired in exchange for salt, as Dzibilchaltún lies near several north coast salt-producing areas. Dzibilchaltún also lies in a marginal agricultural area, and may have traded salt for basic staples with agricultural-based polities in the interior. The economies of other cities located on marginal land near the north coast, such as Chunchucmil, Yalcihóm, and San Fernando, may have operated in similar fashion.

The coast may have also served as a channel for cultural contacts with distant regions, suggested by scattered evidence of Teotihuacan cultural elements and/or trade goods at Dzibilchaltún, Xelhá, and Altun Ha. These data clearly underscore the integration of the Maya coastal networks into larger spheres of Mesoamerican trade and culture contacts by the end of the Early Classic period.

The growing coastal economy also appears to have played a large role in at least one major inland polity at this time, namely, Cobá in central Quintana Roo. Located some 40 km from the coast, Cobá has long attracted attention because of its Peten-style ceramics, architecture, and iconography, suggesting to many the existence of an overland "Peten corridor" up into this region. Recent research suggests that this was a coastal corridor, with trade goods and southern influence channeled through the east coast port of Xelhá. If so, Cobá would have transshipped the trade goods into north central and northwestern Yucatán through its main sacbe, which terminated at Yaxuná. In addition to enjoying a strong agricultural base, Cobá would have further benefitted from its role as a middleman in the north-south long-distance trade networks. Thus, the emerging role of a maritime economy in the political development of the northern lowlands can be traced to this period.

Terminal Classic and Early Postclassic Periods (A.D. 750–1200)

Because of the current uncertainty about the degree of overlap of the ceramic types of these periods, I am considering the Terminal Classic and Early Postclassic as a single period. Occupations have been identified at more than 62 sites. Since the pronounced increase in the volume and diversity of coastal trade during this period has been one of the most heavily discussed topics of Maya archaeology in the last decade, I will not review the large body of data and theory on the subject.

As I have argued elsewhere (Andrews 1978b; Andrews and Robles 1985), one of the main features of the Itzá state was its deployment of an extensive network of outposts along the north and west coasts of the peninsula. Among the more prominent are Champotón, Campeche, Jaina, Canbalam, Xcopté, Punta Cerrito, Isla Cerritos, and Vista Alegre. These outposts not only enabled the Itzá to capitalize on coastal resources and the salt trade, but also allowed them to establish mercantile and military bases that would have ensured their control of the entire coastal trade network. The capital itself has yielded unequivocal evidence of economic ties to the sea and coastal trade; this is further reflected in Itzá iconography, which displays a major concern with maritime themes. The recent investigations at Isla Cerritos underscore these ties, and the evidence leaves little doubt as to the existence of a major Itzá port on the north coast. While the evidence of Itzá control of the east coast is still equivocal, recent work at Cozumel has documented strong evidence of their presence on the island. There is also scattered evidence of Iztá presence along the Caribbean shore, at places such as El Meco, Xcaret, Xelhá, Tancah, Ambergris Cay, and at sites in northern Belize.

Most scholars would agree that the Itzá expansion in northern Yucatán was tied to a growing reliance on a maritime economy; this trend continued in the following period.

Late Postclassic Period (A.D. 1200–1550)

Following the collapse of Chichén Itzá, the occupation of the west and north coast decreased dramatically. Evidence of Late Postclassic occupation has been documented at only 10 sites on the west coast and 7 on the north coast. But on the east coast and offshore islands of Quintana Roo and Belize over 100 sites have Late Postclassic occupations; and for most this was the major period of settlement.

The collapse of the Itzá state also led to the abandonment of many of its outposts on the west and north coasts and the trading networks it supported. The Itzá collapse also led to a political vacuum in northern Yucatán, which was replaced by a mosaic of provincial chiefdoms. Several chiefdoms in the northwest attempted to form a loose confederation based at Mayapan, but that also ultimately failed.

It is interesting to note that despite the political fragmentation and breakdown of the Gulf Coast trade networks, all but four or five of the coastal provinces maintained access to the coast. While the presence of the northwestern provinces on the coast is not archaeologically prominent, it is nonetheless well documented in the sixteenth-century sources. The coasts appear to have been vital to the survival of the late chiefdoms, and conflicts over coastal resources led to wars between the provinces. The coast was clearly where the action was, and most provinces would fight to maintain access to its resources and trade.

The major development of the period was the massive shift to northeast and east coasts, where new centers of power emerged. Prominent coastal communities of the period included Emal, Chiquilá, Ecab, El Meco, Cancún Island, the Puerto Morelos/Mulchi area, Cozumel Island, the Playa del Cármen/Xcaret area, Paamul, Xelhá, Tulum/Tancah, San Miguel, Chacmool, Ichpaatún/Tamalcab, and Santa Rita/Chetumal. These communities made up an almost continuous chain of densely inhabited city states, thriving on a combination of agriculture, marine resources, and trade.

Types and Functions of Maya Ports

The vast majority of coastal sites that appeared on the Lowland Maya coastline originated as fishing camps or hamlets. Some were only briefly occupied. A few, however, evolved into larger communities, serving needs beyond the basic subsistence of their inhabitants. During this development many communities acquired specialized functions, and the archaeological identification of these functions has been a central concern of Mayanists working on the coasts. In the pages that follow I present a review of the major functions of Maya ports, and a preliminary classification of major port types. Because of the wide range of activities that take part in any coastal community, past or present, it is impossible to assign any given coastal site to an exclusive category. Most fit into several, if not all, categories.

Coastal Communities

This is the most embracing category, and includes the majority of coastal sites on the peninsula, communities whose primary function was to exploit marine and coastal resources for basic subsistence. The resources included basic marine faunal food (fish, shellfish, crustacean, and sea mammal meat) as well as marine faunal byproducts (shells, coral, stingray spines, and shark's teeth), and other coastal resources like salt and volcanic pumice. The community's trade of these resources to nearby inland localities in exchange for agricultural staples, pottery, and stone artifacts was a routine activity. Some communities may have had specialized subsistence patterns, such as the exploitation of certain marine fauna or salt, but as is the case with coastal communities today, they most likely exploited all other resources available in the vicinity. Because of their coastal location they also served as ports for local—and occasionally long-distance—coastal trade and transport, sometimes diverting some of this trade to nearby inland communities.

Religious Coastal Centers

The construction of major religious architecture at the edge of the sea has obvious ritual implications. Though these implications are still poorly understood, such construction is evident at many coastal sites and clearly reflects a major intersection of ideology and maritime themes in the Maya world view.

The prominent role of the sea in Mesoamerican ideology is echoed in the maritime themes (mostly shells and sea creatures) that appear in the iconography of many sites far removed from the coasts—examples can be found in the murals of Chichén Itzá, Cacaxtla and Teotihuacán, and in the artwork of many sites in the interior of the Maya Lowlands. Among the Maya, the sea was associated with a variety of themes, most notably those of death and birth, the underworld, and the afterlife. Within this thematic complex, then, the coast was clearly at the edge of the Maya World, and many coastal sites served as outposts of their geographic and spiritual frontiers, as well as gateways to other domains. Many Maya coastal sites were major religious centers, and it is now evident that the construction of religious architecture on the shoreline became a major concern through time.

Cerros, on the north coast of Belize, is the only major coastal Preclassic site with ceremonial architecture. During the Classic period, major ceremonial centers appear at Jaina, Cozumel, Xelhá, and most likely at several other sites where the remains of religious architecture have not yet been dated. The Postclassic saw the culmination of this trend, especially on the northeast and east coasts, where major ceremonial complexes were constructed at scores of coastal sites, from Isla Cerritos to Chetumal Bay.

The isolated coastal shrine, which appears to be a primarily Postclassic construction, is another type of coastal site that reflects the Maya religious orientation to the sea. These are found along the east coast, from Isla Mujeres to Ascención Bay, on major promontories or next to small inlets that served as natural harbors for coastal shipping. In most cases, they appear to be associated with nearby inland sites, and represent an extension of those sites out to the open coast. In other cases, they may represent outposts demarcating the territorial domain of a major coastal community. While several authors have proposed that they may have served as navigational aids, they are nonetheless religious structures, and therefore reflect an abiding religious concern with the sea. Another famous example of this type of shrine was located in Campeche on a rocky promontory off the coast of Champotón.

Island Necropoli

Ever since Charnay uncovered large numbers of burials with elaborate goods at Isla Jaina in 1886, there has been a widespread belief that Jaina and other island sites served as sacred burial grounds for the Maya elite. This belief has been reinforced by discoveries of large numbers of burials at Isla Piedras and Isla Uaymil on the west coast north of Jaina, at Isla Cerritos on the north coast, and at Isla Tamalcab in Chetumal Bay. Looting and local folklore have lent further credence to this notion: at Isla Cerritos, for example, legend has it that the island was the final resting place of the kings of Chichén Itzá.

While it is possible that certain remote island sites may have served as elite burial grounds, the actual evidence in support of this notion is far from conclusive. Jaina, for example, was a major coastal community involved in fishing and trading activities for more than 700 years; thus, it is possible that the burials are the remains of the local population (Piña Chan 1968: 124). Whether members of elites from other sites were buried there remains an open question (López Alonso and Serrano S. 1984).

At Isla Cerritos, recent test excavations have also uncovered evidence of a large burial population (Andrews and Gallareta 1986; Andrews et al. 1986); however, the island was densely occupied for over 1,000 years, and the remains may also be those of local inhabitants.

The islands of Piedras, Uaymil and Tamalcab have never been formally excavated, and the mere presence of large amounts of skeletal remains—exposed by looters—need not indicate a necropolis.

Specialized Trading Ports

Many sites along the coastline of the Maya Lowlands have been identified as major trading ports. In fact, it is probably safe to assume that any major shoreline community with evidence of long-distance trade served such a purpose. Among the more famous trading ports are Xicalango, Champotón, Campeche, Jaina, Isla Cerritos, Chiquilá, Ecab, El Meco, El Rey (Cancún), several sites on Cozumel Island, Xcaret (Polé), Xelhá, Tulúm/Tancah, Santa Rita, and Cerros. The major occupation of most of these sites was during the Terminal Classic or Postclassic period, though some were also prominent ports in earlier periods. Cerros was a major trading port of the Late Preclassic period, while Jaina, Isla Cerritos, Cozumel and Xelhá exhibit evidence of major trading activities during the Classic period. Future excavations will undoubtedly reveal more ports of the Preclassic and Classic periods.

Beyond these general trading ports, Mayanists have identified four more specialized types of ports: (1) Ports of Embarkation to Offshore Islands, (2) "Ports-of-Trade," (3) Coastal Transshipment Ports, and (4) Seaports of Inland Polities.

Ports of Embarkation to Offshore Islands Several coastal sites served as ports of embarkation to offshore islands. As such, they would have also been the island's main trade link to the mainland. The best known of these are Xcaret (Polé) and Playa del Cármen (Xamanhá), which served as points of departure for the island of Cozumel, and El Meco, the main point of embarkation for Isla Mujeres.

Ethnohistoric sources record that Cozumel was the home of the shrine of Ixchel, the goddess of the moon and childbirth, and that pilgrims came from distant lands to pay her homage. The large amount of religious architecture—mostly shrines—found at Xcaret and Playa del Cármen fits well with the historic accounts. As way stations for religious pilgrims, they would have been the locale for rituals of purification and safe passage before embarkation on the hazardous journey across the deep Cozumel channel to the sacred shrine. Isla Mujeres also may have had the status of a holy place, and the religious architecture at El Meco would have served a similar function to that of Xcaret and Playa del Cármen.

Several other coastal sites also served as mainland ports for offshore islands, though this role was not the main reason for the existence of the site. On the far north coast of Quintana Roo, Chiquilá was undoubtedly the main point of departure for the island of Holbox. Travelers to Isla del Cármen, in the Laguna de Términos, would have embarked from a number of sites along the mainland shore of the lagoon. Likewise, travel to the offshore keys of Belize would have been through a variety of shoreline sites; Ambergris Cay, the largest, was likely reached through embarkation at Santa Rita, Cerros, and Sarteneja, all prominent ports on the north coast of Belize. Finally, the short passage to the island of Tamalcab, in Chetumal Bay, would have originated from any of a cluster of sites facing the island on the mainland (San Manuel, Oxtancah, or Ichpaatún).

Ports-of-Trade This type of port has been proposed at several locations around the peninsula by Anne Chapman (1957), at Cozumel by Jeremy Sabloff and William Rathje (1973, 1975), at Tulúm by Arthur Miller (1982), and at Xelhá by Fernando Robles (1981b).

As defined by Chapman (1957: 115–16), a port-of-trade was a locality for exchange

> ... whose specific function was to serve as a meeting place of the foreign traders. The word "port" as employed here need not imply a coastal or riverain, although ports of trade were usually thus situated.... Prior to modern days, the port of trade should therefore be regarded as the main organ of long-distance commerce.... Ports of trade usually developed in politically weak spots ... strangers shunned territories that were incorporated into military empires.... Even powerful rulers were wary of laying their hands on the "port," lest foreign traders and strangers shy off and trade suddenly dry up.

Rathje and Sabloff (1973: 222; Sabloff and Rathje 1957: 7) have listed a general set of attributes that are common to all ports-of-trade:

(1) Location at a transitional zone, created by seasonal and/or geographic factors that require resupply or transshipment facilities, on a trade-transport route;
(2) location among small political units at a distance from powerful resource control centers;
(3) populations in excess of both local food production and mineral resources so that significant quantities of basic materials are imported;
(4) little retail distribution in the center's surrounding area of the total volume of products exchanged.

Chapman's (1957) pioneering work proposed five such entrepots during the Late Postclassic period (A.D. 1200–1517): Xicalango, Acalán, Xoconusco, Chetumal Bay, and the Gulf of Honduras. The study relies entirely on historical information and has several weaknesses. The major problem is that she treats the trading enclaves as areas, and glosses over the fact that the actual location of the ports is unknown. Hence, we have no record of the size of the ports, storage facilities, and so on. Another problem is the political status of Xicalango and Xoconusco: both were under the control of the Aztec empire, and we know little of them prior to the Aztec presence. Chapman suggests that Xoconusco was a port-of-trade before Aztec control, but there is no evidence of such (Dillon 1975; Berdan 1978). During the Late Postclassic period Chetumal Bay was the home of the capital of the province of Chetumal, which was probably located at Santa Rita (D. Chase 1981, 1986)—hardly a marginal political area. In short, there is no solid evidence to corroborate the existence of these ports-of-trade.

Rathje and Sabloff (1973; and Sabloff and Rathje 1975) have proposed that Cozumel Island was a port-of-trade in Early Postclassic times (A.D. 1000–1200). This has yet to be demonstrated, for a variety of reasons. First, the political status of Cozumel during the Early Postclassic has yet to be ascertained; there is some evidence to suggest that it might have served as a trading port for Chichén Itzá. Whether the Itzá presence on the island was purely commercial or military has not been determined. Moreover, while Cozumel was deficient in mineral resources and had to import raw materials for lithic artifacts, it was not deficient in basic foodstuffs. It has ample agricultural land, on which maize, beans, cotton, and garden crops traditionally have been grown, and inexhaustible marine resources in the surrounding seas. Archaeological evidence indicates that the Cozumel Maya exploited a wide spectrum of marine, land, and avian fauna (Hamblin 1984). Finally, there is no conclusive evidence at sites on Cozumel of major wholesale markets, storage facilities, or transshipment of trade goods (for a lengthier discussion of Cozumel as a port-of-trade, see Andrews 1980).

Arthur Miller (1982: 75–76) has proposed that Tulúm also functioned as a port-of-trade during the Late Postclassic period, and Fernando Robles (1981b: 110–12) has proposed the same for Xelhá during the Classic period. Once again, these cases are not easily demonstrated, for many of the same reasons that apply to Cozumel. We do not know what the political status of Tulúm was, and Xelhá appears to have been under the control of Cobá (Andrews and Robles 1985; Robles and Andrews 1986). Both regions are self-sufficient in agricultural and marine resources. Moreover, we have no evidence of wholesale long-distance exchange, storage facilities, or transshipment of trade goods at either site.

While it is most likely that Tulúm, Xelhá and Cozumel were major trading enclaves, they do not fit the formal requirements for a "port-of-trade." The problems encountered by Mayanists suggest a fundamental limitation in the application of the port-of-trade concept. Simply put, it may not be definable on the basis of archaeological and limited historic evidence alone. Classic examples of ports-of-trade from the Old World are historic localities for which there are substantial political and economic information (e.g. Alexandria, Delos, Timbuctoo, and Wydah). To define a site as a port-of-trade, one must have detailed knowledge of the subtleties of the economic and political structures and an understanding of how they operated. This knowledge is particularly necessary if one is to meet the rigorous definition proposed by Rathje and Sabloff. Unfortunately, such information is not now available for prehispanic Maya ports.

Coastal Transshipment Ports   One of the primary concerns of coastal archaeologists is the identification of trading nodes, or way stations where long distance trade goods were transshipped. In fact, it is likely that many proposed ports-of-trade were transshipment nodes, a category of port that is more easily documented through archaeological evidence.

As noted above, most Maya coastal communities participated to some degree in "down-the-line" coastal trade. Some communities, however, appear to have become specialized as points of transshipment in the long-distance trade networks that girded the peninsula. Many of these ports served as nodes not only for coastal trade, but also as points from which long-distance goods were diverted to inland communities.

Among the more prominent transshipment ports are Xicalango and Jaina on the west coast, Isla Cerritos on the north coast, Ecab, El Meco, Cancún, Xcaret, Xelhá, Tulúm/Tancah, Ambergris Cay, Moho Cay, Point Placencia and Wild Cane Cay on the east coast. In addition to these, there are several major ports whose strategic locations at the mouths of navigable rivers suggest that they were major conduits of coastal trade into the interior: these would include several sites on the shores of the Laguna de Términos (*see* Eaton 1978), Champotón, at the mouth of the Champotón river, Ichpaatún, Santa Rita, and Cerros, all located near the mouths of the Hondo and New Rivers in Chetumal Bay, and Moho Cay, at the mouth of the Belize River. Chunyaxché (or Muyil), connected to Boca Paila Lagoon south of Tulúm via canal, may have been another major trade conduit between the coast and the interior.

Many less prominent coastal sites around the peninsula may have also served as minor transshipment nodes as well. These have not been investigated, but their locations and surface remains suggest such a role. Several sites on the north coast of Campeche lie at the mouths of canals that connect to the interior; many of these canals were nineteenth-century logwood canals, but some of them may have been in use in prehispanic times (Andrews 1977, 1978a; Millet Cámara 1984). The site of Canbalám, at the mouth of the Celestún estuary, was likely a major node for trade going into the river and to the inland site of Chunchucmil. Several sites along the central east coast of Quintana Roo, between Playa del Cármen and Tulúm, lie next to rocky inlets that would have served as natural harbors for coastal shipping trade (Andrews IV and Andrews 1975). Also, there are several sites south of Tulúm and on the Xkalak peninsula which may have served as stopping points for passing traders; the Xkalak peninsula has not yet been formally surveyed, but at least 10 sites have been reported (Andrews 1983a, Cortés de Brasdefer 1984).

Several recently investigated sites on the Belize coast and offshore cays have also been proposed as transshipment points: Ambergris Cay (Guderjan, Garber, and Smith n.d.), Moho Cay (McKillop 1981); Point Placencia (McKinnon 1985) and Wild Cane Cay (Hammond 1976; McKillop 1982). On the north coast of Belize, three sites have been tentatively proposed as coastal outposts of inland communities: Ramonal & Condemned Point, for the inland site of Shipstern (Sidrys 1983: 188); Northern River Lagoon Site (or Pibil Luum) for Colhá (Kelly 1980: 56–60), and Marlowe Cay for Altun Ha (Craig 1966: 24).

It is difficult to trace the evolution of transshipment ports through time, as most sites have not been excavated. Still, on the basis of survey, surface collection, and test excavation data, it is evident that many were occupied for prolonged periods. An examination of the occupation data suggests a gradual increase in the number of ports through time, from the Late Preclassic period to the conquest. There is a marked increase in the number of ports during the Terminal Classic and Early Postclassic, and a quantum jump during the Late Postclassic, particularly along the east coast.

Seaports of Inland Polities It is somewhat surprising, given the research conducted to date, that few coastal sites have been linked to inland Maya capitals. At present, documentation for such a linkage exists for only two ports: Isla Cerritos and Xelhá.

Archaeologists working on the east coast have suspected for several years that Chunyaxché, Tancah or Xelhá may have served as the ports for the large Classic period inland polity of Cobá (Robles 1976, 1977, 1981; Benavides 1977; A. Miller 1982; Andrews and Robles 1985; Robles and Andrews 1986). As it has not been excavated, it is not possible to assess the role of Chunyaxché as a port of Cobá. While Tancah exhibits ceramic evidence of a Classic period occupation, it does not have any major architectural complexes dating to the same period; its major occupation was during the Postclassic period (A. Miller 1982).

Recent excavations at Xelhá, however, provide substantial evidence of ceramic and architectural links to Cobá and the Petén (Robles, personal communication); this evidence and the fact that Xelhá is the closest major coastal site to Cobá strongly suggest that Xelhá was the seaport of the inland capital. Xelhá lies next to the largest and deepest rocky inlet on the east coast, which serves as a major natural harbor for coastal shipping. A small shrine and a large defensive wall with a main entrance form part of the harbor facilities. As I have mentioned, Xelhá likely served as the main port in the "Peten Corridor," which linked Cobá to the southern Maya Lowlands.

Isla Cerritos, a small island at the mouth of the Rio Lagartos, was most likely the main port of the Terminal Classic/Early Postclassic capital of Chichén Itzá. The discovery of port facilities—docks and a major harbor wall—and large quantities of Itzá surface ceramics during the 1960s and 1970s (Andrews 1978b) led to detailed surveys and test excavations in 1984 and 1985. The results of this research not only confirmed the existence of close ceramic and architectural ties to the Itzá capital, but also of a wide variety of trade goods from all over Mesoamerica and Central America. In fact, Isla Cerritos appears to be one of the richest trade enclaves on the Maya coast, and all the evidence suggests that it was the main seaport of the Itzá (Andrews et al. 1986; Andrews and Gallareta 1986).

There are a number of other coastal sites that may have linkages to inland polities, but the relationships have not been documented archaeologically.

The site of Canbalám, at the mouth of the Celestún estuary, is only 25 km from the inland city of Chunchucmil, and the predominant occupation of both sites is of Late and Terminal Classic date. One of the largest urban sites in northwest Yucatán, Chunchucmil undoubtedly relied on the coast for resources and trade (Vlcek, Garza, and Kurjack 1978). Control of the nearby salt beds of Celestún would have provided it with a major trade item for exchange with both the interior and the external coastal trade networks (Andrews 1983a). Given such a situation, it is most likely that Canbalám served as a seaport for Chunchucmil.

A similar argument can be advanced for the site of Emal, which lies in the midst of the huge *salinas* of Las Coloradas, on the northeast coast of Yucatán. These are the largest salt beds of Mesoamerica. Occupied from Late Preclassic times to the conquest, Emal was most likely the main administrative center of the salinas. Fourteen kilometers inland lies the site of San Fernando, one of the largest prehispanic communities in the region. This site has not yet been surveyed, but a brief visit revealed a major Classic period occupation. A site the size and location of San Fernando would have undoubtedly maintained a presence on the coast, which suggests that Emal may have served as its seaport.

Finally, Allan Craig (1966: 24) has proposed that Marlowe Cay, in Salt Creek Lagoon on the north coast of Belize, was the main seaport for the large Classic period site of Altun Ha. Given Altun Ha's proximity to the coast and its extensive involvement in Mesoamerican trade networks, this is a logical possibility, but has yet to be verified.

Conclusions

Our knowledge of the Maya coastline has increased substantially over the last 25 years through surveys, test excavations, and large-scale excavations at a few sites. It is now possible to examine the coast as a whole and to discuss regional variations in trade and subsistence patterns, the functions of Maya ports, and, in a few instances, their role in larger political configurations.

One major pattern that emerges from this survey is that Maya coastal communities, and Maya ports in particular, have evolved over a long period of time, from the Preclassic period onward. Many scholars have played up the role of maritime economies during the Postclassic period as a response to the Classic collapse. In doing so, we have, perhaps unwittingly, reinforced a simplified scenario in which the Maya underwent a major shift from a Classic agricultural economy to a largely maritime Postclassic economy. This is partly owing to the nature of the overall archaeological record, which for decades has stressed the contrast between a Classic south and a Postclassic north. Recent research has drastically altered this picture: we now have a much broader vision of the north during Preclassic and Classic times, and evidence of widespread activity in the south during Postclassic times. But the "Old" and "New Empire" metaphor lingers on in subtle ways.

Contrary to the metaphor, a growing body of data challenges the notion that there was a sudden shift to a maritime economy in Postclassic times in the north. While there is clear evidence of a heavier reliance on the sea in Postclassic times, it was not an abrupt response to Classic conditions, but an outgrowth of a long maritime tradition that much earlier. It was this tradition, coupled with a complex and still poorly understood sequence of events in Terminal Classic/Early Postclassic northern Yucatán, that brought about a gradual shift in the economic base that shaped the overall trajectory of Maya state development.

The increasing reliance of the Maya on the sea can now be documented more thoroughly than a decade ago, and the evidence clearly suggests that this pattern was the gradual outcome of a maritime tradition that began in Late Preclassic times, gathered momentum during the Classic period, and culminated in the dominant maritime economies of the Postclassic.

Notes

1. I would like to thank Mary Janis for her comments and editorial assistance and Gabrielle Vail for sharing with me her compilation of data on coastal Belize.

Eleven

Up From the Dust: The Central Lowlands Postclassic as Seen from Lamanai and Marco Gonzalez, Belize

By David M. Pendergast

I have written elsewhere of the long-held view that the Postclassic was a descent into the dust, and of the beginnings of a change in that view that resulted from the early years of excavation at Lamanai, in northern Belize (Pendergast 1986a). That thirteen-year project is now at an end, and the results of the work provide an even more convincing argument than they did some years ago for a revision of our assessment of Postclassic events. Just as the Lamanai work was drawing to a close, Dr. Elizabeth Graham and I began a much smaller-scale project at the comparatively tiny site of Marco Gonzalez, at the swampy south end of Ambergris Cay, the northernmost coral island on Belize's barrier reef (E. Graham and Pendergast 1987; Pendergast and E. Graham 1987). Despite its size, Marco Gonzalez has also shed important light on Postclassic life, and added to the basis for a new evaluation of Maya life from the eleventh century until the Conquest.

It is common practice to take the Classic Maya as one's standard, and to view what followed the Classic as a decadent expression of all in Maya life that was of merit in the esthetic, and perhaps also the social, sense. Such a judgment is perfectly acceptable as long as it is understood as a statement of taste based upon a specific set of values, but it leads automatically to the ascent-pinnacle-descent model with which the terms Preclassic, Classic, and Postclassic are traditionally associated, and is very likely to prevent any valid anthropological or humanistic assessment of events from the tenth century to the arrival of the Spaniards.

The earliest data-based syntheses of Maya prehistory drew their inspiration regarding events in the southern half of the lowlands almost entirely from excavations in the Guatemalan Peten. As a result they pictured the years after the tenth century as a time of desolation and abandonment, from which the survivors emerged to found, or to contribute to the resurgence of, a complex social order in the north. This reconstruction of Maya prehistory divided time and space into Old Empire and New Empire (Morley 1947: 50–97) and obviously ruled out the possibility that anything of significance had occurred in the south after the fall. Less obvious was the debt such a view owed to the perception of cycles of grandeur and decay that was then current in the archaeology of Western Asia. Today we know that neither the Maya nor the peoples of the Near East followed the paths discerned half a century ago in the archaeological record, but the legacy of those early views remains with us nonetheless.

The view in more recent times has been that the southern lowlands were very severely destabilized, and the population decentralized and perhaps driven northward, by the collapse (Culbert 1973). This view owes just as much to the history of archaeological research in the area as does the earlier reconstruction of Maya prehistory. The focus on work in the Peten not only produced the concept of the area as the core of the south and all else in the area as periphery, but also adduced the social processes reflected in the Peten archaeological record as a model for the entire southern lowlands. Based on what was known of Maya sociopolitical structure, the likelihood of the existence of a core/periphery dichotomy, and of a geographically encapsulated model for southern lowlands prehistory, should have been recognized as very small. Instead, the paradigm of rise and fall was seen by most as universally applicable in the south. Out of this perception grew the evaluation of the southern lowlands Postclassic as a time pervaded by decay, with no qualities to parallel those that had made the Classic so grand an era.

The most vocal modern proponent of the idea that the Classic embodied all that was best and brightest in Maya prehistory was J. E. S. Thompson (1966). He surely chose his title quite consciously to recall Gibbon's (1783–90) in order to hark back to the Classical world and set in the reader's mind the image of a Roman level of grandeur in the Maya Classic and a barbarian level of dissolution in all that followed. Thompson's view was very probably that collapse in the southern lowlands was a blessing in disguise, for he saw the Postclassic as a time of unregenerate moral, and perhaps technological degradation where society survived (Thompson 1966: 110–16).

Like others, Thompson wrote off the southern half of the lowlands as a participant in any significant events that followed the collapse, and like others before and after him he may have been led by this assessment to misinterpret the uppermost part of the stratigraphic record. If one is certain that the Postclassic was a time of somnolence born of decay, it follows automatically that all material from the top stratum, especially if it includes dramatically new artifact types, cannot be later than Terminal Classic in date (Thompson 1939: fig. 82a,b). The approach has persisted in more recent times; in the upper Belize Valley the existence of an Early Postclassic occupation is recognized, but the collection includes material of later date (Sharer and Chase 1976). Such interpretations may not only compress a span of centuries into a far briefer period but also eradicate the possibility of evaluating the artifacts, and the society they represent, in their own terms rather than as measured against the standards of the Classic.

The move away from a simplified version of Postclassic events in the south can be said to have begun with the assertion of complex and differing forces as the causes of the collapse (Culbert 1973) and the recognition that a polycausal event is very likely to have had multifarious effects. Yet the sense of the Classic as the yardstick against which all later achievement had to be measured was still strong, and can even be detected in spots in the most recent syntheses of data on the Postclassic (Chase and Rice 1985; Sabloff and Andrews 1986). The belief in the Classic as the best of times, at least in the material and esthetic realms, remains to this day the linchpin of many assessments of Maya culture (Culbert 1985: 61), though countervailing views have begun to be given currency in such places as the exhibition that gave birth to this volume.

It is my view, and I think that others engaged in the study of Postclassic and early Historic Maya remains generally concur, that the Postclassic was not nearly the descent into the dust it was long thought to have been. Furthermore, it is evident that we gain much more by studying the Postclassic on its own terms than we do by measuring it against the standard of earlier centuries. Behind the general principle regarding study of the Postclassic lie very considerable bodies of data from Lamanai, Santa Rita, Negroman-Tipu, and now Marco Gonzalcz, that document the richness, vibrance, and variety of Postclassic Maya life. These excavations, together with work in the Petén, tell us much more than we knew a decade ago about the fabled collapse and its aftermath. At present Lamanai is the only site at which a continuum from the Classic through all the centuries of the Postclassic and on into the early Historic period is clearly in evidence. However, unbroken occupation will very probably be fully documented by further work at Negroman-Tipu, in the Cayo District of Belize, and may well have marked other excavated southern lowlands sites.

Continuing intensive use of Classic sites through the Postclassic years may in fact have been more the rule than the exception in some areas. It is the present impossibility of defining the geographic extent of such Postclassic use that leads me to employ the partly outmoded term "Central Lowlands" to avoid the implication that the phenomena observable at Lamanai and some other Belizean sites were paralleled at most or all southern lowlands centers. The data do not indicate that the collapse did not occur; instead, they argue for revision of our view of the disintegration as pervasive in the southern lowlands, and for reevaluation of events in the centuries that followed.

As work in Belize has revealed masses of new information on the Postclassic, it has made clear the effect of the history of Maya archaeology on our assessment of the region's prehistory. It is to the early focus of research in the Petén that we owe the standard assessment of the extent and impact of the collapse, as well as the view of the time from the tenth century onward as a period of dross and dreariness in the southern lowlands. If excavation had begun in the eastern part of the southern lowlands rather than in the central Petén "heartland," we might long ago have characterized the collapse as an important but not unvarying phenomenon that had its greatest effect in some of the larger centers of the central and western Peten, and was felt to a lesser degree, or at least in spottier fashion, elsewhere. Acceptance of this view would immediately have weakened the argument for a picture of scattered hardy souls wandering about among ruined temples in the Postclassic years. That picture surely reflects reality in many sites but not, as we used to believe, in all.

Just as the Lamanai excavations have contributed to revision of our view of the collapse and its effects, this and other investigations have done much to alter our perception of the nature of life in ensuing centuries. Nevertheless, it is still widely held that the years from A.D. 900 onward saw Maya civilization tumble rapidly and painfully down the rough slope of decadence, both in the areas where Mexican intrusion took place and farther to the south. The same body of thought maintains that no one who savors Classic material culture can possibly see anything other than the unsavory in the products of later times.

For at least two decades we have known that a number of southern lowland sites still had a considerable amount of life left in them as the Classic came to an end. At Altun Ha, for example, at least one ceremonial and administrative structure near the site center was given its final form about A.D. 850–875, and saw some minor modifications thereafter, while neighboring and distant residences were also being rebuilt (Pendergast, in press). Such efforts were carried out in the face of mounting evidence that the fragmentation of Classic society was rapidly spreading to the heart of the fabric; in some cases, at least, life among the ruins seems not to have been a very daunting prospect for ninth- and tenth-century Altun Ha citizens. By about A.D. 1100, however, the burdens had become too much to bear, and Altun Ha, like other sites that suffered the collapse, yields no further evidence of inhabitants.

The picture that emerged from the Lamanai excavations is sharply, and at first glance surprisingly, different from that recognizable at Altun Ha and most excavated southern lowlands sites. There is no conclusive evidence of major change in social structure in the latter part of the Late Classic; transformation of religious practice was clearly less than total, though it is reflected by the decline in or cessation of maintenance of most of the major temples in the Central Precinct. In the late ninth and early tenth centuries, when any percipient Lamanai resident would surely have been aware that political control was disintegrating in many neighboring communities, several parts of the southern end of the site center saw major renewal. The building efforts appear to reflect a focus on the southern part of the site as more northerly temples fell into disuse, but there is persuasive evidence in the and volume of Terminal Classic construction that this internal shift was not accompanied by any significant reduction in Lamanai's population. To all appearances, the community, though changed in shape, was as vibrant both in terms of population and construction activity in A.D. 950 as it had been in A.D. 650.

Although it is possible to document Lamanai's survival through the time of disintegration elsewhere, it is far from possible to pinpoint the sources of the community's strength in the face of hardship. The availability of food resources superior to those obtainable in some communities clearly conferred an advantage on Lamanai's residents, as did the presence of a riverine highway to the outside world, but these or any other environmental factors do not suffice as an explanation of the city's successful passage through the difficulties that marked the ninth and tenth centuries.

Because much of the major-structure modification at Lamanai following the Early Classic, and in fact during this period as well, consisted of the refronting of existing buildings, it is quite likely that the community's leaders demanded smaller amounts of labor from the populace than did the elite at many other centers; this, too, may have contributed to Lamanai's stability during the lowland upheavals. Finally, the quality of leadership, often fundamental to the preservation of communal confidence during confrontations with disaster, may well have been high enough in ninth- and tenth-century

Lamanai to buttress a social structure that might otherwise have toppled. Though possibly as much of a factor as any other in Lamanai's survival, the nature of the community's leaders through the critical years is, of course, undocumented in the archaeological record. There may be other elements of the picture that are equally undetectable, but what we can see surely bespeaks a multifaceted procession of events for which the causes are likely to have been legion.

The clearest expression of Lamanai's apparent confidence in the future during the years of upheaval elsewhere lies in architecture. Whether large or small, the construction efforts of A.D. 900–1000 unquestionably mirror a population still planning for the years ahead; in the case of the largest known effort of the period, the evidence also tells us something about the organization that permitted translation of such plans into stone-and-mortar reality. The greatest undertaking occurred in the southernmost residential and administrative assemblage in the Central Precinct (Plaza N10-3) a complex that had been important for at least 400 years (Pendergast 1986a: 231–32); here the renewal, probably begun in the second half of the tenth century, involved amassing about 21,000 metric tons of stone in a reshaping of the group that was ultimately to span at least a century and perhaps as much as 200 years. The labor represented was obviously at least as staggering as any demanded in earlier times; the work must have consumed much of the community's energy, as well as a considerable amount of wealth deposited in numerous offerings, through much of the Early Postclassic. The ability of Lamanai's elite to marshall and guide communal effort, and the existence of resources equal to those of peak times in the Classic, are both clearly documented by the size and nature of the work; based on these data, one can scarcely fail to conclude that the community's structure and energy continued undiminished through the time of collapse at other centers.

Of much smaller scale, but equally significant as a statement of optimism regarding Lamanai's future, is the ball court (Structures N10-40 and 41) built near the end of the Classic, with its massive marker disc and offering that included the only reported mercury from the Maya Lowlands (Pendergast 1982a; 1986a: 229–30). The court's meaning in the life of the community is difficult to assess fully because no earlier ball courts appear to have graced Lamanai's Central Precinct; one might therefore see the introduction of the ceremonial game as an attempt to stave off the disaster that was befalling other centers, though the ball game is not known to have possessed this protective quality. However, the proximity of the court to the massive construction described above argues for identification of the structure as yet another part of the statement of strength made throughout the site's southern zone in the opening years of the Postclassic.

The vigor of Early Postclassic life at Lamanai reflected in architectural endeavour was paralleled in many other areas of material culture. Continuation of Terminal Classic or earlier forms into the eleventh century was accompanied by innovations of the sort that bespeak a vitality equal to that of preceding centuries; the Maya of Lamanai were clearly still examining, modifying, and inventing, while proceeding along a path that had not diverged greatly from the one they had trod for a great many lifetimes. If they were conscious of upheaval, it must have been almost entirely a matter of news from the outside rather than problems at home.

Continuity through the years of disaster elsewhere seems also to have marked at least some aspects of religious practice, although abandonment of most temples in the Central Precinct might have meant neglect of some gods or the shifting of their sites of worship to far less prepossessing surroundings. In the area that saw greatest activity in Terminal Classic and Early Postclassic times, however, maintenance of the southernmost great temple in the Central Precinct continued not only in these years but in limited form throughout the Postclassic (Pendergast 1986a: 234–35, 241). This surely connotes maintenance of the beliefs and rituals with which the building was associated; whether it also serves as evidence of a tighter religious focus, perhaps on a single deity or related group of deities, is something we could only judge if we understood the relationship between temples and gods at any point in Maya prehistory.

The strengths of Lamanai in the opening centuries of the Postclassic obviously must have rested on a solid economic base. Archaeobotanical studies at the site document continuation of corn production in the Postclassic, and trace-element and stable-isotope analyses of skeletal material show that, following an apparent diminution in its importance near the end of the Classic, corn reemerged as a dominant element in the Lamanai diet by or before the twelfth century (White 1986: 153, Figure 15). These palaeonutritional data do not, of course, shed specific light on the quality of Postclassic diet, since corn might have achieved its preponderant share of the food spectrum simply because other foodstuffs grew scarce. Overall, however, vegetable and animal protein intake appears to have been adequate, and the role of the large lake that fronts Lamanai as a source of fish and turtles was surely significant in this dietary quality. Studies of the Postclassic skeletal material indicate a generally healthy population; this is supported by data from Negroman-Tipu, where the Early Historic population enjoyed surprisingly good health (Cohen et al. 1985). We cannot tell whether Lamanai's agricultural production involved continued maintenance of the small raised field system at the site's north limit, but it is beyond question that the community's Postclassic population found means to assure the stability in food resources necessary to individual and societal good health.

Just as in foodstuffs, Lamanai continued successful exploitation of other local resources required for the variety of manufactures that marked the Postclassic. In addition, it is clear that the site benefitted from trade connections that extended far beyond the local area, with flow of goods—and surely ideas as well—in both directions. Obsidian from Guatemalan sources, a very small amount of ceramics from northern Yucatan, marine shell, and numerous other items reached Lamanai in the Postclassic, probably via the great avenue afforded traders by the New, or Dzuluinicob, River. By the twelfth century, the trade items reaching Lamanai had begun to include copper objects from sources in western and central Mexico, Oaxaca, and lower Central America; though probably a trickle at first, the flow increased in Middle and Late Postclassic times to such an extent that the 152 metal artifacts from the site now constitute the largest collection from controlled excavations in the Maya area, and one of the larger from all of Mesoamerica. Though few items other than the obsidian may have been vital to maintenance of Lamanai's way of life, the quantity and variety of trade goods tell us much about the community's prosperity and about its status in the eyes of traders and manufacturers elsewhere in Postclassic Mesoamerica.

Trade outward from Lamanai is somewhat more difficult to document, but it surely must have equaled the inflow, since the Lamanai city-state could hardly have afforded the balance-of-payments problems that beset many modern nations. Concepts of pottery design and decoration were almost certainly part of the trade package that was transported from Lamanai to sites in the northern Yucatán (Pendergast 1986a: 240), and Lamanai ceramics themselves made their way in small to moderate quantities to the other Belize sites of Altun Ha (Pendergast 1982b: 42, 140, Fig. 81d)), Mayflower, in the Stann Creek District (E. Graham 1983: 569–70, fig. 169a,b), and Tipu, in the Cayo District (E. Graham, 1987). No raw materials can be securely traced to a Lamanai source, and to date we have been unable to identify any artifact type so distinctive of the site that we can be certain of its origins when it appears elsewhere. However, despite the fact that the established inventory of outgoing products and ideas is very far from extensive, there can be little doubt that Lamanai contributed significantly to the Postclassic economy of the Maya Lowlands as more than just a consumer of goods manufactured in northern centers.

The Lamanai trade data bear on a larger issue regarding the nature of the Postclassic, which is that the period is often characterized as a time in which commercial interests held sway—a time of merchants rather than god-kings. The characterization frequently suggests greater emphasis on maritime trade than existed in earlier times, and sometimes identifies the Putun as the prime entrepreneurs of the Postclassic years. Though it is not at all unlikely that waterborne transport played a large role in Lamanai's Postclassic commerce, as it had presumably done in the Classic and earlier, there is nothing at the site that points to specific traders, or even argues persuasively for a more dominant role for merchants after A.D. 1000 than they had had before. As in so many other respects, the community's passage from Late Classic to Postclassic times seems not to have brought with it radical change—though with many former trading partners no longer accessible, the patterns of Lamanai's trade, especially westward, must have been altered beyond all recognition.

What we have examined thus far demonstrates that Lamanai enjoyed a fairly stable existence in a time of instability elsewhere in the lowlands, and managed to maintain a high level of activity and a diversity of external contacts in the Postclassic centuries. It seems to me that there is a solid basis for seeing the quality of life at Lamanai, although different in the Postclassic, as no worse than in the Classic, and perhaps better in some respects. A decrease in population may be reflected in the abandonment of many Central Precinct structures, though a refocusing of energies is an equally plausible explanation of the evidence; in any event, a smaller population does not necessarily reduce the quality of life, and may in fact enhance it. The great variety in pottery vessel form and decoration suggests greater freedom than had existed earlier, and I suspect that here we are on firmer ground than we may be elsewhere in equating ceramics with society. However, it is to esthetic quality that many refer when they speak of the Postclassic as a time of decadence, and it is here that matters of taste are most clearly at issue.

It has been said that no one, having admired the great painted cylindrical vessels from eighth-century sites in the central lowlands, can turn to Postclassic ceramics and fail to conclude that the final centuries of Maya prehistory were a time of decadence. It is my contention that while one may indeed judge a Postclassic vessel to be less attractive, or less well potted, than a Classic piece, that esthetic judgment should not be confused with a culture-historical assessment of Maya achievement. If we are to attempt to evaluate and understand the endeavours of the Maya in the Postclassic, or indeed in any period, surely we must do so within the context of the times rather than by setting the achievements at some point on a personally devised scale.

I see the Postclassic years as a vital and vibrant time in at least some parts of the Maya area, and both the pottery and other manufactures as clear reflections of those qualities. I suspect that an eighth-century Maya would have been appalled by a standard vessel from the hands of his thirteenth-century descendant—a fair judgment when made by the bearer of a tradition that he assumed would live forever, who is suddenly thrust into a world he cannot comprehend. It is equally probable, in my view, that the thirteenth-century potter would have found his ancestor's work effete, bound by excessive restrictions, and perhaps too dainty for words. This, too, would have been a valid judgment, based on culturally moderated individual taste and without any pretense to cultural or historical explanation. Though these two judgments are perfectly acceptable, they are precisely the opposite of the approach required if the material achievements of the Maya in any period are to be appreciated for what they were: functioning parts of a complex cultural system.

Viewed in their own terms, many of the products of Lamanai's Postclassic people can be seen to have the same range that one encounters in the Classic, or the Preclassic; differences in potting ability, in carving skill, in the patience required for stone polishing, and in countless other aspects of quality abound. Here judgments regarding quality are as fully meaningful as they are in any other cultural context, but of course they measure only individual skill and talent, and do not characterize the culture as a whole. Matters of individual variation are the concern of the humanist, and almost an anathema to the social scientist except insofar as they can be subsumed under some larger cultural themes. Luckily the Lamanai data, like those from other Postclassic centers, admit some of the sorts of generalizations that give us a sense of the values on which the culture rested.

Although Postclassic pottery making rarely involved production of vessels as thin-walled as those of the seventh century, there are many superlative examples of the potter's art in the inventory of the period. Many of these involve a sort of confectionary approach to pottery, and it is their complexity rather than their delicacy that posed major challenges for their makers. Overall, however, Postclassic pottery is not as well made as that of earlier times. Censer bodies are often set askew on their bases, bases of these and some other vessel forms had little smoothing after they were "wired off," and rims are often roughly finished. Many vessels vary greatly in thickness, and thicker portions tend to be poorly fired at the center; many are also markedly out of round, perhaps due to a combination of reduced care in finishing and use of clays with undesirable characteristics. At the same time, experiments in form, especially in the feet of tripod vessels and the body shapes of deep bowls and jars, were extremely common, and the quality of carved decoration embodying reptilian and other naturalistic and geometric forms remained high. What seems to be in evidence is, at least in part, a shift in emphasis, both within the pottery-making tradition and in the role of pottery in Maya society.

Most or all of the aspects of lower quality in Postclassic pottery are very probably attributable to a single cause, which is greatly increased production. The potters of Classic times seem to have labored hard until one examines Postclassic middens and burials, where the quantities of ceramics are truly staggering. Any major increase in domestic vessel use is very likely to have been ceremonially dictated, since durability of household wares seems to have remained high enough to obviate the necessity of greater turnover due to increased breakage; hence religion was probably a factor in higher midden ceramic content during the Postclassic. For censers and other specialized forms there is no question that great numbers were required to meet ceremonial needs, and the appearance of mass-produced work is strongest in these vessel categories. The Postclassic inhabitants of Lamanai must have made the same compromise with which we are so familiar: if they wanted more, they would have to settle for lower quality.

In some other areas of portable material culture, the same sort of shift in emphasis, and perhaps the same sort of compromise in quality, can also be documented. In lithics, however, what we can see is surely a combination of changes in resource procurement patterns and the reshaping of the modes of other activities. Sources of jade seem to have diminished or dried up almost entirely, so that the material's previously important role in the economy and in religious practice dwindled very considerably, and often involved re-use or recarving of earlier pieces. By the fifteenth century obsidian also appears to have grown scarce, and both the quantity and the size of artifacts decreased accordingly, with reshaping of small pieces a common feature in late pre-Conquest times. These sorts of resource problems obviously had major impact on life at Lamanai, but their effect may not have been as extensive as that of the single greatest shift in Postclassic lithics, which was from larger projectile points to the characteristic, nearly universal small arrowhead.

The production of small points, generally of chert and most frequently side-notched, had its beginnings just as the Classic was drawing to a close, but did not reach its peak until the Middle Postclassic. The quantities at that time, and through the Early Historic period, suggest manufacture on as large a scale as in the ceramic sphere, but here no particular compromise with quality was necessarily involved. As with pottery, the increase in production was designed to meet a specific need, created in this case by a sharp change in the nature of the activity itself. With spears, the standard weapon of the Classic, the hunter has a reasonable chance of recovering the missile and using it a good many times, since the size of the shaft makes location relatively easy even in the jungle, and the sturdiness of the point reduces the chance of breakage. With bow-and-arrow hunting, breakage probably increases somewhat, and loss becomes a major problem; hence higher production levels are required of the point maker, and to some extent a less carefully crafted artifact may result. The throwaway nature of the object presumably made absence of top-quality craftsmanship unimportant; perhaps, in a sense, the same can be said of ceremonial pottery, meant for short-term or even single use and therefore without the need of the full range of the maker's skills.

Together with the great amount and variety of local manufacture and imports from many sources, the Lamanai Postclassic inventory includes a very considerable number of objects that represent really major artistic and technical achievement. They demonstrate that the atmosphere that encouraged fine craftsmanship, and the resources that made such work possible, were present in the Postclassic just as they had been in earlier times. It would be a mistake, however, to hold these objects up as the lone examples of high quality in Postclassic manufacture; in fact, quality is a matter of the degree to which an object fulfills the purpose for which it is intended, whether that purpose is utilitarian, ceremonial, purely esthetic, or a combination of all three.

The Maya enjoyed the advantage of an absence of advertising, and so presumably never knowingly produced any object that had no function in the material culture. To approach an archaeological assemblage with this in mind is to recognize that understanding of the workings of the culture is permitted only by assessment of the artifacts in context. In this sense, all classes of objects in the Postclassic

Maya cultural assemblage possess adequate quality, and it is only the individual artifacts themselves that vary as the talents of their makers differed. The important point is that Postclassic society embraced a great range of such difference, so that we are as able to see the exalted and the pedestrian handling of a particular object just as clearly here as we can in earlier assemblages.

The Lamanai material gives us a considerable number of insights into the form of Postclassic society at this single center, and a less complete picture of the place of the community in the larger Maya sociopolitical and economic structure. To a great degree, however, the Lamanai data would be reduced in meaning if it could be shown that the survival of the community through the Postclassic was an isolated event in the southern lowlands. The data from Santa Rita and Tipu make it clear that for at least part of the Postclassic other centers functioned much as Lamanai did, but the former site shows few relationships with Lamanai, and the amount and significance of Lamanai links at Tipu remain to be made fully clear. Now, however, we have a body of data from a rather unlikely source that sheds important light on Postclassic life in the lowlands, both in the south and in the north.

The 1986 excavations at the very small site of Marco Gonzalez, at the extreme southern tip of Ambergris Cay on Belize's barrier reef, revealed the presence of a community that had its beginnings in the Late Preclassic, and was very probably still lightly occupied at the time of Spanish entry into Belize in 1544. We cannot yet document continuous occupation over this span of at least 1700 years, but it is clear that the community was functioning in Terminal Classic and Early Postclassic times; trade to the site in that period included plumbate pottery and ceramics from northern Yucatan, and may have extended to central Mexican green obsidian as well. However, this was not the peak period for Marco Gonzalez; its time of greatest construction activity, and probably maximum population, came in the twelfth and thirteenth centuries, when the community was closely allied ceramically with Lamanai.

The peak period at Marco Gonzalez was not simply a small swell in an undistinguished sea; in the twelfth and thirteenth centuries, the community saw construction, rebuilding, or at the least intensive use of every one of its 45 structures, and the amount of hard-goods production, as well as resource exploitation and intersite trade, was exceedingly high. Despite the site's small size, Lamanai-related ceramics occur in quantities greater than those encountered in the richest Lamanai middens; beyond this, the pottery is not simply a trade item, but appears to be of local manufacture. Though the forms and decoration are generally those characteristic of Lamanai, both paste features and vessel sizes, as well as some decorative motifs, distinguish the Marco Gonzalez material from that of its large sister site. In turn, the Lamanai collection contains very small quantities of pottery with motifs that are prevalent at the reef community, so that two-directional exchange may be in evidence.

Trade also linked Marco Gonzalez with more distant locales; Maya Mountains granite sources in Belize provided material for grinding implements, and central Mexican green obsidian was certainly arriving at the site in significant quantity during the Middle Postclassic. The architecture of the period was most unprepossessing, and as might be expected in such a setting, it included no masonry-chambered buildings; but the overall impression at Marco Gonzalez is one of real florescence during a time of great richness at Lamanai.

The Lamanai link, since it is not in evidence at sites along the New River, suggests some special function for Marco Gonzalez that may have been related to Lamanai's control over trade in the headwaters area of the river, and perhaps beyond. Since Marco Gonzalez lies in a logical spot for the exercise of control over the leeward waters around Ambergris Cay, and hence over the water route to Lamanai, it appears quite likely that the small reef site played a part in the Postclassic trade network in which Lamanai was obviously an important element. This tells us that the Postclassic developments at Lamanai had a more extensive effect than could be judged at the major center itself. Together with data from Santa Rita and Tipu, the Marco Gonzalez material suggests strongly that survival through the time of collapse and subsequent flourishing in what used to be thought of as a time of decay may have been a fairly widespread phenomenon in Belize, and perhaps in neighboring areas as well.

Both Marco Gonzalez and Lamanai experienced some decline in population, and in construction activity, as the Postclassic drew near its close, and in fact the reef site has thus far yielded only a few bits of ceramic evidence that point to sixteenth-century occupation. At Lamanai, a principal settlement in the southern part of the site and a smaller, separate village north of the Classic Central Precinct were the scenes of development of a new and distinctive ceramic assemblage (Pendergast 1985; E. Graham, 1987) around the beginning of the sixteenth century, and at least the southern community was still an important force in the area when the Spaniards arrived (*see* Pendergast 1986b). That importance is reflected in the establishment of a church at Lamanai, and the subsequent construction of an imposing masonry and thatch building that persisted in use until the uprising of 1641. Maya occupation at Lamanai ceased late in the seventeenth or early in the eighteenth century, a date that marks the effective end of the Postclassic, since Spanish presence eradicated neither the material culture nor the religious belief and practice of pre-Contact times.

Though the sixteenth-century Lamanai community was smaller than its earlier Postclassic counterparts, it still enjoyed extensive trade contacts in pre-Spanish times, with metal artifacts as the most striking element in the package. There is, in fact, evidence to suggest that here, as at Tipu (E. Graham 1985), production of copper artifacts developed late in the prehistoric period (Pendergast 1985). This may have been an element in Lamanai's economic importance in the area, but we are far from being able to assess this or any other aspect of the relationship between Lamanai and other centers in the last few decades before the Spaniards appeared on the scene.

The data summarized above should suffice to make it clear that the Postclassic was far from a decadent time, and indeed in some cases may have been a time of real florescence. Excavations in the past dozen years have shown that what we call the Classic and Postclassic periods in the southern lowlands possess information of equal value, which cannot be judged in terms of "quality." That Maya society underwent change from the patterns of Late Classic times to those of the Postclassic is beyond question, but we can now see those changes as no greater than many that preceded them, and as part of a period of evolution that began in the Preclassic and continued through the time of Spanish rule.

I have criticized judgments made in the past that the term Postclassic could only be equated with decadence, and have suggested that a kind of archaeocentric view, which hailed the Classic as the time of everything fine in Maya society, lay behind this assessment of the years after A.D. 950. In fact, given the history of Maya archaeology, the judgments are entirely understandable; hence the real criticism should be leveled at the fact that archaeologists allowed the "decadent" rubric to affect their approach to the study of site settlement, chronology, economics, and indeed all aspects of Maya culture history from the tenth century onward. As a result, evidence for Postclassic occupation in the southern lowlands has not, until recently, been treated very effectively or rigorously. Now we can see that evidence as not only important in its own right but also a potential source of information about the Classic, since it provides us with a picture of strategies for survival once the Classic ceased to be. We should understand life after the tenth century as simply different from that of preceding times, a matter of choosing a somewhat divergent track in the broad path of Maya prehistory. We may like or dislike the period's art and architecture as we choose, as long as we recognize that the Postclassic is there, and has its own vital story to tell.

Twelve

Prophets and Idol Speculators: Forces of History in the Lowland Maya Rebellion of 1638

By Grant D. Jones

They were to give obedience to their king and wished them to abandon their town, saying that if they did not do so all would die and be finished, because at such a time the Itzas would come to kill them and there would be many deaths, and hurricanes would flood the land.[1]

And that will be the ending of words:
    The great war.
Risen will be the Chan
    And the Tihosuco plain.
Who will fight
    The Chan War
Of the 1 Ahau
    Katun.
Fires
    And hurricane rains are the burden of the katun.
(*Edmonson 1986: 213*)[2]

Maya prophets concerned themselves deeply with the politics of resistance to Spanish colonial rule. Both quotations above speak to events that were prophesied for Katun 1 Ahau, the period of about twenty years that was to begin in 1638.[3] The first was reported by the Spanish *cabildo*, or town council, at Salamanca de Bacalar in September of that year and spoke to warnings by the leaders of Tipu to the Maya villagers of Belize, encouraging them to abandon their towns and join the resistance at Tipu. The second was recorded in the *Book of Chilam Balam of Tizimin* and clearly refers to the identical prophecy, although it is worded in more global, all-purpose terms. Reports of prophecy as a stimulus for anticolonial resistance appeared frequently throughout the seventeenth century, forcing us to consider the cultural discourse of Maya resistance, the political mechanisms through which resistance was organized, and the political economic conditions that stimulated this resistance.

This essay addresses the latter two issues, leaving the deeper problem of meaning and discourse for a later time. I seek here merely to demonstrate that much colonial period Maya resistance in the Yucatán peninsula was a process of separatism and avoidance of Spanish control, a protracted struggle to withdraw to free and independent zones, far from the rigors of the triumvirate institutions of *encomienda* (Indian tribute), *repartimiento* (forced Indian labor and production), and mission. This resistance was not just an underground of seething discontent: it sometimes broke out into murderous violence that frightened all Spaniards and drove them in turn to retaliate with violence and further repression. Underlying Maya violence and resistance was the message that the colony would be tolerated as long as independent Maya polities beyond a restricted zone of Spanish control were permitted their political and religious freedom.

Maya resistance action signaled a demand for colonial tolerance of another world of Maya activity beyond immediate Spanish control. By and large this tolerance was grudgingly given, but ultimately the price to be paid—particularly in the loss of labor power caused by flight from working encomiendas—was deemed too great, and Spanish authorities commenced to plan for the ultimate destruction of all independent Maya territories. These plans began as early as 1621, but so great was native resistance that Tah Itza[4] on Lake Petén Itzá, the heartland of all Maya independence movements, was not conquered until 1697 (Bricker 1981: 21–24; Villagutierre Soto-Mayor 1933, 1983). The intervening years witnessed a series of extensive anti-Spanish movements, one climax of which was a rebellion centered at Tipu in western Belize in 1638. In order to demonstrate the complexity and protracted nature of the processes that resulted in this rebellion, I shall provide here a summary and interpretation of the historical evidence that is available to us in support of the generalizations that I have just cited.

The Part and the Whole

Several years ago I wrote, based on rather slim evidence, that the southern, largely unknown frontier zone of Spanish colonial Yucatán "comprised far more than a few scattered pagan settlements beyond the pale of civilization. It was, in fact, a critical element in the total colonial society, a force that played a central role in the affairs of Yucatán from the level of the *ranchería*, or hamlet, to the very seats of colonial government" (G. Jones 1983: 64). My vision of that intractable, mysterious frontier was even more clouded then than it is today; but I did have some suggestive evidence for patterns of Maya migration and trade that cross-cut the tribute-paying regions of the north and the "free zones" of the south, with their spiritual headquarters among the Mayas who were living around Lake Petén Itzá and who escaped Spanish conquest until the late date of 1697 (G. Jones 1986).

Even on this slim evidence, I was reacting to another, less holistic view of these southern territories so poorly understood by the Spanish. On the one hand I found inadequate Eric Thompson's view that the Maya settlements of the southern frontier, which he called the Chan Maya region, were but "clusters of huts scattered over a large area, [each] . . . independent under its local chief and sometimes local priest" (Thompson 1977: 24). Thompson, in fact, devoted only half a page to the topic of political and social organization in this area, as his interests were more attuned to the region's cultural or ethnic identity.

Thompson's view of the so-called Chan Mayas as both acephalous and without effective ties beyond the community (except for those at Tah Itza on Lake Petén Itzá), did not make sense to me in view of the fact that many of these people effectively resisted integration into the colony until long after independence. Scholes and Roys' (1968) treatment of the northernmost groups of these people, while historiographically more satisfactory, likewise gave no clear vision that they possessed any social ties of importance beyond the isolated community. All three of these authors were undoubtedly deeply influenced by Redfield's characterizations of "folk" society (1941, 1947). It was here on the edges of colonial Yucatecan civilization that the end of the folk-urban continuum was really to be found: the last of the isolated, recalcitrant small-town, stubbornly pagan folks in all of Yucatán.

More convincing to me is a vision of the frontier Mayas living in a place where plans were constructed across long stretches of forest, where rebel frontiersmen stirred up trouble in peaceful encomienda villages, where refugees from civilization were in constant contact with their tribute-paying kinsmen, and news traveled quickly via an efficient intelligence network from the chambers of government in Mérida to the palace of Can Ek at Tah Itza. This vision of the colonial Maya frontier suggests a place alive with political and ideological struggle, defining new but not always satisfying ways of life for the thousands of runaways from the northern encomiendas and hatching interregional plots to weaken the fragile Spanish hold on their seething but superficially quiet subjects.

From the series of events that I shall describe later I believe that we can see the usefulness of such a view, for these events not only make sense out of a series of apparently disconnected, separate events in colonial Maya history but also force us to glimpse a colonial period Maya world that was far more global in scope that we had previously imagined. We must certainly not abandon the non-Maya world in seeking to understand these processes of rebellion. At one level we learn from these events the overwhelming force of the European-imposed tributary mode of production in affecting daily and long-term Maya life strategies. We learn how ruthless was the partnership of colonial government and ambitious military men and how opposed were the ideological interests of the Franciscans and the material interests of military leaders.

But of far greater implication for a general model of Maya rebellion is the insight that we gain into how Mayas as independent operatives—as "subjects," to use Farriss's term (1983: 19)—worked to avoid Spanish systems of control and even to put the colonial power on the defensive. This Maya world, which is just beginning to invade our consciousness, was centered in the forested zones of the southern peninsula, from just below that part of Yucatán known as the Sierra, all the way south beyond even Lake Petén Itzá; an important subregion was located along the eastern coast of the peninsula. While sparsely populated, the region was so immense that only a few poor, insecure missions were eve established among many thousands of runaway or unconverted Mayas. The only Spanish town was Salamanca de Bacalar, whose poverty and inaccessibility made life there attractive to only a handful of tough, sometimes brutal frontiersmen and their families.

In examining the Mayas who lived on the frontiers of southern colonial Yucatán, we discovered that they were organized around localized "centers" of political activity, populated principally by runaways from encomiendas to the north and often under the leadership of apostate charismatic figures who actively recruited their followings. The continued existence of these centers was dependent upon several factors, the most important of which were as follows:

(1) The highly exploitive nature of the tribute economy of the Yucatecan encomienda system, which stimulated flight to the frontier;
(2) an underground network of information, controlled by the Mayas, about the location of frontier settlements, the individuals who occupied them and their kinship relationships to those in settled encomienda towns, and the identity and reputation of their leaders;
(3) a regularized system of communication among these centers, whose leaders could forward news of importance about Spanish or other activity to leaders of other groups;
(4) a regularized system of trade throughout the frontier, which further fostered the communication of information and which strengthened the authority of local leaders who attempted to control the trade itself;
(5) the existence of the so-called Itza stronghold on Lake Petén Itzá, whose leaders were interested in fomenting anti-Spanish resistance along their distant borders and who at times attempted to exert control over the frontier centers;
(6) the apparent use of katun-based prophecies by all of these leaders in order to legitimize their authority. There is evidence that the primary center of prophecy formulation was in the hands of high priests and other leaders of the Itza confederacy in opposition to efforts by Can Ek, their nominal ruler, to accept Christianity and other political accommodations with the Spanish; the awareness of Franciscans of the power of these prophecies;
(7) finally, the shared Maya-Spanish knowledge that only with the final capitulation of the Itzas would colonial control over the frontiers be achieved.

I shall now attempt to weave this model into a chronological account of the events that led to the rebellion of 1638. My account follows a theatrical metaphor made up of stage setting, prologue, three acts, and epilogue. Through this metaphor I find it possible to place the Maya actors on center stage and to attribute to them, retrospectively, the concept of dramatic action that their keen sense of political timing and prophetic vision provided them.

Setting the Stage

The frontier region that I shall describe comprised the northern half of modern-day Belize, the northeastern quarter of the Petén (including Lake Petén Itzá), and the southeastern portions of Quintana Roo. The Yucatec-speaking provinces that comprised this area at the time of the Spanish conquest are vaguely known today. We do know, however, that Salamanca de Bacalar was located in the southernmost part of the Uaymil province; that the province of Chetumal was confined to northernmost Belize and possibly the southern coast of Quintana Roo; and that Tipu, located on the Macal branch of the Belize River near the Guatemalan border, was the capital town of the recently identified province of Dzuluinicob, which probably extended as far north as New River Lagoon (E. Graham, Jones, and Kautz 1985; G. Jones 1984: 29; G. Jones, Kautz, and Graham 1986).

The political geography of the Petén is very poorly known for the early contact period, although it is certain that the so-called Itza dynasty of the Can Eks at Tah Itzá held together a loose confederacy of political territories that were concentrated around the Central Lakes region of the Petén. Political factions in this confederacy were to play a major role in maintaining the autonomy of this latter region from Spanish control until the end of the seventeenth century. Directly north of this confederacy was a loosely delineated area known as the Cehaches during the late sixteenth and seventeenth centuries, but it is not clear whether this was a Precolumbian province or simply a collection of refugee polities made up predominantly of runaways from the encomiendas of northern Yucatán. To their southeast was a province known in the seventeenth century as Mopan, whose contact period status is also unclear. To the northwest of the Central Lakes region were the Chontal-speaking Putún Acalan, and in southernmost Belize were the Chol-speaking Manches; both of these non-Yucatec groups were probably marginal to the political events that involved the Yucatec-speaking Mayas (G. Jones 1982, 1983; Thompson 1977).

European contact in this region was initiated by Hernán Cortés, who made an ambitious *entrada* through Putún, Cehach, Itzá, Mopan, and Manche Chol territory in 1525. Cortés discovered that the political and economic heartland of much of this vast southern territory was Tah Itza itself and that Can Ek controlled a trade network all the way from Manche Chol territory to Lake Petén. He visited Can Ek at Tah Itza, vowing to return one day and leaving his lame horse under the care of the Itzas (Bricker 1981: 21; G. Jones 1983: 72–73). We shall learn more about this infamous horse later on.

Cortés, of course, never returned to Tah Itza, and it would be nearly a century before official Spanish contact with the Can Eks would be reattempted. From Cortés's time on, Spanish conquest and pacification strategies would focus on the east coast and on the riverine access to the Petén through Belize. The first of these efforts took place in 1528, when the *adelantado* Francisco de Montejo and his lieutenant, Alonso Dávila, set off by sea and land down the east coast of Yucatán in search of a location for a permanent Spanish settlement in the area. They reached the coastal town of Chetumal, probably on Corozal Bay, whose inhabitants they confronted in a battle supposedly led on the Maya side by Gonzalo Guerrero, the shipwrecked mariner who had joined forces with the Mayas. Plans to establish a Spanish settlement in the Chetumal area were postponed until 1531, when Dávila and his troops attempted to pacify the Uaymil and Chetumal provinces and to establish a *villa* (administrative town) at Chetumal itself. His attempts were ultimately unsuccessful, and after about a year he was forced by Maya opposition to abandon his new town of Villa Real (G. Jones 1984: 28–31).

Eleven years later, in late 1543 or early 1544, after the establishment of the city of Mérida and the northern villas of Campeche and Valladolid, Melchor and Alonso Pacheco set out to conquer the provinces of Uaymil, Chetumal, and Dzuluinicob, establishing the new villa of Salamanca de Bacalar near the mouth of the Río Hondo. This was the most notoriously cruel and vicious conquest in the history of Yucatán, and we now know that it was far more ambitious in scope than previously supposed. The Pachecos probably reached southernmost Belize, and it is likely that they conquered and reduced the area around Tipu. They established with their Spanish troops a small number of extensive cacao-producing encomiendas along the rivers of northern Belize and around Salamanca de Bacalar. These encomiendas were never easy to administer, and rebellions broke out in the region as early as 1547. In 1567 and 1568 the villa was said to be once again under a state of virtual siege by hostile Mayas who carried away Maya men and women living around Salamanca de Bacalar, and several pacification entradas were carried out during those years by lieutenant governor Juan Garzón. One of these entradas resulted in the reconquest of Tipu, which was in the center of a particularly rebellious, apostate territory (G. Jones 1984: 31–33).

The effects of Spanish conquest of the region under nominal control by the Spanish at Salamanca de Bacalar were to displace centers of Maya leadership, particularly at Chetumal; to disperse the indigenous population, which initiated a pattern of flight to less controlled areas and to neighboring regions controlled by unconquered Maya groups; to establish encomiendas for the purpose of tribute collection and the formation of missions in native towns subordinate to the villa of Bacalar; and on occasion to congregate hostile and runaway groups nearer the villa itself. The Maya population responded to these activities not only by fleeing to more remote regions (and welcoming into their midst runaways from northern Yucatán) but also by organizing periodic rebellions. The principal aim of these rebellions, about which we know very little, appears to have been to remove the Maya of Belize from encomienda control. To the extent that control over more remote encomiendas such as Tipu appears to have been weak and periodic, these rebellions must have been partially successful. Their success was certainly fostered in part by the weakness of Spanish control at Salamanca de Bacalar, whose tiny Spanish population was unable to quell native conflict without the importation of troops from northern Yucatán (G. Jones 1984: 33).

This, then, was the established setting in which the events that I shall presently describe took place: by the end of the sixteenth century this vast territory was administered by a villa that was nothing more than a poor frontier outpost that probably earned more in contraband coastal trading than in rents from the Maya population. None of the Maya towns in Belize had permanent Spanish residents, but they were a major attraction for refugees fleeing conditions in the north. As I have described elsewhere, there was a lively underground Maya trade in cacao, forest products, metal tools, and cotton cloth that bypassed Spanish controls (G. Jones 1984). There was also trade in pottery idols and a continuously active non-Christian ritual system that drew together the various frontier Mayas and their brethren from the north (G. Jones, Kautz, and Graham 1986).

Spanish efforts to stop such pagan activities in such remote quarters were all but ineffective throughout the sixteenth century. By the seventeenth century conditions on the encomiendas of northern Yucatán had worsened due to the increasingly burdensome extortions of illegal repartimientos, which sent even more Mayas fleeing into the forests of the south, joining not only established encomienda towns such as Tipu but also numerous independent frontier Maya polities under the control of charismatic priests and other Maya leaders. Incessant Spanish attempts to concentrate a dispersed population in a few central settlements were only temporary plugs, and *encomenderos* (recipients of Indian tribute) were alarmed by significant losses of population. Spanish bureaucrats and military men saw only one solution: the destruction of Tah Itza and the conquest of the so-called Itzas, who were viewed as the ideological inspiration and political-military protectors of the entire frontier crisis. As long as the Itzas remained free from Spanish control, the drain on Yucatán's labor resources would continue unabated.

The events that I shall now summarize should be understood in the context of a Spanish effort to open a road, both literally and figuratively, to the Itzas through the refugee zone of southeastern Quintana Roo and from thence through western Belize and Tipu. Tipu was seen by the Spanish as a gateway to the Itzas, as its leaders were on good terms with the Itza hierarchy and were at least nominally Christian. The failure of this effort, which resulted in massive rebellion and Spanish expulsion from virtually all of Belize, was a major setback in Spanish designs on the Petén, which would remain unconquered until the end of the century.

Prologue: The Itza Visit to Mérida

Victoria Bricker recently brought to our attention that a group of Itzas went to Mérida, supposedly in 1614, to declare their submission to the crown. The Spanish source for this visit was López de Cogolludo, who wrote in about 1659 that

> The Itza Indians . . . came to the city of Mérida during the time of this governor. They said that they came to submit themselves to the king, in whose name the governor presented them with alcaldes' staffs of office and named a council. This being done they went back, it being understood that they had voluntarily become subjects. This, however, was later seen to be a deception. (López de Cogolludo 1688: Bk. 9, ch. 2)

Although Bricker accepted the date of 1614 for this event given by Villagutierre, who wrote many years after the event (1933: Bk. 2, ch. 1), it appears that Villagutierre actually invented this date. His own source, López de Cogolludo, stated only that the Itzas' visit to Mérida occurred during the term of Antonio de Figueroa, who governed Yucatán from March 1612 until September 1617.

I recently learned that the Itza visit had been reported as early as 1633 in a garbled account of Lizana, who was apparently López's source (Lizana 1893: 115). He wrote of the visit in the context of the life history of Fray Juan de Orbita, an impulsively devout Franciscan who had visited Tipu and Tah Itza with Fray Bartolomé de Fuensalida in 1618. Lizana wrote,

> This holy religious had already visited Taiza on

another occasion [before 1618]. He had been there two days, was given an excellent reception, and convinced them to offer their vassalage to the king our lord, in whose name he appointed the very same king Can Ek as governor or cacique. He also gave alcaldes' staffs to two Indian *principales* and formed a council and all the rest necessary for the *república*. All were contented. (Lizana 1893: 115)

Apparently Orbita and his companion thereupon returned with 150 inhabitants of Tah Itza to Mérida, where they presented a report of their successes to the Franciscan prelate and to the governor and bishop. The news was well received, and the governor confirmed the appointments they had made, encouraging them to continue their work. Just what later went wrong is not made clear by Lizana, who only laments that "the hour for the conversion of that people must not have arrived" and that God had set them aside to be "firebrands for Hell" (Lizana 1893: 115). We might read into this passage Lizana's understanding that the Itza visit to Mérida was in response to one Itza faction's interpretation of a prophecy that the Itza would accept Christianity and Spanish rule at the end of Katun 5 Ahau, which was to occur in 1618.

Lizana reported that Orbita did not arrive in Yucatán until 1615, after which he learned Maya "scientifically" (1893: 113). If this date is correct, the Itza visit to Mérida could not have been before 1615 and was probably not until 1616 or 1617. It now becomes apparent why Fuensalida and Orbita visited Tah Itza yet again in 1618: they were simply following up on their mandate to pursue the complete conversion of the Itzas as they were instructed by governor Figueroa.

Bricker suggested that passages in the Book of Chilam of Tizimin that pertain to the year 1611, toward the end of Katun 5 Ahau, refer directly to the Itza visit to Mérida and to their ignominious return to Tah Itza, where the representatives may have been seized and beaten (Bricker 1984: 21; Edmonson 1982: 103–106). According to Edmonson's free interpretation of these obscure passages, there may have been conflict at this time between pro-Christian and anti-Christian factions at Tah Itza. This is a fascinating possibility, although I must admit to some skepticism concerning Edmonson's interpretation; and certainly the visit did not occur as early as 1611.

That this visit did occur, probably in 1616 or 1617, is quite certain. It was covered up "in the press," so to speak, for reasons that are not clear. I have been able to find no primary source documentation for an event that must have been considered of major importance—not even a mention of it in correspondence from the governor. Just why the visit was considered by López and Lizana to have been an immediate failure is also not clear, because there is no evidence of Itza hostility or refusal to accept missionaries from Yucatán. It should be pointed out that an almost identical event occurred again in 1695, when a delegation from Tah Itza again visited Mérida through Tipu, precipitating at that time a major split in the Itza confederacy and resulting in similar claims by the Spanish that the visit had been a hoax. This visit, too, was timed to coincide with the end of a katun (Katun 8 Ahau, which was to end in 1697), and like the earlier event was followed by abortive Franciscan efforts to secure voluntary submission and ultimately by plans to take Tah Itza by military conquest. The second time around, however, Spanish forces succeeded in their mission, whereas, as we shall see, the earlier attempt ended in disaster.

This earlier visit was a key event in that we discover in it the seeds of ideologically motivated political ferment—both at Tah Itza and Mérida—to which all of the later events that we shall examine were ultimately answerable.

Act I: The Destruction of Tzimin Chac

Tzimin Chac, or Thunder Horse, was a lime and stone statue of the horse left by Cortés in the care of Can Ek in 1525. The Spanish portrayed it as the Itzas' principal idol, and its destruction by the passionate Fray Juan de Orbita in 1618 so infuriated the Itzas that the event was recalled by Itza troops at the time of the near murder of Fray Bartolomé de Fuensalida and his companions near Tipu twenty-five years later, in 1643. Whatever hope the 1616 or 1617 Itza embassy to Mérida might have provided for a peaceful conquest of the Petén was dashed by Orbita's impetuousness.

Shortly after the departure of the Itza embassy from Mérida, arrangements were made for the Franciscans Fuensalida and Orbita to travel to Tah Itza by way of Tipu, apparently in the hope of solidifying the terms of their capitulation. The details of this trip and their visit to Tah Itza were recorded in a now-lost *relación* written many years later by Fuensalida. This *relación* was fortunately available to the López de Cogolludo, who paraphrased and quoted from it at length.

I have space to mention only one small aspect of their visit to Tah Itza, which was clearly timed to convince Can Ek and other leaders to accept Christianity at the time of the katun change. López de Cogolludo reported that Can Ek and his *principales* answered Fuensalida's impassioned sermon on the power of the gospel to the effect "that it was not time to be Christians (they had their own beliefs as to what they should be) and that they should go back where they had come from; they could come back another time, but right then they did not want to be Christians" (López de Cogolludo 1688: Bk. 9, ch. 9).

At this point the religious were taken on a tour of the island town, which was arranged with about 200 houses along the shore and about 12 large temples in the upper and middle section. It was on this tour that Orbita "lost his cool":

> In the middle of one of them was a great idol shaped like a horse and made of lime and stone. It was seated on the floor of the temple on its haunches with its back legs folded under and its forefeet raised up. They worshiped it as god of thunder, calling it Tzimin Chac, which means horse of thunder and lightning. They had this idol because, as was noted in the first book of these writings, when D. Fernando Cortés passed through that area on his way to Honduras, he left them a horse that could not travel any further. It died on them, and for fear that they could not return it to him alive if he returned and asked for it, they made it into this statue and began to worship it that they might not be blamed for the death of the horse. Because they entrusted it to the Indians saying they would return for it and the Indians believed that it was an animal with reason, they fed it chickens and other meats. They presented it bouquets of flowers as they were accustomed to giving important people. All these honors (which it seems they did) led to the death of the poor horse, who died from hunger. They gave it this name because they had seen some of the Spanish on that expedition firing their harquebuses and muskets above the horses while hunting, and they believed that the horses caused the clamor that seemed like thunder to them and the flash from the muskets and smoke from the powder that seemed like lightning. The devil used this together with the blindness of their superstitions to increase their worship of the statue to the point that when the religious were there it was the principal idol that they honored.
>
> When Father Fr. Juan de Orbita saw it, says his companion Father Fuensalida, it was as if the Spirit of the Lord descended upon him; and filled with a fervent jealousy for God's honor, he picked up a stone in his hand and mounted the statue of the horse and broke it into pieces, scattering them all over the floor. When the Indians who were with him, and there were many, saw that he had destroyed their most cherished idol, they let out a shout saying one to the other: "Kill them, for they have killed our God. They shall die in recompense for the injury that they have done." And so great was the outcry that our Lord must have been working to keep them from carrying it out then, although we would have been fortunate (he says) to die there for his holy love. The uproar did not disturb the religious who with great courage and strength of spirit put all their confidence in God, and the Father *comisario*, carrying the holy Crucifix in his hands, said to the Indians: "Know, oh Itzas, that this idol that you worship here as your god is nothing more than a figure of an irrational beast, as are the deer and other animals that you shoot to eat. In it you worship the devil who has tricked you and blinded you through your idolatries, and that neither he nor you can harm us at all, if our God and true Lord, Creator of heaven and earth and all things, in whom we believe, confess, and worship, does not give you permission to do so. (López de Cogolludo 1688: Bk. 9, ch. 9)

Despite Orbita's rash act and impassioned sermon, the religious stayed on for several more days and were dealt with sympathetically, even supportively, by Can Ek and some of the other inhabitants. However, Can Ek repeated that "the time had not arrived in which their ancient priests had prophesied they would need to give up the worship of their gods, for the present age was one called Ox Ahau (which means third age) and the one that he had indicated to them was not arriving so soon" (López de Cogolludo 1688: Bk. 9, ch. 10).

Nonetheless, Fuensalida and Orbita returned to Tah Itza in 1619 and found Can Ek completely receptive to new overtures. Can Ek even agreed to the naming of a *cabildo* among his leaders, over whom he would serve as hereditary cacique. He also allowed a new cross to be erected in front of his house, which would supplement that left in 1525 by

Cortés. In short order, however, factions opposed to Can Ek and supported by his wife spoke out against such activities, and the religious were forced out of town. They were probably also supported by leaders of Tipu, who were found in 1619 engaged in various "idolatrous" activities that were linked to the bad influences of the Itzas (López de Cogolludo: Bk. 9, chaps. 12 and 13).

From the activities surrounding these first two events—the 1616 or 1617 Itza mission to Mérida and Orbita's destruction of Tzimin Chac in 1618—I hypothesize that during Orbita's first visit to Tah Itza, Can Ek himself had agreed to spearhead a Christianization movement and would accept nominal Spanish rule with himself as cacique of a bitterly divided Itza confederacy. This would almost certainly have been done in return for a ten-year holiday from tribute payments, which would after that time be payable to the crown and not to individual encomenderos. Can Ek thereupon agreed to send the delegation of 150 to meet Governor Figueroa in Mérida, accompanied by the hero of the day, Orbita. There, as Lizana reported, colonial appointments of native leaders were confirmed, and the emissaries returned, probably via Tipu. Can Ek's control of his fractious leaders of a growing population around the lake was weakened primarily by rival prophetic interpretations of the impending Katun 3 Ahau. That katun had already begun when Fuensalida and Orbita arrived at Tah Itza in 1618, having doubtless known of the political situation before they decided to make the journey. Katun 3 Ahau would be controlled by an intensely anti-Spanish, anti-Christian faction that wielded immense influence throughout the frontier, setting the stage for the widespread rebellion that would break out at the beginning of Katun 1 Ahau in 1638. Orbita's destruction of Tzimin Chac was likely the key event to give popular Itza support to the anti–Can Ek faction.

I should note briefly certain striking similarities between the Itza delegation of 1616 or 1617 and that of 1695, when Can Ek sent representatives to Mérida to declare their submission to the crown. Both of these events took place on the eve of a new katun, 3 Ahau and 8 Ahau respectively. Both involved subsequent explicit references by Can Ek to the prophecies, which were apparently well understood by the Franciscan friars. Both were followed by indications of major divisions among the confederation leaders of the Lake Petén Itzá area, placing Can Ek in the position of appearing to be a weak pro-Spanish power seeker, anxious to co-opt any Spanish takeover and act as a colonially sanctioned cacique over the entire confederacy.

In both cases Can Ek lost the internal battle for power. In the earlier case the conservatives managed to gain full control, resulting in the deaths in 1624 of Fray Diego Delgado and his party at Tah Itza and in the Sacalum massacre (discussed below). In the latter one it was already too late, and the Itzas were overcome militarily. History nearly repeated itself.

Act II: The Murder of Fray Diego Delgado and the Sacalum Massacre

Fray Diego Delgado, a native of the villa of Pedroso in Spain, requested in early 1621 a license to reduce fugitives in the forests of Yucatán. The request was approved by his superiors and by a new governor, Diego de Cárdenas, sometime around September 1621. Apparently in late 1621 Delgado, then serving at Hecelchakan near Campeche, recruited a following for his mission (including native church officers) from that town and from the towns in the Sierra (López de Cogolludo 1688: Bk. 10, ch. 2). He probably reached as far as a town called Hopelchen, on the road to an infamous region of rebels and runaways known as La Pimienta, located in southeastern Quintana Roo west of Salamanca de Bacalar. Here he created a full reduction town, returning to Mérida by early 1622.[5] By March 19 he was named to accompany a military entrada with aims to conquer the Itzas, under Captain Francisco de Mirones Lescano. This entrada was to go via Hopelchen, and Delgado was on his way to join it by the beginning of April, 1622.

Mirones was a military man who had served in Spain against the Turks in 1610. He had been for several years a military officer along the northern coast of Yucatán, where he also held the notorious title of *juez de grana*, that is, overseer of cochineal production. Although armed entradas to Tah Itza were forbidden by the Crown, Governor Cárdenas approached Mirones in 1621 with a plan to pursue an armed conquest of the Itzas, apparently from a base at Hopelchen, or possibly at Sacalum, a mission in the Pimienta region that might have been founded as early as 1604. Mirones agreed to the plan, which was promptly submitted to the Council of the Indies.⁶

In a petition (dated 9 November 1621) addressed to governor Diego de Cárdenas offering to carry out an entrada Mirones noted that he learned about the existence of idolatrous Indian provinces where fugitive Indians and "wrongdoers" who had been fleeing from the settled provinces sought refuge. These, he understood, included not only those idolatrous "barbarians" living at the lake of Tah Itza, those of the Lacandon Sierras, and those located in other islands and provinces, but also various "baptized runaways" from Yucatán, including their children and their descendants. These peoples collectively exerted a negative influence on the "natives of these provinces" due to their proximity to them. He noted the entrada of Fuensalida and Orbita in 1618 to Tah Itza, where their successes included saying mass, preaching, the destruction and burning of idols, and the sworn conversion to Christianity of various Itzas. There was no mention, however, of their earlier visit to Mérida.

Once their conversion was sworn to, Mirones argued, the Itzas became rebels whom the crown had the right to pacify by whatever entrada might be necessary. The purpose of his petition was to offer his services to convert and pacify "the said Indians and provinces" under several specific conditions: Mirones would be in full command of the troops and would administer any Spanish town founded by him in the name of the provincial governor. Among his services would be the opening of a road to Guatemala through the towns of Mani, Ticul, Oxkutzcab, and Tekax. He would supply 100 men for the journey, and the Franciscan governing superior would provide a religious. In addition, he could take all the beasts of burden, Indian porters, female Indian millers, and guides that he needed. Two thousand of the conquered Indians would belong to the crown. Of the remaining, Mirones would receive one-third in encomienda; these would pass to his descendants, or, if he had no children, to a successor whom he would name. The other two-thirds would be given in encomienda to his officers and soldiers, and he would pay the crown's taxes on any treasure that he found. He would name officials in any Spanish towns he founded; the Indians residing there would pay no tribute for the first ten years.

Mirones was clearly an ambitious man, and had he succeeded he might have been the richest man in Yucatán. The mood at Tah Itza, however, was not in his favor.

Mirones made a detailed diary (from 9 March to 31 May 1622) of his entrada from Ticul via Pustunich and Oxkutzcab to Hopelchen (Delgado's reduction town) and eventually on to a town called Ixpimienta. The diary contains remarkable details of the social life in the frontier towns and of the process of an armed entrada under the direction of a tough, ruthless, and mercenary military man. The venture began with 20 Spanish soldiers and 80 Mayas recruited from the Sierra towns. More Mayas were recruited by his agents, but he was plagued by desertions that left him with only a handful of men by the time he reached his destination. He took sworn testimonies all along the way, especially at Hopelchen, seeking to learn what he might find at Ixpimienta, where he apparently intended to establish a base from which he would prepare for the final attack on Tah Itza. From this testimony he learned that Hopelchen had been founded by fugitives some sixty years earlier, apparently during Bishop Fray Diego de Landa's inquisition. Fugitives continued to arrive there, primarily in small family groups from the region around Hecelchakan. Contact between Ixpimienta, Hopelchen, and Hecelchakan was active, mediated by relations of trade in wax and copal from the inner forests in exchange for knives, machetes, and salt. Marriages between the frontier and encomienda towns like Hecelchakan were frequent.

He also learned that these lines of communication provided news about events in Mérida almost as soon as they had happened. One informant who had been to Ixpimienta said that the inhabitants there knew about the discussions concerning the proposed road to Verapaz and the plans to reduce the Itzas and other pagans. They had held a meeting to plan for this eventuality at which it was decided that all would be prepared to defend themselves to the death and that spies would be posted to warn of the Spaniards' arrival. Each Indian carried 400 arrows, made by others who were being punished for various crimes.

Ixpimienta was a center of religious activity, administered by four *ah kines* (native priests) who were also called *bobat*, or prophet. These wore Spanish-style priestly vestments and apparently controlled the receipt and distribution of trade goods. Other men from the town wore their hair long in the style of the frontier rebels, even though they sometimes traveled through Spanish-controlled territory to visit their wives at Hecelchakan.

After Delgado's arrival, he and Mirones pushed on to Ixpimienta against great odds that included a shortage of water and continuing desertions. Having sent letters ahead asking for peaceful submission, they entered with a small number of troops on Friday, May 6, and were "received surrounded by Indian men and women carrying palms in their hands and [having placed] a cross at the entrance of the town, before which we all knelt and gave thanks." The Mayas knew how to give a proper reception.

Baptisms of children began immediately, and the church and the priest's house were completed in three days. Over the next several weeks the inhabitants of neighboring settlements were reduced to Ixpimienta, and their children were also baptized.[7]

Sometime during the next months Mirones decided to move his headquarters to a place called Sacalum, further along the proposed road to Tah Itza. By now it must have been obvious to Mirones that his guide had taken him far out of the way. His reinforcements were slow in coming, and he spent the next year and a half firming up his presence in the area and building a proper armed presidio at Sacalum (López de Cogolludo 1688: Bk. 10, ch. 2). Throughout the rest of the year he illegally forced the Mayas to produce goods in return for advances (*tratos y contratos de granjería*), and his behavior was challenged by Delgado as their differences became publicly known. In early 1623 Delgado wrote a letter of complaint to his superior, who advised him that the armed entrada was illegal and that he was under no obligation to follow Mirones' orders; instead he should follow God's inspiration (López de Cogolludo 1688: Bk. 10, ch. 2).

Later that year Delgado left for Tipu, taking Indians who had accompanied him from Hecelchacan and clearing a new path. Learning of this, Mirones sent twelve soldiers to accompany him to Tipu, where Delgado sent a message to the Itzas through Don Cristóbal Na, the cacique of Tipu who had accompanied Fuensalida and Orbita in 1618. The Itzas gave Delgado permission to visit them with the twelve soldiers, and Na recruited eighty Tipuans to accompany the party.

Once at Tah Itza the Itzas fell on their Spanish and Maya visitors immediately after their arrival. First they killed all of the party except Delgado, reportedly offering their hearts to their idols and nailing their heads to stakes on a hill in view of the town. Delgado's captors informed him, according to the witness, that he was to be killed in retribution for the idols that Fuensalida had taken back to Mérida with him on his first visit. Delgado's heart was removed and offered to the idols, even as he continued preaching, his body cut into pieces and his head put on a stake with the others. Don Cristóbal Na of Tipu was among those killed (López de Cogolludo, Bk. 10, ch. 2).

Mirones had meanwhile sent a party of two Spaniards, his servant, Bernardino Ek, and other Mayas of his party to check on Delgado and his party. These learned of the massacre but went on to Tah Itza anyway, where they were put in manacles and locked in a palisaded corral. Ek alone managed to escape, returning to Tipu and then to Bacalar, where he told his story. The alcalde of Bacalar took his deposition, which he sent to Cárdenas (López de Cogolludo 1688: Bk. 10, ch. 3).

Worried by the news of Delgado's and the Spaniards' death at Tah Itza, the governor ordered that Ek be sent to warn Mirones. He also ordered Captain Juan Bernardo Casanova to march quickly with reinforcements from Mani to Sacalum; Casanova was to be accompanied by Fray Juan Fernández, a lay friar who had worked for many years in Florida. Ek had actually arrived at Sacalum before Casanova, but Mirones did not believe him and had him tortured (López de Cogolludo 1688: Bk. 10, ch. 3).

On about January 29, 1624, before Casanova's reinforcements arrived, a group of Mayas attacked the Spaniards while they were defenseless in church and proceeded to kill all the Mayas loyal to the Spanish. The leader of the massacre was Ah Kin Pol (Cárdenas Valencia 1937: 58–59; López de Cogolludo 1688, Bk. 10, ch. 3).

There exist in the Archivo General de Indias detailed documents describing Casanova's rescue mission to Sacalum. The picture of what his party discovered only shortly after the massacre took place is a grisly one, but the nature of the testimony is such that I see no reason why we should not accept it as true. Ten or eleven Spaniards, including Mirones, had been hanged and beheaded, and their bodies were burned. Mirones's chest had been opened and his heart removed. An unspecified number of Maya men and women were also murdered but not beheaded. They found signs of ritual sacrifice, and the entire town was destroyed by fire. A letter in Maya, which has been preserved in Spanish translation, was found intact; it may be interpreted as a communication between leaders of the insurrection.[8]

Rumors abounded that the perpetrators of the Sacalum massacre together with inhabitants of the towns of the Sierra were plotting an attack against the Spanish on Jueves Santo. Over the next two months Casanova and another captain, Antonio Méndez de Canzo, stationed Spanish troops in Oxkutzcab, Mani, and Tekax. Rewards were offered for anyone who could capture Ah Kin Pol, who was reputed to have been the principal leader behind the massacre and to have had a wide following throughout the Sierra towns.[9]

Méndez de Canzo commissioned the Maya governor of Oxkutzcab, Don Fernando Camal, and 150 Maya archers to track down Pol and his followers in the forests. Camals' troops were successful and found with Pol and the others the chalices and other silver from the Sacalum church, as well as a silver-plated dagger and some clothing belonging to Mirones. Pol and others were dragged back to Canzo, who claimed to have tried the prisoners. The prisoners testified to the events of the massacre, presumably under torture, but their account has survived only in summary form. They were then hanged, dragged through the streets, and drawn and quartered. Their heads were displayed in the plazas of the towns of the Sierra. The punishment was precisely the same as that administered in Sacalum and at Tah Itza, only the hearts were not removed as a sacrificial offering (López de Cogolludo 1688: Bk. 10, ch. 3).[10]

So great were the Spanish suspicions of an imminent uprising that even Maya wax traders arriving from the forest at Tizimin, near Chancenote, that infamous den of idolaters, were arrested and sent to the Valladolid jail. This was a long way from Mani or Sacalum, but no Indian stranger was to be trusted.[11]

Act III: The 1638 Tipu Rebellion

Spanish fears in 1624 of a general uprising in the Sierra were probably unfounded, as Maya strategies of rebellion were aimed at protecting Itza autonomy and a wide territory of unconquered rebels across the north and east of Itza territory. The rebellion of 1638 was the final outcome of this strategy, which was fully obvious from the events surrounding the Sacalum massacre of 1624. We may assume, I believe, that all of the preceding events were closely interconnected and coordinated under the most powerful conservative factions around Tah Itza—leaders who had always opposed Can Ek's peaceful overtures to the Spanish on the basis of his interpretation of prophecies of capitulation implicit in Katun 3 Ahau, which began in 1618.

The year 1638 ushered in Katun 1 Ahau, whose prophecies, quoted at the beginning of this essay, suggested a time of natural disaster and rebellion. The events of the period were focused around Tipu, the ancient capital of Dzuluinicob, but there is considerable evidence that, again, the source of the plots was at Tah Itza. Tipuans, who for a brief time had been cooperative with Spanish designs on the Itzas, now joined forces with anti-Spanish factions at Tah Itza and succeeded completely in their efforts to remove Spanish influence from the province.

Tipu and its immediate hinterland had not fared well during the years preceding 1638. In 1614 and 1615 the area had been subjected to forced settlements by the alcalde of Salamanca de Bacalar.[12] In 1618 and 1619 the Franciscans Fuensalida and Orbita had used the town of Tipu as their gateway to their unproductive encounters with the Itzas, and in the latter year the town suffered inquisition and punishment following the priests' discovery of idols hidden in homes. In 1620 the alcalde of Salamanca de Bacalar carried out a round of visits to the native towns for the purpose of collecting fines, and he almost certainly included Tipu in his tour. The encomiendas of Tipu and other Belize towns were reconsolidated in 1622, certainly leading to more effective collection of rents.[13] And in 1623, 80 Tipuans, including their cacique, were murdered while accompanying another Franciscan, Fray Diego Delgado, to Tah Itza.

Tipu was caught between two forces: on one side, Spanish rent collectors, missionaries, and military men bent on using the town in their designs on the Itzas; and on the other, the aggressive, anti-Spanish Itzas. It is hardly surprising, given the harsh treatment to which they were subjected by the Spaniards at Salamanca de Bacalar, that Tipuans opted for an ideologically appealing anti-Spanish movement masterminded at Tah Itza. Leaders at Tipu spread the prophetic message of this movement throughout the Belize encomienda towns and for a time consolidated much of the territory's Maya population around Tipu itself.

The first signs of rebellion appeared in 1630, when the Mayas of Xibun and Soite deserted their towns, fleeing to the forest with the bells and ornaments of their churches. The inhabitants of Xibun, on the Sibun River, had resettled at an inland town called Chululte, where they were found practicing idolatry. But when asked why they had run away, all of the witnesses were mum, replying with characteristic ambiguity that it had simply been their pleasure to do so.[14]

The next several years were quiet in Belize, but in July 1638 the governor of Yucatán, the Marqués de Santo Floro, wrote to the king of reports of more desertions from the Belize encomiendas, including Tipu, discussing in detail the conditions that had led to these activities. The Bacalar cabildo had sent suspect prisoners to him, but the governor had received earlier complaints about the Spaniards themselves through the defender of Indians, who had been personally visited in Mérida by a delegation from Tipu. The complaints focused on the fifty or so non-Maya inhabitants of Bacalar, who extorted the Mayas of the province by selling items in return for cacao. All of his efforts to correct such behaviors had failed due to the distance and isolation of the villa. Nor was he able to correct complaints by Tipuans about the tyrannical behavior of the secular priest sent to them from Bacalar.

Learning of renewed Maya desertions, the governor intervened by sending messengers all the way to Tipu, who returned with two Tipuans sent by the cacique of the town. The Tipuans confirmed the reports, saying that the inhabitants had fled because of fear of an impending visit by people from Bacalar. Nonetheless, several of the cabildo members had remained and sent their names for the customary confirmation by the governor.[15]

By September, the inhabitants of several coastal villages had also fled to the forests, claiming that the Tipuans had sent prophetic messages to them (quoted at the opening of this essay):

> that they were to give obedience to their king and wished them to abandon their town, saying that if they did not do so all would die and be finished, because at such a time the Itzas would come to kill them and there would be great mortalities and hurricanes that would flood the land.[16]

The Bacalareños took the few runaways they were able to capture back to Bacalar, where they were settled in the Barrio of San Juan and at Tamalcab on the coast. By the end of 1638, Pacha, Yumpetén, Soite, Manan, Xibun, and Lamanai were deserted.[17] In 1639 Cárdenas Valencia wrote:

> news has come from Bacalar that those few towns which we have described had been going to the forests, encouraged and deceived by those barbarous infidels of the Tah Itzas, becoming one with them, as a result of which Bacalar will become more deserted and short of people. (Cárdenas Valencia 1937: 97)

His predictions were exactly on the mark. By 1642, after a blackout of reports on the situation, the governor wrote that eight of the rebel towns, consisting of some 300 families, had congregated at Tipu itself. Only about 150 families, presumably of those six villages listed above, remained loyal to the Crown; but of these some had fled to the forests "either out of fear that they would be carried off by the rebels or for not being able to tolerate the weight of work, being so few."[18] Some of these had been repopulated at their original towns, including Lamanai, but specific information is lacking.[19]

Writing later of these events López de Cogolludo (1688: Bk. 11, ch. 12) claimed that the rebels had "completely refused to obey God and the king, horribly rejecting our holy faith. They returned to the vomit of their idolatries. They desecrated the images and burned the temples consecrated to the Divine Majesty and then their towns, and then they fled to the forests. A poignant indication of the truth of this claim is the recent archaeological discovery of a non-Christian offering within the walls of the nave of the church at Tipu. This offering is stylistically similar to one of the offerings discovered in a Maya ceremonial complex only a stone's throw from this church (Elizabeth Graham, personal communication 1986).

Epilogue: Fuensalida's Return and the Destruction of Bacalar

In 1641 Fray Bartolomé de Fuensalida, accompanied by three other Franciscans (one a lay friar), were sent to Bacalar in order to attempt the reconversion of the rebels.[20] The centerpiece of their activities was a futile attempt by Fuensalida and Fray Juan de Estrada, the lay friar and a fine linguist, to reach Tipu, the headquarters of the rebellion. Fuensalida left a detailed narrative of this effort, recorded by López de Cogolludo (1688), as part of his lost relación, only a portion of which I have space to summarize.

The religious found towns burned and deserted from Lamanai to those along the Belize River. Approaching the Belize River they saw

> statues of men dressed like Spaniards scattered about.... These idols guarded the way and would stop and enchant anyone who tried to pass by them. (Bk. 11, ch. 13)

The rebels they saw were armed and had painted their bodies, and their hair was long in the style of non-Christian Indians; some of them were now living in towns in the interior. They witnessed what they considered idolatry, learned that a Maya priest had been carrying out his own version of the mass using tortillas and pozol, and were humiliated by the destruction of the saints' images and the crucifix that they carried with them.

Their mistreatment climaxed while they were at Hubelna. Approached at the house where they had spent a frightened night, they were met by an armed procession accompanied by boys beating on conch shells. The day before, they had read letters from the governor and bishop promising amnesty in return for submission by the Mayas, but now they were tied up and subjected to humiliating insults:

> They said, "Let the governor come. Let the king come. Let the Spanish come. We are ready to fight them. Now go and tell them.... Others threatened to kill him because he and Father Orbita had destroyed the Itzas' idol Tzimin Chac and thereby killed their god. (Bk. 11, ch. 14).

Earlier indications of Itza inspirations for this rebellion were, then, fully confirmed, and the motif of Act I returned to haunt Orbita's one-time companion. Now, although willingly awaiting martyrdom, the religious and their Maya companions from Bacalar were not harmed. Their ignominious departure, however, was accompanied by screams, whistles, and obscene gestures as they were sent running for their lives back to Bacalar.

On November 22, 1642, Bacalar was sacked by the pirate Diego Lucifer de los Reyes el Mulato, whose men profaned the church, chopped up the images of the saints, dressed in the saints' clothes, and made off with goods valued at 12,000 to 14,000 pesos.[21] The villa was sacked again in 1648, this time by a pirate named Abraham (Bk. 12, ch. 12). Pirates became an increasingly troublesome scourge along this coast, and before 1654 the inhabitants of Salamanca de Bacalar had moved the villa to a new location at Pacha along the road to Valladolid.[22] Spanish control over Chetumal and Dzuluinicob was at an end, and the way was open for the British occupation of Belize.

Conclusion

Nancy Farriss recently noted the general absence of colonial rebellions in Yucatán during the colonial period, save for the Can Ek rebellion of 1761 (Farriss 1984: 68). Reports of uprisings were common during this period, as she notes, but rare was the occasion when these movements broke out into violent confrontation. While not disagreeing with her assessment, I have argued here that resistance to colonial rule was in fact deeply rooted as a process of separatism and independence. The events described here were but a few in a rich tapestry of frontier resistance movements that lasted even beyond the final but elusive conquest of Tah Itza in 1697.

The well-known nineteenth-century Caste War of Yucatán becomes all the more remarkable as an exception to this pattern of colonial period resistance, even though fully satisfactory explanations of this rebellion still, in my opinion, elude us. Studies of the Caste War give us a clue, I think, about why anthropologists and historians have not been very successful in understanding the nature of Maya rebellion. These studies have tended to compartmentalize the religious and the secular aspects of that rebellion, perhaps because that rebellion appears to fit so well the social scientific view of modern agrarian movements as being rooted in a struggle by peasant elites for greater participation in state affairs and political and economic self-determination.

Studies of the Caste War of Yucatán have been particularly unsuccessful in coping with the ideological foundations of rebellion and with the ability of the leaders to recruit a passionate following that at the beginning sought accommodation and reform, not violent confrontation. Many studies of that event probably labor under a false assumption that the revitalization movement of the so-called Talking Cross, as a religious movement, actually postdated the war itself. The suggestion that the outbreak itself may have been timed by prophecy suggests otherwise and, if true, could well transform our understanding of the entire event and make it much more similar to events of the Colonial period (Bricker 1981: 28, 328; Edmonson 1976). The Caste War, like the rebellions of the seventeenth century, soon took on an aspect of separatism and autonomy in the formation of the so-called cult of the Talking Cross.

The view presented here suggests that rebellion in Yucatán has been elusive because it was defined primarily in nonconfrontational terms that tend to keep it "underground" and to lead to solutions based more on recruitment of followings to alternative leaderships that were not interested in challenging the existence of the European political hierarchy. Rather, these leaderships offered protection and separatism, along with powerfully convincing religious ideologies. During the Colonial period this form of resistance was predicated on geographical separation on remote frontiers, although the underground network of recruitment penetrated throughout densely settled areas. Rebellion took the form of running away. To a degree the Caste War seemed to have turned things around: beginning with underground recruitment and unsuccessful efforts to reach accommodation, the war broke out like water bursting a dam; only later, with the failure of military engagement, did the process of running away and the contest for the recruitment of native followings begin.

Much more needs to be documented and understood about the dynamics of Maya resistance. By now, however, it should be apparent that we may have to revise old thinking and approach the issue from a comparative perspective that takes into account the entire period since the Spanish conquest began.

Notes

These notes include all references to unpublished primary documentation. The abbreviation AGI refers to the *Archivo General de Indias* in Seville, Spain. References to published works are noted in the text and cited in the bibliography that follows. Portions of this chapter appear in revised and expanded form in Grant D. Jones, *Maya Resistance to Spanish Rule: Time and History on a Colonial Frontier* (Albuquerque: University of New Mexico Press, 1989).

1. Luís Sánchez de Aguilar et al. to Marqués de Santo Floro, 20 Sept. 1638. AGI, México 360.

2. For a somewhat different English interpretation see Roys 1967: 157.

3. The *katun* was composed of periods of 7,200 days (twenty times the Maya *tun* of 360 days). Thirteen such katuns, or about 256 years, made up a full katun cycle. During the Spanish period, beginning in 1539, a particular katun was identified by the name and number of its first day, beginning that year with a Katun 11 Ahau. The next katun began in 1559 and was Katun 9 Ahau. The numerical coefficients of the following katuns, then, were 7, 5, 3, 1, 12, 10, etc. The Maya believed that each 256-year cycle of 13 katuns was in some way a reenactment of those cycles that had come before, so that the characteristics of a particular katun of the previous cycle might be anticipated in the same katun of the current one. For further discussion see Edmonson 1982: 195–99; Morley 1956: 246–49; Roys 1967: 182–87.

4. Although long known as Tayasal, a common seventeenth-century designation for the island capital of the Itzas (now Flores, Petén) was Tah Itza, or location of the Itzas. For a discussion of the location of Tah Itza see G. Jones, Rice, and Rice 1981.

5. López de Cogolludo claimed that Delgado founded the reduction town of Sacalum in the forests of La Pimienta on his 1621 mission (1688: Bk. 10, ch. 2). However, he was apparently mistaken, as that town was apparently not founded until 1623. I believe that López, like later writers, must have confused the Sacalum established by Francisco Mirones de Lezcano that year with the mission town of Sacalum founded in the Cehach zone as early as 1604 (López de Cogolludo 1688: Bk. 8, ch. 9; Scholes and Roys 1968: 279–80, 285–86). Mirones (see below) made it clear in his diary that Delgado had been the founding minister of Hopelchen (AGI, México 141, Documentos respectivos al servicio que prometió hacer a S.M. el Capn. Francisco Mirones y Lezcano, 1622; transcribed in Scholes and Adams 1936–37: 160–73).

6. The following discussion is based on AGI, México 141, Documentos respectivos . . . Mirones y Lezcano, 1622.

7. AGI, México 141, Documentos respectivos . . . Mirones y Lezcano, 1622.

8. AGI, México 246, Méritos y servicios de Juan Bernardo Casanova, 1627

9. AGI, México 246, Méritos y servicios de Juan Bernardo Casanova, 1627; AGI, México 243, El capitán Guillen Peraza de Ayala [pide merced], 1643; AGI, México 925, Comisión al capitán Guillen Peraza de Ayala, 15 March 1624; AGI, México 148, R. 3, N. 40e, El capitán Guillen Peraza de Ayala suplica se le de confirmación de una encomienda, 1629; AGI, México 242, Confirmación de encomienda en capitán Don Andrés de Mendoza, 1672; AGI, México 1962, Cédula, 26 Nov. 1630; AGI, México 3048, Memorial de Doña Maria Romero, 1638; AGI, Escribanía de Cámara 3138, Merced de encomienda en Rodrigo de Vargas Mayorga, 22 Aug. 1628.

10. AGI, México 145, Petition by Francisco Camul, governor of Oxkutzcab et al. 1624; transcribed in Scholes and Adams 1936–37: 273–76.

11. AGI, México 925. Comisión al capitán Guillen Peraza de Ayala, 15 March 1624.

12. AGI, México 148, R. 1, N. 27, Juan Sánchez de Aguilar . . . suplica se le de confirmación de los pueblos de Chanlacan y Yumpeten, 1630. AGI, México 242, Title of the encomienda of towns in the Bacalar province, in Diego Rodriguez, 25 June 1622.

13. AGI, México 242, Title of the encomienda of towns in the Bacalar province, in Diego Rodriguez, 15 June 1622.

14. AGI, México 914, Petición del Alférez Critóbal Sánchez, vecino y regidor de la villa de Salamanca de Bacalar, 1631.

15. AGI, México 360, Marqués de Santo Floro to crown, 10 July 1638.

16. AGI, México 360, Luís Sánchez de Aguilar et al. to governor, 20 September 1638.

17. AGI, México 360, Luís Sánchez de Aguilar to governor, 29 October 1638; AGI, Contaduría 915A, Accounts for 1638.

18. AGI, México 369, Bishop of Yucatán to crown, 5 March 1643.

19. López de Cogolludo (1688: Bk. 11, ch. 13) indicates that in 1643 the town and church of Lamanai had just been burned and deserted upon the approach of Fuensalida and his party, suggesting that it had been resettled since 1638.

20. AGI, México 369, Bishop of Yucatán to crown, 5 March 1643.

21. AGI, México 360, Marqués de Santo Floro to crown, 7 February 1642. AGI, México 369, Bishop of Yucatán to king, 5 March 1643.

22. This move certainly had taken place by 1654 but may well have occurred immediately after the 1648 pirate attack. AGI, México 158, Méritos y servicios del capitán Francisco Pérez, 1661.

Bibliography

ADAMS, RICHARD E.W
1971 *The Ceramics of Altar de Sacrificios.* In Papers of the Peabody Museum of Archaeology and Ethnology, 63(1). Harvard University, Cambridge.
1977 (editor) *The Origins of Maya Civilization,* School of American Research Advanced Seminar. University of New Mexico Press, Albuquerque.
1978 Routes of Communication in Mesoamerica: The Northern Guatemalan Highlands and the Peten. In *Mesoamerican Communications Routes and Cultural Contacts,* Thomas A. Lee Jr. and Carlos Navarrete, eds., pp. 27–35. Papers of the New World Archaeological Foundation, No. 40. Brigham Young University, Provo.
1984 (editor) *Rio Azul Reports, No. 1: The 1983 Season.* San Antonio Center for Archaeological Research, University of Texas at San Antonio.
1985 *Rio Azul Archaeological Project: 1985 Summary Report.* Manuscript. University of Texas at San Antonio.
1986 *Rio Azul Archaeological Project: 1986 Summary Report.* Manuscript. University of Texas at San Antonio.
1987 (editor) *Rio Azul Reports, No. 3: The 1985 Season.* San Antonio Center for Archaeological Research, University of Texas at San Antonio.

ADAMS, RICHARD E.W., WALTER E. BROWN, AND T. PATRICK CULBERT
1981 Radar Mapping, Archaeology and Ancient Maya Land Use. In *Science* 213: 1457–63.

AGRINIER, PIERRE
1978 *A Sacrificial Mass Burial at Miramar, Chiapas, Mexico.* In Papers of the New World Archaeological Foundation, No. 42. Brigham Young University, Provo.

ALVAREZ, TICUL
1982. Restos de mamíferos recientes y pleistocenicos procedentes de las Grutas de Loltún, Yucatán, México. In *Restos de Moluscos y Mamíferos Cuaternarios Procedentes de Loltún, Yucatán, México,* pp. 7–35. Cuaderno de Trabajo No. 26, Departmento de Prehistoria, Instituto Nacional de Antropologia e Historia. Mexico D.F.

ANDREWS, ANTHONY P.
1977 Reconocimiento arqueológico de la costa norte del Estado de Campeche. In *Boletín de la Escuela de Ciencias Antropológicas de la Universidad de Yucatán,* 4 (24): 64–77.
1978a Breve addenda al "Reconocimiento arqueológico de la costa norte del Estado de Campeche." In *Boletín de la Escuela de Ciencias Antropológicas de la Universidad de Yucatán* 6 (33): 40–43.
1978b Puertos costeros del Postclásico Temprano en el norte de Yucatán. In *Estudios de Cultura Maya* 11: 75–93.
1980 *Salt-making, Merchants and Markets: The Role of a Critical Resource in the Development of Maya Civilization.* Ph.D. Dissertation, University of Arizona, Tucson. University Microfilms, Ann Arbor.
1983a *Ancient Maya Salt Production and Trade.* University of Arizona Press, Tucson.
1983b Reconocimiento arqueológico de Tulúm a Punta Allen, Quintana Roo. In *Boletín de la Escuela de Ciencias Antropológicas de la Universidad de Yucatán* 11 (61): 15–31.
1985 The Archaeology and History of Northern Quintana Roo. Part IV of *Geology and Hydrogeology of the Yucatán and Quaternary Geology of Northeastern Yucatán Peninsula,* by W.C. Ward, A.E. Weidie, and W. Back, pp. 127–43. New Orleans Geological Society, New Orleans.

ANDREWS, ANTHONY P. AND TOMAS GALLARETA NEGRON
    1986   The Isla Cerritos Archaeological Project, Yucatán, Mexico. In *Mexicon* 8 (3): 44–48.

ANDREWS, ANTHONY P., TOMAS GALLARETA N., FERNANDO ROBLES C., R. COBOS AND P. CERVERA R.
    1986   Isla Cerritos Archaeological Project. A Report of the 1985 Season. Report submitted to the Committee for Research and Exploration. National Geographic Society, Washington, D.C.

ANDREWS, ANTHONY P. AND FERNANDO ROBLES C.
    1985   Chichen Itza and Coba: An Itza-Maya Standoff in Early Postclassic Yucatan. In *The Lowland Maya Postclassic*, Arlen. F. Chase and Prudence. M. Rice, eds., pp. 62–72. University of Texas Press, Austin.
    in press   *Excavaciones arqueologicas en El Meco, Quintana Roo.* Instituto Nacional de Antropologia e Historia, Mexico.

ANDREWS, E. WYLLYS IV, AND ANTHONY P. ANDREWS
    1975   *A Preliminary Study of the Ruins of Xcaret, Quintana Roo, Mexico, with notes on other archaeological remains on the east coast of the Yucatan Peninsula.* In Middle American Research Institute Publication 40. Tulane University, New Orleans.

ANDREWS, E. WYLLYS IV, AND E. WYLLYS ANDREWS V
    1980   *Excavations at Dzibilchaltun, Yucatan, Mexico.* In Middle American Research Institute Publication 48. Tulane University, New Orleans.

ANDREWS, E. WYLLYS V
    1974   Some Architectural Similarities between Dzibilchaltun and Palenque. In *Primera Mesa Redonda de Palenque, Part I*, M. G. Robertson, ed., pp. 137–47. Robert Louis Stevenson School, Pebble Beach, California.
    1979   Early Central Mexican Architectural Traits at Dzibilchaltun, Yucatan. In *Acts, XLII International Congress of Americanists* (Paris, 1976) 8: 237–49. Paris.
    1986   Olmec Jades from Chacsinkin, Yucatan, and Maya Ceramics from La Venta, Tabasco. In *Research and Reflections in Archaeology and History: Essays in Honor of Doris Stone*, E. Wyllys Andrews V, ed., pp. 11–49. Middle American Research Institute Publication 57. Tulane University, New Orleans.
    1988   Ceramic Units from Komchen, Yucatan, Mexico. In *Cerámica de Cultura Maya* 15: 51–64. Temple University, Philadelphia.

ANDREWS, E. WYLLYS V, WILLIAM M. RINGLE, PHILIP J. BARNES, ALFREDO BARRERA R., AND TOMÁS GALLARETA N.
    1984   Komchen, An Early Maya Community in Northwest Yucatan. In *Investigaciones recientes en el área maya*, Vol. 1, pp. 73–92. XVII Mesa Redonda, Sociedad Mexicana de Antropología (San Cristobal de las Casas, Chiapas, June 1981). Mexico D.F.

ANTOINE, PIERRE P., RICHARD L. SKARIE AND PAUL R. BLOOM
    1982   The Origin of Raised Fields near San Antonio, Belize: An Alternative Hypothesis. In *Maya Subsistence: Essays in Memory of Dennis E. Puleston*, Kent. V. Flannery, ed., pp. 227–36. Academic Press, New York.

ASHMORE, WENDY
    1981   Some Issues of Method and Theory in Lowland Maya Settlement Archaeology. In *Lowland Maya Settlement Patterns*, Wendy Ashmore, ed., pp. 37–69. University of New Mexico Press, Albuquerque.

AVENI, ANTHONY F.
    1990   The Real Venus-Kukulcan in the Maya Inscriptions and Alignments. In *Sixth Round Table of Palenque*, vol. 8. University of Oklahoma Press, Norman.

AYALA FALCÓN, MARICELA
    1987   La Estela 39 de Tikal, Mundo Perdido. In *Memorias del Primer Coloquio Internacional de Mayistas* (August 1985), pp. 599–654. Centro de Estudios Mayas, Universidad Nacional Autónoma de Mexico, Mexico D.F.

BALL, JOSEPH W.
    1974   A Coordinate Approach to Northern Maya Prehistory: A.D. 700–1000. In *American Antiquity* 39 (1): 85–93.
    1977a   An Hypothetical Outline of Coastal Maya Prehistory: 300 B.C.–A.D. 1200. In *Social Process in Maya Prehistory*, Norman Hammond, ed., pp. 167–96. Academic Press, New York.
    1977b   *The Archaeological Ceramics of Becan, Campeche, Mexico.* In Middle American Research Institute Publication 43. Tulane University, New Orleans.
    1983   Teotihuacan, the Maya, and Ceramic Interchange: A Contextual Perspective. In *Highland-Lowland Interaction in Mesoamerica: Interdisciplinary Approaches*, Arthur Miller, ed., pp. 125–45. Dumbarton Oaks

Research Library and Collection, Washington, D.C.

BARRERA RUBIO, ALFREDO
1985   Littoral-Marine Economy at Tulum, Quintana Roo, Mexico. In *Lowland Maya Postclassic,* Arlen F. Chase and Prudence M. Rice, eds., pp. 50–61. University of Texas Press, Austin.

BARRERA VASQUEZ, ALFREDO
1980   *Diccionario Maya Cordemex, Maya-Español, Español-Maya.* Ediciones Cordemex, Merida.

BECKER, MARSHALL
1983   Kings and Classicism: Political Change in the Maya Lowlands during the Classic Period. In *Highland-Lowland Interaction in Mesoamerica: Interdisciplinary Approaches,* Arthur Miller, ed., pp. 159–200. Dumbarton Oaks Research Library and Collection, Washington, D.C.

BENEVIDES CASTILLO, ANTONIO
1977   Los caminos prehispánicos de Cobá. In *XV Mesa Redonda de la Sociedad Mexicana de Antropología* (Guanajuato, 1977) 2: 215–25. Mexico D.F.

BENEVIDES CASTILLO, ANTONIO AND ANTHONY P. ANDREWS
1979   Ecab: poblado y provincia del siglo XVI in Yucatán. In *Cuadernos de los Centros Regionales. Centro Regional del Sureste.* Instituto Nacional de Antropología e Historia, Mexico D.F.

BENSON, ELIZABETH P.
1973   (editor) *Mesoamerican Writing Systems.* Dumbarton Oaks, Washington, D.C.

BERDAN, FRANCES F.
1978   Ports of Trade in Mesoamerica: A Reappraisal. In *Mesoamerican Communication Routes and Culture Contacts,* Thomas A. Lee and Carlos Navarrete, eds., pp. 187–98. Papers of the New World Archaeological Foundation, No. 40. Brigham Young University, Provo.

BERGER, RAINER, JOHN A. GRAHAM, AND ROBERT F. HEIZER
1967   A Reconsideration of the Age of the La Venta Site. In *Studies in Olmec Archaeology:* 1–22. Contributions of the University of California Archaeological Research Facility, No. 3. Berkeley.

BERLIN, HEINRICH
1958   El glifo "emblema" in las inscripciones Mayas. In *Journal la Société des Americanistes* n.s. 47: 111–19. Paris.
1963   The Palenque Triad. In *Journal de la Société des Americanistes* n.s. 52: 91–99. Paris.
1965   The Inscription of the Temple of the Cross at Palenque. In *American Antiquity* 30: 330–42.

BERLO, JANET
1984   *Teotihuacan Art Abroad: A Study of Metropolitan Style and Provincial Transformation in Incensario Workshops.* BAR International Series 199 (i), Oxford, England.

BERNAL, IGNACIO
1968   Teotihuacan. In *Historia de Mexico,* vol. 1, pp. 221–70. Editorial Salvat, Mexico D.F.
1976   *The Olmec World.* Translated by Doris Heyden and Fernando Horcasitas. University of California Press, Berkeley.

BISHOP, RONALD L., MARILYN P. BEAUDRY, RICHARD M. LEVENTHAL, AND ROBERT J. SHARER
1980   Compositional Analysis of Classic Period Painted Ceramics in the Southeast Maya Area. Paper presented at the 45th Annual Meeting of the Society for American Archaeology, Philadelphia.

BLACK, STEPHEN L.
1987   Settlement Pattern Survey and Testing, 1985. In *Rio Azul Reports, No. 3: The 1985 Season.* Richard E.W. Adams ed., pp. 183–21. San Antonio Center for Archaeological Research, University of Texas at San Antonio.

BLACK, STEPHEN L. AND CHARLES SUHLER
1986   The Rio Azul Settlement Survey. In *Rio Azul Reports, No. 2: The 1984 Season.* Richard E.W. Adams ed. San Antonio Center for Archaeological Research, University of Texas at San Antonio.

BLANTON, RICHARD AND GARY FEINMAN
1984   The Mesoamerican World System. In *American Anthropologist* 86: 673–82.

BLOOM, PAUL R., MARY POHL, CYNTHIA BUTTLEMAN, FREDERICK WISEMAN, ALAN COVICH, CHARLES MIKSICEK, JOSEPH BALL, AND JULIE STEIN
1983   Prehistoric Maya Wetland Agriculture and the Alluvial Soils Near San Antonio, Rio Hondo, Belize. In *Nature* 301: 417–19.

BOGGS, STANLEY H.
1950   "Olmec" Pictographs in the Las Victorias Group, Chalchuapa Archaeological Zone, El Salvador. In *Notes on Middle American Archaeology and Ethnology* 4 (99): 85–92. Carnegie Institution of Washington, Department of Archaeology, Cambridge, Massachusetts.

BRAINERD, GEORGE W.
1951   Early Ceramic Horizons in Yucatan. In *The Civilizations of Ancient America. Selected Papers of the 39th International Congress of Americanists*, vol. 1, Sol Tax, ed., pp. 72–78. University of Chicago Press, Chicago.
1958   *The Archaeological Ceramics of Yucatan.* Anthropological Records, 19. University of California, Berkeley and Los Angeles.

BRAUN, BARBARA
1986   Chac's Revenge. In *Art in America*, January 1986, pp. 89–96.

BRICKER, VICTORIA R.
1981   *The Indian Christ, The Indian King: The Historical Substrate of Maya Myth and Ritual.* University of Texas Press, Austin.
1985   Notes on Classic Maya Metrology. In *Fifth Palenque Round Table, 1983*, Merle G. Robertson and Virginia M. Fields, eds., pp. 189–92. Precolumbian Art Research Institute, San Francisco.

BRONSON, B.
1966   Roots and the Subsistence of the Ancient Maya. In *Southwestern Journal of Anthropology* 22 (3): 251–79.

BULLARD, WILLIAM R.
1960   Maya Settlement Patterns in Northeastern Peten, Guatemala. In *American Antiquity* 25: 355–72.

CAMPBELL, LYLE, AND TERRENCE KAUFMAN
1976   A Linguistic Look at the Olmecs. In *American Antiquity* 41: 80–89.

CÁRDENAS VALENCIA, FRANCISCO DE
1937   *Relación historical eclesiástica de la provincia de Yucatán de la Nueva España.* Edited with introduction by F. Gómez de Orozco. Biblioteca Historia de México. Obras Inéditas. Mexico (Original Ms. dated 1639).

CARR, ROBERT F., AND JAMES E. HAZARD
1961   Map of the Ruins of Tikal, El Peten, Guatemala. In *Tikal Reports*, No. 11. University Museum, University of Pennsylvania, Philadelphia.

CEJA TENORIO, JORGE F.
1985   *Paso de la Amada: An Early Preclassic Site in the Soconusco, Chiapas, Mexico.* Papers of the New World Archaeological Foundation, No. 49. Brigham Young University, Provo.

CERVANTES, MARIA A.
1967   Una Estela Olmeca de Dos Caras. In *Boletin de Instituto Nacional de Antropologia e Historia*, 28: 32–35. Mexico D.F.
1969   Dos Elemento de Uso Ritual en el Arte Olmeca. In *Anales de Instituto Nacional de Antropologia e Historia*, Epoca 7a, Tomo 1: 37–51. Mexico D.F.

CHAPMAN, ANNE M.
1957   Port of Trade Enclaves in Aztec and Maya Civilization. In *Trade and Market in the Early Empires*, Karl Polanyi, Conrad M. Arensbert and Harry W. Pearson, eds., pp. 114–53. Glencoe.

CHASE, ARLEN F., AND DIANE Z. CHASE
1987   Putting Together the Pieces: Maya Pottery of Central Belize and Central Peten, Guatemala. In *Maya Ceramics: Papers from the 1985 Maya Ceramic Conference*, Prudence M. Rice and Robert J. Sharer, eds., part i, pp. 47–72. BAR International Series 345(i), Oxford, England.

CHASE ARLEN F., AND PRUDENCE M. RICE
1985   (editors) *The Lowland Maya Postclassic.* University of Texas Press, Austin.

CHASE, DIANE Z.
1981   The Maya Postclassic at Santa Rita Corozal. In *Archaeology* 34(1): 25–33.
1986   Social and Political Organization in the Land of Cacao and Honey: Correlating the Archaeology and Ethnohistory of the Postclassic Lowland Maya. In *Late Lowland Maya Civilization: Classic to Postclassic*, Jeremy A. Sabloff and E. Wyllys Andrews V, eds., pp. 347–77. University of New Mexico Press, Albuquerque.

CHEEK, CHARLES D.
1977   Excavations at the Palanqana and the Acropolis, Kaminaljuyu. In *Teotihuacan and Kaminaljuyu: A Study in Prehistoric Culture Contact*, William T. Sandars and Joseph E. Michels eds., pp. 1–204. Pennsylvania State University Press, Pittsburg.

CLANCY, FLORA S.
1976   Maya Pedestal Stones. In *New Mexico Studies in the Fine Arts*, vol. 1, pp. 10–19. University of New Mexico, Albuquerque.
1980   *Formal Analysis of the Relief-Carved Monuments of Tikal Guatemala.* Ph.D. Dissertation, Yale University. University Microfilms, Ann Arbor.
1983   A Comparison of Highland Zapotec and Lowland Maya Graphic Styles. In *Highland-Lowland Interaction in Mesoamerica: Interdisciplinary Approaches*, Arthur Miller, ed., pp. 223–40. Dumbarton Oaks Research Library and Collection, Washington, D.C.

1985 Maya Sculpture. In *Maya Treasures of an Ancient Civilization*, Charles Gallenkamp and Regina E. Johnson, eds., pp. 58–70. Albuquerque Museum and Harry N. Abrams, Inc., New York.

CLARK, JOHN E. AND THOMAS A. LEE, JR.
1984 Formative Obsidian Exchange and the Emergence of Public Economies in Chiapas, Mexico. In *Trade and Exchange in Early Mesoamerica*, Kenneth G. Hirth, ed., pp. 235–74. University of New Mexico Press, Albuquerque.

COBEAN, ROBERT H., MICHAEL D. COE, EDWARD A. PERRY, KARL K. TURKIAN AND DINKAR P. KHARKAR
1971 Obsidian Trade at San Lorenzo Tenochtitlan, Mexico. In *Science* 174: 666–71.

COE, MICHAEL D.
1957 Cycle 7 Monuments in Middle America: A Reconsideration. In *American Anthropologist* 59(4): 597–611.
1961 *La Victoria: An Early Site on the Pacific Coast of Guatemala*. Papers of the Peabody Museum of Archaeology and Ethnology, 53. Harvard University, Cambridge, Massachusetts.
1962 *Mexico, Ancient Peoples and Places*. Thames and Hudson, New York.
1965 The Olmec Style and Its Distribution. In *Handbook of Middle American Indians*, vol. 3, Robert Wauchope and Gordon Willey eds., pp. 716–38. University of Texas Press, Austin.
1966 An Early Stone Pectoral from Southwestern Mexico. In *Studies in Pre-Columbia Art and Archaeology*, No. 1. Dumbarton Oaks Research Library and Collection, Washington, D.C.
1977 Olmec and Maya: A Study in Relationships. In *The Origins of Maya Civilizations*, Richard E.W. Adams, ed., pp. 183–195. School of American Research Advanced Seminar, University of New Mexico Press, Albuquerque.
1978 *Lords of the Underworld*, Princeton University Press, Princeton.
1980 *The Maya*. Revised ed. Thames and Hudson, New York.
1987 *The Maya*. 4th ed. Thames and Hudson, New York.

COE, MICHAEL D., AND RICHARD A. DIEHL
1980 *In the Land of the Olmec. The Archaeology of San Lorenzo Tenochtitlan*. 2 vols. University of Texas Press, Austin.

COE, MICHAEL D., AND KENT V. FLANNERY
1967 *Early Cultures and Human Ecology in South Coastal Guatemala*. Smithsonian Contributions to Anthropology 3. Smithsonian Press, Washington, D.C.

COE, WILLIAM R.
1959 *Piedras Negras Archaeology: Artifacts, Caches and Burials*. Museum Monographs 18. University Museum, University of Pennsylvania, Philadelphia.
1965 Tikal, Guatemala, and Emergent Maya Civilization. In *Science* 147: 1401–19.
1967 *Tikal: A Handbook of the Ancient Maya Ruins*. University of Pennsylvania, Philadelphia.
1972 Cultural Contact between the Lowland Maya and Teotihuacan as Seen from Tikal, Peten, Guatemala. In *Teotihuacan, 11th Mesa Redonda*, vol. 2, pp. 257–71. Sociedad Mexicana de Antropologia, Mexico D.F.

COE, WILLIAM R., AND WILLIAM A. HAVILAND
1982 Introduction to the Archaeology of Tikal, Guatemala. In *Tikal Reports*, No. 12. University Museum, University of Pennsylvania, Philadelphia.

COGGINS, CLEMENCY C.
1975 *Painting and Drawing Styles at Tikal: An Historical and Iconographic Reconstruction*. Ph.D. Dissertation, Harvard University. University Microfilms, Ann Arbor.
1979a Teotihuacan At Tikal in the Early Classic Period. In *Acts, XLII International Congress of Americanists* (Paris, 1976) 8: 251–69.
1979b A New Order and the Role of the Calendar: Some Characteristics of the Middle Classic Period at Tikal. In *Maya Archaeology and Ethnohistory*, Norman Hammond, ed., pp. 38–50. University of Texas Press, Austin.
1980 The Shape of Time: Some Political Implications of a Four-Part Figure. In *American Antiquity* 45(4): 727–39.
1982 The Zenith, the Mountain, the Center, and the Sea. In *Ethnoastronomy and Archaeoastronomy in the American Tropics*, Anthony F. Aveni and Gary Urton, eds., Annals of the New York Academy of Sciences 385: 111–23.
1984 An Instrument of Expansion: Monte Alban, Teotihuacan, and Tikal. In *Highland-Lowland Interaction in Mesoamerica: Interdisciplinary Approaches*, Arthur Miller, ed., pp. 49–68. Dumbarton Oaks Research Library and Collections, Washington, D.C.

1985 Maya Iconography. In *Maya Treasures of an Ancient Civilization,* Charles Gallenkamp and Regina E. Johnson, eds., pp. 47–57. Albuquerque Museum and Harry N. Abrams, New York.

1987a New Fire and Chichen Itza. In *Memorias del Primer Coloquio Internacional de Mayistas* (August 1985), pp. 427–82. Centro de Estudios Mayas, Universidad Nacional Autónoma de Mexico, Mexico D.F.

1987b The Names of Tikal. In *Primer Simposio Mundial sobre Epigrafia Maya,* pp. 23–45. Instituto Nacional de Antropologia e Historia, y Asociacion Tikal, Guatemala, and National Geographic Society, Washington, D.C.

1988a On the Historical Significance of Decorated Ceramics at Copan and Quirigua and Related Classic Maya Sites. In *Southeastern Classic Maya Zone,* Elizabeth H. Boone and Gordon R. Willey, eds., pp. 95–123. Dumbarton Oaks Research Library and Collection, Washington, D.C.

1988b The Manikin Scepter: Emblem of Lineage. In *Estudios de Cultura Maya,* vol. 17, pp. 123–58. Universidad Nacional Autónoma de Mexico, Mexico D.F.

1988c Classic Maya Metaphors of Death and Birth. in *RES* 16: 64–84. Peabody Museum, Harvard University.

1989 New Sun at Chichen Itza. In *World Archaeoastronomy,* Anthony E. Aveni, ed., pp. 260–75. Cambridge University Press.

1987a Quetzalcoatl, Teothihuacan and the Maya in the Early Classic Period. Paper presented at the Society for American Archaeology Meeting, May 1987, Toronto.

1987b Quetzalcoatl Names at Teotihuacan and Among the Classic Maya. Paper presented at the American Anthropological Association Meeting, November 1987, Chicago.

COHEN, MARK N., SHARON L. BENNETT, MARIE E. DANFORTH, CARL ARMSTRONG, AND HELENE MEKUNAS
1985 An Overview of Skeletal Biology in the Colonial Period Maya Population from Tipu. Paper presented at the 50th Annual Meeting of the Society for American Archaeology, Denver.

COOKE, C. W.
1931 Why the Mayan Cities of the Peten District, Guatemala Were Abandoned. In *Journal of the Washington Academy of Sciences* 21(13): 283–87.

CORTÉS DE BRASDEFER, FERNANDO
1984 El registro de sitios arqueológicos in Quintana Roo. In *Boletín de la Escuela de Ciencias Antropológicas de la Universidad de Yucatán* 12 (68): 13–20.

COWGILL, URSULA M.
1962 An Agricultural Study of the Southern Maya Lowlands. In *American Anthropologist* 64: 273–86.

COWGILL, URSULA M. AND G. EVELYN HUTCHINSON
1966 The Chemical History of Laguna de Petenxil. In *Memoirs of the Connecticut Academy of Arts and Sciences* 17: 121–26.

CRAIG, ALAN K.
1966 Geography of Fishing in British Honduras and Adjacent Coastal Waters. In *Coastal Studies Institute Technical Report,* No. 28. Louisiana State University, Baton Rouge.

CULBERT, T. PATRICK
1973 (editor) *The Classic Maya Collapse.* School of American Research Advanced Seminar. University of New Mexico Press, Albuquerque.

1977 Early Maya Development at Tikal, Guatemala. In *The Origins of Maya Civilization,* Richard E.W. Adams, ed., pp. 27–43. School of American Research Advanced Seminar. University of New Mexico Press, Albuquerque.

1979 The Ceramics of Tikal: Eb, Tzec, Chuen, and Manik Ceramic Complexes. Manuscript, University of Arizona, Tucson.

1985 Maya—Treasures of an Ancient Civilization. In *Archaeology* 38 (2): 60–63.

CULBERT, T. PATRICK AND DONALD S. RICE
1991 (editors) *Precolumbian Population History in the Maya Lowlands.* University of New Mexico Press, Albuquerque.

DAHLIN, BRUCE H.
1979 Preliminary Investigations of Agronomic Potentials in Bajos Adjacent to Tikal, Peten, Guatemala. In *Acts, XLII International Congress of Americanists* (Paris, 1976) 8: 305–12. Paris.

DAHLIN, BRUCE H., J. E. FOSS, AND M.E. CHAMBERS
1980 Project Acalches: Reconstructing the Natural and Cultural History of a Seasonal Swamp at El Mirador, Guatemala; Preliminary Results. In *El Mirador, Peten, Guatemala: An Interim Report,* Ray Matheny, ed., pp. 37–57. Papers of the New World Archaeological Foundation, No. 45. Brigham Young University, Provo.

DEMAREST, ARTHUR A.
1976 A Reevaluation of the Archaeological Sequences of Preclassic Chiapas. In *Studies in Middle American Archaeology*, pp. 75–107. Middle American Research Institute Publication 22. Tulane University, New Orleans.
1986 *The Archaeology of Santa Leticia and the Rise of Maya Civilization*. Middle American Research Institute Publication 56. Tulane University, New Orleans.
1987 Recent Research on the Preclassic Ceramics of the Southeastern Highlands and Pacific Coast of Guatemala. In *Maya Ceramics: Papers from the 1985 Maya Ceramic Conference*, Prudence M. Rice and Robert J. Sharer, eds., part ii, pp. 329–39. BAR International Series 345(ii). Oxford, England.

DEMAREST, ARTHUR A., AND ROBERT J. SHARER.
1982 The Origins and Evolution of Usulutan Ceramics. In *American Antiquity* 47: 810–22.

DENEVAN, WILLIAM M.
1980 Latin America. In *World Systems of Traditional Resource Management*, Gary A. Klee, ed., pp. 217–44. John Wiley & Sons, New York.

DILLON, BRIAN D.
1975 *Notes on Trade in Ancient Mesoamerica*. Contributions of the University of California Archaeological Research Facility, No. 24, pp. 80–135. University of California, Berkeley.

DRUCKER, PHILIP
1952 *La Venta, Tabasco: A Study of Olmec Ceramic and Art*. Bureau of American Ethnology Bulletin 158. Smithsonian Institution, Washington, D.C.

DRUCKER, PHILIP, ROBERT F. HEIZER, AND ROBERT J. SQUIER
1959 *Excavations at La Venta, Tabasco, 1955*. Bureau of American Ethnology Bulletin 170. Smithsonian Institution, Washington, D.C.

DÜTTING, DIETER, AND ANTHONY F. AVENI
1982 The 2 Cib 14 Mol Event in the Palenque Inscriptions. In *Zeitschrift für Ethnologie* 107. Branschweig.

EATON, JACK D.
1975 *Ancient Agricultural Farmsteads in the Rio Bec Region of Yucatan*. Contributions of the University of California Archaeological Research Facility, No. 27, pp. 56–82. University of California, Berkeley.
1978 *Archaeological Survey of the Yucatan-Campeche Coast*. Middle American Research Institute Publication 46, pp. 1–67. Tulane University, New Orleans.

EDMONSON, MUNRO S.
1976 The Mayan Calendar Reform of 11.16.0.0.0. In *Current Anthropology* 17: 713–17.
1982 *The Ancient Future of the Itza: The Book of Chilam Balam of Tizimin*. University of Texas Press, Austin.
1986 *Heaven Born Merida and Its Destiny: The Book of Chilam Balam of Chumayel*. University of Texas Press, Austin.

FARRISS, NANCY M.
1983 Indians in Colonial Yucatan: Three Perspectives. In *Spaniards and Indians in Southeastern Mesoamerica: Essays on the History of Ethnic Relations*, Murdo J. MacLeod and Robert Wasserstrom, eds., pp. 1–39. University of Nebraska Press, Lincoln.
1984 *Maya Society Under Colonial Rule: The Collective Enterprise of Survival*. Princeton University Press, Princeton.

FIALKO, VILMA
1985 Tikal, Mundo Perdido: Identificación de un complejo con implicación astronómica. In *Memorias del Primer Coloquio Internacional de Mayistas* (August 1985), pp. 143–64. Centro de Estudios Mayas, Universidad Nacional Autónoma de Mexico, Mexico D.F.
1987 El Marcador de Juego de Pelota de Tikal: Nuevas Referencias epigráficas para el Clásico Temprano. In *Primer Simposio Mundial sobre Epigrafía Maya*. Instituto Nacional de Antropologia e Historia, y Asociacion Tikal, Guatemala, and National Geographic Society, Washington, D.C.

FIELDS, VIRGINIA
1982 Political Symbolism Among the Olmec. Paper on file, Department of Art History, University of Texas, Austin.

FLANNERY, KENT V.
1968 The Olmec and the Valley of Oaxaca: A Model for Inter-regional Interaction in Formative Times. In *Dumbarton Oaks Conference on the Olmec*, Elizabeth P. Benson, ed., pp. 79–117. Dumbarton Oaks Research Library and Collection, Washington, D.C.

FOLAN, WILLIAM J., ELLEN R. KINTZ, AND
LARAINE A. FLETCHER
    1983   *Coba, A Classic Maya Metropolis.* Academic Press, New York.

FONCERRADA DE MOLINA, MARTA
    1982   Signos glíficos relacionados con Tlaloc en los Murales de la Batalla de Cacaxtla. In *Anales del Instituto de Investigaciones Esteticas* 50(1): 23–33. Universidad Nacional Autonoma de Mexico, Mexico D.F.

FORD, ANABEL
    1986   *Population Growth and Social Complexity: An Examination of Settlement and Environment in the Central Maya Lowlands.* Arizona State University Anthropological Research Papers, No. 35. Arizona State University, Phoenix.

FOX, JAMES A., AND JOHN S. JUSTESON
    1984   Polyvalence in Mayan Hieroglyphic Writing. In *Phoneticism in Mayan Hieroglyphic Writing,* John S. Justeson and Lyle Campbell, eds., pp. 17–76. Institute for Mesoamerican Studies Publication No. 9. State University of New York, Albany.

FREIDEL, DAVID A.
    1979   Culture Areas and Interaction Spheres: Contrasting Approaches to the Emergence of Civilization in the Maya Lowlands. In *American Antiquity* 44(1): 36–54.
    1981   Civilization as a State of Mind: The Cultural Evolution of the Lowland Maya. In *The Transition to Statehood in the New World,* Grant D. Jones and Robert R. Kautz, eds., pp. 188–227. Cambridge University Press, Cambridge.
    1986   The Monumental Architecture. In *Archaeology at Cerros, Belize, Central America. Volume 1, An Interim Report,* Robin A. Robertson and David A. Freidel, eds., pp. 1–22. Southern Methodist University Press, Dallas.
    1987   *Yaxuna Archaeological Survey. A Report of the 1986 Field Season.* Department of Anthropology, Southern Methodist University, Dallas.

FREIDEL, DAVID A., AND ANTHONY P. ANDREWS
    1990   The Loltun Bas Relief and the Origins of Maya Kingship. *Research Reports on Ancient Maya Writing.* Center for Maya Research, Washington, D.C.

FREIDEL, DAVID A., ROBIN ROBERTSON, AND MAYNARD B. CLIFF
    1982   The Maya City of Cerros. In *Archaeology* 35(4): 12–21.

FREIDEL, DAVID A., AND JEREMY A. SABLOFF
    1984   *Cozumel. Late Maya Settlement Patterns.* Academic Press, New York.

FREIDEL, DAVID A., AND LINDA SCHELE
    1988a   Kingship in the Late Preclassic Maya Lowlands, the Instruments and Places of Ritual Power. In *American Anthropologist* 90(3): 547–567.
    1988b   Symbol and Power: A History of the Lowland Maya Cosmogram. In *Maya Iconography,* Elizabeth P. Benson and Gillett G. Griffin, eds., pp. 44–93. Princeton University Press, Princeton.
    1985   Knot Skull the Great Seed: Death, Rebirth and Heroic Amplification in the Lowland Maya Ballgame. Paper presented at the International Symposium on the Mesoamerican Ballgame and Ballcourts, November 1985. Tucson.

FRY, ROBERT
    1969   *Ceramics and Settlement in the Periphery of Tikal, Guatemala.* Ph.D. Dissertation, University of Arizona, Tucson. University Microfilms, Ann Arbor.
    1987   The Ceramic Sequence of South-Central Quintana Roo, Mexico. In *Maya Ceramics: Papers from the 1985 Maya Ceramic Conference,* Prudence M. Rice and Robert J. Sharer, eds., pt. ii, pp. 111–22. BAR International Series 345. Oxford, England.

FUENTE, BEATRIZ DE LA
    1973   *Escultura Monumentul Olmeca.* Instituto de Investigaciones Esteticas, Universidad Nacional Autonoma, Mexico D.F.

GANN, THOMAS
    1900   Mounds in Northern Honduras. In *Nineteenth Annual Report, 1897–1898, Bureau of American Ethnology,* pt. 2: 655–92. Smithsonian Institution, Washington, D.C.

GARBER, J. F.
    1983   Patterns of Jade Consumption and Disposal at Cerros, in Northern Belize. In *American Antiquity* 48(4): 800–807.
    1986   The Artifacts. In *Archaeology at Cerros, Belize, Central America. Volume 1, An Interim Report,* Robin A. Robertson and David A. Freidel, eds., pp. 117–26. Southern Methodist University Press, Dallas.

GARCÍA MOLL, ROBERTO
    1985   *Palenque 1926–1945.* Instituto Nacional de Antropologia e Historia, Mexico D.F.

GENDROP, PAUL
    1984   La Crestería Maya y su Posible Symbolism Dinástico. In *Cuadernos de Arquitectura Mesoamericana* 1: 25–39. Facultad de Ar-

quitectura, Universidad Nacional Autonoma, Mexico D.F.

GIBBON, EDWARD
1783–90 *The History of the Decline and Fall of the Roman Empire.* 12 Volumes. W. Strahan, London.

GIFFORD, JAMES C.
1976 Barton Ramie–Tikal Ceramic Comparisons during the Jenney Creek Ceramic Complex. In *Prehistoric Pottery Analysis and the Ceramics of Barton Ramie in the Belize Valley,* by James Gifford and others, pp. 83–84. Memoirs of the Peabody Museum of Archaeology and Ethnology, 18. Harvard University, Cambridge.

GLIESSMAN, STEPHEN R., BILL L. TURNER II, ROSADO MAY, AND M.F. AMADOR
1983 Ancient Raised Field Agriculture in the Maya Lowlands of Southeastern Mexico. In *Drained Field Agriculture in Central and South America,* J.P. Darch, ed., pp. 91–110. BAR International Series 189. Oxford, London.

GOMEZ-POMPA, A., HECTOR LUIS MORALES, EPIFANIO JIMENEZ AVILA, AND JULIO JIMENEZ AVILA
1982 Experiences in Traditional Hydraulic Agriculture. In *Maya Subsistence: Essays in Memory of Dennis E. Puleston,* Kent. V. Flannery ed., pp. 327–42. Academic Press, New York.

GONZÁLEZ DE LA MATA, ROCIO
1984 Xaman Há—un sitio prehispánico en la costa de Quintana Roo. In *XVII Mesa Redonda de la Sociedad Mexicana de Antropología (1981)* 2: 155–65. Mexico D.F.

GRAHAM, ELIZABETH
1983 *The Highlands of the Lowlands: Environment and Archaeology in the Stann Creek District, Belize.* Ph.D. Dissertation, University of Cambridge. University Microfilms, Ann Arbor.
1985 Postclassic to Historic Period Settlement at Negroman-Tipu, Belize. Paper presented at the 50th Annual Meeting of the Society for American Archaeology, Denver.
1987 Terminal Classic to Historic Period Vessel Forms from Belize. In *Maya Ceramics: Papers from the 1985 Maya Ceramic Conference,* Prudence M. Rice and Robert J. Sharer, eds., part i, pp. 73–98. BAR International Series 345 (i), Oxford, England.

GRAHAM, ELIZABETH, GRANT D. JONES, AND ROBERT R. KAUTZ
1985 Archaeology and Ethnohistory on a Spanish Colonial Frontier: An Interim Report on the Macal-Tipu Project in Western Belize. In *The Lowland Maya Postclassic,* Arlen F. Chase and Prudence M. Rice, eds., pp. 206–14. University of Texas Press, Austin.

GRAHAM, ELIZABETH AND DAVID M. PENDERGAST
1987 Cays to the Kingdom. In *Royal Ontario Archaeological Newsletter,* series 2, No. 18. Royal Ontario Museum, Toronto.

GRAHAM, IAN
1967 *Archaeological Explorations in El Peten, Guatemala.* In Middle American Research Institute Publication 33. Tulane University, New Orleans.

GRAHAM, JOHN A., THOMAS R. HESTER, AND ROBERT N. JACK.
1972 Sources for the Obsidian at the Ruins of Seibal, Peten, Guatemala. In *Studies in the Archaeology of Mexico and Guatemala,* John A. Graham, ed., pp. 111–16. Contributions of the University of California Archaeological Research Facility, No. 16. University of California, Berkeley.

GREEN, DEE F., AND GARETH W. LOWE
1967 *Altamira and Padre Piedra, Early Preclassic Sites in Chiapas, Mexico.* Papers of the New World Archaeological Foundation, Publication 15, Paper no. 20. Brigham Young University, Provo.

GROVE, DAVID C.
1973 Olmec Altars and Myths. In *Archaeology* 26(2): 129–35.

GROVE, DAVID C., AND LOUISE I. PARADIS
1971 An Olmec Stela from San Miguel Amuco, Guerrero. In *American Antiquity* 36(1): 95–102.

GUDERJAN, THOMAS H., J. GARBER, AND H. SMITH
n.d. A Maya Trading Transshipment Point on Northern Ambergris Cay, Belize. Manuscript in authors' possession.

GUILLEMIN, GEORGE F.
1968 Tikal Ceremonial Center. In *Ethnos* 33: 1–35.

GUSSINYER, JORDI
1976 Tercera Temporada de Salvamento Arquelogico en la Presa de La Angostura, Chiapas. In *Anales de Instituto Nacional de Antropologia e Historia,* Epoca 7a, Tomo 5,

1974–75, pp. 63–84. Secretaria de Educacio Publica, Mexico D.F.

HAMBLIN, NANCY L.
1984 *Animal Use by the Cozumel Maya.* University of Arizona Press, Tucson.

HAMMOND, NORMAN
1972 Obsidian Trade Routes in the Mayan Area. In *Science* 178: 1092–93.
1974 The Distribution of Late Classic Maya Major Ceremonial Centers in the Central Areas. In *Mesoamerican Archaeology, New Approaches,* Norman Hammond, ed., pp. 313–34. University of Texas Press, Austin.
1975a (editor) *Archaeology in Northern Belize. British Museum–Cambridge University Corozal Project 1974–1975 Interim Report.* Centre of Latin American Studies, Cambridge University, Cambridge, England.
1975b *Lubaantun: A Classic Maya Realm.* Monographs of the Peabody Museum, No. 2. Harvard University, Cambridge.
1976 Maya Obsidian Trade in Southern Belize. In *Maya Lithic Studies. Papers from the 1976 Belize Field Symposium,* Thomas R. Hester and Norman Hammond, eds., pp. 71–81. Center for Archaeological Research, Special Report No. 4. University of Texas at San Antonio.
1977 The Earliest Maya. In *Scientific American* 236: 116–33.
1980 Early Maya Ceremonial at Cuello, Belize. In *Antiquity* 54: 176–190.
1982a A Late Formative Stela in the Maya Lowlands. In *American Antiquity* 47(2): 396–403.
1982b Pom for the Ancestors: A Reexamination of Piedras Negras Stela 40. In *Mexicon* 3: 77–79.
1983 The Development of Belizean Archaeology. In *Antiquity* 57: 19–27.
1984 The Roads Diverged: A Brief Comment on "Lowland Maya Archaeology at the Crossroads." In *American Antiquity* 49: 821–826.
1985 The Emergence of Maya Civilization. In *Scientific American* 255(2): 106–15.

HAMMOND, NORMAN, SARA DONAGHEY, RAINER BERGER, SUZANNE DE ATLEY, V.R. SWITSUR, AND A. P. WARD
1977 Maya Formative Phase Radiocarbon Dates from Belize. In *Nature* 267: 608–10.

HAMMOND, NORMAN, DUNCAN C. PRING, RAINER BERGER, V.R. SWITSUR, AND A.P. WARD
1976 Radiocarbon Chronology for Early Maya Occupation at Cuello, Belize. In *Nature* 260: 579–81.

HAMMOND, NORMAN, DUNCAN C. PRING, RICHARD WILK, SARA DONAGHEY, FRANK P. SAUL, ELIZABETH S. WING, ARLENE V. MILLER, AND LAWRENCE H. FELDMAN
1979 The Earliest Lowland Maya? Definition of the Swasey Phase. In *American Antiquity* 44: 92–110.

HANSEN, RICHARD D.
1984 *Excavations on Structure 34 and the Tigre Area, El Mirador, Peten, Guatemala: A New Look at the Preclassic Maya.* Master's Thesis, Department of Anthropology, Brigham Young University, Provo.

HARRISON, PETER D.
1977 The Rise of the *Bajos* and the Fall of the Maya. In *Social Processes in Maya Prehistory: Studies in Memory of Sir Eric Thompson,* Norman Hammond, ed., pp. 470–508. Academic Press, New York.
1978 Bajos Revisited: Visual Evidence for One System of Agriculture. In *Prehispanic Maya Agriculture,* Peter D. Harrison and B.L. Turner II, eds., pp. 247–53. University of New Mexico Press, Albuquerque.
1981 Some Aspects of Preconquest Settlement in Southern Quintana Roo, Mexico. In *Lowland Maya Settlement Patterns,* Wendy Ashmore, ed., pp. 259–86. University of New Mexico Press, Albuquerque.
1983 Pulltrouser Swamp and Maya Raised Fields: A Summation. In *Pulltrouser Swamp: Ancient Maya Habitat, Agriculture and Settlement in Northern Belize,* B.L. Turner II and Peter D. Harrison, eds., pp. 246–70. University of Texas Press, Austin.
1985 The Organization of Lowland Maya Culture History: Space and Diversity. In *Fourth Palenque Round Table, 1980,* Merle G. Robertson and Elizabeth P. Benson, eds., pp. 285–89. Pre-Columbian Art Research Institute, San Francisco.

HARRISON, PETER D., AND B.L. TURNER II
1978 (editors) *Prehispanic Maya Agriculture.* University of New Mexico Press, Albuquerque.

HAVILAND, WILLIAM A.
1969 A New Population Estimate for Tikal, Guatemala. In *American Antiquity* 34(4): 429–33.
1981 "Dower Houses" and Minor Centers at Tikal, Guatemala: An Investigation into the Identification of Valid Units of Settlement Hierarchies. In *Lowland Maya Settlement Patterns,* Wendy Ashmore, ed., pp.

335–49. University of New Mexico Press, Albuquerque.

HEIZER, ROBERT F.
1967   Analysis of Two Low-Relief Sculptures from La Venta. In *Contributions of the Archaeological Research Facility*, No. 3, pp. 25–55. Department of Anthropology, University of California, Berkeley.

HELLMUTH, NICHOLAS M.
1969   *Mexican Symbols in the Classic Art of the Southern Maya Lowlands.* Master's Thesis, Brown University.
1975   The Escuintla Hoards: Teotihuacan Art in Guatemala. In *F.L.A.A.R.* 1(2). Guatemala.

HESTER, THOMAS R.
1985   The Maya Lithic Sequence in Northern Belize. In *Stone Tool Analysis: Essays in Honor of Don E. Crabtree*, Mark G. Plew, James C. Woods and Max G. Pavesic, eds., pp. 187–210. University of New Mexico Press, Albuquerque.

HESTER, THOMAS R., AND HARRY J. SHAFER
1984   Exploitation of Chert Resources by the Ancient Maya of Northern Belize, Central America. In *World Archaeology* 16(2): 157–73.

HESTER, THOMAS R., HARRY J. SHAFER, THOMAS C. KELLY, AND GIANCARLO LIGABUE
1982   Observations on the Patination Process and the Context of Antiquity: A Fluted Projectile Point from Belize, Central America. In *Lithic Technology* 11(2): 29–34. Center for Archaeology Research, University of Texas at San Antonio.

HOUSTON, STEPHEN D.
1984   An Example of Homophony in Maya Script. In *American Antiquity* 49(4): 790–805.

HOUSTON, STEPHEN D., AND PETER MATHEWS
1985   *The Dynastic Sequence of Dos Pilas, Guatemala.* Pre-Columbian Art Research Institute, Monograph No. 1, San Francisco.

HOUSTON, STEPHEN D. AND KARL TAUBE
n.d.   "Name-Tagging" in Classic Maya Script: Examples of Objects of Stone and Ceramic. Unpublished ms. on file, Dept. of Anthropology, Vanderbilt University, Nashville.

IGLESIAS, MARIA JOSEFA
1986   *Excavaciones en el grupo habitacional 6D-V, Tikal, Guatemala.* Ph.D. Dissertation, Facultad de Geografia e Historia, Universidad Complutense, Madrid.

JACK, ROBERT N., THOMAS R. HESTER, AND ROBERT F. HEIZER
1972   Geologic Sources of Archaeological Obsidian from Sites in Northern and Central Veracruz, Mexico. In *Studies in the Archaeology of Mexico and Guatemala*, John A. Graham, ed., pp. 117–22. Contributions of the University of California Archaeological Research Facility, No. 16. Berkeley.

JOESINK-MANDEVILLE, LEROY V.
1976   The Significance of Mani Cenote, Yucatan, in the Prehistory of Middle America. In *Ethnos* 41 (I–IV): 146–64. Stockholm.

JONES, CHRISTOPHER
1969   *The Twin Pyramid Group Pattern: A Classic Maya Architectural Assemblage at Tikal, Guatemala.* Ph.D. Dissertation, University of Pennsylvania. University Microfilms, Ann Arbor.

JONES, CHRISTOPHER, AND LINTON SATTERTHWAITE
1982   *The Monuments and Inscriptions of Tikal: The Carved Monuments.* Tikal Reports, No. 33A. University Museum, University of Pennsylvania, Philadelphia.

JONES, CHRISTOPHER, AND ROBERT J. SHARER
1980   Archaeological Investigations in the Site Core of Quirigua. In *Expedition* 23(1): 11–19.

JONES, GRANT D.
1982   Agriculture and Trade in the Colonial Period Southern Maya Lowlands. In *Maya Subsistence: Studies in Memory of Dennis E. Puleston*, Kent V. Flannery, ed., pp. 275–93. Academic Press, New York.
1983   The Last Maya Frontiers of Colonial Yucatan. In *Spaniards and Indians in Southeastern Mesoamerica: Essays on the History of Ethnic Relations*, Murdo J. MacLeod and Robert Wasserstrom, eds., pp. 64–91. University of Nebraska Press, Lincoln.
1984   Maya-Spanish Relations in Sixteenth-Century Belize. In *Belcast Journal of Belizean Affairs* 1(1): 28–40.
1986   The Southern Maya Lowlands during Spanish Colonial Times. In *Ethnohistory*, Ronald Spores, ed., pp. 71–87. Supplement to the Handbook of Middle American Indians, vol. 4, Victoria R. Bricker, ed. University of Texas Press, Austin.
1989   *Maya Resistance to Spanish Rule: Time and History on a Colonial Frontier.* University of New Mexico Press, Albuquerque.

JONES, GRANT D., ROBERT R. KAUTZ, AND ELIZABETH A. GRAHAM
1986 Tipu: A Maya Town on the Spanish Colonial Frontier. In *Archaeology* 39(1): 40–47.

JONES, GRANT D., DON S. RICE, AND PRUDENCE M. RICE
1981 The Location of Tayasal: A Reconsideration in Light of Peten Maya Ethnohistory and Archaeology. In *American Antiquity* 46: 530–47.

JORALEMON, PETER D.
1971 *A Study of Olmec Iconography.* Studies in Precolumbian Art and Archaeology, No. 7. Dumbarton Oaks Research Library and Collection, Washington, D.C.
1974 Ritual Blood Sacrifice among the Ancient Maya: Part I. In *Primera Mesa Redonda de Palenque: II,* Merle G. Robertson, ed., pp. 59–75. Robert Louis Stevenson School, Pebble Beach, California.

JUSTESON, JOHN S., WILLIAM M. NORMAN, LYLE CAMPBELL, AND TERRENCE KAUFMAN
1985 *The Foreign Impact on Lowland Mayan Language and Script.* Middle American Research Institute Publication 53. Tulane University, New Orleans.

KAUFMAN, TERRENCE
1974 *Idiomas de Mesoamérica.* Seminario de Integración Social Guatemalteca Publication 33. Ministerio de Educatión, Guatemala.
1976 Archaeological and Linguistic Correlations in Mayaland and Associated Areas in Meso–america. In *World Archaeology* 8: 101–18.

KELLEY, DAVID H.
1962 Glyphic Evidence for a Dynastic Sequence at Quirigua, Guatemala. In *American Antiquity* 27: 323–35.
1965 The Birth of the Gods at Palenque. In *Estudios de Cultura Maya* 5: 93–134. Universidad Nacional Autonoma de Mexico, Mexico D.F.
1976 *Deciphering Maya Script.* University of Texas Press, Austin.
1982 Notes on Puuc Inscriptions and History. *The Puuc Symposium,* May 1977. Central College, Pella, Iowa.

KELLY, THOMAS C.
1980 The Colha Regional Survey. In *Colha Project. 1980 Interim Report,* Thomas R. Hester, Jack D. Eaton and Harry J. Shafer, eds., pp. 51–69. Center for Archaeological Research, University of Texas at San Antonio.

KIDDER, ALFRED V., JESSE JENNINGS, AND EDWIN M. SHOOK
1946 *Excavations at Kaminaljuyu, Guatemala.* Carnegie Institution at Washington Publication 561, Washington, D.C.

KIRCHHOFF, PAUL
1955 The Principles of Clanship in Human Society. In *Davidson Anthropological Journal* 1:1–11.

KOSAKOWSKY, LAURA J.
1983 *Intra-site Variability of the Formative Ceramics from Cuello, Belize: An Analysis of Form and Function.* Ph.D. Dissertation, University of Arizona, Tucson. University Microfilms, Ann Arbor.
1987a The Formative Ceramic Sequence of Cuello, Belize. In *Maya Ceramics: Papers from the 1985 Maya Ceramic Conference,* Prudence M. Rice and Robert J. Sharer, eds., part i, pp. 15–35. BAR International Series 345. Oxford, England.
1987b *Preclassic Maya Pottery at Cuello, Belize.* Anthropological Papers of the University of Arizona, No. 47. University of Arizona, Tucson.

KOWALSKI, JEFFERY K.
1985 Lords of the Northern Maya. Dynastic History in the Inscriptions. In *Expedition* 27(3): 50–60.

KROCHOCK, RUTH
1990 Dedication Ceremonies at Chichen Itza: The Glyphic Evidence. In *Sixth Round Table of Palenque,* vol. 8. University of Oklahoma Press, Norman.

KUBLER, GEORGE A.
1969 *Studies in Classic Maya Iconography.* Memoirs of the Connecticut Academy of Arts and Sciences, vol. 18, New Haven.
1972 Jaguars in the Valley of Mexico. In *Cult of the Feline,* Elizabeth P. Benson, ed., pp. 19–49. Dumbarton Oaks Research Library and Collection, Washington, D.C.
1973 Science and Humanism Among Americanists. In *Iconography of Middle American Sculpture,* Dudley T. Easby Jr., ed., pp. 163–67. Metropolitan Museum of Art, New York.

KURJACK, EDWARD. B., AND SILVIA GARZA T.
1981 Pre-Columbian Community Form and Distribution in the Northern Maya Area. In *Lowland Maya Settlement Patterns,* Wendy Ashmore, ed., pp. 287–309. University of New Mexico Press, Albuquerque.

LAMBERT, JOHN D.H., AND J.THOR ARNASON
    1983   Ancient Maya Land-use and Potential Agricultural Productivity at Lamanai, Belize. In *Drained Field Agriculture in Central and South America*, J.P. Durch, ed., pp. 111–22. BAR International Series 189. Oxford, England.

LAMBERT, JOHN D.H., ALFRED H. SIEMENS, AND J.THOR ARNASON
    1984   Ancient Maya Drained Field Agriculture: Its Possible Application Today in the New River Floodplain, Belize. In *Agriculture, Ecosystems and Environment* 11: 67–84.

LANGE, FREDERICK W.
    1971   Marine Resources: A Viable Subsistence Alternative for the Prehistoric Lowland Maya. In *American Anthropologist* 73(3): 619–39.

LAPORTE, JUAN PEDRO
    1984   El Complejo Manik: Dos Depósitos Sellados, Grupo 6C-XVI, Tikal. Proyecto Nacional Tikal. Guatemala.
    1985   El "talud-tablero" en Tikal, Petén: Nuevos Datos. Paper presented for the Symposium, *Vida y Obras de Román Piña Chan*, 1985. Instituto de Investigaciones Antropológicas, Universidad Nacional Autónoma de Mexico, Mexico D.F.
    1987   El Grupo 6C-XVI, Tikal Petén: Un Centro Habitacional del Clásico Temprano. In *Memorias del Primer Coloquio Internacional de Mayistas* (August 1985), pp. 221–44. Centro de Estudios Mayas, Universidad Nacional Autónoma de Mexico, Mexico D.F.

LAPORTE, JUAN PEDRO, AND VILMA FIALKO
    1985   (editors) *Reporte Arqueologico (1979–1984): Mundo Perdido y Zonas de Habitacion, Tikal, Peten*. Proyecto Nacional Tikal, Guatemala.
    1986a   La Cerámica del Clásico Temprano desde Mundo Perdido, Tikal, una Reevaluación. Paper presented at the Conferencia de Cerámicas Mayas. Proyecto Nacional Tikal.
    1986b   Una Visión Preliminar de Mundo Perdido, Tikal, durante el Preclásico de las Tierras Bajas Maya. Manuscript, Proyecto Nacional Tikal, Guatemala.

LAPORTE, JUAN PEDRO, AND LILIAN VEGA DE ZEA
    1986   Aspectos dinásticos para el Clásico Temprano de Mundo Perdido, Tikal. Paper presented for the Congreso de Epigrafía Maya. Museo de Arqueología y Ethnología, Guatemala.

LEVENTHAL, RICHARD M.
    1983   Pusilha. Survey and Excavations, 1979 and 1980. Unpublished manuscript in possession of author.

LEVENTHAL, RICHARD M., GORDON R. WILLEY, AND ARTHUR A. DEMAREST
    1987   The Cultural and Social Components of Copan. In *Polities and Partitions: Human Boundaries and the Growth of Complex Societies*. Anthropological Research Papers, No. 37. Arizona State University, Tucson.

LINICK, T. W.
    1984   La Jolla Natural Radiocarbon Measurements X. In *Radiocarbon* 26: 75–110.

LINNE, SIGVALD
    1934   *Archaeological Researches at Teotihuacan, Mexico* 5: 1. Ethnographic Museum of Sweden.

LIZANA, BERNARDO DE
    1893   Historia de Yicatán. Devocionario de nuestra señora de Izamal y conquista espiritual. Imprenta del Museo Nacional, Mexico. (Originally published in 1633.)

LÓPEZ ALONSO, SERGIO, AND C. SERRANO S.
    1984   Prácticas funerarias prehispánicas en la Isla de Jaina, Campeche. In *XVII Mesa Redonda de la Sociedad Mexicana de Antropologia* 2: 441–52. Sociedad Mexicana de Antropologia, Mexico D.F.

LÓPEZ DE COGOLLUDO, DIEGO
    1688   *Historia de la Provincia de Yucatan*. Madrid.

LOTHROP, SAMUEL K.
    1924   *Tulum. An Archaeological Study of the East Coast of Yucatan*. Carnegie Institution of Washington Publication 335. Washington, D.C.

LOUNSBURY, FLOYD G.
    1973   On the Derivation and Reading of the "Ben Ich Prefix." In *Mesoamerican Writing Systems*, Elizabeth P. Benson, ed., pp. 99–143. Dumbarton Oaks Research Library and Collection, Washington, D.C.
    1976   A Rationale for the Initial Date of the Temple of the Cross at Palenque. In *The Art, Iconography, and Dynastic History of Palenque, Part III: Proceedings of the Sequnda Mesa Redonda de Palenque*, Merle G. Robertson, ed., pp. 211–24. Robert Louis Stevenson School, Pebble Beach, California.
    1980   Some Problems in the Interpretation of the Mythological Portion of the Hieroglyphic Text of the Temple of the Cross at

Palenque. In *Third Palenque Round Table, 1978*, vol. 2, Merle G. Robertson, ed., pp. 99–115. University of Texas Press, Austin.

1985   The Identities of the Mythological Figures in the Cross Group Inscriptions of Palenque. In *Fourth Palenque Round Table, 1980*, Merle G. Robertson and Elizabeth P. Benson, eds., pp. 45–58. The Pre-Columbian Art Research Institute, San Francisco.

LOVE, BRUCE
1987   *Glyph T93 and Maya "Hand-scattering" Events.* Research Reports on Ancient Maya Writing, No. 5. Center for Maya Research, Washington, D.C.

LOWE, GARETH
1960   The Mound 1 Caches. In *Mound 1, Chiapa de Corzo, Chiapas, Mexico,* Gareth Lowe and Pierre Agrinier, eds., pp. 55–64. Papers of the New World Archaeological Foundation, No. 8. Brigham Young University, Provo.

1971   The Civilizational Consequences of Varying Degrees of Agricultural and Ceramic Dependence within the Basic Ecosystems of Mesoamerica. In *Observations on the Emergence of Civilization in Mesoamerica,* Robert F. Heizer and John A. Graham, eds., pp. 212–48. Contributions of the University of California Archaeological Research Facility, No. 11. Berkeley.

1977   The Mixe-Zoque as Competing Neighbors of the Early Lowland Maya. In *Origins of Maya Civilization,* Richard E.W. Adams, ed., pp. 197–248. School of American Research Advanced Seminar. University of New Mexico Press, Albuquerque.

1978   Eastern Mesoamerica. In *Chronologies in New World Archaeology,* R.E. Taylor and Clement W. Meighan, eds., pp. 331–93. Academic Press, New York.

1981   Olmec Horizons Defined in Mound 20, San Isidro, Chiapas. In *The Olmec and their Neighbors: Essays in Memory of Matthew W. Stirling,* Elizabeth P. Benson, ed., pp. 231–55. Dumbarton Oaks Research Library and Collections, Washington, D.C.

LUNDELL, CYRUS L.
1934   Preliminary Sketch of the Phytogeography of the Yucatan Peninsula. In *Carnegie Institution of Washington Publication 436,* pp. 255–355. Washington, D.C.

1937   *The Vegetation of the Maya.* Carnegie Institution of Washington Publication 478. Washington, D.C.

MACKINNON, J. JEFFERSON
1985   The Point Placencia Archaeological Project: 1984–1985 Fieldwork. In *Mexicon* 8(5): 80–83.

MACNEISH, RICHARD S.
1982   *Third Annual Report of the Belize Archaic Archaeological Reconnaissance.* R.S. Peabody Foundation, Andover, Massachusetts.

MCANANY, PATRICIA A.
1986   *Lithic Technology and Exchange Among Wetland Farmers of the Eastern Maya Lowlands.* Ph.D. dissertation, University of New Mexico. University Microfilms, Ann Arbor.

1987   *K'axob: A Formative and Classic Period Settlement at Pulltrouser Swamp, Belize.* Manuscript in possession of editors.

MCDONALD, ANDREW J.
1983   *Tzutzuculi: A Middle Preclassic Site on the Pacific Coast of Chiapas, Mexico.* Papers of the New World Archaeological Foundation, No. 47. Brigham Young University, Provo.

MCKILLOP, HEATHER
1981   *Moho Cay, Belize: Preliminary Investigations of Trade, Settlement and Maritime Resource Exploitation.* Master's thesis, Trent University, Peterborough, Canada.

1982   Wild Cane Cay Archaeological Project, 1982 Season. In *Mexicon,* 4(5/6): 88–89.

MARCUS, JOYCE
1976a   *Emblem and State in the Classic Maya Lowlands.* Dumbarton Oaks Research Library and Collections, Washington, D.C.

1976b   The Origins of Mesoamerican Writings. In *Annual Review of Anthropology* 5: 35–67.

1983   Lowland Maya Archaeology at the Crossroads. In *American Antiquity* 48: 454–82.

MARTINEZ HERNANDEZ, JUAN
1929   *Diccionario de Motul, Maya-Español. Atribuido a Fray Antonio de Cuidad Real y arte de lengua por Fray Juan Coronel.* Compania Tipografica Yucatec, Merida.

MATHENY, RAY T.
1970   *The Ceramics of Aguacatal, Campeche, Mexico.* Papers of the New World Archaeological Foundation, No. 27. Brigham Young University, Provo.

1976   Teotihuacan Influence in the Chenes and Rio Bec Areas of the Yucatan Peninsula, Mexico. In *XIV Mesa Redonda Sociedad Mexicana de Antropologia* (Tegucigalpa,

1975) 2: 45–54. Mexico D.F.

1986 *Early States in the Maya Lowlands during the Late Preclassic Period: Edzna and El Mirador.* Manuscript, Brigham Young University, Provo.

MATHEWS, PETER
1985 Maya Early Classic Monuments and Inscriptions. In *A Consideration of the Early Classic Period in the Maya Lowlands,* Gordon R. Willey and Peter Mathews, eds., pp. 5–54. Institute for Mesoamerican Studies Publication 10. State University of New York, Albany.
n.d. On the Glyphs "West" and "Mah K'ina." Maya Glyph Notes, No. 6. Manuscript in possession of author.

MATHEWS, PETER, AND LINDA SCHELE
1974 Lords of Palenque—The Glyphic Evidence. In *Primera Mesa Redonda de Palenque,* part I, Merle G. Robertson, ed., pp. 63–76. Robert Louis Stevenson School, Pebble Beach, California.

MAUDSLAY, ALFRED P.
1889– *Archaeology: Biologia Centrali-Americana,*
1902 vol. 4. London.

MAYER GUALA, PABLO
1977 Cancún: Informe Preliminar. In *XV Mesa Redonda de la Sociedad Mexicana de Antropologia* (Guanajuato, 1977) 2: 207–13. Mexico D.F.

MEDELLIN ZENIL, ALFONSO
1971 *Monolitos Olmecas y Otros en el Museo de la Universidad de Veracruz.* Volume V of *Corpus Antiquitatum Americanesium.* (Union Academique Internationale) Instituto Nacional de Antropologia e Historia, Mexico D.F.

MERWIN, ROBERT E., AND GEORGE C. VAILLANT
1932 *The Ruins of Holmul, Guatemala.* Memoirs of the Peabody Museum of American Archaeology and Ethnology, 3(2). Harvard University, Cambridge.

MICHELS, JOSEPH E.
1979 *The Kaminaljuyu Chiefdom.* Pennsylvania State University Press, Pittsburg.

MIKSICEK, CHARLES H.
1983 Macrofloral Remains of the Pulltrouser Swamp Area: Settlements and Fields. In *Pulltrouser Swamp. Ancient Maya Habitat, Agriculture and Settlement in Northern Belize,* B.L. Turner II and Peter D. Harrison, eds., pp. 94–104. University of Texas Press, Austin.

MILES, SUZANNE
1965 Sculpture of the Guatemalan-Chiapas Highlands and Pacific Slopes and Associated Hieroglyphs. In *Handbook of Middle American Indians,* vol. 2, Gordon Willey, ed., pp. 237–75. University of Texas Press, Austin.

MILLER, ARTHUR G.
1982 *On the Edge of the Sea: Mural Painting at Tancah-Tulum, Quintana Roo, Mexico.* Dumbarton Oaks Research Library and Collections, Washington, D.C.

MILLER, MARY E.
1986 *The Murals of Bonampak.* Princeton University Press, Princeton.

MILLET CÁMARA, LUIS
1984 Logwood and Archaeology in Campeche. In *Journal of Anthropological Research* 40(2): 324–28.

MILLON, RENE
1981 Teotihuacan: City, State and Civilization. In *Archaeology,* Jeremy A. Sabloff, ed., pp. 198–243. *Supplement to the Handbook of North American Indians,* vol. 1, Victoria R. Bricker, general editor. University of Texas Press, Austin.

MIRANDA F.
1959 Rasgos Fisiograficos (de interes para los estudios biologicos). In *Recursos Naturales del Sureste y su Aprovachamiento,* vol. 2, pt. 2, Estudios Particulares, E. Baltran, ed. Instituto Mexicano Recursos Renovables, Mexico.

MOHOLY-NAGY, HATTULA
1986 Variability in Early Classic Burials at Tikal, Guatemala. Paper presented at the Society for American Archaeology, New Orleans.

MORLEY, FRANCES R., AND SYLVANUS G. MORLEY
1938 The Age and Provenance of the Leyden Plate. In *Contributions to American Anthropology and History,* No. 24. Carnegie Institution of Washington, Washington, D.C.

MORLEY, SYLVANUS G.
1938– *The Inscriptions of Peten.* 5 volumes. Carne-
1939 gie Institution of Washington Publication 347. Washington, D.C.

MORLEY, SYLVANUS, G., AND GEORGE W. BRAINERD
1956 *The Ancient Maya.* 3d edition. Stanford University Press, Stanford.

MORLEY, SYLVANUS G., GEORGE W. BRAINERD, AND ROBERT J. SHARER
    1983   *The Ancient Maya*. 4th edition. Stanford University Press, Stanford.

NAVARRETE, CARLOS
    1974   *The Olmec Rock Carvings at Pijijiapan, Chiapas, Mexico and Other Olmec Pieces from Chiapas and Guatemala*. Papers of the New World Archaeological Foundation, No. 35. Brigham Young University, Provo.

NELSON, FRED W., JR.
    1985   Summary of the Results of Analysis of Obsidian Artifacts from the Maya Lowlands. In *Scanning Electron Microscopy 1985* II: 631–49.

NELSON, FRED W., JR., DAVID A. PHILLIPS, JR., AND ALFREDO BARRERA RUBIO
    1983   Trace Element Analysis of Obsidian Artifacts from the Northern Maya Lowlands. In *Investigations at Edzna, Campeche, Mexico*, vol. 1, part 1: *The Hydraulic System*, by Ray T. Matheny et al., Appendix A, pp. 205–19. Papers of the New World Archaeological Foundation, No. 46. Brigham Young University, Provo.

NELSON, FRED W., JR., RAYMOND V. SIDRYS, AND RICHARD D. HOLMES
    1978   Trace Element Analysis of X-Ray Fluorescence of Obsidian Artifacts from Guatemala and Belize. In *Excavations at Seibal, Department of Peten, Guatemala: Artifacts*, by Gordon R. Willey, pp. 153–161. Memoirs of the Peabody Museum of Archaeology and Ethnology 14(1). Harvard University, Cambridge.

NODELMAN, SHELDON
    1967   Sixties Art: Some Philosophical Perspectives. In *Perspecta 11. The Yale Architectural Journal*, pp. 73–89. New Haven.

NORMAN, V. GARTH
    1973   *Izapa Sculpture, Part I: Album*. Papers of the New World Archaeological Foundation, No. 30. Brigham Young University, Provo.
    1976   *Izapa Sculpture, Part II: Text*. Papers of the New World Archaeological Foundation, No. 30(2). Brigham Young University, Provo.

OCHOA, LORENZO
    1983   El medio Usumacinta: un eslabón en los antecedentes olmecas de los mayas. In *Antrhopología e historia de los mixe-zoques y mayas (Homenaje a Frans Blom)*, Lorenzo Ochoa and Thomas A. Lee, eds., pp. 147–74. Centro de Estudios Mayas, Universidad Nacional Autonoma de Mexico and Brigham Young University, Mexico D.F.

OCHOA, LORENZO, AND LUIS CASASOLA
    1978   Los Cambios del patrón de asentamiento en el área del Usumacinta. In *Estudios preliminares sobre los Mayas de las Tierras Bajas Noroccidentales*, Lorenzo Ochoa, ed., pp. 19–43. Centro de Estudios Mayas, Universidad Nacional Autonoma de Mexico, Mexico D.F.

OROZCO-SEGOVIA, ALMA D.L., AND STEPHEN R. GLIESSMAN
    1986   The *marceno* in Flood-Prone Regions of Tabasco, Mexico. In *Mexican Agroecosystems: Past and Present*, A. Gonzalez and Stephen Gliessman, eds.

PALERM, A., AND ERIC R. WOLF
    1957   Ecological Potential and Cultural Development in Mesoamerica. In *Social Science Monographs*, vol. 3, pp. 1–38. Pan American Union.

PANOFSKY, ERWIN
    1972   *Renaissance and Renascences in Western Art*. Icon Editions. Harper and Row, New York.

PARSONS, LEE A.
    1969   *Bilbao, Guatemala: An Archaeological Study of the Pacific Coast Cotzumalhuapa Region*, vol. 2. Publications in Anthropology, No. 12. Milwaukee Public Museum, Milwaukee.
    1978   The Peripheral Coastal Lowlands and the Middle Classic Period. In *Middle Classic Mesoamerica A.D. 400–700*, Esther Pasztory, ed., pp. 25–34. Columbia University Press, New York.
    1986   *The Origins of Maya Art: Monumental Stone Sculpture of Kaminaljuyu, Guatemala, and the Southern Pacific Coast*. Studies in Pre-Columbian Art and Archaeology, No. 28. Dumbarton Oaks Research Library and Collection, Washington, D.C.

PASZTORY, ESTHER
    1978   Artistic Traditions of the Middle Classic Period. In *Middle Classic Mesoamerica A.D. 400–700*, Esther Pasztory, ed., pp. 100–42. Columbia University Press, New York.

PEARSON, G.W., AND MINZE STUIVER
    1986   High-precision Calibration of the Radiocarbon Time Scale, 500–2500 B.C. In *Radiocarbon* 28: 839–62.

PENDERGAST, DAVID M.
    1971   Evidence of Early Teotihuacan–Lowland

	Maya Contact at Altun Ha. In *American Antiquity* 36: 455–59.
1982a	Ancient Maya Mercury. In *Science* 217 (4559): 533–35.
1982b	*Excavations at Altun Ha, Belize, 1964–1970*, vol. 2. Royal Ontario Museum, Toronto.
1985	The Terminal Postclassic and Early Historic Community at Lamanai. Paper presented at the 50th Annual Meeting of the Society for American Archaeology, Denver.
1986a	Stability Through Change: Laminai, Belize, from the Ninth to the Seventeenth Century. In *Late Lowland Maya Civilization: Classic to Postclassic,* Jeremy A. Sabloff and E. Wyllys Andrews V, eds., pp. 223–49. School of American Research Advanced Seminar. University of New Mexico Press, Albuquerque.
1986b	Under Spanish Rule: The Final Chapter in Laminai's Maya History. In *Belcast Journal of Belizean Affairs* 3(1 & 2): 1–7.
1990	*Excavations at Altun Ha, Belize, 1964–1970,* Volume 3. Royal Ontario Museum, Toronto.

PENDERGAST, DAVID M., AND ELIZABETH GRAHAM
    1987   No Site Too Small: The ROM's Marco Gonzalez Excavations in Belize. *Rotunda* 20(1). Royal Ontario Museum, Toronto.

PIJOAN, CARMEN, AND MARIA ELENA SALAS
    1984   Costumbres funerarias en Mundo Perdido, Tikal. Paper presented at the symposium, *La Plaza de la gran Piramide, Mundo Peridod, Tikal.* Museo de Arqueologia, Guatemala.

PIÑA CHAN, ROMÁN
    1968   *Jaina, La Casa en el Agua.* Instituto Nacional de Antropologia e Historia, Mexico D.F.

POLLOCK, HARRY, E.D.
    1965   Architecture of the Maya Lowlands. In *Archaeology of Southern Mesoamerica,* Part 1, Robert Wauchope and Gordon R. Willey, eds., pp. 378–40. Handbook of Middle American Indians, vol. 2. University of Texas Press, Austin.
    1980   *The Puuc: An Architectural Survey of the Hill Country of Yucatan and Northern Campeche, Mexico.* Memoirs of the Peabody Museum of Archaeology and Ethnology, 19. Harvard University, Cambridge.

POTTER, DANIEL R.
    1982   Some Results of the Second Year of Excavation at Operation 2012. In *Archaeology at Colha, Belize: The 1981 Interim Report,* Thomas R. Hester, Harry J. Shafer, and Jack D. Eaton, eds., pp. 98–122. Center for Archaeological Research, University of Texas, and Centro Studi e Ricerche Ligabue (Venezia), San Antonio, Texas.

POTTER, DANIEL R., THOMAS R. HESTER, STEPHEN L. BLACK, AND FRED VALDEZ, JR.
    1984   Relationships between Early Preclassic and Early Middle Preclassic Phases in Northern Belize: A Comment on "Lowland Maya Archaeology at the Crossroads." In *American Antiquity* 49: 628–31.

PREM, HANNS J.
    1971   Calendrics and Writing. In *Observations on the Emergence of Civilization in Mesoamerica,* Robert F. Heizer and John A. Graham, eds., pp. 112–32. Contributions of the University of California Archaeological Research Facility, No. 11. Department of Anthropology, University of California, Berkeley.

PRING, DUNCAN C.
    1975   The Ceramic Sequence in Northern Belize. In *Archaeology in Northern Belize: British Museum–Cambridge University Corozal Project 1974–75 Interim Report,* Norman Hammond, ed., pp. 190–205. Centre of Latin American Studies, Cambridge University, Cambridge, England.
    1977   *The Preclassic Ceramics of Northern Belize.* Ph.D. Dissertation, London University. University Microfilms, Ann Arbor.

PRING, DUNCAN C., AND NORMAN HAMMOND
    1982   The Stratigraphic Priority of Swascy Ceramics at Cuello, Belize. In *Cerámic de Cultura Maya* 12: 43–48. Temple University, Philadelphia.

PROSKOURIAKOFF, TATIANA
    1946   *An Album of Maya Architecture.* Carnegie Institution of Washington Publication 588. Washington, D.C.
    1968   Olmec and Maya Art: Problems of Their Stylistic Relation. In *Dumbarton Oaks Conference on the Olmec,* Elizabeth P. Benson ed., pp. 119–34. Dumbarton Oaks Research Library and Collection, Washington, D.C.

PULESTON, DENNIS E.
    1968   *Brosimum alicastrum as a Subsistence Alternative for the Classic Maya of the Central Lowlands.* Master's Thesis, University of Pennsylvania. University Microfilms, Ann Arbor.

1974   Intersite Areas in the Vicinity of Tikal and Uaxactun. In *Mesoamerican Archaeology: New Approaches,* Norman Hammond, ed., pp. 303–11. University of Texas Press, Austin.

1983   *The Settlement Survey of Tikal.* In Tikal Reports No. 13, William A. Haviland, vol. ed. University Museum, University of Pennsylvania, Philadelphia.

PULESTON, DENNIS E., AND OLGA S. PULESTON

1971   An Ecological Approach to the Origins of Maya Civilization. In *Archaeology* 24: 330–37.

QUIRARTE, JACINTO

1973   *Izapan-Style Art. A Study of Its Form and Meaning.* Studies in Pre-Columbian Art and Archaeology, No. 10. Dumbarton Oaks Research Library and Collections, Washington, D.C.

1976   The Relationship of Izapan-Style Art to Olmec and Maya Art: A Review. In *Origins of Religious Art and Iconography in Preclassic Mesoamerica,* Henry B. Nicholson, ed., pp. 73–85. UCLA Latin American Center Publications. Ethnic Arts Council, Los Angeles.

1977   Early Art Styles of Mesoamerica and Early Classic Maya Art. In *Origins of Maya Civilizations,* Richard E. Adams, ed., pp. 249–83. School of American Research Advanced Seminar. University of New Mexico Press, Albuquerque.

1979   Sculptural Documents on the Origins of Maya Civilization. In *Acts, 42d International Congress of Americanists (1976)* 8: 189–96. Paris.

RAISH, MARTIN

1984   *An Iconographic Study of Olmec and Izapan Monumental Stone Sculpture.* Ph.D. Dissertation, University of New Mexico. University Microfilms, Ann Arbor.

RANDS, ROBERT L.

1969   *Mayan Ecology and Trade: 1967–1968.* Mesoamerican Studies, Research Records of the University Museum. Southern Illinois University, Carbondale.

1974   A Chronological Framework for Palenque. In *Primera Mesa Redonda de Palenque,* part 1, Merle G. Robertson, ed., pp. 33–39. The Robert Louis Stevenson School, Pebble Beach, California.

1977   The Rise of Classic Maya Civilization in the Northwestern Zone: Isolation and Integration. in *The Origins of Maya Civilization,* Robert E.W. Adams, ed., pp. 159–80. School of American Research Advanced Seminar, University of New Mexico Press, Albuquerque.

1987   Ceramic Patterns and Traditions in the Palenque Area. In *Maya Ceramics: Papers from the 1985 Maya Ceramic Conference,* part i, Prudence M. Rice and Robert J. Sharer, eds., pp. 203–38. BAR International Series 345, Oxford, England.

RATHJE, WILLIAM L., AND JEREMY A. SABLOFF

1973   Ancient Maya Commercial Systems: A Research Design for the Island of Cozumel, Mexico. In *World Archaeology* 5: 221–31.

RATTRAY, EVELYN C.

1984   El Barrio de los Comerciantes en Teotihuacan. In *XVII Mesa Redonda de Sociedad Mexicana de Antropologia (1981)* 1: 147–64. Mexico D.F.

REDFIELD, ROBERT

1941   *The Folk Culture of Yucatan.* University of Chicago Press, Chicago.

1947   The Folk Society. In *American Journal of Sociology* 52: 293–308.

RICE, DON S.

1976   Middle Preclassic Maya Settlement in the Central Maya Lowlands. In *Journal of Field Archaeology* 3: 425–45.

RICE, DON S., AND DENNIS E. PULESTON

1981   Ancient Maya Settlement Patterns in the Peten, Guatemala. In *Lowland Maya Settlement Patterns,* Wendy Ashmore, ed., pp. 121–56. University of New Mexico Press, Albuquerque.

RICE, DON S., AND PRUDENCE M. RICE

1980   The Northeast Peten Revisited. In *American Antiquity* 45: 432–54.

RICE, PRUDENCE M.

1979   Ceramic and Non-ceramic Artifacts of Lakes Yaxha-Sacnab, El Peten, Guatemala. Part I. The Ceramics. Section A, Introduction and the Middle Preclassic Ceramics of Yaxha-Sacnab, Guatemala. In *Cerámica de Cultura Maya* 10: 1–36. Temple University, Philadelphia.

RICKETSON, EDITH B.

1937   The Artifacts. In *Uaxactun, Guatemala: Group E—1926–1931,* by Oliver G. Ricketson and Edith B. Ricketson, pp. 181–314. Carnegie Institution of Washington Publication 477. Washington, D.C.

RICKETSON, OLIVER G., AND EDITH B. RICKETSON

1937   *Uaxactun, Guatemala: Group E—1926–1931.* Carnegie Institution of Washington

Publication 477. Washington, D.C.

RINGLE, WILLIAM M.
1985 *The Settlement Patterns of Komchen, Yucatan, Mexico.* Ph.D. Dissertation, Tulane University. University Microfilms, Ann Arbor.

RINGLE, WILLIAM M., AND E. WYLLYS ANDREWS V.
1988 Formative Residences at Komchen, Yucatan, Mexico. In *Household and Community in the Mesoamerican Past,* Richard R. Wilk and Wendy Ashmore, eds., pp. 171–97. University of New Mexico Press, Albuquerque.
1991 The Demography of Komchen, an Early Maya Town in Northern Yucatan. In *Precolumbian Population History in the Maya Lowlands,* T. Patrick Culbert and Don S. Rice, eds. University of New Mexico Press, Albuquerque.

RIVERA DORADO, MIGUEL
1982 *Los Mayas, Una Sociedad Oriental.* Editorial de la Universidad Complutense, Madrid.

ROBERTSON, MERLE G., EDWARD B. KURJACK, AND ROBERTO MALDONADO C.
1985 Ball Courts of the Northern Maya Lowlands. Paper presented at the International Symposium on the Mesoamerican Ballgame and Ballcourts, November. Tucson.

ROBERTSON, ROBIN A., AND DAVID A. FREIDEL
1986 (editors) *Archaeology at Cerros, Belize, Central America, Volume 1, An Interim Report.* Southern Methodist University Press, Dallas.

ROBERTSON-FREIDEL, ROBIN A.
1980 *The Ceramics from Cerros: A Late Preclassic Site in Northern Belize.* Ph.D. Dissertation, Harvard University. University Microfilms, Ann Arbor.

ROBISCEK, FRANCIS, AND DONALD HALES
1981 *The Maya Book of the Dead. The Ceramic Codex.* The University of Virginia Museum, Charlottesville. (Distributed by the University of Oklahoma Press, Norman.)

ROBLES CASTELLANOS, FERNANDO
1976 Ixil, centro agrícola de Cobá. In *Boletín de la Escuela de Ciencias Antropológicas de la Universidad de Yucatán* 4(20): 13–43.
1977 Evidence for Late Classic Political Units among the Maya: The Sacbes of Northern Yucatan. Paper presented to the 42d Annual Meeting of the Society for American Archaeology, April. New Orleans.
1980 *La Secuencia Cerámica de la Región de Cobá, Quintana Roo.* Tesis profesional, Escuela Nacional de Antropologia e Historia. Instituto Nacional de Antropologia e Historia, Mexico D.F.
1981a (editor) *Informe Anual del Proyecto Arqueológico de Cozumel, 1980.* Fideicomiso Caleta de Xelha y del Caribe, Mexico.
1981b Xelha: un proyecto de investigación. In *Memoria del Congreso Interno 1979,* pp. 101–21. Centro Regional del Sureste. Instituto Nacional de Antropologia e Historia, Mexico D.F.
1986 Cerámica de Loltun, Yucatán, en el Peabody Museum de la Universidad de Harvard. Seminar paper for Anthropology 325, Harvard University, Cambridge.

ROBLES CASTELLANOS, FERNANDO, AND ANTHONY P. ANDREWS
1986 A Review and Synthesis of Recent Postclassic Archaeology in Northern Yucatan. In *Late Maya Civilization: Classic to Postclassic,* Jeremy Sabloff and E. Wyllys Andrews V, eds., pp. 53–98. School of American Research Advanced Seminar, University of New Mexico Press, Albuquerque.

ROYS, RALPH L.
1933 *The Book of Chilam Balam of Chumayel.* Carnegie Institution of Washington Publication 438. Washington, D.C.
1967 *The Book of Chilam Balam of Chumayel.* Reprint. University of Oklahoma Press, Norman.

RUZ LHUILLIER, ALBERTO
1958 Exploraciones arqueologicas en Palenque: 1953–56. In *Anales del Instituto Nacional de Antropología e Historia* 10. Instituto Nacional de Antropología e Historia, México D.F.
1969 La costa de Campeche en tiempos prehispánicos. In *Serie Investigaciones* 18. Instituto Nacional de Antropología e Historia, México D.F.

SABLOFF, JEREMY A.
1975 *Excavations at Seibal, Department of Peten, Guatemala: Ceramics.* Memoirs of the Peabody Museum of Archaeology and Ethnology, 13(2). Harvard University, Cambridge.
1977 Old Myths, New Myths: The Role of Sea Traders in the Development of Maya Civilization. In *The Sea in the Precolumbian World,* Elizabeth P. Benson, ed., pp. 67–88. Dumbarton Oaks Research Library and Collection, Washington, D.C.
1986 Interaction among Maya Polities: A Preliminary Examination. In *Peer Polity Inter-*

action and Socio-Political Change. Colin Renfrew and J.F. Cherry, eds., pp. 109–16. Cambridge University Press, Cambridge, England.

SABLOFF, JEREMY A., AND E. WYLLYS ANDREWS V.
1986 (editors) *Late Lowland Maya Civilization: Classic to Postclassic.* School of American Research Advanced Seminar, University of New Mexico Press, Albuquerque.

SABLOFF, JEREMY A., AND WILLIAM L. RATHJE
1973 A Study of Changing Precolombian Commercial Patterns on the Island of Cozumel, Mexico. In *Acts of the 40th International Congress of Americanists* (Rome-Geneva, 1972), I: 455–63. Tilgher, Geneva.
1975 A Study of Changing Pre-Colombian Comercial Systems. *The 1972–73 Seasons at Cozumel, Mexico.* In Monographs of the Peabody Museum, No. 3. Harvard University, Cambridge.

SABLOFF, JEREMY A., PATRICIA A. MCANANY, BERND FAHMEL BEYER, TOMAS GALLARETA N., SIGNA L. LARRALDE, AND LUANN WANDSNIDER
1984 *Ancient Maya Settlement Patterns at the Site of Sayil, Puuc Region, Yucatan, Mexico: Initial Reconaissance (1983).* Research Paper Series 14. Latin American Institute, University of New Mexico, Albuquerque.

SAENZ, CESAR
1975 Xochicalco, Mexico. In *Los Pueblos y Senorios Teocraticos,* Part 1: 55–102. Instituto Nacional de Antropologia e Historia, Mexico D.F.

SALAS, MARIA ELENA, AND CARMEN PIJOAN
1982 Estudio osteológico de los entierros procedentes de las exploraciones del Proyecto Nacional Tikal, Temporadas 1980–1982. *Informe, Proyecto Nacional Tikal, Guatemala y Departamento de Antropologia Fisica.* Instituto Nacional de Antropologia e Historia, Mexico D.F.

SANDERS, WILLIAM T.
1960 *Prehistoric Ceramics and Settlement Patterns in Quintana Roo, Mexico.* Contribution No. 60. Carnegie Institution of Washington Publication 606. Washington, D.C.
1972 Chiefdom to State: Political Evolution at Kaminaljuyu, Guatemala. In *Reconstructing Complex Societies,* C. Moore, ed., pp. 97–121. American Schools of American Research, Massachusetts Institute of Technology, Cambridge.
1976 The Agricultural History of the Basin of Mexico. In *The Valley of Mexico,* Eric Wolf, ed., pp. 59–67. University of New Mexico Press, Albuquerque.
1979 The Jolly Green Giant in Tenth-century Yucatan, or, Fact and Fancy in Classic Maya Agriculture. In *Reviews in Anthropology* (Fall): 493–506.

SANDERS, WILLIAM T., JEFFERY R. PARSONS, AND ROBERT S. SANTLEY
1979 *The Basin of Mexico.* Academic Press, New York.

SANDERS, WILLIAM T., AND ROBERT S. SANTLEY
1983 A Tale of Three Cities: Energetics and Urbanization in Pre-Hispanic Central Mexico. In *Prehistoric Settlement Patterns,* Evon Z. Vogt and Robert M. Leventhal, eds., pp. 243–92. University of New Mexico Press, Albuquerque, and Peabody Museum, Cambridge.

SANTLEY, ROBERT S.
1983 Obsidian Trade and Teotihuacan Influence in Mesoamerica. In *Highland-Lowland Interaction in Mesoamerica: Interdisciplinary Approaches,* Arthur Miller, ed., pp. 69–124. Dumbarton Oaks Research Library and Collections, Washington, D.C.

SCARBOROUGH, VERNON
1983 A Preclassic Maya Water System. In *American Antiquity* 48(4): 720–44.
1986 Drainage Canal and Raised Field Excavations. In *Archaeology at Cerros, Belize, Central America, Volume 1, An Interim Report.* Robin A. Robertson and David A. Freidel, eds., pp. 75–87. Southern Methodist University Press, Dallas.

SCHAPIRO, MEYER
1969 On Some Problems in the Semiotics of Visual Art: Field and Vehicle in Image-Signs. In *Semiotica* 1(3). Mouton and Company, The Hague, Netherlands.

SCHOLES, FRANCE V., AND ELEANOR ADAMS
1936– Documents Relating to the Mirones Ex-
1937 pedition to the Interior of Yucatan, 1621–24. In *Maya Research* 3: 153–76 (pt. 1) and 251–76 (pt. 2).

SCHOLES, FRANCE V., AND RALPH L. ROYS
1968 *The Maya Chontal Indians of Acalan-Tixchel: A Contribution to the History and Ethnography of the Yucatan Peninsula.* 2d edition. University of Oklahoma Press, Norman.

SCHELE, LINDA
1974 Observations on the Cross Motif at Palenque. In *Primera Mesa Redonda de Pal-*

	enque, part 1, Merle G. Robertson, ed., pp. 41–62. Robert Louis Stevenson School, Pebble Beach, California.
1976	Accession Iconography of Chan-Bahlum in the Group of the Cross at Palenque. In *The Art, Iconography, and Dynastic History of Palenque, Part III. Proceedings of the Segunda Mesa Redonda de Palenque,* Merle G. Robertson, ed., pp. 9–34. Robert Louis Stevenson School, Pebble Beach, California.
1978–1987	*The Workbook of the Workshop on Maya Hieroglyphic Writing at Texas.* Institute of Latin American Studies, University of Texas, Austin. (*Workbooks* for the years 1978, 1981, 1984, and 1987.)
1979	Genealogical Documentation in the Tri-figure Panels at Palenque. In *Tercera Mesa Redonda de Palenque,* vol. 4, Merle G. Robertson, ed., pp. 41–70. Pre-Columbian Art Research. Palenque and Herald Printers, Monterey, California.
1981	Sacred Site and World-View at Palenque. In *Mesoamerican Sites and World-Views,* Elizabeth P. Benson, ed., pp. 87–117. Dumbarton Oaks Research Libraries and Collection, Washington, D.C.
1984	*The Workbook for the Maya Hieroglyphic Writing Workshop at Texas, 1984.* Institute of Latin American Studies, University of Texas, Austin.
1985a	The Hauberg Stela: Bloodletting and the Mythos of Maya Rulership. In *Fifth Palenque Round Table, 1983,* vol. 7, Merle G. Robertson and Virginia M. Fields, eds., pp. 135–49. Pre-Columbian Art Research Institute, San Francisco.
1985b	Some Suggested Readings of the Event and Office of Heir-Designate at Palenque. In *Phoneticism in Mayan Hieroglyphic Writing,* Lyle Campbell and John S. Justeson, eds., pp. 287–307. Institute for Mesoamerican Studies, State University of New York, Albany.
1987	*The Workbook for the Maya Hieroglyphic Writing Workshop at Texas, 1987.* Institute of Latin American Studies, University of Texas, Austin.
1986	The Tlaloc Complex in the Classic Period: War and the Interaction between the Lowland Maya and Teotihuacan. Paper presented at the symposium The New Dynamics. Kimbell Art Museum, Fort Worth.

SCHELE, LINDA, AND DAVID FREIDEL
1985   The Maya Message: Time, Text, and Image. A paper presented at the Conference on Art and Communication, January 1985. Israel Museum, Jerusalem.

SCHELE, LINDA, AND PETER MATHEWS
1979   *The Bodega of Palenque, Chiapas, Mexico.* Dumbarton Oaks Research Library and Collection, Washington, D.C.

SCHELE, LINDA, AND JEFFERY H. MILLER
1983   *The Mirror, The Rabbit, and the Bundle: "Accession" Expressions from the Classic Maya Inscriptions.* Studies in Pre-Columbian Art and Archaeology, No. 25. Dumbarton Oaks Research Library and Collection, Washington, D.C.

SCHELE, LINDA, AND MARY E. MILLER
1986   *The Blood of Kings: Dynasty and Ritual in Maya Art.* Kimbell Art Museum, Fort Worth, and George Braziller, New York.

SCHORTMAN, EDWARD M.
1988   Maya/Non-Maya Interaction along the Late Classic Southeast Maya Periphery: The View from the Lower Motagua Valley, Guatemala. Manuscript in author's possession.

SCOTT, JOHN F.
1971   *Post-Olmec Art in Preclassic Oaxaca, Mexico.* Ph.D. Dissertation. Columbia University, New York.
1977   El Meson, Veracruz, and Its Monolithic Reliefs. In *Baessler-Archive,* neue folge, Band 25, pp. 83–138. Verlag von Dietrich Reimer, Berlin.

SEDAT, DAVID W., AND ROBERT J. SHARER
1972   Archaeological Investigations in the Northern Maya Highlands: New Data on the Maya Preclassic. In *Studies in the Archaeology of Mexico and Guatemala,* John A. Graham, ed., pp. 23–35. Contributions of the University of California Archaeological Research Facility, No. 16. Berkeley.

SELER, EDUARD
1902   Die Monumente von Copan und Quirigua und die Altarplatten von Palenque. In *Gesammelte Abhandlungen sur Americanischen Sprach- und Alther Thumskunde von Eduard Seler,* vol. 1: 721–91. H. Asher, Berlin.

SHAFER, HARRY J.
1983   The Lithic Artifacts of the Pulltrouser Area: Settlements and Fields. In *Pulltrouser Swamp: Ancient Maya Habitat, Agriculture and Settlement in Northern Belize,* B.L. Turner II and Peter D. Harrison, eds., pp. 212–45. University of Texas Press, Austin.

SHARER, ROBERT J.
1976   The Jenney Creek Ceramic Complex at

Barton Ramie. In *Prehistoric Pottery Analysis and the Ceramics of Barton Ramie in the Belize Valley,* by James C. Gifford and others, pp. 61–63. Memoirs of the Peabody Museum of Archaeology and Ethnology, 18. Harvard University, Cambridge.

1978 *Pottery and Conclusions. The Prehistory of Chalchuapa, El Salvador,* vol. 3, Robert J. Sharer, gen. ed. University Museum Monographs, University of Pennsylvania Press, Philadelphia.

SHARER, ROBERT J., AND WENDY ASHMORE
1979 (editors) *Quirigua Reports I.* University Museum Monographs 37. University of Pennsylvania Press, Philadelphia.

SHARER, ROBERT J., AND ARLEN F. CHASE
1976 New Town Ceramic Complex. In *Prehistoric Pottery Analysis and the Ceramics of Barton Ramie in the Belize Valley,* by James C. Gifford and others, pp. 288–311. Memoirs of the Peabody Museum of Archaeology and Ethnology, 18. Harvard University, Cambridge.

SHARER, ROBERT J., AND JAMES C. GIFFORD
1970 Preclassic Ceramics from Chalchuapa, El Salvador, and their Relationships with the Maya Lowlands. In *American Antiquity* 35: 441–62.

SHARER, ROBERT J., AND DAVID W. SEDAT
1987a *Archaeological Investigations in the Northern Maya Highlands, Guatemala: Interaction and the Development of Maya Civilization.* University Museum Monograph 59. University of Pennsylvania Press, Philadelphia.
1987b Preclassic Ceramics from the Salama Valley, Baja Verapaz, Guatemala. In *Maya Ceramics: Papers from the 1985 Maya Ceramic Conference,* Prudence M. Rice and Robert J. Sharer, eds., part ii, pp. 241–76. BAR International Series 345. Oxford, England.

SHOOK, EDWIN M., AND ROBERT HEIZER
1976 An Olmec Sculpture from the South (Pacific) Coast of Guatemala. In *Journal of the New World Archaeology* 1(3): 1–8. Institute of Archaeology, University of California, Los Angeles.

SIDRYS, RAYMOND V.
1983 *Archaeological Excavations in Northern Belize, Central America.* In Institute of Archaeology Monograph 17. University of California, Los Angeles.

SIDRYS, RAYMOND V., AND JEROME KIMBERLIN
1979 Use of Maya Obsidian Sources through Time: Trace-Element Data from El Balsamo, Guatemala. In *Journal of Field Archaeology* 6: 116–22.

SEIMANS, ALFRED H.
1978 Karst and the Prehispanic Maya in the Southern Lowlands. In *Prehispanic Maya Agriculture,* Peter D. Harrison and B.L. Turner II, eds., pp. 117–43. University of New Mexico Press, Albuquerque.
1982 Prehispanic Cultural Use of the Wetlands of Northern Belize. In *Maya Subsistence: Studies in Memory of Dennis E. Puleston,* Kent V. Flannery, ed., pp. 205–25. Academic Press, New York.
1983a Oriented Raised Fields in Central Veracruz. In *American Antiquity* 48: 85–102.
1983b Modeling Prehispanic Hydroagriculture on Levee Backslopes in Northern Veracruz, Mexico. In *Drained Field Agriculture in Central and South America,* J.P. Darch, ed., pp. 27–54. BAR International Series 189. Oxford, England.

SEIMANS, ALFRED H., AND DENNIS E. PULESTON
1972 Ridged Fields and Associated Features in Southern Campeche: New Perspectives on the Lowland Maya. In *American Antiquity* 37: 228–39.

SISSON, EDWARD B.
1976 *Survey and Excavation in the Northwestern Chontalpa, Tabasco, Mexico.* Ph.D. Dissertation. Harvard University, Cambridge.

SMITH, A. LEDYARD
1950 *Uaxactun, Guatemala: Excavations of 1931–1937.* Carnegie Institution of Washington Publication 588. Washington, D.C.
1972 *Excavations at Altar de Sacrificios: Architecture, Settlement, Burials, and Caches.* Papers of the Peabody Museum of Archaeology and Ethnology, 62(2). Harvard University, Cambridge.
1982 *Excavations at Seibal, Department of Peten, Guatemala: Major Architecture and Caches.* Memoirs of the Peabody Museum of Archaeology and Ethnology, 15(1). Harvard University, Cambridge.

SMITH, CAROLE
1976 Analyzing Regional Social Systems. In *Social Systems,* vol. 2 of *Regional Analysis,* Carole Smith, ed. Academic Press, New York.

SMITH, RICHARD T.
1983 Drained Field Agriculture and Soil Fertility. In *Drained Field Agriculture in Central and South America,* J.P. Darch, ed., pp. 251–63. BAR International Series 189. Oxford, London.

SMITH, ROBERT E.
1937   A Study of Structure A-1 Complex at Uaxactun, Peten, Guatemala. In *Contributions to American Archaeology*, No. 19. Carnegie Institution of Washington Publication 456. Washington, D.C.
1955   *Ceramic Sequence at Uaxactun, Guatemala.* 2 vols. Middle American Research Institute Publication 20. Tulane University, New Orleans.

SMITH, VIRGINIA G.
1984   *Izapa Relief Carving.* Studies in Pre-Columbian Art and Archaeology, No. 27. Dumbarton Oaks Research Library and Collections, Washington, D.C.

STIRLING, MATTHEW
1943   *Stone Monuments of Southern Mexico.* Bulletin 138. Smithsonian Institution, Bureau of American Ethnology, Washington, D.C.

STUART, DAVID
1983   Epigraphic Evidence of Political Organization in the Usumacinta Drainage. Paper on file at the Center for Maya Research, Washington, D.C.
1984   Blood Symbolism Among the Maya. In *RES* 7/8: 6–20. Peabody Museum, Harvard University.
1985   The "Count of the Captives" Epithet in Classic Maya Writing. In *Fifth Palenque Round Table, 1983*, vol. 7, Merle G. Robertson and Virginia Fields, eds., pp. 97–101. Pre-Columbian Art Research Institute, San Francisco.
1986   The "*Lu*-bat" Glyph and its Bearing on the Primary Standard Sequence. Paper presented at the *Primera Conferencia Internacional de Jeroglíficos Mayas*, August. Guatemala City.
1987   Ten Phonetic Syllables. In *Research Reports on Ancient Maya Writing*, No. 14. Center for Maya Research, Washington, D.C.

STUART, GEORGE E.
1981   Maya Art Treasures Discovered in Cave. In *National Geographic Magazine* 160: 220–35.
1987   A Carved Shell from the Northeastern Maya Lowlands. In *Research Reports on Ancient Maya Writing*, No. 13. Center for Maya Research, Washington, D.C.

STUIVER, MINZE, AND G. W. PEARSON
1986   High-precision Calibration of Radiocarbon Time Scale, A.D. 1950–500 B.C. In *Radiocarbon* 28: 805–38.

STUIVER, MINZE, AND P.J. REIMER
1986   A Computer Program for Radiocarbon Age Calibration. In *Radiocarbon* 28: 1022–30. (Rev. 1.3, Radiocarbon Calibration Program, 9 Jan '87. Quaternary Isotope Laboratory, Quaternary Research Center AK-60, University of Washington, Seattle).

SUGIYAMA, SABURO
1986   Recent Excavations at the Temple of Quetzalcoatl and Their Significance. Paper presented at the Society of American Archaeology, New Orleans.

TATE, CAROLYN
1986   Maya Astronomical Rituals Recorded on Yaxchilan Structure 23. In *The Rutgers Art Review* 7: 1–20.

TEDLOCK, DENNIS
in press   The Sowing and Dawning of all the Sky-Earth: Astronomy in the Popol Vuh. In *Ethnoastronomy: Astronomical and Cosmological Traditions of the World*, John B. Carlson and Von del Chamberlain, eds. Smithsonian Institution Press, Washington, D.C.

TEEPLE, JOHN E.
1930   Maya Astronomy. In *Contributions to American Archaeology*, No. 2, pp. 29–115. Carnegie Institution of Washington Publication 403, Washington, D.C.

THOMPSON, J. ERIC S.
1930   *Ethnology of the Mayas of Southern and Central British Honduras.* Field Museum of Natural History Anthropological Series, 17(2). Chicago.
1931   *Archaeological Investigations in the Southern Cayo District, British Honduras.* Field Museum of Natural History Anthropological Series, 17(3). Chicago.
1939   *Excavations at San Jose, British Honduras.* Carnegie Institution of Washington Publication 506. Washington, D.C.
1954   Memoranda on Some Dates at Palenque, Chiapas. In *Notes on Middle American Archaeology and Ethnology*, 5(120): 45–52. Carnegie Institution of Washington, Division of Historical Research, Washington, D.C.
1960   *Maya Hieroglyphic Writing: An Introduction.* University of Oklahoma Press, Norman.
1962   *A Catalog of Maya Hieroglyphics.* University of Oklahoma Press, Norman.
1966   *The Rise and Fall of Maya Civilization.* 2d edition. University of Oklahoma Press, Norman.
1970   *Preliminary Decipherments of Maya Glyphs, no. 5. Ku [k'u] as a Value of the Cauac Glyph.* Ashdon. (Abbreviated version of a

paper read at the 37th International Congress of Americanists, Mar de Plata, Argentina, 1966. Not published in Proceedings.)

1974 "Canals" of the Rio Calendaria Basin, Campeche, Mexico. In *Mesoamerican Archaeology: New Approaches*, Norman Hammond, ed., pp. 297–302. University of Texas Press, Austin.

1977 A Proposal for Constituting a Maya Subgroup, Cultural and Linguistic, in the Peten and Adjacent Regions. In *Anthropology and History in Yucatan*, Grant D. Jones, ed., pp. 3–42. University of Texas Press, Austin.

TURNER, B. L. II
1974 Prehistoric Intensive Agriculture in the Mayan Lowlands. In *Science* 185: 118–24.

1983 *Once Beneath the Forest: Prehistoric Terracing in the Rio Bec Region of the Maya Lowlands.* Dellplain Latin American Studies, No. 13. Westview Press, Boulder, Colorado.

TURNER, B. L. II, AND PETER D. HARRISON
1981 Prehistoric Raised-Field Agriculture in the Maya Lowlands. In *Science* 213: 399–405.

1983 (editors) *Pulltrouser Swamp: Ancient Maya Habitat, Agriculture and Settlement in Northern Belize.* University of Texas Press, Austin.

VAIL, GABRIELLE
1987 *The Archaeology of Coastal Belize, Central America.* Bachelor's Thesis, New College of the University of South Florida, Sarasota.

VAILLANT, GEORGE C.
1928 Report on the Excavations in the Plaza of Group E at Uaxactun. In *Carnegie Institution of Washington Yearbook* 27: 313–17. Washington, D.C.

VALDÉS, JUAN ANTONIO
1984 Uaxactun durante el Clasico Temprano. Manuscript, Proyecto Nacional Tikal, Guatemala.

1986a Report de las Actividades Realizadas en Uaxactun, 1983–1985. Proyecto Nacional Tikal, Guatemala.

1986b Los Masarones Preclásicos de Uaxactun: El Caso del Grupo H. Paper presented at the Congreso de Epigrafía. Museo de Arqueología y Etnología, Guatemala.

1986c Uaxactun: Recientes Investigaciones. In *Mexicon* 7(6): 125–28.

VALDEZ, FRED JR.
1987 *The Prehistoric Ceramics of Colha, Northern Belize.* Ph.D. Dissertation, Harvard University. University Microfilms, Ann Arbor.

VALDEZ, FRED JR., AND RICHARD E.W. ADAMS
1982 The Ceramics of Colha after Three Field Seasons: 1979–1981. In *Archaeology at Colha, Belize: The 1981 Interim Report,* Thomas R. Hester, Harry J. Shafer, and Jack D. Eaton, eds., pp. 21–30. Center for Archaeological Research, University of Texas and Centro Studi e Ricerche Ligabue (Venezia), San Antonio.

VARGAS PACHECO, ERNESTO
1978 Los Asentamientos Prehispanico y la Arquitectura en la Isla Can Cun, Quintana Roo. In *Estudios de Cultura Maya* 11: 93–112.

VELÁZQUEZ VALADÉZ, RICARDO
1980 Recent Discoveries in the Caves of Loltun, Yucatan, Mexico. In *Mexicon* 2(4): 53–55.

1981 Etapas de funcionalidad de las Grutas de Loltún. In *Memoria del Congreso Interno 1979,* pp. 139–44. Instituto Nacional de Antropología e Historía, Centro Regional del Sureste. Mexico D.F.

VILLAGUTIERRE SOTO-MAYOR, JUAN DE
1933 Historia de la conquista de la provincia de el Itzá, reducción y progresos de la de el Lacandón.... 2d edition. Guatemala City: Biblioteca "Goathemala" de la Sociedad de Geografía e Historía, vol. 9. Guatemala: Tipografía Nacional. (Originally published in 1701.)

1983 History of the Conquest of the Province of the Itzas. Translated by Brother Robert D. Wood, S.M. and edited by Frank E. Comparato. Labyrinthos, Culver City, California.

VLCEK, DAVID T., SILVIA GARZA T. DE GONZÁLEZ, AND EDWARD B. KURJACK
1978 Contemporary Farming and Ancient Maya Settlements: Some Disconcerting Evidence. In *Prehispanic Maya Agriculture,* Peter D. Harrison and B.L. Turner II, eds., pp. 211–23. University of New Mexico Press, Albuquerque.

VON EUW, ERIC
1978 Xultun. In *Corpus of Maya Hieroglyphic Inscriptions,* Ian Graham, ed. vol. 5, pt. 1. Peabody Museum, Harvard University, Cambridge.

VOORHIES, BARBARA
1969 *San Felipe. A Prehistoric Settlement in Eastern Guatemala.* Ph.D. Dissertation, Yale University.

WALLERSTEIN, IMMANUEL
1974a   *The Modern World-System: Capitalist Agriculture and the Origins of the European World-Economy in the Sixteenth Century.* Academic Press, New York.
1974b   The Rise and Future Demise of the Capitalist World-System: Concepts for the Comparative Analysis. In *Comparative Studies in Society and History* 16: 387–415.

WHITE, CHRISTINE D.
1986   *Paleodiet and Nutrition of the Ancient Maya at Lamanai, Belize: A Study of Trace Elements, Stable Isotopes, Nutritional and Dental Pathologies.* Master's Thesis, Trent University, Ontario.

WILK, RICHARD
1981   *Agriculture, Ecology and Domestic Organization among the Kekchi Maya.* Ph.D. Dissertation, University of Arizona, Tucson. University Microfilms, Ann Arbor.

WILK, RICHARD, AND NORMAN HAMMOND
1976   Explorations at Nimli Punit, Toledo District, 1976. In *Archaeology in Northern Belize.* Centre of Latin American Studies, University of Cambridge, Cambridge, England.

WILLEY, GORDON R.
1970   Type Descriptions of the Ceramics of the Real Xe Complex, Seibal, Peten, Guatemala. In *Monographs and Papers in Maya Archaeology,* William R. Bullard, Jr., ed., pp. 313–55. Papers of the Peabody Museum of Archaeology and Ethnology, 61. Harvard University, Cambridge.
1973   Mesoamerican Art and Iconography and the Integrity of the Mesoamerican Ideological System. In *The Iconography of Middle American Sculpture,* Dudley T. Easby, ed., pp. 153–62. Metropolitan Museum of Art, New York.
1977a   External Influences on the Lowland Maya: 1940 and 1975 Perspectives. In *Social Process in Maya History,* Norman Hammond, ed., pp. 58–72. Academic Press, New York.
1977b   The Rise of Classic Maya Civilization: A Pasion Valley Perspective. In *The Origins of Maya Civilization,* Richard E.W. Adams, ed., pp. 133–57. University of New Mexico Press, Albuquerque.
1977c   The Rise of Maya Civilization: A Summary View. In *The Origins of Maya Civilization,* Richard E.W. Adams, ed., pp. 383–423. University of New Mexico Press, Albuquerque.
1978   *Excavations at Seibal, Department of Peten, Guatemala: Artifacts.* Memoirs of the Peabody Museum of Archaeology and Ethnology, 14(1). Harvard University, Cambridge.

WILLEY, GORDON R., AND RICHARD M. LEVENTHAL
1979   A Preliminary Report on Prehistoric Maya Settlement in the Copan Valley. In *Maya Archaeology and Ethnohistory,* Norman Hammond and Gordon R. Willey, eds., pp. 75–102. University of Texas Press, Austin.

WILLEY, GORDON R., WILLIAM R. BULLARD, J.B. GLASS, AND JAMES C. GIFFORD
1965   *Prehistoric Maya Settlement in the Belize Valley.* Papers of the Peabody Museum of Archaeology and Ethnology, 54. Harvard University, Cambridge.

WILLEY, GORDON R., A. LEDYARD SMITH, GAIR TOURTELLOT III, AND IAN GRAHAM
1975   *Excavations at Seibal. Introduction: The Site and Setting.* Memoirs of the Peabody Museum of Archaeology and Ethnology, 13(1). Harvard University, Cambridge.

WILLEY, GORDON R., RICHARD M. LEVENTHAL, AND WILLIAM L. FASH
1978   Maya Settlement in the Copan Valley. In *Archaeology* 31(4): 32–43.

WILLEY, GORDON R., ROBERT J. SHARER, R. VIEL, ARTHUR DEMERAST, RICHARD M. LEVENTHAL, AND EDWARD M. SCHORTMAN
1980   A Study of Ceramic Interaction in the Southeastern Maya Periphery. Paper presented at the 45th Annual Meeting of the Society for American Archaeology. Philadelphia.

WRIGHT, A.C.S., D.H. ROMNEY, R.H. ARBUCKLE, AND V.E. VIAL
1959   *Land in British Honduras.* Colonial Research Publication 24. London.

ZEITLIN, ROBERT N.
1978   Long-Distance Exchange and the Growth of a Regional Center: An Example from the Southern Isthmus of Tehuantepec, Mexico. In *Prehistoric Coastal Adaptations: The Economy and Ecology of Maritime Middle America,* Barbara L. Stark and Barbara Voorhies, eds., pp. 183–210. Academic Press, New York.

Index

Abelino Red, 7, 10
Abraham (pirate), 191
Acalán, 164
Achiotes Unslipped, 9, 14
Agriculture, viii, ix, 105; chinampa, 101; intensive, x, 100, 110–12, 116, 124n1; milpa, 99–101, 104, 107, 110; types of, 103; wetland, 115–18, 124
Aguada, description of, 124
Aguateca, 93
Aguatepic Thick, 8
Aguila Group, 40, 59, 61, 62
Ahau, 67, 74, 77, 78, 85
Ah Bolon Tun, 89, 93
Ah kines, 187
Ah Pam, 7
Akbal sign, 45
Albion Island, 107; drained fields at, 116
Altar de Sacrificios, 2, 3, 6–8, 10, 13–15, 18n5, 19n11, 19n12, 21, 22, 59, 160; obsidian at, 12
Alta Verapaz, 12; surveys in, 9
Altun Ha, 59, 96n5, 160, 166, 167, 171, 173
Ambergris Cay, 161, 164, 165, 176
Anthropomorphs, 37, 41
Archaeobotanical studies, 172–73
Architecture, styles of, 64–66, 126–27
Archivo General de Indias, 188

Bacalar, 188; destruction of, 190–91
Bajo de Santa Fe, 112
Bajo Mirador, 112
Bajo Morocoy, 111–12, 115; chinampa agriculture in, 101; raised fields at, 116
Bajos, 105; description of, 100–101, 117; ecology of, 117, 119–24; escoba, 115–17, 119–23; excavation of, 120–24; exploitation of, 101, 111–12, 115–16; patterning in, 103 tintal, 116, 117, 122–24. *See also* Wetlands
Baktun, viii, 79, 81–82; Seibal and, 86, 89, 93, 96
Baktun Seven, 79
Baktun Eight, 79, 82–84, 96n8

Baktun Nine, 85, 86, 89, 93
Balakbal, 64
Balam Ahaw Chan (Jaguar Lord Sky), 42
Balanza Group, 59, 61, 62
Ball Court Marker (Tikal), 46, 48, 51–53, 56, 59, 64, 97n13; discovery of, 33
Ball courts, 77, 131–32, 172; discovery of, 138–39
Ball Game Mural (Tikal), 52, 54
Barra phase, 11
Barrio of San Juan, 190
Barton Ramie, 3, 6–8, 15
Basaltic columns, 21, 27, 31; Late Preclassic, 32, Middle Preclassic, 22, 24, 25, 30, 32
Beans *(Phaseolus* spp.), 103
Becan, 46, 59, 97n11
Belize Red, 128
Black Chunhinta, 14
Bladen phase, 5–8, 10, 15
Bloodletting, 64, 145, 146, 149
Bobat, 187
Bolay phase, 5, 7, 8, 10, 11
Bombolales, 122
Book of Chilam Balam of Tizimin, 179
Boulder monuments, 21; Late Preclassic, 25, 27, 32; Middle Preclassic, 22, 24, 27, 32; Terminal Preclassic, 32
Brechas, descriptions of, 122–23
Buena Vista, 107, 109
Burials, 40–41, 64, 139, 163; multiple, 62; offerings for, 42, 45, 60–62

Cacao, 148, 183
Cacaxtla, 64, 162
Cahal, 74, 77
Calakmul, 64
Caldero Buff Polychrome, 59, 61
Calendar Round, 89
Calzadas Carved, 8
Camal, Fernando, 189
Camaño Coarse, 9
Campeche, 161, 163, 165, 182
Canals, 104, 105, 112, 116, 117, 121, 124; pattern of, 119; soil profiles of, 120

Canbalam, 161, 166
Cancún Island, 162, 163, 165
Canderleros, 128
Cárdenas, Diego de, 186–87
Carving, 174; relief, 24–25, 30–31
Casanova, Juan Bernardo, 188–189
Caste War, 191–92
Cauac phase, 35, 37, 39, 64, 81, 96n3
Cauac Sky, 84, 96n5
Cayo District, 170, 173
Cehaches, 182
Ceibal, 57. *See also* Seibal
Censers, 175
Central Acropolis (Tikal), 156
Central Precinct, 171, 172, 174, 177
Ceramics, 9, 14, 61, 128, 174–76; development of, 1; reconstructions through, 2
Ceremonial complexes, 86, 107; coastal, 162. *See also* Commemorative Astronomical Complexes
Cerro de la Piedra, stela from, 21, 32
Cerros, 71, 72, 160, 163–65; raised fields at, 112
Chaacal, 74
Chacmool, 162
Chacsinkin, 68, 73
Chac Zutz, 74
Chalchihuitl, 86
Champotón, 161, 163, 165
Chan-Bahlum I, 143, 147, 155
Chan-Bahlum II, 143, 147, 149, 156n3
Chan Maya region, 180
Chawacol, 107
Chaya *(Cnidoscolus)*, 103
Chenes, architecture of, 127
Chetumal, 162, 164, 191; villa at, 182
Chicanel, 3, 6, 57
Chicen Itza, 77, 89, 97n11; collapse of, 161–64; lintels at, 148
Chiquilá, 160, 162, 163
Chiuaan complex, 3, 8
Cholan languages, 154
Chuen phase, 35, 37, 64
Chululte, 190
Chunchucmil, 160, 166
Chun complex, 9
Chunyaxché, 160, 165, 166

Ciudadela (Teotihuacan), 59
Classic period, viii, 177; maritime activities of, 159, 160
Cloth, 183; trade for, 128
Coba, 77, 161, 165; ports for, 166
Cocas Chicanel ceramics, 105
Cocos Chicanel, 106
Colhá, 106, 123, 166
Colonial period, viii, 180
Commemorative Astronomical Complexes, 33, 35–45, 48, 59, 64–66. *See also* Ceremonial complexes
Compositional fields: multi-panel, 22; panel, 22–24; recto-verso, 22, 25, 27; wraparound, 22, 25, 29, 31, 32
Conchas Orange, 13
Condemned Point, 165
Conquest, 180–81
Copador, 128
Copan, 96n1, 129, 143, 147, 150, 154; Emblem glyph, 149; settlement of, 126
Copper, 177
Corn *(zea mays)*, 103, 172–73
Cortés, Hernán, 182, 184, 185
Cozumel Island, 161–65
Cream-to-buff Dzudzuquil, 14
Crisanto Black, 7, 8
Cuello, 6, 107, 109, 110
Curl Nose, 52, 57, 58, 62, 83, 89, 97n13

Data bases, expansion of, 125
Dávila, Alonso, 182
Decoration, 2, 5, 127
Delgado, Diego, 192n4; murder of, 186–89
Delirio Plano Relief type, 62
Door jambs, 152–53, glyphs on, 154
Dos Pilas, 57, 81, 86, 93
Double-line break, 7–8
Dumbarton Oaks plaque, 68–69, 71, 72
Dzibilchaltún, 15, 46, 89, 160
Dzuluinicob, 181, 182, 189, 191

Ear-flare assemblages, 72–73
Early Classic period, viii, 125
Early Postclassic period, 172; time activities of, 161
East Platform (Mundo Perdido Tikal), 35, 39, 45, 48, 65
Eb phase, 3, 6, 11, 14–16, 33
Ecab, 162, 163, 165
Economy, x; maritime, 159–62, 167
Edzna, 64
Ek, Bernardino, 188
Ek, Can, 180–182, 184–86, 189, 191
El Chayal, obsidian from, 12–13
El Cuyo, 160
El Meco, 161–63, 165
El Mirador, 64
El Pedernal, 117, 119, 120, 122, 123
El Peru, 99
El Ray, 163
El Zapote, 58
El Zotz, 99

Emal, 160, 162, 166
Encomenderos, 183
Encomiendas, 179, 181, 183, 187, 190
Entradas, 182
Epigraphy, changes in, 1. *See also* Iconography
Equus conversidens, remains of, 17
Escuintla tripod vessels, 51
Estrada, Juan de, 191
Ethnic identity, 10–12

Feathers, trade for, 128
Fernández, Juan, 188
Fernandez, Miguel Angel, 156
Fertilization, 100
Fields (agriculture): constructing, 105; drained, 104, 116; enclosing, 123–24. *See also* Raised fields
Figueroa, Antonio de, 183–84, 186
"Fire" Dedication Events, 150
Fishing camps, 160, 162
5 Eb 5 Kayab events, 152–54
5 Imix 17 Mol bloodletting passages, 145
Flor Cream, 9
Food, 173; marine, 100; population and, 110; sources of, 99, 100; transporting, 111
Franciscans, 180–81, 184, 186, 191
Free zones, 180
Fuensalida, Bartolomé de, 183–85, 187–91, 193n19

Garzón, Juan, 182
Gateway Hill, 131, 138
Glyphs, 31, 41, 45, 51, 56, 68–69, 72, 77, 82, 93, 125–28, 129, 131, 134, 143, 154
God C, 93, 149, 151, 154, 156
God I, 67, 143
God K, 74, 84, 85, 89, 93, 96
Great Ball Court (Chichen Itza), 77
Group 6C-XVI (Tikal), 33; plan of, 34
Group E (Uaxactun), 33, 35, 39
Group of the Cross (Palenque), 143, 149, 151, 152, 155, 156n4; dedication of, 156
Guerrero, Gonzalo, 182
Guitara Incised, 8

Harvard University-Copan Valley Settlement Project, 129
Hauberg Stela, 52, 74, 155
Hecelchakán, 187–88
Herbaceous tintal, description of, 123
Hero Twin Hun Ahua, 151
Hieroglyphs. *See* Glyphs, Petroglyphs
Holmul, excavations at, 2
Hopelchen, 187, 192n5
House dedication, 154–56
Household wares, 175
House of GI, 151–52
House platforms, 106–7
Hubelna, 191
Huetche White, 7

Ichpaatún, 162, 164, 165
Iconic mode, description of, 22

Iconography, x, 21–22, 30, 127–28, 131, 134, 139, 143, 156n1; Jaguar Paw, 45; maritime, 162; Maya, 126; Olmec, 28, 67
Images, relief-carved, 30, 31n3
Initial Series Inscriptions, 81, 84
Inner Sanctuaries, 152, 154
Intermarriage, 128
Isla Cerritos, 161–63, 165, 166
Isla Jaina, 161–63, 165
Isla Piedras, 163
Isla Tamalcab, 163
Isla Uaymil, 163
Itza, 161, 164, 166, 179, 182–84, 186–88, 190
Ixcanrio Orange Polychrome, 9, 40
Ixchel, shrine of, 163
Ixpimienta, 187–88
Ixtabai complex, 6
Izapa, 27, 29

Jade, 175; trade for, 128
Jaguar Paw I, 42; sacrifice of, 86
Jaguar Paw II, 42
Jaguar Paw III, 45, 46, 65
Jaguar Paw lineage, 35–45, 52, 57, 65, 66, 79, 83, 86, 96, 156
Jaguar Paw Skull, 45, 58
Japon Resist, 61
Jenney Creek phase, 6–8, 11
Jester God, transformation of, 67–69, 71–74, 77–78
Joventud Red, 10, 13, 14
Jueves Santo, 189
Jupiter, 146, 149, 156n5

Kaminaljuyu, 29, 46, 59, 60 83, 96n1
Kan Boar, 52, 57, 62
Kan Cross, 62, 85
K'an discs, description of, 86
Katun 1 Ahau, 186, 189; prophecies of, 179
Katun 3 Ahau, 186, 189
Katun 5 Ahau, 184
Katun 8 Ahau, prophecies of, 184
Katun, 96n8, 192n3; prophecies, 179, 181, 184; Toltec warriors and, 82–83
K'axob, 104, 106, 107, 109, 110
K'inich K'uk' glyphs, 147
Kin sign, 45
Kokeal, 106, 107; population of, 103
Komchen, 160; ceramics from, 1
K'u, 82, 84–85, 93
K'uk', concept of, 82, 84, 93, 96n4, 96n5
K'uk' Ka'an, 84–85, 96n5, 97n13
K'uk'ulkan (Quetzalcoatl), 83, 89, 96, 96n5

La Amelia, 57
Ladyville site, 17
Laguna de Términos, 160, 164, 165
Laguna Verde Incised, 9
Laguna Zope, obsidian at, 12
Lake Petén Itzá, 179–182, 186
Lamanai, 170, 173–77, 190, 193n19; ball court at, 172; drained fields at,

116; excavation of, 169; population of, 171
Landa, Diego de, 187
La Pimienta, 186
La Providencia, 160
Las Coloradas, 160
Late Classic period, 125, 137, 138, 177
Late Postclassic period, maritime activities of, 161–62
Late Preclassic period, 176; maritime activities of, 160
La Venta, 8, 10; obsidian at, 12–13
La Victorias, boulder monument from, 25
Leyden Plaque, 42, 45, 52
Lintels, 148, 149, 155
Loltun Cave, 17, 74
Long Count, 79, 81, 82
López e Cogolludo, 183–85, 190, 191, 192n4
Lord X, 57
Lower Motagua Valley, 129; settlement of, 126
Labaantun, viii, 129; ball courts at, 138; work at, 131, 138
Lucha Incised, 59, 61; dish rims, 8

Ma'Cuch title: lineage of, 45–57; lineage of (Uaxactun), 57–62, 64–66, 97n3
Mah K'ina, 146, 149, 154
Mah K'ina K'uk,' 147, 149
Majan Red-and-cream-to-buff, 14
Mamon phase, 3, 5–9, 13–16, 19n12; relationships for, 10
Manan, 190
Manche Chol, 182
Mani, 187–89
Manik 1 phase, 36, 39, 40, 46, 59, 66
Manik 2 phase, 35, 37–43, 46, 49, 52, 65, 66
Manik 3 phase, 46, 48, 58–62, 65
Marco Gonzalez, 169, 170, 176
Marlowe Cay, 166
Masks, 37
Maya Mountains, 137, 139–40
Maya language, divergence of, 12
Mayapan, 161
Maya Realm, 131
Mayflower, 173
Méndez de Canzo, Antonio, 189
Merchants, 173
Mérida, 180, 182–84, 186, 190
Metal artifacts, 173, 177, 183
Mexican Year Sign, 51
Middle Preclassic Horizon style, 67
Mirones Lescano, Francisco de, 186–89, 192n4
Mixe-Zoque, 10–13, 15, 16. *See also* Zoque
Mixtec Vienna Codex, 152
Models, 141; development of, 125–27
Moho Cay, 165
Monte Alban, 46
Montejo, Francisco de, 182
Monuments: free-standing, 21–22; Late Preclassic, 25, 27–30; Middle Preclassic, 22, 24–25; relief-carved, 30, 31; sculptured, 56–57; Terminal Preclassic, 30–31; types of, 21
Moon Zero Bird, 42
Mopan, 182
Mopila, 77
Mundo Perdido (Tikal), 47, 48, 59, 62, 64–66, 83, 97n12; evolution of, 33–35
Mural of the Ball Players (Tikal), The: description of, 54–56
Muxanal Red-on-cream, 14

Na, Cristobal, 188
Nabanche phase, 15, 16, 19n13
Nacaste phase, 8
Nakbe, 64
National Geographic Society, 137
Negroman-Tipu, 170, 173
New Empire, 167, 169
New River, 105
Nim Li Punit, 71, 129, 132, 134, 137–40; ball courts at, 138, 140; map of, 133; work at, 131–32, 134, 138
Nohmul, 107, 109, 110
North Acropolis (Tikal), 33, 35, 37, 42, 52, 57, 59, 62, 64, 65, 71
Northern River Lagoon Site, 166

Obsidian, 173, 176; early distribution of, 12–13; trade for, 128
Old Empire, 167, 169
Old God, 51, 52
Olmec, 5, 10–12, 15, 71, 73, 78; iconography of, 28
Orbita, Juan de, 183–89, 191
Ox Ahau, 185
Oxkutzkab, 187, 189
Oxtancah, 164

Paamul, 162
Pacal, 145–46
Pacha, 190
Pacheco, Alonso, 182
Paddler Gods, 156
Palacio, Joseph, 131
Palenque, 64, 74, 75, 85, 89, 129, 143–45, 149, 152, 153, 155
Pastes, 2, 7
Pedestals, 21; block, 24; Late Preclassic, 28–30, 32; relief-carved, 30; Terminal Preclassic, 32. *See also* Stela
Peten, 166, 170, 171, 181–84
Petroglyphs, 31. *See also* Glyphs; Hieroglyphs
Piedras Negras, 83, 97n11
Pirates, 193n22; raids by, 191
Pital Cream, 14
Playa del Cármen, 162, 163, 165
Plaza organization, Maya, 126
Plazuela, 48
Point Placencia, 165
Points, description of, 175
Pol, Ah Kin: massacre by, 188, 189
Polvero Black, 9
Population: Classic period, 100; estimate of, 107; fluctuation of, x, 99, 101, 110, 125
Ports: coastal transshipment, 165–66; of embarkation, 163–64; function of, 162–63; for inland polities, 166; role of, 167; of-trade, 163–65; types of, 163–66
Prehispanic Maya Agriculture (Harrison and Turner), 101
Primary Standard Sequence, 143, 147
Principal Bird Diety, 151
Problematic deposits, 62, 97n12
Proyecto Arqueologico Copan, 129
Proyecto Nacional Tikal, 33
Pucte, 59
Puerto Morelos, 162
Pulltrouser Swamp, 104, 106, 112, 113n3, 116; ceremonial centers at, 107; intensive agriculture in, 111; map of, 102, 108; population of, 108, 110; spacing relationships in, 103, 109
Pulltrouser Swamp, Ancient Maya Habitat, Agriculture, and Settlement in Northern Belize (Turner and Harrison), 103
Pulltrouser Swamp Project, 111
Punta Cerrito, 161
Pure Florescent, 15
Pusilha, 129, 137; ball courts at, 138, 139; map of, 132; work at, 131, 138
Putún, 173, 182
Puuc, 77; architecture of, 127
Pyramids, 37, 59, 86; false, 127; radial, 35, 86

Quadripartite Badge, 155
Quadripartite God, 156
Quirigua, excavation of, 129

Radiocarbon, 6
Raised fields, 101, 109–12, 124n1; description of, 103–5, 116. *See also* Fields (agriculture)
Ramonal, 165
Ramon cropping, 100. *See also* Agriculture
Ranchería, 180
Real phase, 3, 7, 8, 10, 15, 18n5, 19n11
Rebellion, 191; forms of, ix; Mayan, 180–81
Regionalism, 141; concepts of, 128–29
Repartimientos, 179, 183
Revisionism, Maya studies and, vii–viii
Reyes el Mulato, Diego Lucifer de los, 191
Rims, 8; shape of, 5, 7; Tecomate, 10
Rio Azul, 46, 58, 59, 99, 115, 119, 121; excavation near, 120; intensive agriculture at, 112; map of, 119; tintal bajo in, 122–24; wetland agriculure at, 116–17
Rio Azul Project, work of, 117
Rio Bec, architecture of, 127

Sacalum, 192n4; massacre at, 186–89
Sacbe, 77, 134

Sacrifice, 62; mass, 40–41
Salamanca de Bacalar, 179, 181–83, 186, 189–91
Salt pans, 160
San Antonio (Belize), 107
San Estavan (Belize), 107, 109, 110
San Felipe (Belize), 137
San Gervasio (Quintant Roo), 160
San Lazaro (Belize), 107, 109
San Lorenzo (Belize), 107, 109
San Lorenzo Tenochtitlan, 12, 22
San Luis (Belize), 107
San Martin Jilotepeque, obsidian from, 12–13
Santa Rita Corozal, 6, 160, 162–65, 170, 176
Santa Floro, Marqués de, 190
Sapote Striated, 9
Sarteneja, 164
Saturn, 146, 149, 156n5
Sedge tintal, description of, 122–23
Sedimentation, 104–7
Seibal, 3, 6–8, 10, 14, 15, 19n12, 68, 79, 96, 160; baktun and, 86, 89, 93, 96; Emblem Glyph, 93, 96; obsidian at, 12; Stelae, 89–93. *See also* Ceibal
Serpent-bird, 82, 84
Serpents, 52, 64, 83, 127, 155, 156
Settlements, 100; patterns for, 107–10
Shipstern, 166
Sierra Red, 9, 13
Silver Creek, 129
Sky event, 151–52
Slips, 2, 5, 7, 9, 14–15; varieties of, 10
Smoking Ax, 51, 52
Smoking Frog, 46, 52, 57, 58, 62, 65, 97n13
Soil profiles, 116, 12–21
Soite, 190
Solar observatory, 86
Southern Belize Archaeological Project, 132
South Plaza (Mundo Perdido Tikal), 36–37
Spacing relationships. *See* Settlements, patterns for
Spears, 175
Stelae, 21, 40, 41, 52, 74, 79, 80, 83–85, 89–92, 94, 95, 137, 138, 155; Late Preclassic, 27–30, 32, plain, 27; plaza, 131, 134; relief-carved, 30; Terminal Preclassic, 30, 32. *See also* Pedestals
Stone polishing, 174
Stormy Sky, 52, 57, 62, 83–86, 93, 97n13
Sugar cane, 104
Sun God, 84
Surface depressions, 117, 119
Swasey phase, 5–6, 8, 10, 11, 15, 16, 18n5, 19n3, 106
Symbolism, 84–85

Tablet of the Slaves (Palenque), 74, 75
Tah Itza, rebellion at, 179–91, 192n4
Tajumulco, obsidian from, 13
Talking Cross, 192
Talud-tablero mode, 46, 48, 59, 65–66
Tamalcab, 162, 164, 190
Tamarindito, 57
Tancah, 160–63, 165, 166
Tatagapa Red, 8
Tekax, 187, 189
Tempers, 2
Temple of Quetzalcoatl (Teotihuacan), 59
Temple of the Cross (Palenque), 143–45, 152, 155
Temple of the Foliated Cross (Palenque), 143–45
Temple of the Seven Dolls (Dzibilchaltun), 160
Temple of the Sun (Palenque), 143–45, 157n9
Temples, 185; dedication of, 155–56
Tenochtitlan-Mexica Aztecs, 127
Teotihuacan, 46, 51, 59, 79, 86, 96n1, 96n7, 97n11, 125, 127, 162
Terminal Classic period, 171, 172, 176; maritime activities of, 161
Te-tun (stone tree), 149
Thin Orange ware, 59, 62
3 Caban 15 Mol event, 144, 146–49, 151, 149
Tibaat, description of, 106, 113n5
Ticul, 187
Tierra Mojada Resist, 13–14
Tikal, 3, 6, 33, 37, 41, 42, 45, 57–59, 64, 71, 79, 83, 96, 96n1, 96n8, 97n13, 117, 128, 155, 156, 160; Emblem Glyph, 84–86
Tipu, 173, 176, 177, 179, 180, 182–84, 188–90
Tlaloc, 62, 64, 66
Tok phase, 12, 18n5
Toledo District, 131, 137; map of, 130
Toltec warriors, *k'atun* and, 82–83
Trade, 173, 176; coastal, 160, 161, 165; local, 127, 162; long-distance, 127, 128, 160, 162, 165
Triad gods, 151, 154, 155, 157n5
Triadic Pattern Architecture, 64–66
Tula-Toltecs, 127
Tular Black and White, 9
Tulum, 162–65
Twin Pyramid Complexes, 86
2 Cib 14 Mol series, 143–46, 156n4, 157n5
Two Coyote, 52
Tzakol 2 Phase, 57, 65
Tzakol 3 Phase, 57, 58, 65
Tzemé, 160
Tzimin Chac (Thunder Horse), 191; destruction of, 184–86

Uaxactun, 2–3, 33, 35, 39, 58, 59, 64, 71, 83, 96n1, 97n13, 128, 156
Underworld, 56, 89, 162
Urita Gouged-Incised type, 59
Uxbenka, 129; map of, 136; stelae at, 134, 138; work at, 134, 137

Valladolid, 182
Venus, 79, 81, 83, 86, 89, 96, 97n14
Venus Crocodile-Serpent, 83
Veracruz: drained fields at, 116; obsidian at, 12
Verapaz Project, 9
Vessel forms, 2, 5
Villas, establishing, 182
Villagutierre, 183
Villa Real, 182
Vision Serpent, 52, 155, 156
Vista Alegre, 161

Wakah Chaan, 152, 154, 155
Wetlands: ecology of, 115–16; escoba, 123; modification of, 115–16, 122; soil profile of, 116. *See also* Bajos
Wild Cane Cay, 165
World Tree, 155–56
Writing system, Maya, 126

Xcalumkin, 77
Xcambó, 160
Xcaret, 161–63, 165
Xcopté, 161
Xelhá, 160–66
Xe phase, 3, 5, 6, 7–10, 15, 16, 17, 18n5, 19n11
Xibun, 190
Xicalango, 163–65
Xnaheb, 129, 137–39; map of, 135; stela at, 134; work at, 134
Xochicalco, 51, 97n11
Xoconusco, 164
Xox phase, 9, 12, 16
Xtampu, 160

Yalcihóm, 160
Yax-Pac, 154
Yaxchilan, 57, 149, 155; Emblem glyph, 154
Yaxha, 46, 58, 59, 64, 128
Yax K'an, 84, 85, 89, 93, 97n9, 97n13; death of, 83
Yax-K'uk'-Mo, 149
Yaxuná, 161
Yo Creek, 107, 110
Yo Tumben, 107

Zoomorphs, 37, 41, 42
Zoque, 12, 16. *See also* Mixe-Zoque